PHILOSOPHY AT THE EDGE OF CHAOS: GILLES DELEUZE AND THE PHILOSOPHY OF DIFFERENCE

From the early 1960s until his death, French philosopher Gilles Deleuze (1925–1995) wrote many influential works on philosophy, literature, film, and fine art. One of Deleuze's main philosophical projects was a systematic inversion of the traditional relationship between identity and difference. This Deleuzian philosophy of difference is the subject of Jeffrey A. Bell's *Philosophy at the Edge of Chaos*

Bell argues that Deleuze's efforts to develop a philosophy of difference are best understood by exploring both Deleuze's claim to be a Spinozist, and Nietzsche's claim to have found in Spinoza an important precursor. Beginning with an analysis of these claims, Bell shows how Deleuze extends and transforms concepts at work in Spinoza and Nietzsche to produce a philosophy of difference that promotes and, in fact, exemplifies the notions of dynamic systems and complexity theory. With these concepts at work, Deleuze constructs a philosophical approach that avoids many of the difficulties that linger in other attempts to think about difference. Bell uses close readings of Plato, Aristotle, Spinoza, Nietzsche, Heidegger, Derrida, and Whitehead to illustrate how Deleuze's philosophy is successful in this regard and to demonstrate the importance of the historical tradition for Deleuze. Far from being a philosopher who turns his back on what is taken to be a mistaken metaphysical tradition, Bell argues that Deleuze is best understood as a thinker who endeavoured to continue the work of traditional metaphysics and philosophy.

(Toronto Studies in Philosophy)

JEFFREY A. BELL is a professor in the Department of Philosophy at Southeastern Louisiana University.

JEFFREY A. BELL

Philosophy at the Edge of Chaos:

Gilles Deleuze and the Philosophy of Difference

UNIVERSITY OF TORONTO PRESS
Toronto Buffalo London

© University of Toronto Press Incorporated 2006
Toronto Buffalo London
Printed in Canada

ISBN 13: 978-0-8020-9128-8 (cloth)
ISBN 10: 0-8020-9128-8 (cloth)

ISBN 13: 978-0-8020-9409-4 (paper)
ISBN 10: 0-8020-9409-0 (paper)

Printed on acid-free paper

Library and Archives Canada Cataloguing in Publication

Bell, Jeffrey A.
  Philosophy at the edge of chaos : Gilles Deleuze and the philosophy of
difference / Jeffrey A. Bell.

  Includes bibliographical references and index.
  ISBN 13: 978-0-8020-9128-8 (bound)
  ISBN 10: 0-8020-9128-8 (bound)
  ISBN 13: 978-0-8020-9409-4 (pbk.)
  ISBN 10: 0-8020-9409-0 (pbk.)

  1. Deleuze, Gilles.   2. Difference (Philosophy).   I. Title.   II. Title: Gilles
Deleuze and the philosophy of difference.

  B2430.D454B44 2006   194   C2006-901760-3

University of Toronto Press acknowledges the financial assistance to its
publishing program of the Canada Council for the Arts and the Ontario
Arts Council.

University of Toronto Press acknowledges the financial support for its
publishing activities of the Government of Canada through the Book
Publishing Industry Development Program (BPIDP).

For Elizabeth, Leah, and Rebecca
and
To the memory of my father

Contents

Acknowledgments

It would be impossible to acknowledge all the individuals who have contributed in so many ways to this book. Throughout the years, numerous colleagues and students at Southeastern Louisiana University have been extremely supportive through their listening and feedback, enabling me to develop and shape the arguments that would eventually make their way into this book. Among my colleagues, I owe a special thanks to Pete Petrakis, whose intellect and friendship have been a continual source of inspiration and guidance throughout the process of writing and researching this book. I must also thank Michael Zimmerman and John Glenn for their early and continuing support of my work. It was this support, in particular, that gave me the confidence to submit and eventually publish an early version of chapter 3 in the journal *Philosophy Today* (vol. 39, no. 4, 1995). University of Toronto Press, and Len Husband, in particular, has from start to finish been especially easy to work with, providing along the way whatever assistance I needed. I also cannot thank enough the anonymous readers for their invaluable suggestions for improving the manuscript. They were both extremely thorough and professional, and this book would not be nearly as good as it is if it were not for their efforts. And finally I must thank my wife, Elizabeth, for her love and support, and my daughters, Leah and Rebecca, for their sustaining love and energy. It is this support and love which makes all the difference.

PHILOSOPHY AT THE EDGE OF CHAOS:
GILLES DELEUZE AND THE PHILOSOPHY OF
DIFFERENCE

Introduction

'To think is to create – there is no other creation – but to create is first of all to engender "thinking" in thought.'[1] This line from *Difference and Repetition* expresses one of the more important themes of Deleuze's entire philosophical project, which is to make of thinking, and in particular philosophic thinking, an enterprise that is truly creative and hence not subordinate to factors that predetermine what this thinking should be. As Deleuze otherwise states the objective of his project, it is to lay out a philosophy of difference that truly thinks difference without reducing it to a predetermining identity.[2] Deleuze, moreover, is not alone in his efforts, for as we will see Heidegger and Derrida are equally committed to 'thinking difference,' to developing a philosophy of difference that shows how it is identity that is conditioned by a fundamental difference rather than difference itself being conditioned by an already established and predetermining identity, such as the difference between identities.[3]

The difference between Derrida and Deleuze, however, is key, and it becomes most evident in comparing their respective views concerning systematic thought, or thinking in terms of systems. For Derrida, with his development of the concept 'differance,' the very identity of a system presupposes, he claims, a fundamental difference that prevents the system from ever attaining any sense of completion or closure. This position is itself simply the extension of his argument that every identity or presence, every attempt to establish the self-identical, self-present grounding and meaning from which all other meanings can then arise, presupposes its other, a difference and/or absence which perpetually defers the closure necessary to attain true self-presence. Derrida thus defines the term 'differance' as 'an economic concept designating the production of differing/deferring';[4] and it is this continual production that defers and subverts (i.e., deconstructs) any system from attaining completion (i.e., closure or self-identity). For Deleuze, by contrast, in his single-authored works and then with Guattari, what is implicilty developed is the notion of a fundamental both/and or difference that is inseparable from dynamic systems that are at the 'edge of chaos.' A dynamic system, on this understanding, presupposes both the stable, structured strata that are in some sense *complete*, and it entails the unstable, unstructured, deterritorializing flows. As Deleuze and Guattari proceed to develop the implications of this thinking, or as they develop a philosophy at the 'edge of chaos,' they neither create concepts which solve, once and for all, philosophical problems, nor do they slip into a state of anarchical relativism. Rather, philosophy, as with a living organism at the 'edge of chaos,' must maintain both its stable strata and its unstable, deterritorializing flows. Without the former, a living organism dies (or a philosophy slips into disordered nonsense and says nothing), and without the latter, an organism is unable to adapt and will also die (or a philosophy falls into a mindless repetition of clichés and platitudes). Unlike Derrida, therefore, there is the need for systems, dynamic systems, and systems whose very completeness staves off a collapse into the destructive consequences of an either/or (e.g., either nonsense or cliché).[5]

In *A Thousand Plateaus*, the concept that carries much of the weight in explicating this philosophy at the 'edge of chaos' is the notion of an 'abstract machine.' The abstract machine, as understood by Deleuze and Guattari, entails a fundamental both/and, or what they will call a double articulation, a double bind, and it is this both/and that is inseparable from and allows for the possibility of dynamic systems. This double articulation, which we will discuss more fully in later chapters, involves a first articulation whereby unstructured, deterritorialized flows – what Deleuze and Guattari will refer to as the Body without Organs (BwO) – comes to be drawn into a plane of consistency such that, in the second articulation, this consistency can be actualized as determinate, identifiable entities, systems, etc. Expressed in the terms of dynamic systems theory, a dynamic system at the edge of chaos is a system such that only when there is sufficient consistency to the system (first articulation) can it then actualize and engender new, unpredicted systems and identities (second articulation).[6] The abstract machine is precisely this double articulation, the fundamental both/and (ordered and chaotic, or chaosmos), that is inseparable from identities and from the transformations and becomings of these identities. By arguing, then, that Deleuze and Guattari understand identities in terms of abstract machines, where such machines, as dynamic systems, presuppose the fundamental both/and of order and chaos, we can see more clearly how, unlike Derrida's understanding of 'differance,' the abstract machine is not a fundamental both/and condition which subverts completion. To the contrary, the fundamental difference, Deleuze's difference in itself, is instead the immanent condition presupposed by dynamic systems, and by the completeness and stability such systems require.[7]

As Deleuze and Guattari develop the concept of the abstract machine, along with the related concepts that support it or are connected to it (e.g., BwO, plane of consistency, double articulation, event, rhizome, and others as will be discussed in later chapters), it is important to recognize that despite the apparent novelty of this terminology, Deleuze and Guattari's project is nonetheless much in line with the transcendental tradition in philosophy, especially the Kantian tradition. In fact, *A Thousand Plateaus* is in many ways a Kantian critique which attempts to delineate the appropriate limits within which the abstract machine is the condition for a functioning, dynamic system, and they seek, through advocating a form of experimentalism, to determine the limits beyond which the abstract machine fails to actualize such a system but instead collapses into either the cancerous body of uncontrolled proliferation and chaos or the fascist body of smothering identity.[8] Deleuze and Guattari, however, explicitly differentiate their transcendental project from other similar attempts, especially Kant's. How they differ is that the concepts Deleuze and Guattari develop in carrying forward their transcendental project are not to be understood as predetermining identities, in the vein of Kant's categories, but rather are to be used as tools for experimenting with and questioning various identities and systems. In short, what Deleuze and Guattari seek to do with concepts such as the abstract machine is to provide concepts that are abstract enough to be applied to all types of identifiable systems and that are yet not too abstract so that they fail to account for the transformative processes that are the transcendental conditions inseparable from the identifiable systems they make possible. To clarify this project, we can see how Deleuze and Guattari contrast it from others. Deleuze and Guattari, for example, will criticize Bertrand Russell's and Noam Chomsky's efforts to understand the *identifiable* system of language in terms of an abstract transcendental logic or grammar:

All methods for the transcendentalization of language, all methods for endowing language with universals, from Russell's logic to Chomsky's grammar, have fallen into the worst kind of abstraction, in the sense that

they validate a level that is both too abstract and not abstract enough ...
'Behind' statements and semioticizations there are only machines.[9]

By accusing Chomsky's and Russell's transcendentalization of language with being *too abstract*, Deleuze and Guattari believe Chomsky
and Russell failed to adequately address social contexts, or the concrete,
material processes of economics, politics, desire, etc., and their roles
(i.e., *abstract machinic* roles) in the generation and transformation of language systems.[10] Chomsky's grammar, and Russell's logic, are *too*
abstracted and hence disconnected from these other processes, and as a
result their transcendentalization of language is, in Deleuze and
Guattari's opinion, seriously incomplete and inadequate.[11]

On the other hand, Chomsky's and Russell's approach is also *not
abstract enough*. What is meant by this is that Russell's logic and Chomsky's grammar are not abstract enough to apply to *identifiable* systems
other than language. Deleuze and Guattari, with their concept of the
double articulation of the abstract machine, clearly feel they have
avoided the 'worst kind of abstraction' that inflicted Russell and Chomsky, for these concepts are *abstract enough* to apply to an indefinite multiplicity of other systems. In the closing words to *A Thousand Plateaus*,
this sense of abstract machines as conceptually abstract enough to be
applied to indeterminately other identities is clearly evident:

> Every abstract machine is linked to other abstract machines, not only
> because they are inseparably political, economic, scientific, artistic, eco-
> logical, cosmic – perceptive, affective, active, thinking, physical, and
> semiotic – but because their various types are as intertwined as their oper-
> ations are convergent. Mechanosphere.[12]

At the same time the concepts they develop are not too abstract so that
they leave one unable to understand the transformative processes
whereby established, actualized identities come to be. It is at this
moment that it becomes most helpful, in our attempt to understand
Deleuze's project, to turn to Deleuze's early work on Nietzsche and
Spinoza. There are numerous reasons why this is so, but the most important reason is that a careful examination of the concepts that Spinoza and
Nietzsche developed will show the profound extent to which Deleuze,
and Deleuze and Guattari, were, in their own conceptual formulations
and practices, innovative Spinozists and Nietzscheans.

We can begin to see this by beginning, as does Spinoza in his *Ethics*,
with God. In *A Thousand Plateaus* Deleuze and Guattari define God in

what at first might appear to be a tongue-in-cheek way: 'God is a Lobster, or a double pincer, a double bind.'[13] With what we have said so far, and with what subsequent chapters in this book will reveal, we can begin to see that this is in fact a philosophically sophisticated formulation. First, by defining God as a 'Lobster, or a double pincer, a double bind,' Deleuze and Guattari in effect define God as 'double articulation.' In other words, as double articulation God is both the first articulation, or the Abstract machine whereby the chaos (BwO) is drawn into a plane of consistency, and God is the second articulation, or the Abstract machine that enables the plane of consistency to be actualized into identifiable, functioning states and systems. Placed into the context of the concepts at work in Spinoza, especially Spinoza's *Ethics*, the relationship between the two aspects of double articulation becomes the relationship between substance as absolutely indeterminate and the attributes, defined by Spinoza as that which the infinite intellect perceives of the substance, constituting *its* essence (1D4).[14] What we will see in our chapter on Spinoza is that many of the apparent problems commentators have had with Spinoza's philosophy can be largely resolved if we understand Spinoza's philosophy in light of what Deleuze will later do with his concepts – namely, develop the notion of abstract machines and double articulation. In particular, applying Deleuze's concept of double articulation wherein the first articulation draws chaos (BwO) into a plane of consistency while the second articulation actualizes the consistency into an *identifiable* state, for Spinoza the first articulation is the drawing or expressing of substance in an attribute, and the second articulation is the actualization or modification of the attribute. There is consequently the necessity for the modification of an attribute – infinite thought – to be that which perceives substance and constitutes its *identifiable*, actualized essence, and it is this dependency of the attributes upon a mode that has caused commentators many problems.[15]

Stating Spinoza's point in Deleuze and Guattari's terminology, the first articulation is only identifiable as actualized, or as a result of the second articulation. Thus for Deleuze when the BwO is drawn into a plane of consistency it is, as Deleuze puts it, real but not actual. When a monkey, to use one of Deleuze's examples, learns that its food is in 'one particular colour amidst others of various colours,' there occurs, in the process of learning, 'a paradoxical period during which the number of "errors" diminishes even though the monkey does not yet possess the "knowledge" or "truth" of a solution in each case.'[16] In other words, the monkey first achieves a level of consistency, or a plane of consistency is drawn upon the monkey's initially random choices, and this consistency is real but not yet actualized as 'knowledge,' and it is only as actualized that one can speak of a determinate, identifiable 'essence,' 'rule,' 'knowledge,' etc., in the sense Spinoza and Deleuze intend. Similarly, it is only as actualized within an infinite mode that the attribute which expresses substance can be identified, and identified as the determinate and constitutive essence of substance that it *is*. In short, stating this again in Deleuze and Guattari's terms, God is the double articulation – the lobster – that is the process whereby absolutely indeterminate substance, what they will refer to as THE BwO, becomes determinate and known. It was for this reason, then, that Deleuze and Guattari rhetorically ask, '[I]s not Spinoza's *Ethics* the great book of the BwO?'[17]

It is at this point where the significance of Nietzsche shines through, for while concepts from Spinoza's *Ethics* may very well have been crucial to Deleuze and Guattari's transcendental project, it was Nietzsche, perhaps more than any other philosopher, who sought to restore to philosophy the importance of becoming. Nietzsche's writings are replete with lines such as the following: 'Heraclitus will remain eternally right with his assertion that being is an empty fiction';[18] 'The character of the word in a state of becoming as incapable of formulation, as "false," as "self-contradictory."'[19] Since an essential part of Deleuze's transcendental project, as noted above, is to determine the conditions whereby the abstract machine can allow for the emergence of new beings – that is, an engendering of '"thinking" in thought' – it is thus the coming-into-being, the becomings, of identities that is of key concern, and as a result the influence of Nietzsche should not be surprising. This influence can be seen in the use Deleuze makes of one of Nietzsche's most enigmatic concepts – that is, the concept of eternal recurrence. As we will see Deleuze argue in chapter 3, Nietzsche's notion of eternal recurrence entails a double affirmation (a double articulation), the affirmations of Dionysus and Ariadne. As Deleuze puts it, 'Dionysian becoming is being, eternity, but only insofar as the corresponding affirmation is itself affirmed.'[20] As the paradoxical both/and that allows for the emergence of identities, becoming is, as Deleuze understands it, and as detailed in subsequent chapters, non-identifiable. It is only as the object of a second affirmation (second articulation), an affirmation that repeats the first, that one can then say of becoming that it is something that *is*. The first affirmation is indeed an eternal affirmation, for the Dionysian affirmation of becoming cannot be reduced to the identities of the present, or to what Deleuze will frequently refer to as the measurable time of *chronos*

– chronological time. In contrast to chronological time, the Dionysian affirmation exceeds it, or is eternal – Deleuze will frequently contrast the term *aion* to *chronos*, where *aion* is the immeasurable eternity that cannot be reduced to measurable, chronological time.[21] Consequently, Ariadne's second affirmation is a recurrence of the eternal – it is eternal recurrence; and it is with the concept of eternal recurrence, Nietzsche believes, where we have 'the closest approximation of a world of becoming to a world of being.'[22]

Returning now to Deleuze and Guattari, when they put forth the concept of the Abstract machine, in contrast to the abstract machines, we can see, with Nietzsche's concept of eternal recurrence in hand, that the Abstract machine is God as a lobster, the double articulation which entails a difference in itself that cannot be reduced to identity, and this Abstract machine is only identifiable as the result of expressions that repeat the paradoxical, immeasurable nature of the Abstract machine. Here the Spinoza-Nietzsche connection becomes most clear, for the concept Deleuze believed to be central to Spinoza's *Ethics* was the concept of 'expression,' and it is with this concept that Spinoza, according to Deleuze, is able to account for the relationship between substance and its attributes, for the attributes, as Spinoza defines them, are expressions of substance (1D6: 'By God I understand a being absolutely infinite, i.e., a substance consisting of an infinity of attributes, of which each one *expresses* an eternal and infinite essence' [emphasis mine]). With the conceptual resources of Nietzsche added to Spinoza, we come to the position that, in the terminology of *A Thousand Plateaus*, the Abstract machine is the affirmation of becoming that allows for the second affirmation whereby becoming becomes identifiable. The abstract machines are these secondary affirmations (second articulations), or they are the eternal recurrence of becoming, the 'closest approximation of a world of becoming to a world of being.' Moreover, the *identifiable* abstract machines, as expressions of the Abstract machine, express in their *own* way (i.e., *identifiable* way) the paradoxical double bind of determining and identifying the non-identifiable nature of becoming – in short, these abstract machines are dynamic systems at the edge of chaos. As a result, the abstract machines, as identifiable dynamic systems, are indeed identities, but identities that are assured of becoming other, becoming another identifiable dynamic system. As Deleuze and Guattari put it, 'there is no genetics without genetic drift.'[23] God is a lobster, then, a double pincer, a double bind, a double articulation, precisely because it is this condition that is necessary to, and inseparable from, each and every identity. Deleuze and Guattari, therefore, reaffirm (eternal recurrence) Spinoza's claim that 'God is Nature' (*Deus sive Natura*), and for them this is precisely their transcendental project of detailing the double articulation, the eternal recurrence, that is inseparable from each and every natural process that comes to be identified, and comes to be identified as expressions of the Abstract machine, expressions that *are* only as an approximation of becoming to being.

In the chapters which follow, we will further elaborate how the concepts of Nietzsche and Spinoza come to form the basis for Deleuze's philosophy of difference. As these concepts come to be developed by Deleuze, moreover, we will see that Deleuze is able to avoid the residual difficulties which remain in the philosophies of difference as set forth by Heidegger and Derrida. These difficulties remain, as will be argued in chapters 4 and 5, precisely because Heidegger and Derrida do not develop the notion of a dynamic system at the edge of chaos, a system that is *both* complete, ordered, *and* incomplete and chaotic. In the concluding chapters we will return to Deleuze's own efforts, efforts that have been sketched here, to show how, in his own works and in his writings with Guattari, an unending concern of his was to engender '"thinking" in thought.'

PART ONE

Thinking Difference

1 Systematic Thinking and the Philosophy of Difference

If to engender 'thinking' in thought entails encountering the condition for the possibility of common thoughts and opinions, then 'thinking' involves the instilling of aberration and movement into thought, or it brings this thought to the edge of chaos so that 'thinking' can indeed become creating. Success is not guaranteed, of course, but if it happens it happens, as we will argue, precisely because 'thinking' has become systematic thinking, or it has become a dynamic system that is the condition of possibility for new, stable thoughts, beliefs, and systems. This condition, moreover, is not to be confused with the conditioned, and thus it is more correct to argue that engendering 'thinking' is to think the uncommon condition for the possibility of every common and identifiable system. We will define this uncommon condition as *paradoxa*, using the ancient Greek term which can be translated to mean contrary (*para*) to what is common, and in particular to common opinion and belief (*doxa*). In thinking the whole of reality (i.e., system), this thinking inevitably thinks paradoxa, paradoxa as the condition for the possibility of any and all systems, and the condition of impossibility for a closed, complete system, meaning a system that reduces the uncommon to the common. This condition, as we will see, is inseparable from the systems of which it is the immanent condition, and yet it is not to be identified with these systems; consequently, in doing philosophy one necessarily encounters that which cannot be identified with what is common (e.g., the system of practical, everyday interests). Philosophy is inevitably uncommon and hence subject to the charge of uselessness.

This necessary uselessness of philosophy has long been recognized. Plato, for example, in his *Republic*, attempts, by analogy, to defend philosophy against those who find it useless. In analogizing the ruling of the city-state to the sailing of a ship, Socrates argues that for 'the true pilot it is necessary to pay careful attention to year, seasons, heaven, stars, winds ...' The true pilot will not do what is commonly done aboard ships, namely, try to gain favour through persuasion, flattery, politicking, etc., with the hopes of gaining power. Rather, the true pilot will often be found alone, staring at the movement of the stars; consequently, as Socrates continues, 'the true pilot will be called a stargazer, a prater and useless to them,' useless to those who attempt to get ahead in the common way.[1] The uselessness of philosophy, as Plato's analogy attempts to show, is precisely its greatest strength.

Philosophy is not the only discipline whose usefulness has been questioned. In the sciences, for example, the theories and formulas that have been developed are often far removed from any practical application or relevance. In current cosmological theory, for example, theoreticians have constructed mathematical theories which involve many dimensions beyond those which are practically relevant (e.g., the widely accepted version of string theory calls for eleven dimensions). There is a crucial difference between the cosmologist and the philosopher, however, and this difference is critical for understanding the place and role of philosophy. With the cosmologist, theoretical physicist, or mathematician, the investigation pursued is of an already assumed reality, or their theories in some way connect with, or represent, this reality. As a result, these theories have the potential to be linked up with practical or useful action, even if this potential is not realized immediately. With philosophical investigations, on the other hand, the philosopher does not assume reality but attempts to achieve an all-encompassing view of reality, or he/she attempts to arrive at an understanding of the conditions which account for the reality of the real. In doing metaphysics, therefore, the philosopher is thus forced to step outside the sphere of practical, everyday reality in order to gain a perspective on the whole of reality. The philosopher, in doing metaphysics, must be useless if he/she is to understand the reality wherein practical, useful action occurs. To charge philosophers with pursuing an impractical and useless discipline is, from the perspective of the philosopher doing metaphysics, to accuse them of doing what they should be doing.

It is precisely at this point where the philosophical critique of metaphysics comes into prominence. Beginning with Nietzsche, and continuing through Heidegger to Derrida, Foucault, Deleuze, and others, the argument has been made that it is just this effort to achieve an all-encompassing view of reality that is an impossible and misguided task; moreover, Nietzsche would argue that such an effort denies *this* life, and presumably the practical everyday concerns of this life. One might expect, then, that with the contemporary critique of metaphysics, with the philosophical call for the end of philosophy, that the result would be a philosophy more attuned to common, practical concerns. This is not what one finds. Quite to the contrary, Heidegger, Derrida, and others are routinely criticized for being obscure. Not only do many not see any practical relevance for much of what Heidegger, Derrida, and others have written; many have difficulty simply making sense of the texts themselves. If anything, then, the common view of writers such as Derrida is that they are even more removed from common understanding than their more traditional philosophical counterparts. The same person who can make sense of Aristotle's *Poetics* may find Derrida's *Of Grammatology* unreadable.

Why has more recent philosophy failed to connect with the common interests and practical concerns of society at large, especially given that much of contemporary philosophy has been critical of the metaphysical tradition, a tradition which implicitly justified neglecting the everyday, common world so as to grasp the whole of reality? The reason for the continued perception of philosophy as useless, or as out of step with the common interests and practical concerns of society, is simply because contemporary philosophy continues, insofar as it attempts to engender 'thinking' in thought, to attempt to think that which is uncommon. From this perspective, therefore, a proper philosophical approach is one which thinks the uncommon in everyday activity, or which confronts the uncommon condition for the possibility of common activities and/ or knowledge claims. To this extent, then, we shall largely break with many of the assumptions that are made concerning the 'critique of metaphysics' or 'end of philosophy' traditions.[2] To state our position baldly, to the extent that the 'philosophies' within the 'critique of metaphysics' and 'end of philosophy' traditions attempt to think the uncommon condition for the possibility of common, everyday practices and beliefs, then they are doing what metaphysicians and philosophers ought to be doing. They are, in short, doing philosophy.

To clarify what we believe to be the necessary and inevitable role of philosophy, we need to clarify what it means to think the whole or system, and more importantly why this thinking inevitably leads to thinking the uncommon condition for the possibility of this system (i.e., paradoxa). What is the nature of this *necessary* relationship between the condition and the conditioned? What is the relationship between thought and this necessary condition? What is meant by system, thought, and necessary conditions? And finally (though not exhaustively), how is it that paradoxa can be inseparable from yet not identifiable with the systems it conditions? To begin answering some of these questions, we turn first to Hegel. In Hegel, too, philosophy's necessary and inevitable role is to think the whole or system, and in thinking this system philosophy necessarily encounters its own condition of possibility, a condition it only thinks when it thinks the system.

In Hegel's understanding of system, there is a glaring difference with what we have argued occurs in thinking the system. Whereas we claim that in thinking the system one necessarily confronts the uncommon condition (paradoxa) for the possibility of this stable, identifiable system, Hegel argues that this thinking confronts what is ultimately common. To be more precise, Hegel argues that anything that might appear to thought as something uncommon, novel, or unprecedented, is in reality merely part of the emerging transparency of the Notion to itself. The Notion, as Hegel claims in his *Science of Logic*, is the ultimate reality that is coming into an ever-increasing comprehension of itself. This self-comprehension must occur through an object that is other, or self-comprehension is necessarily mediated through something other – that is, something different, uncommon. This other, however, is only apparently other, for this other is simply the determinate content necessary for the Notion to achieve self-comprehension. As Hegel argues, 'The Idea is itself the pure Notion that has itself for subject matter and which, in running itself through the totality of its determinations, develops itself into the whole of its reality, into the system of the science [of logic], and concludes by apprehending this process of comprehending itself ...'[3] In other words, the determinate reality, including the novel and uncommon, is ultimately subordinate to the Notion, and in thinking this Notion, or in thinking the totality of these determinations, one inevitably, according to Hegel, arrives at 'the science (or system) of logic' wherein one has 'the self-comprehending pure Notion.'[4] And from the perspective of this science there is nothing truly other, nothing truly uncommon: 'determination [whereby through mediation the Notion comes to comprehend itself] has not issued from a process of becoming, nor is it a transition. On the contrary, the pure Idea in which the determinateness or reality of the Notion is itself raised into Notion, is an absolute liberation for which there is no longer any immediate determination that is not equally posited and itself Notion.'[5] In other words, there is no 'immediate determination,' no thing, no matter how unique or uncommon, that is not a positing and determination of Notion itself. As Hegel continues, 'the simple being to which the Idea determines itself remains perfectly transparent to it and is the Notion that, in its determination, abides with itself.'[6] It is thus this self-transparency, or the identity of the Notion with itself, that is, for Hegel, the condition for the possibility of all systems, and the condition for the possibility of the absolute, completed system. The uncommon, in short, is subordinate to the self-identity of the Notion, or the uncommon is ultimately reducible to the common (i.e., Notion) that is the condition for the possibility of all the determinations of the system.

The difference between our position concerning the thinking of system and that of Hegel's is clear. For Hegel the uncommon is not the condition of possibility for any and all systems, as we claim paradoxa is. The common, or Notion, is this condition. And whereas we argue that the uncommon is inseparable from the system it conditions and *is not* to be identified with it, Hegel argues that the Notion is inseparable from the determinations it conditions but would argue that it *is* to be identified with them. Despite this obvious difference, we remain agreed that philosophy ought to think the condition for the possibility of system. Our disagreement emerges when Hegel identifies this condition as the self-identical Notion common to all determinations, and subsequently when he reduces the uncommon to the common.

This is also Nietzsche's disagreement with Hegel. Nietzsche repeatedly criticized the tendency to reduce the uncommon to the common, and in particular the herd tendency for individuals to become common, to be like everyone else. Anything of value, for Nietzsche, is always unique, exceptional, and rare: 'whatever can be common always has little value.'[7] In response to this tendency to reduce the uncommon to the common – in other words, in response to the tendency epitomized by Hegel – Nietzsche sets forth his famous dictum: 'become who you are.' And to become who you are entails, as Nietzsche clarifies in *The Gay Science*, becoming the unique, exceptional, and uncommon individual we all are: 'We, however, want to become those we are – human beings who are new, unique, incomparable, who give themselves laws, who create themselves.'[8] This contrasts sharply with Hegel, for although Hegel does say that 'spirit ... makes itself that which it is,'[9] what it makes itself, or what it becomes, is, as we have seen, that which is self-identical and common to all the determinations of spirit (i.e., Notion).

Despite Nietzsche's overturning of Hegel, or his call for becoming a unique, uncommon individual as opposed to an individual who is merely an expression of what is common, Nietzsche nonetheless recognizes the necessity of reducing the uncommon to the common. The result of this need to reduce the uncommon to the common is 'knowledge.' Nietzsche is clear on this point: 'What is it that the common people take for knowledge? What do they want when they want "knowledge"? Nothing more than this: Something strange is to be reduced to something familiar ... isn't our need for knowledge precisely this need for the familiar, the will to uncover under everything strange, unusual, and questionable something that no longer disturbs us? Is it not the instinct of fear that bids us to know?'[10] It is for this reason that Nietzsche refers to 'knowledge' as a 'condition of life';[11] that is, in order to live and thrive we must have a sense of familiarity and commonality with our environment. Without this familiarity, we might perish. In fact, Nietzsche will go on to argue that the strength of an individual can be measured by how much one can cope with the strange and unfamiliar.[12]

With this understanding of knowledge, Nietzsche clearly comes down against Hegel's theory of Absolute Knowledge. Absolute Knowledge, according to Hegel, is the knowledge of the system, or it is the complete self-conscious realization of Spirit, the self-comprehending Notion. In other words, it is that which is common to all determinations, including all novelty, etc., recognizing itself as self-transparently present within these determinations. Nietzsche, to the contrary, understands knowledge as a necessary condition for life, and thus it is what one needs to 'know' in order to thrive. For example, in his famous discussion of master and slave morality, Nietzsche argues that the 'knowledge' they each arrive at is a function of their strength. In master morality, therefore, one is in a position of strength and is thus better able to cope with that which is different, strange, and unfamiliar, and consequently one does not perceive the strange and unfamiliar as a threat. As for what is common to the masters, it is precisely their strength, dominance, etc., with which they are familiar, and thus when they identify that which is good they naturally point to themselves. What one in master morality 'knows' to be good is one's self. Slave morality, on the other hand, arises from the slaves' position of weakness; consequently, that which is strange, different, and unfamiliar – in particular, he who is strong, dominant, and able to destroy them – is perceived as a threat. In order to thrive, however, they must eliminate this threat; but being in a position of weakness where this is not possible, they subsequently eliminate instead the values embraced by the strong and affirm what is familiar to themselves – being weak, meek, and downtrodden. What one in slave morality 'knows' to be good is to be meek, selfless, and subject to a force greater than oneself (e.g., God); and one also 'knows' that it is evil to be strong, fear-inspiring, selfish, and to live by one's own values. What Nietzsche argues in contrasting master and slave morality is that the 'knowledge' which arises in each case is perfectly legitimate from the perspective of one who is either strong or weak. Belief in the truths of slave morality, after all, was and probably continues to be a source of strength for many people. As a condition of life, the knowledge master and slave morality professes is not an absolute knowledge, *à la* Hegel, but is what enables one in a given life-condition to thrive.

This understanding of knowledge is more commonly known as Nietzsche's theory of perspectivism. Nietzsche's perspectivism, in fact, is explicitly contrasted with Hegel, with what Nietzsche refers to as 'the dangerous old conceptual fiction that posited a "pure, will-less, painless, timeless knowing subject" ... "absolute spirituality," "knowledge in itself,"' and to this he claims 'there is only a perspective seeing, only a perspective "knowing"; and the more affects we allow to speak about one thing, the more eyes, different eyes, we can use to observe one thing, the more complete will our "concept" of this thing, our "objectivity," be.'[13] This perspectivism is not to be confused with relativism. Although the perspectives of slave and master morality arise in response to their respective life-conditions, this does not mean that one perspective is as good as another. For Nietzsche both absolutism and relativism with respect to values are 'equally childish.'[14] Furthermore, as any reader of Nietzsche is well aware, Nietzsche does not hold back in his criticisms of slave morality. Nietzsche thus clearly embraces a criterion or standard whereby he judges the merits of a given perspective. This standard is simply that of life itself: if a perspective or 'knowledge' enhances the ability to live, which entails thriving, growing, and becoming dominant, then it is better than one which leads to a decline. And accumulating a number of 'different' perspectives, or acquiring the 'objectivity' of many 'different eyes,' enables one to be better able to adapt to changing circumstances. It is good for life, and consequently a more 'objective' person will be more likely to cope with an uncommon, unexpected circumstance than one who dogmatically clings to a single perspective.

This latter claim lies at the basis of Nietzsche's critique of metaphysics. The desire to 'know,' to have certainty in an uncertain world, the common in the face of the uncommon, reaches its pinnacle with religion and metaphysics. In fact, Nietzsche, in line with the argument sketched above, states that 'how much one needs a faith in order to flourish ... is a measure of the degree of one's strength (or, to put the point more clearly, of one's weakness).'[15] And he places metaphysics in this category as well: it is the faith in absolute certainties, in a reality that transcends the perspectives of life; and thus, as with religion, 'metaphysics is still needed by some.'[16] Metaphysics, including (perhaps especially) the philosophy of Hegel, exemplifies the need to know, the need to reduce the uncommon to the common, so that those who are weak, or who cannot endure that which is strange and different, can live and flourish. It is this move to reaffirm the uncommon, Nietzsche's call to become who you are in response to the perceived tendencies of religion and metaphysics which call for one to become the common, the certain, which has influenced, beginning with Heidegger, much of the twentieth-century critique of metaphysics. Before we turn to a discussion of Heidegger and this critique, however, we must first, in light of what we have said so far, examine the relationship between the uncommon and system in Nietzsche's writings.

To discuss the significance of system in Nietzsche's philosophy might seem misguided, unless of course one intends to discuss Nietzsche's *critique* of system and systematic philosophy, such as his critique and rejection of Hegel. Nietzsche, however, does not reject system or systematic philosophy. What Nietzsche rejects is a system which claims to transcend the perspective of one's life-condition (as with Hegel, for example). It is in this vein, then, that, in the preface to his early work on the pre-Socratics, Nietzsche praises the systematic philosophy of the pre-Socratics. This philosophy, or the fragments that remain of it, however, do not express an absolute truth of the world; rather, the fragments of the pre-Socratics express the personality (i.e., perspective) of the philosopher. As Nietzsche puts it, these 'philosophical systems are wholly true for their founders only. For all subsequent philosophers they usually represent one great mistake, for lesser minds a sum of errors and truths'; and yet, Nietzsche continues, 'whoever rejoices in great human beings will also rejoice in philosophical systems, even if completely erroneous. They always have one wholly incontrovertible point: personal mood, color.'[17] In a later preface, he reiterates this point more strongly: 'The only thing of interest in a refuted system is the personal element. It alone is what is forever irrefutable.'[18] In approaching a philosophical system, therefore, Nietzsche is not looking for a timeless, eternal truth, nor is he looking for a few shreds of truth scattered in among the errors. This latter task is only what those with 'lesser minds' do. What Nietzsche looks for is the unique, incomparable perspective which infuses the various claims that are made, much as, to use Nietzsche's own analogy, one can come to an understanding of the soil by studying what grows in this soil.[19] Similarly, a philosophical system grows from the perspective of the philosopher; or the philosopher's philosophy, as Nietzsche says much later in *Beyond Good and Evil*, is simply 'the personal confession of its author and a kind of involuntary and unconscious memoir; also that the moral (or immoral) intentions in every philosophy constituted the real germ of life from which the whole plant had grown.'[20]

In *Beyond Good and Evil* it becomes much clearer what perspective Nietzsche looks for in attempting to account for and understand a philosophical system – namely, the moral (or immoral) perspective. In particular, Nietzsche studies a philosophical system to see whether it is the expression of an ascending or descending life. To the extent that Nietzsche does this, it appears, then, that though Nietzsche stresses the significance of the uncommon, unique, and incomparable, and rails against metaphysics for reducing the uncommon to the common, Nietzsche nonetheless does much the same thing. By setting forth the criterion and standard which is based upon what is life-enhancing, one could argue that Nietzsche, too, is doing metaphysics insofar as the uncommon (e.g., the unique, incomparable perspective expressed within a philosophical system) is reduced to that which is common, or what Nietzsche will most frequently refer to as will to power – that is, our *common* tendency as living beings to do what it takes to thrive. This is roughly the criticism Heidegger makes of Nietzsche. Nietzsche, Heidegger believes, was on the right track in attempting to overcome the metaphysical tradition, and in many ways Heidegger believes Nietzsche completely reversed the tradition, but by simply reversing it Nietzsche remained within the grips of metaphysics and failed to overcome it; or, Nietzsche was the last metaphysician.

In his critique of Nietzsche, Heidegger pays particularly close attention to Nietzsche's self-proclaimed attempt to move beyond Platonism and, with this, beyond Christianity, which Nietzsche called 'Platonism for "the people."'[21] At the basis of Nietzsche's move beyond Platonism, and the justification for his critique of Christianity, is an understanding of life as will to power. Nietzsche is explicit on this point: anything that 'is a living and not a dying body ... will have to be an incarnate will to power, it will strive to grow, spread, seize, become predominant – not from any morality or immorality but because it is living and because life simply is will to power.'[22] Nietzsche will thus criticize Platonism for emphasizing the eternal life of the soul that is distinct from the body, from 'incarnate will to power' (note Nietzsche's criticism of Socrates for accepting death as a cure for the illness of life); and he will say much the same about Christianity and its valorization of the weak, downtrodden, and self-sacrificing, while simultaneously giving greatest significance to the eternal life after the death of this body. Heidegger recognizes the importance life plays as a standard whereby Nietzsche judges various perspectives. Most notably, Heidegger, in his book on Parmenides, recognizes the necessity for life, as will to power, to seek a continual aggrandizement of power: 'Power can only be assured by the constant enhancement of power. Nietzsche recognized this very clearly and declared that within the realm of essence of the will to power the mere preservation of an already attained level of power already represents a decrease in the degree of power.'[23] Therefore, as Heidegger notes, because Nietzsche thinks 'in accord with the usual "biological" way of thinking of the second half of the nineteenth century,' he thinks will to power as life, or more precisely as the process whereby life is promoted through the control, domination, and securing of one's environment. The result of will to power, then, is an environment that is predictable, calculable, comfortable, and thus an environment wherein a living being, an 'incarnate will to power,' can thrive.

It would be a mistake, however, as Heidegger was correct to point out, simply to identify Nietzsche's thought with the 'biological' way of thinking, or of a reductionism based on biology, what Nietzsche's critics have called 'biologism.' In the appropriately titled chapter from his work on Nietzsche, 'Nietzsche's Alleged Biologism,' Heidegger claims that 'this current and, in a way, correct characterization of Nietzschean thinking as biologism presents the main obstacle to our penetrating his fundamental thought.'[24] This obstacle consists in assuming that a biological way of thinking has already decided which beings are being questioned and examined, namely, living beings, when the real guiding question, as Heidegger reads Nietzsche, concerns the nature of beings as a whole. In extending the use of biological terms beyond the realm of living beings, Nietzsche is not to be accused of a category mistake, which is one of the criticisms of Nietzsche's alleged biologism. This accusation is symptomatic, according to Heidegger, of the failure to understand Nietzsche's 'fundamental thought.' When Nietzsche extends the use of biological terms, he does so, Heidegger concludes, in order to think 'beings as a whole [systematically],' and thus 'he is not thinking biologically [i.e., scientifically]. Rather, he grounds this apparently merely biological worldview metaphysically.'[25] Nietzsche's thought is more than an example of the typical thinking of the nineteenth century; his thinking is rare and exceptional – that is, he attempts to think beings as a whole, or Being.

Heidegger understands Nietzsche's theory of perspectivism in terms of this attempt to think beings as a whole. Heidegger does not read Nietzsche's notion of perspectivism to mean, in the manner of Leibniz, that there are an indefinite number of perspectives upon one, self-identical being.[26] The perspectives are not the manner in which an underlying reality appears, but instead reality is itself perspectival. As Heidegger puts it, 'all appearance and all apparentness are possible only if something comes to the fore and shows itself at all. What in advance enables such appearing is the perspectival itself ... [or] being-real is in itself perspectival, a bringing forward into appearance ...'[27] Nietzsche, in his theory of perspectivism, is not simply thinking 'biologically,' but more profoundly Nietzsche is thinking metaphysically, thinking Being as a whole, and with perspectivism Heidegger claims 'Reality, Being, is Schein in the sense of perspectival letting shine.'[28]

In thinking metaphysically, however, Nietzsche's thought and philosophy are not, according to Heidegger, to be interpreted as simply another link in a long chain of metaphysical philosophies and systems. Nietzsche's philosophy and metaphysical thinking also bring an end to metaphysics: 'Nietzsche's philosophy is the end of metaphysics.' But as end we are not to read closure or completion of metaphysics; but, rather, Nietzsche thinks the event which began metaphysics. Consequently, Heidegger claims that Nietzsche's philosophy is the end of metaphysics 'inasmuch as it reverts to the very commencement of Greek thought in a way that is peculiar to Nietzsche's philosophy alone.'[29] This same idea will be expressed in Heidegger's late essay 'The End of Philosophy and the Task of Thinking,' when he says that 'the end of philosophy is the place, that place in which the whole of philosophy's history is gathered in its most extreme possiblity,'[30] and hence the task of thinking is to think this 'extreme possibility,' or the very condition and possibility for thinking beings as a whole, that is, for thinking metaphysically. And this possibility is, as is well known, what Heidegger refers to as Being, as aletheia and unconcealment; moreover, in returning to the commencement of metaphysics, to the Greeks, we return to the 'extreme possibility' they did not, could not, think: 'What do ground and principle and especially principle of all principles mean? Can this ever be sufficiently determined unless we experience aletheia in a Greek manner as unconcealment and then, above and beyond the Greek, think it as the opening of self-concealing?'[31] The Greeks, in particular Parmenides and Heraclitus according to Heidegger, did experience beings as a whole as Being, as aletheia, but they could not think the 'self-concealing' of Being in beings, the self-concealing that is the condition of possibility for metaphysics. They could not think this, for though their thought was the event which marks the commencement of metaphysics, they could not think this possibility for it had not yet come to be. Thus, they did not do metaphysics, or think Being as being, as presence, logos, etc. With the metaphysics of Plato and Aristotle, being as a whole is thought, but it is not thought as presencing and unconcealment (Being as aletheia), but rather as presence, or as logos (being). It is the self-concealment of Being which is the 'extreme possibility' of metaphysics, and Parmenides and Heraclitus could not think this for they were experiencing Being, and neither could Aristotle and Plato for Being had been forgotten. It is to this commencement of metaphysics, then, that Heidegger claims Nietzsche's philosophy returns.

In returning to this commencement, however, Heidegger believes that Nietzsche did not ultimately think the commencement in its 'extreme possibility,' but rather thought Being not as presencing but as presence. For example, in returning to Parmenides and Heraclitus, Heidegger argues that Nietzsche's own philosophy is an attempt to embrace both apparently contradictory aspects of their thought – that is, Parmenides' claim that Being is and Becoming is not, and Heraclitus's claim that Becoming is and Being is not. Nietzsche does this, Heidegger claims, by emphasizing the permanence of each: 'Nietzsche argues that being is as fixated, as permanent; and that it is in perpetual creation and destruction.'[32] To justify this reading, Heidegger will cite the famous passage where Nietzsche claims: 'To stamp Becoming with the character of Being – that is the supreme will to power.'[33] In other words, the permanence of Parmenides' Being is its stability, its perdurance, and the same is true of Heraclitus's Becoming, whereby Becoming is the *permanent* nature of reality. Therefore, following the above-cited quote of Nietzsche, Heidegger reads it to mean that 'the sense is not that one must brush aside and replace Becoming as the impermanent – for impermanence is what Becoming implies – with being as the permanent. The sense is that one must shape Becoming as being in such a way that as becoming it is preserved, has subsistence, in a word, is.' And it is precisely this shaping of Becoming, this preservation of Becoming which gives it subsistence, that is the role of will to power.

It is this understanding of will to power which leads Heidegger to criticize Nietzsche as yet another metaphysician who fails to think

Being. By making the supreme will to power that function which pre-serves and shapes Becoming such that it *is*, Nietzsche thus thinks being as a whole not as presencing, as Being, but as presence, as what *is* (being). When Nietzsche claims, then, that 'the world viewed from inside, the world defined and determined according to its "intelligible character" – it would be "will to power" and nothing else,'[34] Nietzsche continues to adhere to the metaphysical tradition which thinks Being as being and as a whole,[35] or Being as presencing has been en-framed, boxed in, contained and preserved as the presence of being and that which *is*, that which has been stamped with being. Heidegger states this criticism quite clearly when, after again quoting Nietzsche's statement that the supreme will to power is 'to stamp Becoming with the character of Being,' he says: 'Why is this the supreme will to power? The answer is, because will to power in its most profound essence is nothing other than the permanentizing of Becoming into presence.'[36] And later Heidegger will criticize Nietzsche's notion of 'eternal recurrence' for precisely the same reason that Nietzsche criticized Hegel – that is, he reduced the uncommon to the common, the unstable to the stable:

> Eternal recurrence [of the same] is the most constant permanentizing of the unstable. Since the beginning of Western metaphysics, Being has been understood in the sense of permanence of presencing, whereby perma-nence has ambiguously meant both fixity and persistence. Nietzsche's concept of the eternal recurrence of the same expresses the same essence of Being. Nietzsche of course distinguishes Being as the stable, firm, fixed, and rigid, in contrast to Becoming. But Being nonetheless pertains to will to power, which must secure stability for itself by means of permanence, solely in order to be able to surpass itself; that is, in order *to become*.[37]

Nietzsche's philosophy attempts to put an end to metaphysics, as Heidegger correctly noted, by returning to the commencement of meta-physics and the event which led to the decline that made metaphysics possible; but with Nietzsche's understanding of will to power and eter-nal recurrence, however, he in the end does not think this commence-ment and remains committed to the tradition of metaphysics which arrested this commencement:

> Neither Nietzsche nor any thinker prior to him – even and especially not that one who before Nietzsche first thought the history of philosophy in a philosophical way, namely, Hegel – revert to the incipient commence-

ment. Rather, they invariably apprehend the commencement in the sole light of a philosophy in decline from it, a philosophy that arrests that commencement – to wit, the philosophy of Plato.[38]

It is for this reason that Heidegger believes Nietzsche's self-proclaimed effort to twist free from Plato is destined to fail. Nietzsche's inversion of Plato, Heidegger claims, 'represents the entrenchment of that position.'[39] In other words, Nietzsche continues to adhere to the notion that there is a true, ultimate reality. Thus, in inverting Plato, Heidegger states that for Nietzsche 'the vacant niches of the "above and below" are preserved, suffering only a change in occupancy, as it were. But as long as the "above and below" define the formal structure of Platonism, Platonism in its essence perdures.' The overcoming of Platonism is successful only when 'the "above" in general is set aside as such, when the former positing of something true and desirable no longer arises, when the true world – in the sense of the ideal – is expunged.'[40] To the extent that Nietzsche's understanding of will to power is such that it is what is real, what is true, then Nietzsche does not successfully escape Platonism.

This is exactly how Heidegger, in his book *Parmenides*, interprets Nietzsche's understanding of the will to power. Here, too, Heidegger argues that 'the entire thinking of the Occident from Plato to Nietzsche thinks in terms of this delimitation of the essence of truth as correctness.'[41] Rather than thinking truth as unconcealedness, as aletheia, and thus truth as the 'extreme possibility' for thinking and for thinking beings, the being or reality of thought and beings is assumed, and truth becomes the correct correspondence between thought and beings. Truth as *aletheia*, as the unstable Being and clearing which allows for the presencing of thinking and being, is stabilized and replaced by the Roman view of truth as *veritas*, as correctnes. And the Roman view arose, according to Heidegger, for the sake of maintaining their imperial command and security, whereby any instability and novelty must be dominated and contained within an order-ing command, a command which establishes a reality that corresponds to its will.[42] In the case of Nietzsche, will to power completes this Roman view by also being understood in the sense of a command ('will to power, as expressly determined by Nietzsche, is in essence command'),[43] or will to power molds and shapes Becoming, the unstable and uncommon, so that becoming can be preserved as that which is. To preserve becoming as that which is, to constitute (schematize) a knowledge and enhancement of power which is a necessary condition for life, this will to power must constantly reflect upon its own status, or it must continually determine that it is in agreement with its will and necessity as will to power. Heidegger is explicit on this point: 'In the essence of assurance [i.e., assurance that there has been an "enhancement of power"] there resides a constant back-relatedness to itself, and in this lies the required self-elevation.'[44] With this move Heidegger believes that the Roman turn to truth as veritas becomes completed when truth as certainty of correspondence becomes absolutized to being the certainty of self-presence: 'In Hegel's metaphysics and in Nietzsche's, i.e., in the nineteenth century, the transformation of veritas into certitudo is completed. This completion of the Roman essence of truth is the proper and hidden historical meaning of the nineteenth century.'[45] Thus, despite his professed break with Hegel, Nietzsche remains firmly entrenched, on Heidegger's reading, to the Hegelian view that all novelty, all that is uncommon and unstable, is ultimately reducible to the certainty of self-presence, to what is essentially true and common to all (Spirit for Hegel and will to power for Nietzsche). It is for this reason, finally, that Heidegger concludes: 'Nietzsche's metaphysics, and with it the essential ground of "classical nihilism," may now be more clearly delineated as a metaphysics of the absolute subjectivity of will to power.'[46]

To think the end of metaphysics and philosophy, Heidegger agrees that one must, as did Nietzsche, return to the commencement of metaphysics in order to think its 'extreme possibility.' But in doing this one does not simply abandon the traditional metaphysical question 'what is being?' or 'what is being as a whole?' Rather, one inquires into the beingness of being, or the Being of being. Nietzsche abandoned the effort to answer the metaphysical question because he saw any answer as a mere fiction one constructs in order to give oneself a sense of security and comfort.[47] But by accounting for this need for security and comfort in terms of will to power, Nietzsche does not leave metaphysics behind, but remains firmly within its grasp as what Heidegger calls the 'last metaphysician.' To inquire into the beingness of beings, the Being of beings, however, or to return to the commencement of metaphysics and the thinking of Being as a whole, one will not find the uncommon reduced to the common; to the contrary, one will find the uncommon within the common. Consequently, in his reading of Parmenides, Heidegger finds that at the commencement of metaphysics the experience of Being – the experience that conditioned the metaphysician's pursuit of an answer to the question 'what is being?' – involved an experience of the uncommon, non-identifiable absence at the heart of what is common. Heidegger thus claims that when 'Being comes into focus, there the extraordinary announces itself, the excessive that strays "beyond" the ordinary, that which is not to be explained by explanations on the basis of beings. This is the uncanny.'[48] The end of metaphysics and philosophy, therefore, does not mean an end to philosophical thinking, unless by that one means the reduction of what is uncommon to that which is common and ordinary; instead, with the end of metaphysics comes the task of thinking the extraordinary within the ordinary, the uncommon within the common, or what Heidegger calls the 'uncanny.'

It is perhaps this effort of Heidegger's to think the uncommon within the common, the extraordinary within the ordinary, which has had the most influence upon contemporary Continental thought, in particular the work of Jacques Derrida. Derrida's philosophy, in fact, as even Derrida himself admits, is largely a continuation of the critique of metaphysics begun by Heidegger. In particular, Derrida narrows in on the claim made by Heidegger in his book *Parmenides*, and discussed above, that 'the entire thinking of the Occident from Plato to Nietzsche thinks in terms of ... truth as correctness.'[49] 'The essence of truth as *veritas* (i.e., correctnes),' Heidegger adds, 'is *without space* and without ground.'[50] There is no space, no distance, between our true thoughts concerning a state of affairs in the world and that state of affairs: the two coincide. The result is the *presence* of truth as self-evidence, or the presence of thought to itself in the manner of self-identity. 'What is lacking,' as we have seen Heidegger develop his critique of metaphysics, 'is the essential space of aletheia, the unconcealedness of things and the disclosing comportment of man, a space completely covered over by debris and forgotten.'[51] What is absent in traditional metaphysics is precisely a thinking sensitive to the unconcealedness which allows for the presencing of that which presents itself, and thus the spacing which allows for the ability to think in terms of *veritas* and *rectitudo*.

Derrida is very much in agreement with Heidegger on this issue. In *Speech and Phenomena*, for example, Derrida claims that the Western emphasis upon the phonetic alphabet accounts in large part for the understanding of truth as self-presence, or as the reduction and forgetting of space: 'hearing oneself speak is experienced as an absolutely pure auto-affection, occurring in a self-proximity that would in fact be the absolute reduction of space in general.'[52] But what Derrida will continually argue and remind us is that 'auto-affection' or 'self-presence' already presupposes a 'pure difference ... and in this pure difference is rooted the possibility of everything we think we can exclude from auto-affection: space, the outside, the world, the body, etc.'[53] And the term most used by Derrida to characterize this pure difference which entails the space auto-affection, or truth as veritas, thought it had expunged, is *differance*; and the function of differance, this pure difference, is to delay the coming to identity and presence of self, or it pollutes identity with a trace of otherness, a space that cannot be reduced: 'this pure difference, which constitutes the self-presence of the living present, introduces into self-presence from the beginning the impurity putatively excluded from it. The living present springs forth out of its nonidentity with itself and from the possibility of a retentional trace. It is always already a trace.'[54] Again, in *Of Grammatology*, Derrida will refer to differance as 'an economic concept designating the production of differing/deferring.'[55] Differance is therefore the pure difference which allows for the possibility of a self coming into presence with itself (i.e., as veritas), and yet it forever defers complete presence and self-identity because it harbours a trace of space and otherness that subverts this identity. More importantly, the fullness and plentitude of self-presence, the plentitude of hearing oneself speak and of having a substantiality intimately tied to the vocalized expression of our ideas, is not the condition for understanding self-presence (though this *is* the implicit, unquestioned assumption of traditional ontotheological metaphysics according to Derrida); rather, Derrida argues that differance (or what he also calls trace) is the condition for this plentitude, and hence for traditional metaphysics: 'The (pure) trace is differance. It does not depend on any sensible plentitude, audible or visible, phonic or graphic. It is, on the contrary, the condition of such a plentitude.'[56] Derrida's deconstructive readings of texts, subsequently, involve thinking or observing the effects of this trace, the play which allows for the presence of the ideas in a text, but which also prohibits closure and complete self-presence.

An obvious target of such a deconstructive reading is the system of Hegel. Hegel's system, as we saw, involved the coming to self-presence of the Notion, or what Hegel called the 'self-comprehending pure Notion.' In his reading of Hegel, therefore, Derrida would argue that there is a pure difference or trace which allows for the possibility of Hegel's system, though a difference which renders impossible the successful completion of this system. Differance forever exceeds system, or is the condition for system that cannot be identified with system: 'differance ... cannot, as the condition of all linguistic systems, form a part of the linguistic system itself and be situated as an object in its field.'[57] And with this claim we see, finally, the manner in which we can begin to understand our earlier claim that paradoxa is the condition for the possibility and impossibility of all systems, a condition that is inseparable from systems though not to be identified with them. Differance is the condition for the possibility of a Hegelian-styled system, and it is inseparable from such a system for Derrida is clear that differance is not to be understood as absence, or as the negation of presence; instead, differance leaves a trace, or an element of play and excess within every system, and it is precisely the effort to read and uncover these excesses and elements of play, the uncommon within the common, that is the 'proper' task of deconstruction as Derrida sees it.

Derrida makes these points quite explicitly in his essay on Bataille, or more precisely on Bataille's reading of Hegel. Derrida highlights Bataille's understanding of sovereignty, and contrasts it with that of the Lord. The latter involves the subordination of everything to the Lord's own positivity. Thus, for example, in his reading of Hegel, Bataille believes that Hegel confronted the negativity of death and yet sought to overcome it within the positivity of thought or system. As Derrida describes it: 'The blind spot of Hegelianism, around which can be organized the representation of meaning, is the point at which destruction, suppression, death and sacrifice constitute so irreversible an expenditure, so radical a negativity ... that they can no longer be determined as negativity in a process or a system.'[58] In Hegel, of course, this negativity is always subordinated to the ultimate positivity of the Idea or Notion, and thus Hegel's blind spot, his Lord function, is to understand negativity as 'the underside and accomplice of positivity,' or as what we have also called the plentitude of self-presence. In his reading of Hegel, Bataille uncovers this blind spot, or reveals the play of a sovereign operation at the very heart of Hegel's system. This 'sovereign operation,' as Derrida defines it, 'is neither positive nor negative. It cannot be inscribed in discourse, except by crossing out predicates or by practicing a contradictory superimpression that then exceeds the logic of philosophy.'[59] As with differance, then, the sovereign is neither absence nor presence; it is inseparable from systems but not to be identified with them; it is the excess beyond and within system which Bataille, and Derrida, attempt to think.

Bataille also attempts to write this excess, or attempts to write the sovereign, in a way that is not subordinate to some positivity à la Hegel. Such a sovereign writing would neither be a writing subordinate to a dominant meaning, nor would it involve a relation to an ultimate standard and criterion; rather, this writing would 'institute a relation in the form of a nonrelation, [it would] inscribe rupture in the text, [and would] place the chain of discursive knowledge in relation to an unknowledge which is not a moment of knowledge.'[60] To write in this manner, however, entails, as Derrida goes on to clarify, passing between 'two dangerous straits.'[61] On the one hand, one 'must not isolate notions as if they were their own context,' or as if one could understand the meaning of what one is saying independently of its relationship to the other notions and concepts that are at play in one's writing. On the other hand, 'one must not submit contextual attentiveness and differences of signification to a system of meaning.' [62] In other words, one is to write (or read) the uncommon within the common, the excess and beyond of a system that is inseparable from the system, but one is to do so without either subordinating the meaning of what one is saying to the totality of a system, or by abandoning system and the interrelationships of meaning altogether. As Derrida puts it, 'this transgression of discourse [associated with sovereign writing] must, in some fashion, and like every transgression, conserve or confirm that which it exceeds.'[63] In Bataille's understanding of the sovereign function (and sovereign writing), therefore, there is a key similarity with Hegel's theory of the Aufhebung, which also emphasizes the transgression and surpassing that simultaneously conserves. Derrida notes a crucial difference, however, in that whereas 'the Hegelian Aufhebung is produced entirely from within discourse, from within the system or the work of signification ... [and thus] the Aufhebung is included within the circle of absolute knowledge, never exceeds its closure, never suspends the totality of discourse, work, meaning, law, etc.'; Bataille's Aufhebung, to the contrary, is an 'empty form of the Aufhebung,' or it is used 'in an analogical fashion, in order to designate, as was never done before, the transgressive relationship which links the world of meaning to the world of nonmeaning.'[64] Consequently, when one successfully steers a path between the two dangerous straits, one does not abandon systematic thinking or writing, one does not abandon what is common; one simply allows for the effects of play and excess to enter the scene.[65]

Derrida thus recognizes the importance of system, the need for systematic interrelationships, or what is often referred to as the interdependence of texts, but this system is placed in relation to a nonmeaning, to a trace and pure difference whose spacing keeps the system forever open to an outside, to new possibilities. Thus in his famous essay 'Differance,' Derrida notes that Saussure was partially correct to say that the meaning of any given word in a language is dependent upon its relationship to all the other words in the language, or this meaning is dependent upon how it *differentiates* itself from the other words of the language. As Derrida puts it, 'Saussure had only to remind us that the play of difference was a functional condition, the condition of possibility, for every sign.'[66] The meaning of a word can therefore not be understood independently of its relationship to the other words of the language, or to the context of the language itself. The meaning of each word is not, as a consequence of Saussure's view of the differentiality of language, a self-contained identity and fullnes; rather, 'the system of signs is constituted by the differences between the terms, and not by their fullness.'[67] At the same time, and this is where Derrida believes Saussure was incorrect, Saussure continued to understand the differentiality of language in terms of the complete, full system of language itself. Derrida even quotes Saussure's claim that '"Whether we take the signified or the signifier, language has neither ideas nor sounds that existed before the linguistic system, but only conceptual and phonic differences *that have issued from the system*."'[68]

It is on this point where we can see that Derrida's reading of Hegel will apply to a reading of Saussure. Just as Hegel understood the significance of terms, concepts, and events as being in a relationship of subordination to the totality of the system (or Notion), so too does Saussure understand the differential relationships between linguistic terms to be subordinate to, and dependent upon, the totality of the system of language. Derrida will reverse this relationship, and thus, as was the case in his reading of Hegel, difference and differential relations are not to be conditioned by the totality and fullness of a system, but instead it is a pure difference (differance or trace) which is the condition for any and all possible systems. Derrida is straightforward on this point: 'differance – is no longer simply a concept, but the possibility of conceptuality, of the conceptual system and process in general.'[69] And a little later he reiterates this point: 'we shall designate by the term differance the movement by which language, or any code, any system of reference in general, becomes "historically" constituted as a fabric of differences.'[70] Consequently, Derrida will argue that to find 'a way out of the closure' of Saussure's system, or the tradition of metaphysics which thinks presence as self-presence, or totality and closure as a coming back and into oneself, one needs to think system, presence, etc., not as conditions for difference and differential relations, but one needs to think system and presence 'as a "determination" and an "effect."' That is, system and presence are 'effects' of differance. Derrida thus does not abandon system and systematicity, as we showed above, but rather than posit a closed, total system such as Hegel and Saussure, Derrida argues for an open system, a system of differance: 'Presence is a determination and effect within a system which is no longer that of presence but that of differance.'[71]

Derrida's understanding of system as an effect of differance has had its critics. Among them is Manfred Frank. Frank argues that Derrida's 'radical outbidding of Saussure' – that is to say, his claim that the system of language is an effect of the play of differance rather than a condition for such play – leaves Derrida unable to account for any identifiable meaning. For Frank, 'without a moment of relative self-identity differentiation could not be established at all, differentiation would lack a criterion and would be indistinguishable from complete inertia.'[72] Without at least a minimum of self-contained identity, a moment of significance that is full and identifiable, Frank believes there is no way to establish the differences between terms, or there is no criterion whereby one can say a term is excluded from another. Frank will then cite what appears to be Derrida's own recognition of this need:

> Iterability requires a minimal remaining (restance) (like an, albeit limited, minimal idealisation) for identity to be repeatable and identifiable in, through, and even with a view to alteration. For the structure of iteration – another decisive trait – implies at the same time identity and difference.[73]

However, because differance forever delays and defers the return to presence, or forever subverts the possibility of self-contained, identifiable meaning, Frank argues that Derrida's own premises have left him unable to account adequately for what he readily admits is needed. And Derrida clearly and explicitly admits he is not abandoning the standards and criteria of truth, which would leave us without a means for determining whether a given text has been read and interpreted truthfully or not. An interpreter cannot, Derrida argues, 'add any old thing' to the text that has not been 'rigorously prescribed' by the text, 'by the logic of play' of this text.[74] 'The value of truth,' Derrida points out, 'is never contested or destroyed in my writings.'[75] Derrida will even go so far as to say that Searle, in his critique of Derrida, in his reading and interpretation of Derrida's writings, has not followed its 'logic of play,' and he has thus read him wrong, or falsely. But if pushed to supply the logic, the protocol or criteria which one ought to

remain 'true' to, or the guard rails which would prevent one from add-
ing 'any old thing' to the text, Derrida confesses that 'I have not found
any that satisfy me.'[76] Frank's criticism of Derrida, as we have seen, is
that Derrida will forever remain unsatisfied, will never find an acceptable criterion, unless he abandons his premises concerning differance,
and in effect 'relinquishes his position.'[77]

Throughout this book it will be argued that the difficulty Frank cites
regarding Derrida is avoidable, and more importantly it will be argued
that Gilles Deleuze has set forth what we believe to be an important
example of how to avoid it. The problem for Derrida arises in that he
understands system (i.e., Saussure's and Hegel's view of system) as an
'effect' of differance. Derrida therefore does not have Saussure's complete system (*langue*) at his disposal in order to account for identifiable
meanings, or for a criterion. Derrida's theory of differance accounts
quite well for the undermining of self-contained meaning and self-presence, but runs into difficulties in explaining how there can be identifiable meanings in the first place, how there can be acceptable criteria and
standards. Derrida is correct, we argue, to claim that the complete system of Saussure is undermined by differance; however, Derrida then
proceeds to prioritize differance over system, and hence the understanding of system as an 'effect.' We will claim that there is a reciprocal
presupposition between system, that is, system as closed and complete
(if only provisionally so, as we will see) and differance. We will use the
term 'chaosmos' in referring to this reciprocal presupposition of completion and differance, system and paradoxa.

We have chosen the term 'chaosmos' for a straightforward reason –
namely, it captures the sense that both chaos and cosmos are reciprocally presupposed.[78] Cosmos corresponds to the sense of system as
order, or system as traditionally understood by Hegel and others; that is,
system as the gathering of determinations and differences (e.g., the
novel and uncommon) in accordance with, or as subordinate to, an Idea
or Identity. In the case of Hegel, this identity was the emerging self-consciousness and self-presence of the Idea, and the entire system of
Nature, as we saw, was gathered and subordinate to this Idea. Chaos, on
the other hand, corresponds to what is beyond and exceeds system; it is
what Bataille and Derrida attempt to think when Bataille writes (of) the
sovereign function and Derrida writes of the functioning of differance.
Chaosmos, therefore, entails both a closed, self-contained system and a
chaos which exceeds it. While exceeding cosmos, however, chaos also
contains or preserves it. This is the sense in which Bataille's sovereign

writing transgresses while it preserves and affirms what is transgressed – Bataille's *Aufhebung*. Foucault notes much the same with respect to Bataille when he argues that transgression (excess) simultaneously affirms the prohibitions it goes beyond (i.e., *system* of laws). Where we differ with this line of argument, and with Derrida in particular, is in our position that chaos is not to be seen as a simple function (*à la* differance), a differing/deferring function; rather, chaos is the limit functioning must forever stave off while not being a function itself. Derrida does say that differance is likewise the condition of possibility for a text, a condition a text must repress or stave off if it is to function as a meaningful text. But differance, as condition for presence and fullness, is not to be identified with fullness; in fact, Derrida states quite explicitly, as we have seen, that presence and fullness are 'effects' of differance.[79] The argument set forth here, and detailed further in chapter 5, is that while agreeing with Derrida's position that chaos is non-identifiable, we differ fundamentally with Derrida in claiming chaos is precisely the very fullness of identifiable beings, rather than an absence or trace presupposed by such beings. Chaos is thus non-identifiable, or not to be confused with the fullness of presence, for the reason that it exceeds the limits necessary for identification and for presence.

In our chapter on Derrida, we will further examine Derrida's claim that plentitude and fullness is an 'effect' of differance. As the argument comes to be developed below, it will be shown that Derrida's critique of fullness and plentitude is symptomatic of a motif common to traditional metaphysics: namely, the reduction of the complex, chaotic, and multiple to the simple. Derrida indeed recognizes this tendency in the metaphysical tradition and will routinely reveal the excessive play that lurks unquestioned within a text. Derrida's understanding of deconstruction, in fact, consists in large part in revealing and thinking that which is uncommon, unique, non-identifiable, excessive, and complex; and he thinks or reads this within a text which at one level claims to be setting forth truths that are simple, pure, and common. We saw how Derrida read Hegel in this way. Despite these moves, Derrida's understanding of plentitude and fullness as conditioned by the productive function of difference will in effect reduce the uncommon excess to being something ultimately related to a functional process that is common to all, in particular to all texts.[80] Couple this with Derrida's further claim that 'there is nothing outside of the text,'[81] and it follows that everything has one thing in common: they are all 'effects' of differance. As we understand chaosmos, and as it will be argued Deleuze understands multiplicities, plateaus, bodies without organs, etc., it is, as Derrida argues with respect to differance, non-identifiable, but it is non-identifiable precisely because of its excessive plentitude and fullness, or because it is inseparable from the systems it conditions. Chaosmos is only identifiable, we claim, when its excessive fullness is filtered, sustained, and contained. Such a containment process does not arise *ex nihilo*; that is, it does not create identity out of nothing (this was essentially Frank's problem with Derrida); it always already has elements of containment, a system, to work with. Chaos is inseparable from an identifiable system, from a cosmos, and hence the term 'chaosmos.'

What this approach offers is an answer to the problem concerning criteria we saw Frank draw attention to with respect to Derrida. In the succeeding chapters of this book, it will be argued that chaos and cosmos are and ought to be in equilibrium, if only precariously so. Neither chaos nor cosmos should be realized to the exclusion of the other. A functioning system would collapse under either of the two possibilites – pure chaos would destroy just as readily as pure cosmos, for to function a system needs order and predictability (cosmos), but to be able to adapt to novel, unforeseen situations a system needs to experiment with untried, uncommon methods (chaos). Both chaos and cosmos are necessary, or, to recall the point made in the introduction, a functioning dynamical system functions best at the edge of chaos. The criterion, then, is chaosmos, or the necessity of maintaining the equilibrium between chaos and cosmos. And with this we can further clarify our position with respect to Derrida. In particular, the functioning of differance, as a functioning and 'production' of 'effects,' is a function which is possible only on the condition of this precarious equilibrium, or on the basis of a system at the edge of chaos (chaosmos).

In affirming and writing of differance, Derrida does affirm its both/and quality (Derrida often refers to such both/ands as undecidables),[82] but in extending Derrida we argue that system – that is, a closed system which enables the identification and relation of terms, *à la* Saussure – is not simply an 'effect,' but is equally affirmed in that which exceeds it (chaos). Moreover, in affirming system, or cosmos, we affirm what Bataille refers to in discussing Hegel's system: the concrete totality of all that is. In rejecting Hegel's system, and in thinking the play of differance which undermines Hegel's system by instilling a play of meaning which defers the closure of this system, Derrida is ultimately led to ignore the play of differance within the concrete totality, and hence the relative lack of political engagement on Derrida's part with political systems. Rather than examining the textual effects of differ-ance within texts, we will, beginning with Spinoza and continuing throughout the remaining chapters of this book, show how important concepts of key philosophers come, in Deleuze's hands, to be used to think concrete totalities, totalities which are inseparable from, and affirm, the uncommon (chaos) that transforms these totalities into a multiplicity of other totalities – a thousand plateaus. Deleuze's effort, in the end, is to think the uncommon within the concrete, common reality, the chaos in the cosmos; in short, Deleuze is doing philosophy.

2 Ironing Out the Differences: Nietzsche and Deleuze as Spinozists

Friedrich Nietzsche's critique of traditional philosophy is well known. Much of his philosophical venom, as we shall see in more detail in the next chapter, is directed against what he sees as the life-denying intellectual legacy that originated with Plato. Included among Nietzsche's flurry of criticisms, however, is an important and influential critique of Descartes. In particular, Nietzsche argues that Descartes' claim to have established the certainty of the *cogito* is far from certain and instead presupposes a 'grammatical habit: "Thinking is an activity; every activity requires an agent; consequently –."'[1] The eventual lesson Nietzsche draws from Descates' case, as well as a host of others, is that any philosopher's claim to have uncovered a bedrock of certainty is ultimately nothing other than a coping mechanism that satisfies a need, what Nietzsche refers to as a 'metaphysical need.'[2]

It should come as quite a surprise, then, that Nietzsche, in a letter to Overbeck, writes, 'I am amazed, utterly enchanted! I have a precursor, and what a precursor! I hardly knew Spinoza ...'[3] This should be especially surprising to Spinoza scholars for two reasons, and perhaps more. First, Spinoza, as the influential Spinoza scholar Martial Gueroult has argued, goes even further than Descartes in arguing for the ability of human beings to acquire absolute, certain knowledge. As Gueroult points out, although Descartes and Leibniz both believe there are things we can know, and know with certainty, God is not one of these things; and yet, for Spinoza, God can be known with certainty.[4] The other reason Nietzsche's praise should come as a surprise is that many commentators interpret Spinoza in light of Descartes. Although differences between Spinoza and Descartes are noted, Spinoza is widely seen to have been profoundly influenced by Descartes and to be continuing the Cartesian project, even if to the extreme.[5] Nietzsche's criticisms of Descartes should therefore apply to Spinoza. Spinoza, in fact, seems to have carried the 'metaphysical need' to lengths that not even Descartes dared to take it.

Nietzsche does indeed criticize Spinoza at a number of places. For instance, Nietzsche refers to the 'hocus pocus of mathematical form with which Spinoza clad his philosophy – really "the love of *his* wisdom,"'[6] and he criticized Spinoza for emphasizing self-preservation (what Spinoza calls *conatus*) to the neglect of will to power, of which 'the struggle for existence is only an *exception*.'[7] And finally, though not exhaustively, Nietzsche was very critical of Spinoza's efforts to 'so naively [advocate] the destruction of the affects through their analysis and vivisection.'[8] Yet despite these criticisms Nietzsche does not group Spinoza with Descates as one who claims to have grounded knowledge on the certainty of the *cogito* and its clear and distinct ideas; to the contrary, in the previously cited letter to Overbeck, Nietzsche states that in addition to their shared tendency to 'make knowledge the most powerful affect,' there are five other points where they agree: 'he [Spinoza] denies the freedom of the will, teleology, the moral world-order, the unegoistic, and evil.' By seeing Spinoza as a philosopher who identified knowledge with the affects, and with the most powerful affect, Nietzsche places Spinoza at odds with the Cartesian claim that knowledge and the will are distinct, or that error comes in when our will and passions extend beyond the clear and distinct ideas our mind (*cogito*) presents. This interpretation is further reinforced, at least in Nietzsche's mind, by Spinoza's denial of the freedom of the will. This chapter shall therefore take Nietzsche's claims regarding Spinoza as a precursor seriously, and by doing this we will see how this reading of Spinoza can address many of the central problems and controversies that have plagued Spinoza's commentators, problems and controversies we feel result from an implicit and at times explicit reading of Spinoza as a Cartesian (i.e., as a metaphysical dualist). This reading will enable us to clarify two themes that were important to both Spinoza and Nietzsche – the critique of teleology and the effort to account for how a finite, mortal person can live eternally. Finally, by taking Nietzsche's claims concerning Spinoza as a precursor seriously, we can come to a greater understanding of the powerful influence both Spinoza and Nietzsche had on the work of Deleuze. Thus, despite what many see as Deleuze's excessive Nietzscheanism,[9] a Nietzscheanism that is certainly present, it is also important to recall and account for the fact that Deleuze claimed to be a Spinozist: '... I consider myself to be a Spinozist ... Spinoza is for me the "prince" of philosophers.'[10]

I

Of the controversies and criticisms which Spinoza's writings have generated, Part 5 of his *Ethics* has received perhaps the harshest and least forgiving of criticisms. Even scholars who are generally sympathetic to what Spinoza is doing find it difficult to accept many of the claims he makes in Part 5. Jonathan Bennett, for example, in his book on Spinoza, is quite forthright in his criticism of Part 5, in particular the last half of this part: 'Those of us who love and admire Spinoza's philosophical work should in sad silence avert our eyes from the second half of Part 5.'[11] Of the many problems Bennett finds here, one of the most troubling for him is Spinoza's discussion concerning the eternal part of the mind. Bennett claims that Spinoza unsuccessfully attempts to argue that the eternal part of the mind does not undergo change and is always and eternally what it is and will be, and yet at the same time he argues the eternal part of the mind can be enlarged, though with 'great effort.'[12] Bennett believes this inconsistency is 'unhealable' and claims that many of the remarks Spinoza makes in the latter pages of Part 5 betray an effort to 'hide' it.

Edwin Curley largely echoes these complaints, with his primary concern being Spinoza's claim that the more we understand of the body under the species of eternity, the more our mind itself will be eternal. Had Spinoza simply said that our *consciousness* of the eternity of the mind would have increased, and not the eternity of the mind itself, then Curley could have agreed. But to say that an increased understanding of the eternity of the mind also entails an increase in the eternity of the mind itself is something Curley finds 'completely unintelligible.'[13] On Curley's reading of Spinoza, what is eternal in a mind are certain facts that are common to all minds; therefore, with increased understanding we have not an increase in the eternity of a particular mind, but an increase in the understanding of the eternity of mind in general. This is not, however, what Curley believes Spinoza actually says; it is only what he feels he should have said.

What seems to be common to both Bennett's and Curley's difficulties with Part 5 is a distinction they make between an *act of intuition* and the *object intuited*. The object of an intuition is distinct from, and ought not to be confused with, the intuition itself. I can understand

and have an intuitive sense of how another might be feeling, but it does not follow from this that I am feeling that way. To claim, then, that understanding what is eternal in the mind actually increases the eternity of the mind would thus seem to confuse the object of an intuition with the intuition itself, and it is precisely this type of confusion which Bennett and Curley accuse Spinoza of making.

There is textual evidence to support Bennett's and Curley's position. For example, Spinoza states in 5P33S that 'the mind has had eternally the same perfections which, in our fiction, now come to it.' The fiction he alludes to is the necessity of speaking about the mind *as if* it were beginning to acquire, and we were beginning to understand, its eternity. Such a fiction allows for 'an easier explanation,' and yet the assumption is clear: the mind is already as eternal as it will be. Though we can come to a conscious awareness and understanding of the eternal perfections of the mind, such an understanding is distinct from the object intuited. Bennett and Curley thus seem to think that Spinoza should, if he were going to be consistent, have remained true to a fundamental, Cartesian distinction between an act of intuition and the object intuited. Spinoza, however, goes on to argue that 'the more the mind understands things by the second and third kind of knowledge, the greater the part of it that remains unharmed' (5P38D). In other words, the more the mind understands its eternal nature, the more of it that becomes eternal. Spinoza thus appears to fall afoul of Descartes' metaphysical dualism, and the working assumptions this entails, and it is this which Curley finds 'unintelligible.'

The difficulty here seems to be quite serious, and because of this problem, along with others, Bennett recommends we 'avert our eyes from the second half of Part 5,' suggesting we do this rather than attempt 'some rescuing interpretation.' Such an interpretation, Bennett argues, does not hold Spinoza to 'a more demanding standard,' and consequently does not show Spinoza's thought the respect it deserves; rather, rescuing interpretations blindly assume that Spinoza 'is always or usually right.'[14] However, by suggesting as Bennett and Curley do that Spinoza *should* have consistently maintained the dualistic assumption of there being a fundamental distinction between the understanding and that which is understood, one subsequently holds Spinoza to a standard that brings with it new difficulties. For example, because Spinoza defines the attributes as that which 'the intellect perceives of a substance, as constituting its essence' (1D4), he seems to be presupposing the mode of an attribute (i.e., the attribute of thought) in his very definition of attributes. A related problem would be Spinoza's claim that God is a substance which consists of an 'infinity of attributes,' a claim that is often interpreted to mean that the attributes are distinct predicates of a distinct subject, substance,[15] while others have stressed the strict identity of the attributes and substance by arguing that the attributes are not simple predicates of substance, but substance pure and simple.[16] Alan Donagan, Gilles Deleuze, and others have recognized the contradictory and problematic nature of these positions, and have attempted to reconcile them by emphasizing Spinoza's claim that each attribute '*expresses* an eternal and infinite essence.'[17] In other words, by understanding the attributes as expressions of substance, they believe we can resolve the difficulties that stem from the dualistic assumption that there is a hard and fast, irreconcilable difference between the attributes as that which an intellect perceives of substance, and substance itself, or the difference between an *act of intuition* and the *object intuited*.

The awareness of these difficulties can be traced back to the earliest commentators on Spinoza's *Ethics*.[18] In the remainder of this chapter, we propose to follow a Nietzschean, non-dualistic reading of Spinoza by arguing that substance, or God/Nature (*Deus sive Natura*), is to be understood as absolutely indeterminate self-ordering becoming. We adopt the term 'absolutely indeterminate' from H.F. Hallett, though for slightly different reasons.[19] The term is appropriate, we feel, for at least two reasons that are essential to Spinoza's project. First, since God is defined as absolutely infinite (1D6), God can in no way be limited or be in any way determinate. This is why God is *absolutely* infinite rather than infinite in its own kind. For God to be infinite in its own kind would require being a determinate and hence limited substance, a substance that presupposes something other than this substance, a substance of an *other* kind that limits and determines this one. Spinoza's monism clearly rules out this possibility. The second and related reason why 'absoutely indeterminate' is appropriate follows from Spinoza's claim in his letter to Jelles (Letter 50) that anyone who 'calls God one or single has no true idea of God' because one is forming a determinate, limited idea of God. Furthermore, since 'determination is negation,'[20] a person who develops a determinate conception of God thus lacks, for Spinoza, a true understanding of God.

With this understanding of God (or Nature), we propose to understand the attributes as the determinate order of identities immanent to absolutely indeterminate substance – that is, the order immanent to self-

ordering becoming. Modes shall be understood to be the actualization of this order, or more precisely they are the condition that allows for the possibility that the order immanent to self-ordering becoming comes to be determinate and identifiable. The attributes, then, are not identities waiting to be discovered; rather, they are identifiable as such only as modified. This suggested way of reading Spinoza might appear to force Spinoza's philosophy into addressing a set of concerns that were not his (i.e., the problem of being and becoming).[21] This criticism would seem to be especially valid to those who take Spinoza to understand substance as an eternal, unchanging being, or as a static substrate for attributes and modes.[22] There is a long tradition of contrasting interpretations, however, that stress the dynamic nature of substance, and it is with this camp that this chapter sides, at least initially.[23] Later we will see that it is only by unduly stressing the order immanent to substance, the being immanent to becomings, that many are led to argue for the nature of substance as static being (i.e., as subordinate to static laws of nature).

To show that our reading of the relationship between attributes and substance is not forced but actually illuminates many of Spinoza's explicit concerns and themes – in particular, his critique of teleology and the notion of living eternally – we begin by turning our attention to 2P8. The importance of this proposition has been noted, especially as it appears to reveal an apparent inconsistency in Spinoza's understanding of substance as necessarily and exhaustively actualized.[24] There should be no possibilities of substance that are not actualized, and yet that seems to be precisely what the proposition states: 'The ideas of singular things, or of modes, that do not exist must be comprehended in God's infinite idea in the same way as the formal essences of the singular things, or modes, are contained in God's attributes' (2P8). Spinoza bases this argument on 2P7, or his famous argument for the parallelism of ideas and things – 'The order and connection of ideas is the same as the order and connection of things' – but most especially he claims that 2P8 follows from the scholium to 2P7.

In this scholium, Spinoza reminds his readers that 'whatever can be perceived by an infinite intellect as constituting an essence of substance pertains to one substance only, and consequently that the thinking substance and the extended substance are one and the same substance, which is now comprehended [*comprehenditur*] under this attribute, now under that.' For our purposes, the key to this scholium is to clarify what is meant by saying that substance is 'comprehended' under an attribute.

As a preliminary answer, we claim that for the attributes to comprehend substance is to function as a condition for the possibility that the absolutely indeterminate becomes actualized in an infinite number of possible finite, determinate modes.[25] Thus Spinoza adds that the same substance that is comprehended in different ways continues to be the same, 'but [is] expressed in two ways.' The attributes thus comprehend different *manners* of actualization, and the modes are these actualizations. The attributes therefore comprehend absolutely indeterminate substance by allowing for an infinite number of actualizations in an infinite number of determinate ways; or, as Spinoza argues in 1D4, the attributes constitute the essence of substance ('By attribute I understand what the intellect perceives of a substance, as [*tanquam*] constituting its essence').

This returns us to our initial difficulty, however, for it appears that an infinite mode of an attribute (the infinite intellect) is used in the very definition of an attribute. It is no wonder, then, that this definition has led to many disputes among commentators. As Curley notes, *tanquam* can be translated by 'as' or 'as if.' The latter translation is proffered in support of subjective interpretations (e.g., Wolfson, Joachim, Kline, and others)[26] whereby the attributes are not taken to be real, and hence really distinct from each other, but are simply intellectual constructs. The objective interpretation by commentators as diverse as Gueroult, Curley, and Donagan holds that the attributes are really distinct constituents of the essence of substance. We side with the realist position, but shall argue that by understanding substance as the self-ordering becoming that is the condition for the actualization of determinate beings, we believe we can shed light on this debate. To see this, let us return to 2P7.

In an example from the scholium to 2P7 that foreshadows the claims made in 2P8, Spinoza claims 'a circle existing in nature and the idea of the existing circle, which is also in God, are one and the same thing, which is explained through different attributes.' In other words, despite the two ways of conceiving a circle, as an extended circle actually existing in nature or the idea of this circle, they each reflect 'one and the same order, or one and the same connection of causes.' Spinoza then reminds the reader that the idea we have of the circle is only as a mode of thought, a mode caused by another mode, and so on to infinity, and the circle as extension is caused by another mode, the drawing hand, and so on. He concludes the scholium to P7 by stating that 'God is really the cause [of the parallel order of causes] insofar as he consists of infinite attributes. For the present, I cannot explain these matters more clearly.'[27] Part of the lacking explanation, we argue, is that God's essence is his power, the power of self-ordering becoming as the condition for the possibility of determinate being, and hence for the possibility that a determinate, infinite intellect can differentiate between substance and its attributes, and hence perceive what constitutes the essence of substance. The lacking explanation thus relies, on our argument, on assumptions that are radically non-dualistic, and the significance of 2P8 is that it lays the groundwork for the explanation as it emerges in the latter half of Part 5.

Yet another reason 2P8 is so important is that it brings to bear an important distinction between durational and eternal existence. The former applies to the causal series of singular things. As Spinoza puts it in the corollary to P8, 'when singular things are said to exist, not only insofar as they are comprehended (*comprehenditur*) in God's attributes, but insofar as they are said to have duration, their ideas involve the existence through which they are said to have duration [i.e., other existing finite modes *ad infinitum*].' Spinoza then moves on to the scholium to explain this further by bringing in the example of a circle wherein 'there are contained infinitely many rectangles that are equal to one another.' 'Nonetheless,' Spinoza continues, 'none of them can be said to exist except insofar as the circle exists, nor also can the idea of any of these rectangles be said to exist except insofar as it is comprehended [*comprehenditur*] in the idea of the circle.' With this move, Spinoza parallels the relationship between the 'infinitely many rectangles' *comprehended* by the idea of the circle and the infinitely many singular things that are *comprehended* by God's attributes, and adds to this a third parallel to non-existent modes. Thus, the infinitely many singular things are *comprehended* by the attributes; the rectangles are *comprehended* in the idea of a circle; and the non-existent modes are *comprehended* in God's infinite ideas, that is, by an infinite mode. Once one of the infinitely many rectangles comprehended by the idea of the circle becomes actualized, however, one can then say that there is both the idea of the rectangle as comprehended in the idea of the circle *and* there is the idea of the rectangle that actually exists. In the case of the former, the idea exists 'only insofar as they involve the existence of the circle,' and in the case of the latter the idea involves the determinate, finite mode of the actualized rectangle, a finite mode dependent on another finite mode, *ad infinitum*. As for the controversy over non-existent modes, it stems from unduly stressing the order immanent to substance, an order taken to be actualized (*in actu*) rather than a mere possibility (*in potentia*). Claiming there are non-existent modes appears to contradict this view. On the reading of Spinoza put forth here, however, substance is *in actu* as absolutely indeterminate, and it is only as an infinite mode, the intellect, perceives and comprehends the modes as determinate that one can say they exist. To argue, therefore, as Spinoza does, that the ideas of modes 'that do not exist must be comprehended in God's infinite idea' (2P8) is simply to argue for the relationship between an infinite mode and the absolutely indeterminate substance it allows to become determinate. God's infinite idea comprehends the absolutely indeterminate, and in doing this comprehends that which is not determinate, and therefore non-*existent*; but it is this same idea that facilitates the becoming determinate of the indeterminate.

This reading helps us to explain the important difference between the infinitely many rectangles comprehended by the idea of a circle and substance as comprehended by the attributes, and infinite modes of these attributes, a substance Spinoza describes in his famous letter to Lodewijk Meyer as the 'infinite enjoyment of existing.'[28] This 'infinite enjoyment of existing,' or substance as eternity rather than duration, is placed by Spinoza on the side of *natura naturans* as distinct from *natura naturata*, where the infinitely many rectangles would be placed. This is an important distinction for Spinoza, but it returns us to our earlier problem. If the attribute, as Spinoza defines it, is 'what the intellect perceives of a substance, as constituting its essence,' then the infinite intellect, which Spinoza places on the side of *natura naturata* and not *natura naturans* (i.e., substance),[29] would be used to define the supposed condition for *natura naturata* – that is, *natura naturans*. Our reading resolves this apparent circularity for we argue that an attribute is indeed substance, or is self-ordering becoming, but it is a substance that can only be said to have determinate and determinable *identity* when this becoming becomes resisted and actualized within determinate and determinable modes. The modifications of substance, as actualizations of absolutely indeterminate substance, are precisely this resistance that allows for the possibility that becomings become determinate and identifiable, where, in short, one can say that becomings *are* and in what determinate and determinable manner they *are*. This is why it is an infinite modification of substance, the infinite intellect, that perceives attributes as constituting the essence of substance. It is not that the attributes are an already existent property (predicate) of a substance (subject) just waiting to be perceived as constituting the essence of substance; rather, the very process wherein the infinite mode perceives the attribute as a deteminate, identifiable attribute of substance is precisely the act of constituting the determinable essence of substance – it is substance as self-caused. Substance only *is*, and is of such and such a determinate and determinable nature, when 'the infinite enjoyment of existing' becomes resisted – that is, when it becomes a modification (actualization) of substance. An infinite mode (the infinite intellect) is indeed then the condition that allows for the determination of absolutely indeterminate substance, and thus it constitutes its determinate, identifiable essence.

We can now see the significance of the parallel Spinoza establishes in 2P8: just as the infinitely many rectangles are determinate and determinable only insofar as they are comprehended under the idea of the circle, so too the infinite enjoyment of existing is determinate and determinable only insofar as it is comprehended under an attribute, an attribute that is itself only determinate and determinable when perceived by a determinate, actualized mode of an attribute. The parallel is not perfect, as Spinoza himself admits,[30] for the relationship between the idea of a circle and the infinitely many rectangles that may come to have a durational existence is a relationship between determinate entities. The relationship of substance to the attributes is that of the absolutely indeterminate to the determinate, and the determinate nature of the attributes, the identity immanent to self-ordering becoming, is itself, as we have seen, reciprocally dependent upon an actualized modification of this identity. Unlike the rectangles that do have a determinate reality distinct from the circle that comprehends them, the attribute is not a pre-existent identity separate and distinct from the conditions that enable its identification.

Despite the rough fit of the analogy, it is fruitful in clarifying the relationship between attributes and substance, and with this clarification we can begin to situate our position relative to other interpretations of Spinoza. In Pierre Macherey's interpretation of Spinoza, for instance, he argues that there is a double-movement at work throughout the *Ethics*. Macherey cites the shift in emphasis from 1P15 to 1P16 as emblematic of this double-movement. 1P15 reads as follows: 'Whatever is, is in God, and nothing can be or be conceived without God.' Here is 1P16: 'From the necessity of the divine nature there must follow infinitely many things in infinitely many modes, (i.e., everything which can fall under an infinite intellect.)' According to Macherey, P15 expresses the centripetal movement whereby all things are *in* God and there is nothing that can come into being or even be conceived without the power of God. P16 expresses the centrifugal movement whereby all determinate things – namely, 'everything which can fall under an infinite intellect' – follow *from* the nature of God. Stated in our terms, the first movement is the power of God as self-ordering becoming, and all things that are or can be conceived presuppose the infinite power whereby they come into being, or the determinate presupposes the absolutely indeterminate. The second movement is that of finite or infinite modes that result when substance as self-ordering becoming becomes resisted. This resistance is the modification that allows for the possibility that a determinate thing 'can fall under an infinite intellect.' The absolutely indeterminate, in other words, presupposes the determinate modifications that enable the infinite intellect to perceive and hence constitute the determinate and infinitely determinable essence of substance. All determinate things ultimately express the essence and power of God, and these determinate things are in turn comprehended and made determinate by virtue of the attributes and modifications of God. This double movement of 'comprehending' and 'expressing,' centripetal and centrifugal, Macherey finds to be a pervasive aspect of Spinoza's *Ethics*, and with it he claims to resolve many of the outstanding problems among Spinoza commentators.[31]

We can now further expand upon our discussion of the relationship between attributes and substance and turn to a frequent problem, even among Spinoza's early commentators, regarding the precise relationship between the attributes and the substance whose essence these attributes express. What is this essence? Commentators such as Bennett find the very relationship between attributes and substance problematic. Others such as Curley and Donagan believe that what is expressed are laws of nature. Another problem is the problem of the infinite attributes – that is, how can we know God adequately, as Spinoza claims we can, if we know only two of the infinite attributes? This problem was brought to Spinoza's attention by Tschirnhaus, and Spinoza's response is seen by many to be inadequate. Gueroult offers an innovative interpretation to resolve this problem. He argues that although we may not know the other attributes, these attributes are distinct constituents of the essence of a unique substance, God, and this unique substance has a single attribute that we can come to know.[32] Donagan finds Gueroult's solution to the problem problematic and argues instead that Spinoza is at bottom a dualist; consequently, the two attributes we know are all there is to know, and this knowledge is achieved by coming to know the 'laws of nature' these two attributes, Thought and Extension, express.[33] Without entering into all the intricacies of this debate, I believe our approach supplements Donagan's interpretation. By understanding the essence that is expressed by the attributes as 'self-ordering becoming,' the laws of nature are understood here to be the immanent order that the intellect can grasp through careful study of the becomings of nature; however, by stressing the *becoming* of self-ordering becoming, we mean to contrast our position from one that understands the laws of nature in the manner of an already established, predetermining law that is imposed on a pliant substance.[34] Such a predetermination is contrary to the notion that substance is absolutely indeterminate. What is assumed, ultimately, is that substance is a determinate, static substance, a substance identical to the laws of nature. From the perspective that substance is dynamic and absolutely indeterminate, however, the contrasting view set forth here is that the laws of nature are simply one of the ways in which substance comes to have, by virtue of the intellect, a determinate essence.

We can now summarize our reading of the relationship between substance and attributes. Both are understood by Spinoza to be examples of *natura naturans*, meaning they are for Spinoza to be understood through themselves and not by means of a transcendent other. That said, substance as we understand it is the eternity of becoming, or the infinite enjoyment of existing that cannot be reduced to a limiting, predetermining identity (e.g., being, laws of nature, transcendent God, etc.), and the attributes are the intelligible identity and order immanent to self-ordering becoming. This identity is not an already established identity simply waiting for an intellect to discover it. Rather, the attributes are the immanent, determinate identities that are only determinable as self-ordering becoming becomes ordered and actualized. These actualizations, the modes (e.g., infinite intellect), are then the condition for conceiving substance as determinate and existing. This is the uniqueness of self-cause, a uniqueness that accounts for Spinoza's difficulty with explaining the process by way of analogy to circles comprehending rectangles.

For Spinoza, then, the infinite intellect functions as the model, or useful fiction, for explaining the process whereby absolutely indeterminate becoming becomes infinitely determinate and determinable beings, and thus this fiction parallels the one discussed earlier where one believes that one comes to acquire more eternity. The infinite intellect, as a useful fiction, enables Spinoza to explain how self-ordering becoming *becomes* ordered, much as the fiction regarding an increase of the eternal perfections of the mind, the *becoming* perfect of the mind, facilitated, as Spinoza put it, 'an easier explanation' (5P33S).[35] This effort to think the relationship between being and becoming anticipates Nietzsche's own efforts, with his notion of 'will to power,' to do the same.

With this last point, we see perhaps the most important and profound reason for the fact that Nietzsche saw in Spinoza's philosophy a precursor to his own thought. This is further validated when one considers that Spinoza begins his *Ethics* by defining self-cause: 'D1: By cause of itself I understand that whose essence involves existence, or that whose nature cannot be conceived except as existing.' Much of the commentary on Spinoza's work seems either to discount this first definition as unimportant or to see it as an unnecessary relic of the scholastic tradition; and still others see it as merely preliminary to more important definitions, such as the definition of God (D6).[36] As we understand this first definition, however, it is absolutely crucial to the entire project of the *Ethics*. If substance is self-ordering becoming, the absolutely indeterminate and infinite enjoyment of existing, then this substance can only be conceived as existing by virtue of the attributes, and modifications of the attributes, that themselves presuppose self-ordering becoming as their condition of possibility. This self-ordering nature of becoming is how we understand this first definition, and its implications run throughout the *Ethics*, as our arguments have illustrated. Moreover, Nietzsche's own notion of 'will to power' echoes these very same issues. In a note written about the same time that he wrote *Beyond Good and Evil*, Nietzsche claims, 'To impose upon becoming the character of being: that is the supreme will to power';[37] and again, in *Beyond Good and Evil*, Nietzsche's Spinozistic monism becomes even more apparent: 'The world viewed from inside, the world defined and determined according to its "intelligible character" – it would be "will to power" and nothing else.'[38] It is no wonder, then, that Nietzsche, if he at all read Spinoza as we propose reading him, saw in Spinoza a precursor. These similarities between Nietzsche and Spinoza become even more obvious when we examine their critique of teleology and their claim that to live an affirmative, joyful life is to live eternally. These points are themselves built upon the arguments we have set forth heretofore, and thus by discussing these points we will further clarify our proposed reading of Spinoza. It is to this discussion that we now turn.

II

A likely reason why Spinoza's critique of teleology appealed to Nietzsche, and on a number of levels, derives from the fact that Spinoza ties teleology to the appetitive concerns of the body: 'By the end for the sake of which we do something I understand appetite' (4D7). Our body, however, as Spinoza argues in the *Ethics*, continuing arguments begun in his *Short Treatise*,[39] is understood to be identified as a proportion of motion and rest. For example, Spinoza claims that a body made up of many smaller bodies, such as our body is, will continue to be the same singular body as long as these bodies 'communicate their motions to each other in a certain fixed manner' (2L3Def.). And again, '2L5: If the parts composing an individual become greater or less, but in such a proportion that they all keep the same ratio of motion and rest to each other as before, then the individual will likewise retain its nature, as before, without any change of form.' Such an individual composed of many parts is still considered by Spinoza to be the same singular thing insofar as the parts are maintained within a fixed proportion and ratio of motion and rest.[40] And finally it is this proportion of motion/rest which defines a body as this body and no other, or it is that feature without which the body would not be this body; in short, this proportion of motion and rest is the singular finite essence of our body, a claim which follows from Spinoza's very definition of essence: '2D2: I say that to the essence of any thing belongs that which, being given, the thing is necessarily posited and which, being taken away, the thing is necessarily taken away; or that without which the thing can neither be nor be conceived, and which can neither be nor be conceived without the thing.'

We can now elucidate the meaning of Spinoza's claim that our appetite is the end for the sake of which we act. Appetite, as Spinoza makes clear, is nothing but our striving to persevere in our being, and this striving, 'as related to the mind and body together, it is called appetite' (3P9S). As related to our body, therefore, our appetite is the striving to persevere in a given proportion of motion and rest. Spinoza refers to this striving as the 'actual essence of the thing' (3P7), as opposed to the formal essence of the thing, which is 'the essence of each thing insofar as it exists and produces an effect, having no regard to its duration' (4Preface). The formal essence, or our proportion of motion and rest, is independent of its duration in the face of external objects, objects which could, if they caused our body to lose this proportion, kill the body.[41] The formal essence of the body is the idea of the body as com-prehended under the attribute of extension, in contrast to the actual essence of the body that has durational existence. Understood in the context of other bodies, that is, actually and not formally, our striving is to maintain the proportion of motion and rest in the face of external differences (other bodies) which might lead to the death and dissolution of our body. One of the functions or effects of our appetites, therefore, is to *select against* excessive differences and determinations. Such a selection process is simply part and parcel of the striving to persevere in one's own being with its proportion of motion and rest.[42] God, on the other hand, as absolutely indeterminate, self-caused substance, is the infinite enjoyment of existing that affirms all differences. Since God is not absolutely indeterminate substance *in potentia*, but *in actu*, and because God does not have to select against difference (i.e., there is nothing lacking in God), God is the most perfect being. Finite and determinate beings, however, must select against difference if they are to persevere in their being. This is their appetite, with its proper goal and end. At the same time, however, it is not clear what differences we must select against, or how much we can endure and still persevere in our being in the face of differences. Consequently, through processes of experimentation and learned association, we can become more perfect; that is, the more difference we do not have to select against, the more perfect we become; and it is in this light that Spinoza argues, in 3P12, for the existence of ideas that 'aid the body's power of acting.'[43] By arguing for the effectiveness of such ideas, Spinoza is not being inconsistent with his earlier claims that the 'decisions of the mind are nothing but the appetites.' To the contrary, the decisions of the mind which aid the body's acting by selecting against difference, or by reducing difference to a common, known form, are nothing but the appetite itself, or our striving to persevere in our being.

This further explains why the human striving to persevere in its being by selecting against difference is carried out in two ways. One is the tendency of our *body* to recognize and then assimilate differences. In 3P52, for example, Spinoza states: 'If we have previously seen an object together with others, or we imagine it has nothing but what is common to many things, we shall not consider it so long as one which we imagine to have something singular.' Stopping to rest upon those things we imagine to have something singular, and passing over those that are common and familiar, is only the first step in the perceptual process of familiarizing ourselves with this singularity, the first step in reducing it to what is common and identifiable. We tend to ignore the sounds our car makes, for example, unless it makes an unfamiliar sound. The other way is the tendency of the *mind* to reduce singularities to something common through the use of language and concepts, or what Spinoza refers to as common notions or beings of reason. Such common notions iron out the differences and lead us to overlook the singular differences and peculiarities of an individual. Rather than perceive the particular details of an individual tree, we see simply what we take to be common and universal to all trees. Such a 'Being of reason,' Spinoza claims in the Appendix to his work on Descartes, 'is nothing but a mode of thinking, which helps us to more easily retain, explain, and imagine the things we have understood' (I/233). In other words, it assists us in identifying or classifying the things we have understood, or it irons out the differences for the sake of easy comprehension.[44] This process is precisely our striving to persevere in our own being; or, it is the appetite which is the end for the sake of which we act.

This clarifies an important confusion which surrounds Spinoza's critique of teleology. In particular, we can see that to make a conscious decision to bring about a certain state of affairs, a decision which prompts certain actions and behaviours, is not inconsistent with Spinoza's claim that the mind can have no effect on the body (5 Preface), nor with his claim that our decisions are determined by our appetites (1 Appendix).[45] The reason is simple: any conscious decision or determination one makes negates, or selects against, other possibilities (recall Spinoza's famous statement 'determination is negation' in Letter 50). To make such a decision is not necessarily a conscious decision to select against difference, though it could be; rather, the decision itself is determined by the process of selecting against difference – that is, it is determined by our appetites. Furthermore, this tendency to select against difference characterizes both the mind and the body; consequently, the conscious decision to bring about some state of affairs is simply the mental counterpart to a bodily process of selecting against difference. This follows both from the fact that for Spinoza 'the order and connection of ideas is the same as the order and connection of things' (2P7) and from his understanding of appetite as the striving to persevere, a striving that is expressed by both the mind and body. Spinoza's critique of teleology, in summary, is thus not a critique in the sense that conscious decisions to do things (i.e., act for the sake of some good or goal) are in some way empty or illusory; his critique ought instead to be understood in the manner of a Kantian critique – namely, an attempt to reveal the conditions for the possibility of making such goal-oriented decisions. And the condition for this possibility is the tendency to select against difference; or, as Spinoza defines it, it is our appetites. Furthermore, it is precisely Spinoza's understanding of teleology in terms of appetites and selecting against difference which most appealed to Nietzsche. For reasons discussed in the next chapter, Nietzsche, too, with his notion of the 'will to power,' will understand our motivations in appetitive terms and in terms of a need to iron out the differences.

III

We can now return to some of the statements in the latter half of Part 5 which have caused many problems for commentators, in particular the statements concerning the difficulty and yet desirability of achieving the goal of increasing the eternity of our mind through an increase in the third kind of knowledge. This is an aspiration that Spinoza had had since his earliest work, *Treatise on the Emendation of the Intellect*. In this work he sought to find a method whereby one could overcome the unhappiness and misery which accompanies our love of finite, perishable things, and replace this with a love for that which is eternal. Much this same sentiment is expressed in the *Ethics*: '... it should be noted that sickness of the mind and misfortunes take their origin especially from too much love toward a thing which is liable to many variations and which we can never fully possess' (5P20S). After noting this, Spinoza then turns to the second half of Part 5, wherein he discusses the love of God, or a love that realizes the eternal and non-perishable. The theme with which Spinoza began his earliest work thus continues to be a concern of his up to the end of his latest works.

There are some crucial differences, however, with respect to the manner in which Spinoza sought to understand the love of the eternal in his *Treatise*, and how it comes to be understood in the *Ethics*. In both works Spinoza ties the love of the eternal to a knowledge of the eternal, but in his early work the majority of the discussion concerns the method which will best suit us in pursuing such knowledge, and in the *Ethics* one could say that Spinoza is using the method he spoke of in his early work. But much more needs to be said. For one thing, the *Treatise* was left unfinished, and thus for whatever reason Spinoza felt he needed to begin again in his efforts to clarify the love of the eternal. The reason Spinoza felt dissatisfied with his early work has to do, we believe, with the difficulty he encountered in explaining how the love of the eternal and infinite could be founded upon the finite and determinate.[46]

This difficulty begins about halfway through the *Treatise* when Spinoza claims that the truth and certainty of an idea 'is nothing but the objective essence itself, i.e., the mode by which we are aware of the formal essence is certainty itself. And from this, again, it is clear that, for the certainty of the truth, no other sign is needed than having a true idea' (§35, II/15). In other words, the truth of an idea does not depend upon some independent criterion or method which will in turn be subject to independent verification, and so on to infinity; rather, the mode in which a true idea is grasped is the truth and certainty of this idea. The method for achieving the love of the infinite and eternal, therefore, will thus be seen by Spinoza to be dependent upon a true idea, or dependent upon the manner in which an idea is grasped: '... Method is nothing but a reflexive knowledge, or an idea of an idea; and because there is no idea of an idea, unless there is first an idea, there will be no Method unless there is first an idea. So that Method will be good which shows how the mind is to be directed according to the standard of a given true idea' (§38, II/15).

The truth of a given idea is thus to be our standard; furthermore, the method founded upon such truths, what Spinoza discusses in this work as developing thoughts from 'true and legitimate definitions,' will reflect the mode of the intellect itself. Thus, late in the *Treatise*, Spinoza returns to the theme of attaining knowledge of eternal things and claims that

> when the mind attends to a thought – to weigh it, and deduce from it, in good order, the things legitimately to be deduced from it – if it is false, the mind will uncover the falsity; but if it is true, *the mind will continue successfully, without any interruption*, to deduce true things from it. This, I say is required for our purpose. For our thoughts cannot be determined by any other foundation. (§104, II/37–8, emphasis added)

If the mind has a true idea, its activity will continue unimpeded and will be able to deduce other true ideas from it; however, if the mind has a false idea, its activity will stall, and it will only be able to go so far. This activity of the mind, whether unimpeded or impeded, is the only foundation upon which the truth of our thoughts is to be determined.[47] Consequently, in returning to the proper method for achieving knowledge of eternal things, Spinoza states that our thoughts ought to be directed by the method which reflects 'this foundation.' But since a method is nothing but 'reflexive knowledge itself,' Spinoza concludes that the proper method 'can be nothing other than knowledge of what constitutes the form of truth, and knowledge of the intellect, and its properties and powers' (§105, II/38). In other words, since it is a mode of activity of the intellect which will serve as the foundation for acquiring knowledge of eternal things, an adequate method must reflect this activity. The method of beginning with true and legitimate definitions, and then deducing other truths on the basis of these definitions, only succeeds because of the power of the mind; and yet to say how such a method would actually proceed requires clarifying the powers of the mind. This is where the difficulty arises, for though Spinoza recognizes the necessity of understanding the activity of our mind, he admits to lacking such an understanding:

> But so far we have had no rules for discovering definitions. And because we cannot give them unless the nature, or definition, of the intellect, and its power are known, it follows that either the definition of the intellect must be clear through itself, or else we can understand nothing. It is not, however, absolutely clear through itself ... (§107, II/38)

Because the intellect is not clear through itself, it appears all might be lost. Spinoza is not willing to throw in the towel, however, and begins, in the final paragraphs of the *Treatise*, to show how the nature of the mind can be understood on the basis of the properties of the mind. Spinoza never completed this and left the *Treatise* unfinished. Part of the reason for this is probably that Spinoza was dissatisfied with having to say that if the mind cannot be known through itself, then it must be known through its proximate cause, or by virtue of properties of the mind.[48] The difficulty with this is if the method for directing the mind towards knowledge of the eternal is founded upon a knowledge of the proximate cause of the mind, then the method depends upon something which transcends the mind, and we can therefore ask what determines the truth of our knowledge of the proximate cause, and so on *ad infinitum*. Spinoza would later criticize Descartes for understanding the mind in terms of its proximate, transcendent cause (i.e., God), and it is therefore unlikely that Spinoza would do the same, especially considering that the *Treatise* and his work on Descartes were written within months of each other.[49] Understanding the mind on the basis of the properties of the mind is equally dissatisfying for Spinoza. As Spinoza would claim later in the *Short Treatise*, properties, or 'Propria,' do 'indeed belong to a thing, but never explain what it is' (ST 1.vi.6). What Spinoza ultimately feels he must do, though at the time of the *Treatise* felt he could not do, is to come to an understanding of how a knowledge of the eternal and infinite could be founded upon a knowledge of the essence of our singular, finite mind rather than basing the emendation of the intellect on a truth that transcends the intellect. Because of Spinoza's dissatisfaction with the alternatives he had before himself in the *Treatise*, he abandoned this work so that he could address the issue of the love of the eternal from a different perspective, a perspective which emerges with the *Ethics*.

What is most noteworthy about the position which emerges in the *Ethics* is the manner in which the eternity of our singular, finite mind is related to the essence of God. Crucial to this new position is the role self-cause plays in enabling Spinoza to relate the finite and determinate to the eternal. More importantly, what emerges in the *Ethics* is Spinoza's argument that a finite, singular mind can come to know God and increase the eternal part of the mind. To demonstrate briefly how this argument unfolds, let us return to our earlier discussion of 2P8, and especially to the corollary of that proposition. We noted at the time that this proposition played an important role in later arguments for the eternity of the mind; so, as we address these arguments, let us recall the corollary itself:

> ... so long as singular things do not exist, except insofar as they are comprehended in God's attributes, their objective being, or ideas, do not exist except insofar as God's infinite idea exists. And when singular things are said to exist, not only insofar as they are comprehended in God's attributes, but insofar as they are said to have duration, their ideas also involve the existence through which they are said to have duration.

The important point to note here is the manner of existence of singular things, including singular minds. Singular things can exist 'insofar as they are comprehended in God's attributes,' but even then only 'insofar as God's infinite idea exists.' They can also exist in the manner of having duration whereby they 'involve the existence through which they are said to have duration,' meaning another singular thing and so on *ad infinitum*. Existence in the first sense is eternal existence. What does this mean? Applying the conclusions reached earlier, to exist as a singular thing 'comprehended in God's attributes' is to exist within the identity immanent to self-ordering becoming, to the 'infinite enjoyment of existing,' but even then only 'insofar as God's infinite idea exists' – that is, only when there exists a determinate mode that facilitates the determination of the absolutely indeterminate. This infinite enjoyment of existing, as we saw earlier in discussing Spinoza's letter where this description is used, brings with it the difference between Eternity and Duration. As Spinoza says in this letter, 'it is only of Modes that we can explain the existence by Duration. But [we can explain the existence] of Substance by Eternity, i.e., the infinite enjoyment of existing ...' The idea of a non-existent mode, therefore, which was precisely the theme of 2P8, is not inconsistent with Spinoza's argument that substance is necessarily and exhaustively actualized. For Spinoza substance as eternity, as infinite enjoyment of existing, is, stating it in the manner we have been using, the absolutely indeterminate self-ordering becoming that is absolutely and infinitely determinable, exhausting and exceeding, moreover, each and every actual and possible determination. The infinite determinations of substance – that is, the infinite attributes – are themselves reciprocally dependent upon modifications that in turn allow for the possibility of perceiving the attributes as infinitely determinate and determinable identities that comprehend infinitely many singular things. Stated in a manner that recalls Nietzsche's project, the attributes immanent to self-ordering becoming must be stamped with 'the character of being'[50] in order to be identified and known, and the modes provide the stamp.

With this argument in mind, we can begin to clarify the proposition from the latter half of Part 5 that has caused so much controversy – P23: 'The human Mind cannot be absolutely destroyed with the Body, but something of it remains which is eternal.' Bennett and others argue that this proposition is a hopeless attempt to appease religious critics of Spinoza's philosophy. On closer examination of the demonstration that supports this proposition, however, coupled with our analysis of 2P8, we can see that such a dismissal is not only premature but ultimately misguided for it fails to appreciate the deeper concerns of Spinoza's project. Key to resolving the difficulty in our view is to differentiate the something of the mind that remains from the mind that Spinoza defines as being nothing but the idea of the body (2P13).[51] What this differentiation brings into play is the distinction between eternity and duration, and thus as the demonstration to 5P23 proceeds, it should not be surprising that Spinoza cites 2P8C. Here is the demonstration:

> In God there is necessarily a concept, *or* idea, which expresses the essence of the human Body (by P22), an idea, therefore, which is necessarily something that pertains to the essence of the human mind (by 2P13). But we do

not attribute to the human Mind any duration that can be defined by time, except insofar as it expresses the actual existence of the Body, which is explained by duration, and can be defined by time, i.e. (by 2P8C), we do not attribute duration to it except while the Body endures. However, since what is conceived, with a certain eternal necessity, through God's essence itself (by P22) is nevertheless something, this something that pertains to the essence of the Mind will necessarily be eternal, q.e.d.

To state this point using our earlier conclusions, the human Mind that is eternal is not the determinate, identifiable mind, but rather the immanent condition for the possibility of such a determinate identification – in short, it is the power of self-ordering becoming that allows for the possibility of determinate, singular bodies, and for the determinate singular minds that are the ideas of these bodies. Furthermore, understood in this way we can explicate the reasoning behind two other key claims by Spinoza, the first being how the knowledge of God results in increasing the eternity of the mind and secondly the late proposition in Part 5 (P39) that claims, 'He who has a Body capable of a great many things has a Mind whose greatest part is eternal.' In justifying this latter claim, Spinoza parallels the ordering of bodily affections with the order of the intellect, and hence with relating the affections of the body 'to the idea of God' wherein something of the human mind remains. This idea of God is not a determinate idea in the sense the analogy from 2P8 might imply. The analogy was not perfect, as Spinoza admitted, and this was because the 'idea of God' is the condition that facilitates the process whereby absolutely indeterminate self-ordering becoming becomes determinate, and this process is what Spinoza equates with God's power (1P34: 'God's power is his essence').[52] This power is the eternal 'infinite enjoyment of existing.' Consequently, the more one is 'capable of a great many things' with one's body, then the less one needs to iron out the differences, and hence the more one expresses the power of God and can embrace and affirm the *coming into being* of other determinate identities, the determinate identities comprehended by the 'idea of God.' God as eternal, indeterminate power is the self-ordering becoming that is inseparable from the determinate and determinable beings with which human beings are continuously engaged. Thus the more one knows God and, more importantly, knows, loves, and affirms that God's essence is power, then the more one lives God's power as a condition for the possibility that other determinate beings can come into being. Much as a State in Spinoza's mind is strengthened by allowing for the freedom to philosophize since this better facilitates the possibility of allowing for the immanent order of nature (or God) to become determinate and known, similarly for Spinoza the more one is able to do with one's body, the more one allows for the possibility that the order immanent to self-ordering becoming can become determinate. Stated in yet another way, the more one comes to know God, the more one lives and experiences God's power, a consequence will be that, as lived and experienced, the *act of intuition* becomes nothing other than the *object intuited* – it is the infinite enjoyment of existing. To live in this manner is to live eternally.[53] This is the most powerful affect, the joy of which we are capable, and it is a joy beyond the dualistic determinations of subject *or* object, act of intuition *or* object intuited. This most powerful affect is beyond good and evil.

Nietzsche would most certainly agree with this conclusion. This was, after all, one of the primary reasons why Nietzsche saw Spinoza as a precursor. But the convergence of thought between the two goes even further, for a primary concern of Nietzsche's was, as we have shown it was for Spinoza, to relate the singular and finite to the eternal. Moreover, this is precisely where Deleuze takes on the projects of both Spinoza and Nietzsche. As Deleuze puts it in *Expressionism in Philosophy: Spinoza*, 'What interested me about Spinoza wasn't his Substance, but the composition of finite modes. I consider this one of the most original aspects of my book. That is: the hope of making substance turn on finite modes, or at least of seeing in substance a *plane of immanence* in which finite modes operate.'[54] In other words, rather than attempt to explain how substance is related to the already identified modes and attributes, an attempt that has left a wake of controversy and difficulties among Spinoza scholars, Deleuze instead calls for understanding the determinate, identifiable nature of substance as being from the start tied to the finite modes rather than being a distinct reality from which finite modes arise. The plane of immanence, or what will be discussed in the next chapter as 'plateaus,' is, to apply the terminology used here, self-ordering becoming as the power that exhausts and exceeds the determinate modifications and actualizations, and yet it is the power that is inseparable from the finite, from the coming-into-being of determinate, finite modes and singular existents. Deleuze also turns to Nietzsche for conceptual help on these matters, for with Nietzsche too a central preoccupation was to account for the relationship between singular, finite identities and the eternal, an effort that takes its most recognizable form with Nietzsche's concept of 'eternal recurrence.'

Without venturing into the many debates surrounding the enigmatic concept of 'eternal recurrence,' debates taken up in the next chapter, one point that Nietzsche does seem to make quite clear is that the notion of eternal recurrence can serve as a barometer of the extent to which one affirms one's *singular* life. If one can affirm that one's life, 'all in the same succession and sequence,' ought to repeat itself again and again into eternity, and affirm it without deleting unwanted sequences, then imagine, Nietzsche asks rhetorically, 'how well disposed would you have to become to yourself and to life *to crave nothing more fervently than this ultimate eternal confirmation and seal?*'[55] This 'eternal confirmation and seal,' on our reading, is the affirmation of becoming and the order or being immanent to self-ordering becoming. Nietzsche explicitly identifies eternal recurrence with the affirmation of becoming later in the same note cited earlier where Nietzsche claims that 'to impose upon becoming the character of being ... is the supreme will to power.' He adds the following claim: 'That *everything recurs* is the closest *approximation of a world of becoming to a world of beings*: – high point of the meditation.'[56] To state Nietzsche's view in slightly different terms, eternal recurrence is the affirmation of the power whereby becoming actively becomes being, beings that in turn become yet other beings, and so on *ad infinitum*. Thus, as Nietzsche nears the end of *Thus Spoke Zarathustra*, Zarathustra urges the 'higher men' to say yes to all things, to affirm the becoming that allows for the eternal return of beings: 'All anew, all eternally, all entangled, ensnared, enamored – oh, then you loved the world. Eternal ones, love it eternally and evermore; and to woe too, you say: go, but return! *For all joy wants – eternity.*'[57]

It becomes clear now why Nietzsche saw a precursor in Spinoza, a philosopher who shared with him the same tendency to 'make knowledge the most powerful affect.' This affect, moreover, is positive and absolutely affirmative – what they both call joy. To live such an affirming life requires, for Nietzsche and for Spinoza, an affirmation of the power of becoming, a power that is, in the end, inseparable from one's finite, mortal self. Nietzsche and Spinoza are also not interested in a quantitative eternity, an eternity that is simply an unending duration. The eternity Spinoza seeks is the 'infinite enjoyment of existing,' an eternity that exceeds and overflows any determinate and determinable conceptions of eternity, and an eternity that is experienced through the love and joy of a God that is the power of absolutely indeterminate, self-ordering becoming. To capture and live a life of joy, a life that recognizes and affirms the determinate and singular, including one's self, as being inseparable from the absolutely indeterminate power that is God, or what Nietzsche calls will to power, is to live the 'infinite enjoyment of existing' – it is to live eternally. Moreover, this shared concern between Nietzsche and Spinoza for living eternally was for Spinoza something that was central to his intellectual labours for the greater part of twenty years. It is also this concern for living eternally that occupies Deleuze. In the hands of Deleuze (and Guattari), living eternally will also mean to live a life that affirms becoming, and affirms it without predetermination. This is the meaning of Deleuze and Guattari's call to become a body without organs, a call that will become of increasing focus over the next three chapters. Far, then, from seeing the final half of Part 5 to Spinoza's *Ethics* as an unnecessary appendage to Spinoza's corpus, we must conclude that the concerns and arguments of this part are not only of integral and essential concern to Spinoza's work, but they also anticipate and influence, as an important 'precursor,' the work of Nietzsche and Deleuze. We would be advised, therefore, not to 'in sad silence avert our eyes' from Part 5.

3 Philosophizing the Double Bind: Deleuze Reads Nietzsche

I say unto you: one must still have chaos in oneself to be able to give birth to a dancing star. I say unto you: you still have chaos in yourselves.
— Nietzsche, 'Zarathustra's Prologue'

Spinoza would also claim that one must still have chaos in oneself to be able to give birth to a dancing star. With his discussion of the third kind of knowledge, Spinoza, as we have seen, argued that we ought to strive to the point where we do not have to select against difference – that is, to the point where one can still have chaos in oneself. One could argue, of course, that for Spinoza God, who does not have to select against difference, is far from chaotic. Nevertheless, if we understand *chaos* as the absolutely indeterminate and indeterminable condition for the possibility of determination (a position we will argue for below), then our argument here will be much in line with our previous discussion of Spinoza. However, as we turn now to Nietzsche, it will be important not only to situate Nietzsche's thought within the terrain charted by Spinoza, but also, and more importantly, to contrast Nietzsche's approach with the general philosophical tradition of the West. In this way, we can begin to establish the uniqueness of the philosophical path upon which Spinoza, Nietzsche, and others have walked, or, as Nietzsche might put it, danced. This will shed light on recent work in philosophy, in particular the work of contemporary French philosophers such as Derrida and Deleuze, who state, following Nietzsche, that their task is to reverse the Western philosophical tradition they trace back to Plato.

On the surface, at least, there are some important similarities between Plato and Nietzsche, for Plato too was well aware of this 'chaos in oneself.' In *The Republic*, for example, we find the recognition of this chaos, a recognition that necessitates the attempt to explicate both the reasons why order needs to be imposed upon this chaos, and the manner in which this is to be done. This need is particularly true of children, for, as Plato notes, the soul of young children is very malleable, or plastic, and thus can be molded into an *indefinite* number of shapes; consequently, throughout *The Republic* it is stressed that this plasticity and indeterminacy which forever threaten to subvert and de-stabilize order (i.e., justice) must be contained and ordered. The plasticity within oneself thus harbours potential disorder and chaos, and must, from the time we are young, be molded and stamped with a simple, identifiable form:

> Don't you know that the beginning is the most important part of every work and that this is especially so with anything young and tender? For at that stage it's most plastic, and each thing assimilates itself to the model whose stamp anyone wishes to give to it. (377b)[1]

The young and tender soul is at its most *impress*-ionable stage, and thus this is the time when a simple, ordered model can be most successfully impressed upon the 'chaos in oneself.' Similarly, in a fragment from *Will to Power* (§515), Nietzsche, too, will claim that we need 'to impose upon chaos as much regularity and form as our practical needs require.' Both Plato and Nietzsche are agreed, then, that it is necessary to impose order upon chaos.

Why is it necessary to impose order upon chaos? Plato's and Nietzsche's answer to this question is on the surface quite simple. As presented in *The Republic*, chaos and disorder are incompatible with justice (i.e., order), and since the stated goal is to find the conditions which make justice possible, and allow for its continued existence, one must then find a way to institute this order upon the plasticity of oneself. For Nietzsche the imposing of order upon chaos is necessary for life. Order, regularity, and predictability are necessary simply to survive:

> ... it might be a basic characteristic of existence that those who would know it completely [the 'chaos in oneself'] would perish, in which case the strength of a spirit should be measured according to how much of the 'truth' one could still barely endure – or to put it more clearly, to what degree one would require it to be thinned down, shrouded, sweetened, blunted, falsified [i.e., how *necessary* it is to impose order upon chaos].[2]

In order for us to get on with our lives, to get started, the chaos in one-self needs to be diluted and *falsified*. We thus begin with the false. Only later, with enough strength, will we *perhaps* be able to peer 'into the chaos and labyrinth of existence'[3] without perishing or needing this chaos to be ordered, diluted, falsified. In the meantime, we have our lies, our falsifications, that serve as our necessary antidote for 'truths' that might otherwise prove fatal – 'No one dies of fatal truths nowadays: there are too many antidotes.'[4]

We also begin with the false in *The Republic*, and at two crucial points in the text. The first occurs with respect to molding the plasticity of the soul. To educate and mold the young and tender soul most effectively, one would do best to begin with the telling of tales that are, on the whole, false:

> 'Won't we begin educating in music before gymnastic?'
>   'Of course.'
>   'You include speeches in music, don't you?' I said.
>   'I do.'
>   'Do speeches have a double form, the one true, the other false?'
>   'Yes.'
>   'Must they be educated in both, but *first in the false*?'
>   'I don't understand how you mean that,' he said.
>   'Don't you understand,' I said, 'that first we tell tales to children? And surely they are, as a whole, false, though there are true things in them too. We make use of tales with children before exercises.' (376e–377a, emphasis added)

In further clarifying and attempting to address Adeimantus's doubts about beginning with what is false, Socrates first discusses the plasticity of the young and tender soul (quoted above), and then adds that children cannot differentiate between what is true in these tales, what he refers to as the 'hidden sense' of the tale, and what is not: 'A young thing can't judge what is hidden sense and what is not; but what he takes into his opinions at that age has a tendency to become hard to eradicate and unchangeable' (378e). The child will naturally conform to the truth ('hidden sense') of the tale without recognizing this truth *as* truth, and thus a great emphasis will be placed upon telling tales which, although on the whole may be false (i.e., they might be fantastical tales of great exploits, adventures, etc., which could in no way be true, but attract and 'grip' children precisely because of their fantastical nature), must nevertheless have a hidden sense that conforms to a true and ideal model – the model of justice for example.

The second instance of beginning with the false occurs when Socrates attempts to clarify what the truth and ideal (*eidos*) of justice is. To do this, Socrates proposes constructing a city in speech. If they can construct a city in speech which would function in perfect harmony, then the assumption is that not only must this city be just, but that by analogy an individual's soul would also be just if it were structured just as the city was. This would also return us to the theme of how best to mold and order the plasticity of the soul. But after constructing a city with which Socrates feels satisfied, a city wherein one's necessities are met with only a few minor 'relishes,' Glaucon urges Socrates to consider a more 'conventional' city, a city much more like Athens; in short, Glaucon wants Socrates to consider a 'luxurious city.' Socrates concedes to Glaucon's request but adds that 'the true city is in my opinion the one we just described – a healthy city, as it were. But, if you want, let's look at a feverish city, too' (372d). And it is indeed the feverish city, the unhealthy falsification of 'the true city,' which will hereafter become the topic of discussion. Not only is the 'luxurious city' a copy or representation of a city, a city in speech, it is a false copy (i.e., *phantasma*); and hence the tale of this city is a fantastical tale.

Plato, as with Nietzsche, will also call for the necessity of lies and falsifications as an antidote for preventing terrible consequences. Lies are 'useful against enemies, and as a preventive, like a drug, for so-called friends when from madness or some folly they attempt to do something bad' (382c); and lies are useful for rulers to tell the ruled in cases when the ruled are unable to grasp the true reasons for the ruler's actions (e.g., the 'noble lie' of bronze, silver, and gold in the soul [414c–415c]). Therefore, just as children should first be told stories that are false, so too should adults be told lies, and the reason in each case is the same: to secure the health and justice of society and the individual. Beginning with the false is a necessary remedy and preventive, but a remedy that in time one will *perhaps* be able, with enough strength, to do without.

Let us pause for a moment. There are, on the surface at least, clear *similarities* between Plato and Nietzsche,[5] but, and as Nietzsche would be the first to point out, we must not conclude that Plato and Nietzsche have the *same* concerns. In a very important sense, Nietzsche claims to be doing, or to be concerned with, the inverse of what Plato is doing. Nietzsche consequently claims to be righting Plato's 'standing of truth on her head and [his] denying [of] perspective.'[6] And with this move Nietzsche launched what has come to be called the critique of metaphysics, a critique taken up most notably by Heidegger and Derrida. Heidegger, however, has remarked with respect to Nietzsche that Nietzsche's inversion of Plato, *as an inversion and reversal*, remains fully inscribed within that which is being reversed.[7] So is Nietzsche's critique a failure? This very same criticism, furthermore, has also been levelled against the other major proponents of the critique of metaphysics, including Heidegger. Jürgen Habermas, John Searle, and Fredric Jameson, to name only a few, are all agreed, although they differ in many other respects, that the critique of metaphysics as found in the thought of Nietzsche, Heidegger, Derrida, and others, is fundamentally flawed because of an implicit commitment and adherence to the very *same* tradition they are criticizing.[8]

This critical strategy is not new. One can see it at work in the Platonic dialogues when, for example, Socrates' interlocutors end up contradicting their initial position, thus affirming the very position they initially rejected (e.g., Thrasymachus, *Republic* 349b–350c). What is new, perhaps, is that the critique of metaphysics claims to be reversing the entire tradition of metaphysics since Plato. This reversal, however, does indeed, as is often acknowledged, *resemble* the tradition that is being reversed, yet despite this resemblance it is not to be seen as part of the *same* tradition. The reason for this is that the crucial aspect of metaphysics which the contemporary critique attempts to reverse is, paradoxically, the very notion of reversal itself, and the binary opposition such a notion presupposes.

In this chapter we will attempt to justify this notion of a 'reversal of reversal' by continuing our discussion of the relationship between Nietzsche and Plato, and we will also elaborate upon themes discussed in earlier chapters; in particular, we will discuss how Nietzsche's 'reversal of reversal' entails reversing the traditional emphasis upon a fundamental either/or and emphasizes instead, as did Spinoza (though not as explicitly as Nietzsche), a fundamental, non-identifiable both/and condition – namely, paradoxa. To do this, our discussion will centre upon three themes. The first theme will be the need for *remedies* – the need for lies, falsifications, order, etc. Derrida's discussion of this topic, in his essay on the *pharmakon* (Greek for remedy), will help us to begin to direct our attention to the criticisms that have been directed against the critique of metaphysics. This will also help us to situate Nietzsche's thought with respect to Plato. Our second theme will be the notion of plasticity, and in particular the tendency for the plasticity within oneself to become an imitation, representation, and approximation of some model. In this context we will discuss the theme of mimesis and the implications of our tendency, or weakness, as Nietzsche refers to it, to see the similar as being the same. In this section we will continue to explore the intricate relationship between Nietzsche and Plato. In the third section we will analyse the relationship between Nietzsche and Plato in terms of Nietzsche's notion of will to power. At this point we will draw significantly from the work of Deleuze, and we will once again return to the issue of Nietzsche's inversion of Plato and the critique of metaphysics, and more importantly to Nietzsche's understanding of will to power as a fundamental, non-identifiable both/and condition. Moreover, we hope to demonstrate that a Nietzschean-styled critique need not be a reversal, inversion, or negation of that which is critiqued, nor need it be a Kantian-styled critique which reveals *identifiable* 'conditions of possibility'; rather, what will be sketched is an understanding of critique as that which forever confronts its conditions of impossibility, a critique that reveals both the impossibility *and* necessity of reversal – in short, a critique without redemption.

Pharmakon

The poison of which weaker natures perish strengthens the strong – nor do they call it poison.

– Nietzsche, *The Gay Science* (§19)

They might, in fact, even call it a remedy, a preventive or antidote. Thus the very same substance, if substance is the *proper* word, can either strengthen or destroy, enhance or diminish. But how do we decide, or is it even possible to decide, what the effect will be in each instance? 'Will this make me stronger, or will it kill me?' Is there a standard, criterion, or test we can use in answering this question? Indeed there is a standard or protocol of experimentation and observation that is common to biochemists, pharmacists, etc., and the result is a list of known effects, symptoms, or side-effects that correspond to each drug (or substance). Yet this protocol assumes that the substance in question, or what is referred to when asking what the effects of *this* will be, has been identified. Once this substance has been identified, it is a rather straightforward procedure which will lead us to state whether *this* will strengthen or weaken; and yet even here things are not so simple. Although most researchers would agree upon the protocol and procedures to use in determining whether a substance is harmful or not, there is often significant disagreement concerning the conclusions of this research. But what if we have yet to, or cannot, identify what it is that might help or hurt us? Is there the possibility of a standard or protocol in this case that will allow us to know something about something we don't know (or haven't identified)? More importantly, can we even ask the question. 'Will this help or harm me?' if we don't already implicitly know what *this* is?

These questions lead us to one of the problems of most renown in Plato's thought: the problem of the Meno, or the problem of accounting for how we can teach that which we do not know (in this case, virtue), or, conversely, how we can learn something if we already know it. Socrates claims this problem is simply the result of a 'trick argument' (*Meno*, 80e), the 'trick' being the assumption that knowledge is something one can teach or impart. Socrates denies this assumption and claims that 'there is no such thing as teaching, only recollection' (82a). Everything we come to know is something the soul already knows (we implicitly know what *this* is) but we have forgotten due to our bodily nature. And Socrates' dialectic and speech, his *logos*, is a remedy for this forgetfulness, for our having forgotten what *this* (e.g., virtue) is. Socrates' subsequent task and passion, and his hope for philosophy, is to cure us of our forgetfulness, and save us from the evils that result from it – hence Socrates' claim that the we do evil only out of ignorance, that is, forgetfulness. Nietzsche is therefore correct to note that 'he [Socrates] seemed to be a physician, a savior.'[9]

The Socratic therapy and cure, his remedy for our forgetfulness, has as its end the knowledge of what is good, or 'the idea of the good,' and hence Socratic therapy is the highest of all pursuits, 'the greatest study' (*Republic*, 504d–505b). And yet the good itself, as Socrates makes explicit, exceeds his capacity to discuss it, is out of his range (506e), though he is willing 'to tell what looks like a child of the good and most similar to it ...'; and that which first comes to mind as 'a child of the good' is the sun:

> ... the sun is an offspring of the good I mean – an offspring the good begot in a proportion with itself: as the good is in the intelligible region with respect to intelligence and what it intellected, so the sun is in the visible region with respect to sight and what is seen. (508b–c)

Just as the the illumination of the sun allows for the possibility of perception, for the relationship between perceiver and perceived, so too does the good allow for the possibility of intelligence, for the relationship between the intellect and the intellected. Furthermore, with this analogy, we see that not only does Socrates find himself incapable of knowing the good directly (he must go through the offspring of the good), but to know the good directly, to recall it completely, would bring annihilating harm:

> ... it occurred to me that I must guard against the same sort of risk which people run when they watch and study an eclipse of the sun; they really do sometimes injure their eyes, unless they study its reflection in water or some other medium. I conceived of something like this happening to myself, and I was afraid that by observing objects with my eyes and trying to comprehend them with each of my other senses I might blind my soul altogether. So I decided that I must have recourse to theories, and use them in trying to discover the truth about things. (*Phaedo*, 99d–e)

We therefore need a remedy, a supplement, or something *other* between ourselves and the good itself, something that will protect us from some harm. But with this move our earlier question returns: 'will that which we do not know, the good, help us or harm us?' It does seem that if we are to know the good through our senses without being harmed, we need 'theories,' or we need to know the good through something *other* than the good, through the 'child of the good,' for example. Yet the good itself is to be understood as something simple, as something that does not entail *otherness*. Thus, in the *Lysis*, after remarking that the good is a 'medicine [*pharmakon*] for evil,' for humans that are 'between evil and good,' Socrates observes that 'where there is no disease, there is, we are aware, no need of medicine. This, then, it appears, is the nature of good' (220d). The good is incapable of being harmed, of suffering disease, etc., and for this reason it neither requires anything other (i.e., medicine), nor does it assist anything other – 'it is,' as Socrates puts it, 'of no use.' Similarly, in *The Republic*, when determining the manner in which the gods are to be portrayed, it is concluded that the gods must be presented such as they are, and not as anything other than what they are. And since the gods are 'really good,' they must not be portrayed as anything other than good; hence the gods must not be depicted as being the cause of bad, evil, or harmful things (379a–c). But with this claim a tension arises which is central to Plato's thought: namely, there is both the necessity of otherness, and the necessity to suppress and eliminate otherness. To know the good, we need 'otherness,' but if the good is to be established, we need to eliminate 'otherness.' It is this tension and ambiguity, this double bind, that interests Derrida. In fact, the method of deconstruction itself (if you can call it a method) is one of revealing, as Alan Schrift has noted, that which has been *necessarily* retained yet suppressed within a given text: 'Derrida's deconstructive reading seeks to indicate those assumptions which a text acknowledges [e.g., the necessity of knowing the good through something other] but must suppress in order to function [e.g., the necessity, in *The Republic*, of suppressing otherness so that justice, and its principle of 'to each his own,' can function].'[10]

In turning to Derrida's interpretation, it is important to note that there has been a shift in our questioning. We were first concerned with how one decides if something (*this*) is *either* helpful *or* harmful, but this quickly became the problem of understanding how otherness can be *both* helpful *and* harmful. Derrida would claim that the shift to another ambiguous both/and is far from accidental. In Derrida's long essay on Plato, 'Plato's Pharmacy,' but also in his work as a whole, it is precisely some ambiguous, undecidable both/and which allows for the possibility of deciding with respect to an either/or. Decisions regarding an either/or necessarily refer to, or depend upon, some problematic, undecidable both/and, yet in the process of deciding, this undecidability must be suppressed. It is precisely this process which deconstruction investigates. For example, in his reading of Plato, Derrida focuses upon the Greek word *pharmakon*, which can be translated to mean either remedy or poison, and he refers to the several places where it is ambiguous what the *proper* meaning is; in short, the question is precisely whether the *pharmakon* will help or harm.

Derrida first cites the *Phaedrus* where Pharmacia (*Pharmakeia*) is referred to as that which caught up Orithyia and blew her into the abyss and killed her (229d); and then just a little later, the texts Phaedrus brought with him are compared by Socrates to a remedy or cure: '... you seem to have discovered a remedy [*pharmakon*] for getting me out' (230e). The administering of the *pharmakon* produces *both* harms *and* benefits, though perhaps the benefits of getting out of the city are not too clear (Derrida notes that it was hot and 'getting out' allowed Socrates to cool off by the river, the same river in which Orithyia was thrown, and hence the ambiguity returns once more). Derrida will later cite the *Phaedo* in which Socrates attempts to find a remedy or cure for the childish terrors and fear of death that the 'little boy' in each of us has. This is the fear that once the soul leaves the body 'the wind may really puff it away and scatter it.' To remedy this situation, Socrates says that one must 'say a magic spell over him [the child] every day until you have charmed his fears away' (77e). And there is no greater magician, as Simmias and others were well aware, than Socrates himself. Just recall Meno's reaction to Socrates:

> Socrates, even before I met you they told me that in plain truth you are a perplexed man yourself and reduce others to perplexity. At this moment I feel you are exercising magic and witchcraft upon me and positively laying me under your spell until I am just a mass of helplessness. (*Meno*, 80a)

Although it is a magician's magic and spells that are a cure and remedy for the childish fear of death, this magic is to be distinguished from the magical wizardry of the imitators, a magic that must be eliminated. For example, in *The Republic* the gods are *not* to be represented by the poets as being anything like 'a wizard, able treacherously to reveal himself at different times in different ideas [*eidos*] ...' (380d). A god is what he is, and need not, nor should not, be anything *other* than what he is. Similarly, with the poets if one

> who is able by wisdom to become every sort of thing and to imitate all things should come to our city, wishing to make a display of himself and his poems, we should fall on our knees before him as a man sacred, wonderful, and pleasing; but we would say that there is no such man among us in the city [and we would therefore] ... send him to another city ... (398a)

This banishment need not be permanent but must be maintained until a remedy or antidote for the speeches of the poets has been found. Thus, when the theme of the poets returns in Book X, Socrates implies that although imitative poetry seems 'to maim the thought of those who hear them [the poets] and do not as a remedy [*pharmakon*] have the knowledge of how they really are' (595b), such poetry is permissible, and perhaps desirable (we will discuss this in the next section), for those who do have such a remedy, since they will have established a resistance to the poet's magic.

There is thus the magic and wizardry of dispersal, of things not being what they are, or for things that are changing, in flux, unpredictable; and this is a magic that captivates us and has us 'on our knees.' But then there is the magic and wizardry of *eidos*, of things being what they are, static, repetitive, predictable; and this is also a magic that captivates us and leaves us as 'just a mass of helplessness.' It is the speech and discourse of the second magic which gets directed against the intoxicating effects of the first, and for this reason this second magic is referred to in the *Laws* as an antidote: 'The one certain touchstone of all is the text of the legislator. The good judge will possess the text within his own breast as an antidote [*alexipharmaka*] against other discourse [in particular, discourses of 'poesy with its eulogies and its satires, or utterances in prose ... with their contentious disagreements' – i.e., their tendency for dispersal], and thus he will be the state's preserver as well as his own' (XI 957d). The *pharmakon* is administered against itself. The good drug and remedy – Socratic dialectics in the service of *eidos* – is necessary to counter the intoxicating effects of the bad drug – imitative poetry and discourse which promotes dispersal and otherness; but this Socratic treatment would not be possible, Derrida argues, 'if the pharmako-logos did not already harbor within itself that complicity of contrary values,'[11] if it were not in 'some sense' already both a poison and a remedy. I use the qualification 'some sense' because the *pharmakon* is not to be seen as being *identifiably* a poison and a remedy, nor does it have a 'proper' sense; rather, Derrida understands it to be the non-identifiable element which is prior to, and allows for the possibility of, making identifiable distinctions:

> The 'essence' of the *pharmakon* lies in the way in which, having no stable essence, no 'proper' characteristics, it is not, in any sense (metaphysical, physical, chemical, alchemical) of the word, a *substance*. The *pharmakon* has no ideal identity; it is aneidetic ... It is rather the prior medium in which differentiation in general is produced, along with the opposition between the *eidos* and its other; this medium is *analogous* to the ... transcendental imagination, that 'art hidden in the depths of the soul,' which belongs neither simply to the sensible nor simply to the intelligible, neither simply to passivity nor simply to activity.[12]

To make a decision, however, to identify whether this is helpful or harmful, the non-identifiable and hence undecidable medium of the *pharmakon* must be left behind. It is precisely this move which Derrida believes Plato makes:

> Plato decides in favor of a logic that does not tolerate such passages between opposing senses of the same word ... And yet ... the pharmakon, if our reading confirms itself, constitutes the original medium of that deci-

sion, the element that precedes it, comprehends it, goes beyond it, can never be reduced to it, and is not separated from it by a single word.[13]

This logic which Plato decides in favour of is nothing less than the logic of either/or, and Plato uses this logic, Derrida argues, in his 'attempts to master, to dominate [i.e., dominate ambiguities such as *pharmakon* that are both poisons and cures] by inserting its definition [e.g., *pharmakon*, whose definition or 'essence' is ambiguous, 'aneidetic,' and undecidable] into simple, clear-cut oppositions: good and evil, inside and outside, true and false, essence and appearance.'[14] Derrida's critique of Plato is therefore both a critique of Plato's decision, or what Derrida also refers to as the decision of metaphysics, to favour the logic of either/or, and it is a critique in the Kantian sense in that it reveals the conditions which make this decision possible.

But this is already Nietzsche's position. Early in *Beyond Good and Evil*, Nietzsche claims that 'the fundamental faith of the metaphysicians is the faith in opposite values.'[15] In particular, he notes the 'typical prejudice' of metaphysicians that something cannot 'originate out of its opposite.' Truth cannot originate in error; selfless deeds in selfish deeds; and, as we have seen in *The Republic*, the goodness of the gods cannot originate in, or even participate in, evil. In contrast to this 'prejudice,' however, Nietzsche argues:

> It might even be possible that what constitutes the value of these good and revered things is precisely that they are insidiously related, tied to, and involved with these wicked, seemingly opposite things – maybe even one with them in essence. Maybe![16]

That the word 'maybe' is emphasized and repeated should be noted, for, as with Derrida, the condition which 'constitutes the value of these good and revered things,' although 'insidiously related' to the opposite of these things, is itself, in 'essence,' the undecidable medium which allows for the possibility of deciding whether something is good *or* evil. In itself, however, one cannot decide with respect to this medium; one is left simply saying, 'Maybe!' The terms Nietzsche most often associates with this undecidable medium are 'will to power,' 'life,' and 'dionysian frenzy.' Thus it is life, will to power, etc., which constitutes value (i.e., allows for the possibility of decisions between good and evil, etc.), but they in turn cannot be evaluated, cannot be decided, and are in short 'unapproachable':

One would require a position outside of life, and yet have to know it as well as one, as many, as all who have lived it, in order to be permitted even to touch the problem of the value of life; reasons enough to comprehend that this problem is for us an unapproachable problem.[17]

Life, as will to power,[18] is always evaluating and deciding between good and evil, helpful and harmful, etc., but life itself cannot be evaluated. Life is the non-identifiable, aneidetic medium which, to use the previously quoted phrase of Derrida, 'harbors within itself that complicity of contrary values.' The logic of either/or is thus made possible by a non-identifiable life wherein the opposite values are 'insidiously related' (i.e., undecidable both/and).

We are now in a better position to understand Nietzsche's inversion or reversal of Plato. To claim that Nietzsche is simply reversing or inverting terms, or that he is simply taking the opposite stance, would be missing the point of Nietzsche's critique. Most especially, this would be assuming that Nietzsche uncritically accepts a faith in opposite values when it is precisely this faith, as we have shown, which he questions. The 'reversal of reversal' is, for Nietzsche, a critique of the metaphysician's fundamental 'faith in opposite values,' and yet it is just this faith that forms the basis of many of the criticisms that have been directed against Nietzsche and the 'critique of metaphysics.'[19] Foucault refers to this tendency as 'Enlightenment blackmail': either you accept the logic of either/or and the faith in opposite values, or you are an irrationalist and a relativist.[20] But the point of the 'reversal of reversal' is not that something is being *opposed* to the logic of either/or, but rather it is an attempt to reveal, within this either/or, a non-identifiable, undecidable, aneidetic medium wherein both the *either* and the *or* are 'insidiously related.' Foucault, for example, attempts both to criticize the Enlightenment and maintain a vigilant acceptance of rationality, and for this reason he expresses his agreement with Habermas's claim that 'if one abandons the work of Kant or Weber ... one runs the risk of lapsing into irrationality.' For Foucault, reason can neither dispense with the irrational, nor should the irrational dispense with reason, but we are in 'this sort of spiral' wherein there is both rationality and irrationality.[21] Foucault's critique, as with Nietzsche's,[22] is therefore both a critique of the decision to favour the logic of either/or, and it is a critique in the Kantian sense in that it argues for a fundamental both/and at the heart of this either/or, or it reveals the fundamental both/and which is the condition of possibility for this logic.

There are, however, questions and potential problems with this approach. First, is this position also not, in 'some sense,' Plato's position? Does not the plasticity within oneself harbour a 'complicity of contrary values' insofar as this plasticity can be molded into either a good or evil form; thus the concern for censoring and banishing the evil forms? And is this plasticity also not the reason for the ultimate failure and fall of justice in that this plasticity cannot be contained within, or be completely reduced to, a simple form? It is necessary for the philosopher-king to eliminate otherness, but this otherness is there from the start: it is the non-identifiable plasticity of the soul, a plasticity that can come to be identified as any of an indefinite number of types; but as the possibility and medium for this identification, whatever type or model does get stamped on the soul will always contain the possibility of becoming an-*other* type. It is this possibility that results in a double bind that is central to Plato's thought: it is both necessary and impossible to eliminate otherness.[23] An instance of this double bind in *The Republic* concerns the necessity and impossibility of eliminating the poets, poetry, and the imitative arts. But does not Plato implicitly recognize this double bind,[24] and moreover does he not also acknowledge a fundamental both/and which is the condition for deciding in favour of a logic of either/or? Does not Nietzsche's and hence Derrida's critique of Plato subsequently entail a fundamental mis-reading; in short, are they not criticizing him for not doing or being aware of something he is doing and aware of? 'Maybe!' But to conclude from this that they are all doing the same thing, or that they are all part of the same tradition, would in turn be a mistake. There are indeed clear similarities between them, but to say of *similar* things that they are the *same* thing is itself a fundamental error, an error of which Nietzsche was well aware. It is to a discussion of this error that we now turn, and, by continuing to follow the contours between Plato and Nietzsche, we will address many of these questions.

Mimesis

Seeing things as similar and making things the same is the sign of weak eyes.
— Nietzsche, *The Gay Science* (§228)

Integral to the process of 'making things the same' that are merely similar is what Heidegger will call, in extending Nietzsche's work, the 'fictioning essence of reason.' This term arises in the context of a discussion of Nietzsche's schematism, or of the necessity of imposing order upon chaos. Heidegger cites a fragment from *Will to Power* (no. 515): 'Not "to know" but to schematize – to impose upon chaos as much regularity and form as our practical needs require.'[25] Our practical needs thus entail that what is strange be reduced to what is familiar because, as Nietzsche continues, 'only when we see things coarsely and made equal do they become calculable and usable to us [i.e., conform to our "practical needs"].' This point is made even more clearly in *The Gay Science* (§111, 'Origin of the Logical'): 'The dominant tendency ... to treat as equal what is merely similar – an illogical tendency for nothing is really equal – is what first created any basis for logic.' Later in this same book, Nietzsche will stress that our need for knowledge is nothing more than a need for the familiar, for the same.[26] But, as Nietzsche points out, 'nothing is really equal,' nothing is really the same, and therefore the schematism is in the end nothing more than the imposition of a useful fiction (or, as Nietzsche will often refer to it, a 'necessary lie'). Nietzsche is also clear in saying that 'no pre-existing "idea" was here at work';[27] in other words, the categories, ideas, etc., under which what comes to be known is subsumed, are themselves the *result* of the schematism, and are not something which *precedes* it. These categories and ideas are, as Heidegger puts it, fictioned: 'That which is fictioned in such a fiction is categories. That which properly appears to us and shows itself under its aspect: this same thingness of the thing – what in Greek would be referred to as "Idea" – thus created, is originally fictioned.'[28]

With Nietzsche's interpretation of the schematism, his reversal or inversion of Plato becomes more clear. First, for Nietzsche, unlike Plato, the ideas (*eidos*) do not pre-exist their being applied to the realm of practical, day-to-day necessity; they are a consequence of this necessity, of our 'practical needs.' And related to this reversal is that of the fictioning process itself. For Plato, as Heidegger discusses this point in referring to the *Phaedrus*, when he 'tells the myth of the descent of the "idea" from a place above heaven, *hyperouranios topos*, into the human soul, this myth is ... none other than the Greek interpretation of the fictioning essence of reason.'[29] The fictioning of the 'ideas,' in other words, occurs in the supersensuous realm 'above heaven.' For Nietzsche, on the other hand, the fictioning occurs within the sensuous realm of life, and it is only as a consequence of the necessities of life that the notion of supersensuous 'ideas' comes about (i.e., are fictioned). Nietzsche thus inverts or reverses the Platonic interpretation of the relationship between the sensuous and the supersensuous; however, it is precisely this reversal that Heidegger finds problematic:

But what does that [Nietzsche's inversion] mean – the sensuous stands above all? It means that it is the true, it is genuine being. If we take the inversion strictly in this sense, then the vacant niches of the 'above and below' are preserved, suffering only a change in occupancy, as it were. But as long as the 'above and below' define the formal structure of Platonism, Platonism in its essence perdures. The inversion does not achieve what it must ... namely, an overcoming of Platonism in its very foundations. Such overcoming succeeds only when the 'above' in general is set aside as such, when the former positing of something true and desirable no longer arises, when the true world – in the sense of the ideal – is expunged.[30]

What Heidegger believed Nietzsche failed to overcome is the very opposition between an 'above' and a 'below,' and thus he maintained the metaphysician's faith in opposing values. Did he? Heidegger grants that Nietzsche did come to question this faith in opposing values, but that he did so 'only in his final creative year (1888).'[31] What we have tried to show is that Nietzsche was well aware of this faith in opposing values, and questioned it not only in *Beyond Good and Evil* (1886), but also in his early work *Human, All Too Human* (1878). The latter work begins by noting that 'metaphysical philosophy' responds to the problem of 'how something can arise from its opposite' by 'denying the origin of one [e.g., logic] from the other [its opposite, e.g., the illogical].' Nietzsche proposes, by contrast, that a 'historical philosophy' would pursue 'a chemistry of moral, religious, aesthetic ideas and feelings ... [a] chemistry [that] *might* end with the conclusion that, even here, the most glorious colors are extracted from the base, even despised substances.'[32] This 'chemistry' *might* find that the glorious and the logical are 'insidiously related' to their 'supposed' opposites, to the despised and the illogical, 'maybe even one with them in essence. Maybe!' One must therefore question Heidegger's claim that Nietzsche's inversion and reversal of Platonism 'means' that the sensuous 'is the true ... genuine being [as opposed to a false and counterfeit being].' This is in effect Derrida's criticism of Heidegger's reading of Nietzsche: 'Nietzsche has written what he has written. He has written that writing – and first of all his own – is not originarily subordinate to logos and to truth.'[33] Even though Nietzsche does emphasize the importance of the sensuous life, and the practical necessities of life, life itself is ultimately 'undecidable,' and thus cannot be subordinated to truth, or to what is *genuine* and 'proper.'

What, then, are we to make of Nietzsche's reversal of Platonism? If there is the double bind that fictioning, the poets, is both necessary and impossible (i.e., impossible in that becoming cannot be fictioned), and if this is a double bind that even Plato seems to have been aware of, then how is Nietzsche doing something *fundamentally different* than Plato? This is the question that underlies Heidegger's critique: Nietzsche's overcoming of Plato is not successful for he is not, in the end, doing anything *fundamentally different*. But what would count as doing something fundamentally different? Is there a criterion or standard which will allow us to decide? Can we say that since Plato and Nietzsche are *similar* in fundamental ways, that they are doing the *same* thing? This is the problem of mimesis, the double bind of mimesis – in short, we can and we must say that they are the same, we must decide, but these decisions are in turn impossible, are always 'improper.'

This very problem was even brought to Nietzsche's attention.[34] In a letter to Nietzsche from his friend Edwin Rohde, Rohde remarks, 'The Persian sage is no doubt yourself ... Plato created his Socrates and you your Zarathustra.'[35] Not only does Rohde identify Nietzsche with Zarathustra (which at times Nietzsche seems to be inviting us to do), but he identifies the relationship between Nietzsche and Zarathustra with that between Plato and Socrates. The implication is that Nietzsche and Plato are not merely similar, they are doing the same thing. Nietzsche's response to this identification, to Rohde's 'decision,' is straightforward: 'Everything in it [*Thus Spoke Zarathustra*] is mine alone, without model, comparison, or precursor; a person who has once lived in it will return to the world with a different face.'[36] Rohde's claim that there is a model with which Nietzsche's work can be compared is therefore, as Nietzsche sees it, 'improper.' Why? An initial reason is that Rohde's remark challenges Nietzsche's belief that he is reversing Platonism, or that he is doing something fundamentally different. For the sake of consistency, therefore, Nietzsche must reject Rohde's suggestion. A more fundamental reason for this rejection, and this directs us to the core of what we take to be Nietzsche's project, is that Nietzsche is concerned with that which is absolutely unique, singular, incomparable, and, yes, undecidable.

It is at this point where we again confront the double bind. If Nietzsche's concern is with the absolutely unique, singular, and incomparable, and if this cannot be fictioned but cannot not be fictioned, then it seems the double bind is our fate. Indeed, it is our fate, but it is precisely our fate which Nietzsche affirms – *amor fati*:

My formula for greatness in a human being is *amor fati*; that one wants nothing to be different, not forward, not backward, not in all eternity. Not merely bear what is necessary, still less conceal it – all idealism is mendaciousness in the face of what is *necessary* – but love it.[37]

If it is our fate that fictions cannot be eliminated, if lies are always already present and necessary, does this then mean that anything goes, that we might as well get along with any fiction, with any lie? For Nietzsche, the answer is 'No!' What, then, is the criterion whereby one can say this lie is better than that one? We will address these questions more directly in the next section, but for the moment we can say that 'strength' is Nietzsche's 'standard.'[38] Fictions that are the result (i.e., were fictioned) of strength are better than fictions that are the result of weakness, or fictions that enhance life's power are better than those that diminish it. Nevertheless, we cannot do without fictions altogether – they are our fate. What we can do, and this is where we begin to see the motivation behind Nietzsche's unrelenting critiques, is to demonstrate that what had been taken to be a fundamental, ultimate 'truth' is merely a convenient and necessary fiction. But this is a critique without end, a critique without redemption, for there is, as Nietzsche argues, no final truth that will ground all our decisions; no 'reality' that will sweep away all our fictions; and no knowledge that will transcend all our opinions. There are nothing but fictions and opinions, and consequently Nietzsche will not attempt to exit the cave of opinion. Nietzsche's critique, rather, is an attempt to dig deeper within this cave, to find an even deeper cave – to enter the abyss. As the hermit argued – can we identify the hermit with Nietzsche? Would they each have said the *same* thing? This is still our problem, the problem of mimesis – the cave is our *necessary* state:

> The hermit ... will doubt whether a philosopher could *possibly* have 'ultimate and real' opinions, whether behind every one of his caves there is not, *must* not be, another deeper cave – a more comprehensive, stranger, richer world beyond the surface, an *abysmally* deep ground behind every ground, under every attempt to furnish 'grounds.' ... Every philosophy is a foreground philosophy ... Every philosophy also *conceals* a philosophy; every opinion is also a hideout, every word also a mask.[39]

Plato was also well aware of the necessity of being in the cave, but the effort such an awareness motivates is (perhaps) quite different from

Nietzsche's. Whereas Nietzsche is concerned with revealing beneath the 'known' (i.e., familiar) causes and the dominant 'habitual explanations' that which is unique and unfamiliar,[40] Plato, on the other hand, attempts to reveal that which is always the same within that which is new and unfamiliar. Nietzsche's critique, although recognizing and affirming the fact that one is fated to fiction the unfictionable (i.e., fated to see the similar as the same), is nonetheless a critique which attempts to reveal the uniqueness and novelty from which the same, the fiction, emerges. Plato seeks to do the reverse: the goal here is to ascend from the cave of similarity, novelty, and difference, and emerge into the light of that which is forever the same. For Plato the necessity of being in the cave merely reflects the fact that this is where the process of acquiring knowledge begins, or it is that from which we seek to get outside. This analogy is *reversed* by Nietzsche: he seeks to get deeper and deeper inside, to the caves behind the caves, to the abyss.

But things are not quite this simple. Both Plato's and Nietzsche's use of a cave analogy reflects a recognition of a fundamental impossibility. For Nietzsche this is the impossibility of getting to a final, ultimate reality or ground (the last cave), wherein fictions would be unnecessary; and for Plato this is the impossibility of reconciling Being with Becoming, or of reconciling Being with the necessity of telling fictions to those in the world of Becoming. For example, when presenting the cave analogy, Socrates (or is it Plato?) asserts that moving from the darkness to the light is a possibility inherent in the soul; consequently, and this returns us to our earlier discussion of the problem of the *Meno*, he claims that 'education is not what the professions of certain men [i.e., sophists] assert it to be. They presumably assert that they put into the soul knowledge that isn't in it, as though they were putting sight into blind eyes' (518b). They presume, in short, that the knowledge of what is – Being – can come into being (becoming), but this is a contradiction in terms for Socrates. What Socrates argues for, as we have seen, is for the recollection of a knowledge that is always already there, that has not come-into-being. However, for humans that have necessarily forgotten the truth of what *is*, for those in the cave, the process of recollection entails a temporary transition from the same to the unique and unfamiliar. The 'habitual explanations,' the dominant beliefs and assumptions about reality, these are unsettled, and one is left disoriented before the strange and unfamiliar. But this is only temporary, and eventually that which is strange will be seen to be similar to what used to be taken to be real, and then this in turn will lead to the re-cognition (i.e., recollection) of that which remains the same and is the cause of the many similar appearances. It is this recollection of Being which is the always already given possibility of the soul:

> ... this power [recollection] is in the soul of each, and ... the instrument with which each learns – just as an eye is not able to turn toward the light from the dark without the whole body – must be turned around from that which *is coming into being* together with the whole soul until it is able to endure looking at that which *is* and the brightest part of that which *is*. (518c)

Thus, Nietzsche's project of revealing the unique and unfamiliar beneath the familiar and habitual is for Plato only a necessary and temporary evil (i.e., *pharmakon*). It is part of the process whereby *bad* habits (i.e., opinion, turned towards Becoming) are replaced by *good* habits (i.e., knowledge, turned towards Being). At this point, however, we encounter the problem of how best to mold the plasticity of the soul, how best to instil one with good habits, and Plato's favoured solution to this problem, as discussed earlier, is to tell a fantastical tale, a tale that might not be true, a tale that might, in fact, be false. It is precisely these fantastical tales, the tales told to children, that were seen to be an excellent means of instilling 'proper' habits in children, habits that will become 'hard to eradicate and unchangeable' (378e). But this applies to adults as well, and to the 'little child' in each adult that fears death. The aging Cephalus, for example, confesses at the beginning of Book I of *The Republic* that, 'the tales told about what is in Hades – that the one who has done unjust deeds here must pay the penalty there – at which he laughed up to then, now make his soul twist and turn because he fears they might be true' (330e). Cephalus at first laughed at the 'childish' fear that upon death 'the wind may really puff it [the soul] away and scatter it' (*Phaedo*, 77e), and he attempted to achieve all he could in this life, in the life that would end at death, even if this meant doing 'unjust deeds.' But in the twilight of his life, Cephalus begins to wonder whether it 'might be true' that the soul does not 'scatter,' but that it continues on to suffer the consequences of the unjust deeds done during his life; consequently, the fear of death becomes transformed into the fear of a punishment without end, and it is this fear which motivates Cephalus to attempt to rectify his unjust actions, to do what is 'proper' and right.

The problem with the telling of such tales is, as Adeimantus pointed out (379a), deciding whether a tale is 'proper' or not, whether it conforms to the model of justice or not. It was in response to this problem that Socrates proposed to construct a 'city in speech.' With this construction, Socrates hoped to show why he feels 'injustice is never more profitable than justice' (354a), even though injustice often seems to be more profitable. But, as we saw, they did not construct a true or healthy city; rather, they constructed a 'feverish' city, a city that needed medicines (i.e., *pharmakon*) in order to be returned to health (Socrates the 'physician'). The medicines necessary to cure such a city were, in many instances, lies (noble lies), and hence the necessity of that which might not be true, that which might be fiction. And in Book X this necessity becomes even more obvious when they return to the question of showing that 'injustice is never more profitable than justice.' At this point, and to Glaucon's surprise, the argument turns on showing that the soul is immortal (608d–611a). The assumption is made that when one is unjust, even if one appears just to others, this injustice 'doesn't escape the notice of (the) gods' (612e). The gods can discern and decide whether one *is* just or not; they won't be fooled by appearances or by the changing flux of Becoming. From here it is an easy transition to the tale of Er, to a tale which recounts how the gods punish an immortal soul for the injustices done during life (i.e., while in the realm of Becoming): 'For all the unjust deeds they had done anyone and all the men to whom they had done injustice, they had paid the penalty for every one in turn, ten times over for each' (615a). It is therefore this tale of Er, a tale that 'might be true,' which, if we are 'persuaded by it' (621c), will motivate us to be concerned, not with the realm of change, similarity, and becoming, but rather with the realm of the stable, with that which is forever the same – namely, Being. To 'persuade' us to be just and 'proper,' to be concerned with the sameness of Being, *The Republic* thus depends upon tales that might be false (i.e., they are, at the very least, fictions), such as the tale of Er or the tale of the feverish city. They are necessary fictions. *The Republic* as a whole, in fact, can be seen as a series of these necessary fictions that fiction that which cannot be fictioned. And the reason for a series of fictions is that each fiction entails the fictioning process, a process which is itself the gap or passage from like to same, and it is precisely this gap that remains forever unthought and thus subject to yet another fiction to fiction the unthought, and so on *ad infinitum*. Plato's fictions, his analogies, are substitutes for, or eternal recurrences of, the incomparable and unthinkable.

What has become of Nietzsche's inversion of Plato? Is it nothing more than a difference in the fictions that are used to fiction the fictioning process, fictions that *necessarily* fail to represent this process? Does Nietzsche, to restate Rohde's claim, have his Zarathustra, and Plato his Socrates? If both ultimately confront and fail to think the unthinkable, generating instead a series of fictions, then is not both Nietzsche's and Plato's thought confronted with a double bind? If so, how are we to understand Nietzsche's self-proclaimed break with traditional metaphysics? Is he, as many of his recent critics seem to suggest, merely deluding himself? To begin answering this question, we will direct our attention to a discussion of 'necessity.' Both Plato and Nietzsche recognized the necessity of lies, fictions, analogies, etc., and both also implicitly recognized the necessity of mimesis – that is, the necessary transition from seeing something as similar to seeing it as the same, or, to put it another way, the necessity of habits. What is the condition for this necessity, or why is the 'necessary' necessary? Does Nietzsche have an answer to this question which will help us to address the problem of how a philosophical discourse is to proceed, how it will supply a *needed* truth and knowledge; or are the critics right to say that Nietzsche, and those who have been influenced by him (e.g., Derrida, Heidegger, Deleuze et al.), have no answer to this question, and that as a result philosophy sinks into an abyss of anarchical relativism? Nietzsche does, as we will see, have an answer to this question, and an answer which will demonstrate that his inversion of Plato both is and is not a reversal (it is a 'reversal of reversal'). His answer, in short, is 'will to power.'

Thumos

The world viewed from inside, the world defined and determined according to its 'intelligible character' – it would be 'will to power' and nothing else.

– Nietzsche, *Beyond Good and Evil* (§36)

'Will to power' is the world 'viewed from inside'; it is not the world viewed from outside, from some privileged perspective beyond the world. This is also true of life, and it was for this reason that the problem of the value of life was seen to be an 'unapproachable problem' by Nietzsche. To resolve this problem 'would require,' Nietzsche claims, 'a position outside of life,' but it is precisely such a position Nietzsche denies. We cannot step outside our lives; we cannot get beyond will to power: 'life simply *is* Will to Power.'[41] Or, as Nietzsche also puts this, our fate, our necessity, is to be part of a whole, to be the whole, where the whole is not understood as a Being, but rather as a becoming:

One is necessary, one is a piece of fatefulness, one belongs to the whole, one is in the whole; there is nothing which could judge, measure, compare, or sentence our being, for that would mean judging, comparing, or sentencing the whole. But there is nothing besides the whole ... the world does not form a unity either as a sensorium or as 'spirit' – that alone is the great liberation; with this alone is the innocence of becoming restored.[42]

We are a piece of fatefulness, a piece of the whole that does not form a unity. And this whole that does not form a unity is a whole that cannot be completely known, or it is infinitely variable,[43] and this variability cannot be unified or represented by a model or schema which would allow us to predict this variability; there is always an element of chance. Each prediction is a 'roll of the dice.' In short, the world, or Nature, as Nietzsche also refers to it, is characterized by 'chance': 'Nature is *chance*.'[44] Since Nature is chance, it is unpredictable and infinitely variable; it cannot be adequately represented; it cannot be unified. In other words, Nature, as well as life, the world, will to power, and our self, is at bottom 'chaos,' and hence any representation, theory, or order which is imposed upon this chaos is, as discussed earlier, a necessary falsification, a necessary lie. These necessary falsifications, however, are not without some merit, or they do not arise without reason. These falsifications are necessary, and Nature itself, as Nietzsche argues, is nothing but these necessities:

Let us beware of saying that there are laws in nature. There are only necessities: there is nobody who commands, nobody who obeys, nobody who trespasses. Once you know that there are no purposes, you also know that there is no accident; for it is only beside a world of purposes that the word 'accident' has meaning.[45]

Nature is neither to be understood to be completely random, a jumbled manifold of fortuitous events, nor is it to be understood to be *ordered* by *unifying* laws. Rather, Nature is characterized by Nietzsche to be *both* chance *and* necessity, or it is a dynamical system. What happens by chance and what happens by necessity are not mutually exclusive; there is no either/or here, and this is precisely because the 'innocence of becoming' is the condition that makes this either/or possible. Becoming cannot be grasped, represented, or unified within this logic of either/or – it is 'undecidable' – but it is the both/and that allows for the possibility of deciding with respect to an either/or. We see this in *Twilight of the Idols*, for example, when Nietzsche argues:

If there is to be art, if there is to be any aesthetic doing and seeing, one physiological condition is indispensable: frenzy ... What is essential in such frenzy is *the feeling of increased strength and fullness*. Out of this feeling one lends to things, one forces them to accept from us, one violates them – this process is called idealizing.[46]

By idealizing, Nietzsche does not mean a process of 'subtracting or discounting the petty and inconsequential,' but rather a 'tremendous drive to bring out the main features so that the others disappear in the process.' A decision is made, an aesthetic differentiation, and it is the dionysian frenzy, or the chaos and becoming within oneself, that makes this possible. This dionysian frenzy, with its 'increased strength and fullness,' is the medium of this decision, the condition for this difference (i.e., difference between the 'main features' and the 'others' that disappear). But when referring to a state of 'increased strength and fullness,' a strength that is discharged or expended as the medium of a decision or difference, Nietzsche will most often use the term 'will to power.'[47] Consequently, 'will to power' is to be understood, and this is how Deleuze will interpret it, as the medium or condition which makes decisions (i.e., differentiation) possible. 'Will to power,' as Deleuze puts it, is 'the genealogical element of force, both differential and genetic.'[48] As the differential element, what is differentiated by will to power are, Deleuze argues, forces, the forces, as quoted above, that are part of the 'feeling of increased strength and fullness.' It was this force that both forced the 'main features' to the fore and forced the 'others' to disappear, and hence the decisions or differences that are made possible by will to power are decisions and differences of force. Therefore, if the world or Nature as 'viewed from inside' is nothing but 'will to power,' then Nature itself is nothing but forces, an infinite variability of forces, a dynamical system of forces.

The importance of 'force' within Nietzsche's thought has long been recognized, at least since Heidegger.[49] Deleuze, however, does not follow Heidegger when Heidegger *identifies* force as simply another name for will to power;[50] rather, Deleuze argues that for Nietzsche 'will to power' is the *non-identifiable* differential element which allows for the identification of forces and the evaluation of the differences between them (e.g., active and reactive). At the same time, 'will to power' is not something separate from these forces, something which 'lacks' force; on the contrary, 'will to power' 'inheres or subsists,' to use a phrase of Deleuze's, within the forces of which it is the 'differential element,' and yet it is not to be identified with them.

This notion of a non-identifiable differential element is perhaps the most 'central' notion of Deleuze's work, and he will use a number of different terms throughout his writings to refer to it: 'singularity,' 'aleatory point,' 'event,' 'inclusive disjunction,' 'incorporeal transformation,' and 'becoming-x' (e.g., 'becoming-animal,' 'becoming-woman,' 'becoming-imperceptible'). In *Logic of Sense*, for example, Deleuze claims that an 'event,' as with his understanding of 'will to power,' neither is separable from actual bodies or states of affairs (or forces), – it 'inheres or subsists'[51] in them – nor is it to be identified with them; it forever eludes such identification:

> With every event, there is indeed the present moment of its actualization, the moment in which the event is embodied in a state of affairs, an individual, or a person, the moment we designate by saying 'here, the moment has come'. The future and the past of the event are only evaluated with respect to this definitive present. On the other hand, there is the future and past of the event considered in itself, sidestepping each present, being free of the limitations of a state of affairs, impersonal, pre-individual, neutral.[52]

The 'event' thus has, as Deleuze notes, a 'double structure.' An event is not separable from the 'present' of some body or state of affairs (it inheres or subsists in them); and an event eludes this present, being simultaneously past and future. This 'double structure' also characterizes, as Deleuze reads Nietzsche, 'will to power.' On the one hand, Deleuze claims that the will to power is 'never separable from particular, determined forces, from their quantities, qualities and directions.'[53] On the other hand, Deleuze cautions that 'inseparable does not mean identical,' that will to power and force do differ, or that 'force is what can, will to power is what wills.' In other words, for Deleuze 'forces will remain indeterminate unless an element which is capable of determining them from a double point of view is added to force itself.'[54] This element is will to power, and the double point of view is that of quantity and quality. Will to power is simultaneously the differential element for quantitative differences between forces (i.e., the 'mechanistic' interpretation of forces) and for the qualitative differences between active and reactive, master and slave, etc. (i.e., the genealogical interpretation of forces). In itself, however, will to power is the 'difference that makes a difference,' the non-identifiable, differential element which is not to be identified with force. Thus, will to power forever eludes being reduced to some identity, even the quantitative identity and equality of forces. It is for this reason that Deleuze believes Nietzsche favours quality over quantity (i.e., genealogy over mechanism), because, as Deleuze puts it, 'quality is distinct from quantity but only because it is that aspect of quantity that cannot be equalized, that cannot be equalized out in the difference between quantities.'[55] As the differential element, therefore, the double structure of will to power is inseparable from particular, identifiable, interpretable forces; and yet, as the non-identifiable element that allows for this identification and interpretation, it 'itself' eludes identification.

But now the problem, as Deleuze is well aware, is interpretation itself. How do we interpret these forces? What interprets them? What is our criterion? Or, to return to our earlier question, how is a philosophical discourse to proceed? The answer to all these questions, on Deleuze's *interpretation* of Nietzsche, is will to power.[56] It is the will to power that interprets, and the standards and criteria used in this interpretation are those of will to power itself; that is, Deleuze feels there is a dual distinction to will to power (i.e., a double structure) which is expressed within the interpretations that are will to power; and then there is a dual distinction which is the repetition of will to power, or it is the *interpreted* distinction between active and reactive forces: 'active and reactive designate the original qualities of force but affirmative and negative designate the primordial qualities of will to power.'[57] It is this notion of repetition that is key, for it is here where the will to power is fundamentally related to Nietzsche's idea of eternal recurrence. Active and reactive forces are the recurrence and repetition of affirmative and negative will, a will that is both their condition of possibility, and their limit, or that which is forever beyond them. As Deleuze states the relationship between them:

> It is as if affirmation and negation were both immanent and transcendent in relation to action and reaction; out of the web of forces they make up the chain of becoming. Affirmation takes us into the glorious world of Dionysus, the being of becoming and negation hurls us down into the disquieting depths from which reactive forces emerge.[58]

It is therefore with respect to becoming, and the being of becoming, that we must turn in order to clarify these relationships – that is, the relationship between active and reactive, affirmation and negation, will to power and force – as well as to clarify the role of interpretation as Deleuze understands it. There are two additional reasons for making this move: first, this will place Nietzsche's discussion of will to power, force, eternal return, etc., within the context of his desire for 'the great liberation...[whereby] the innocence of becoming is restored';

and secondly, with becoming we find again the double structure Deleuze claimed to be characteristic of the 'event' and 'will to power,' and with Nietzsche's understanding of becoming we will find the deeper motivation and reason for these characterizations (i.e., his effort to think difference).

That much of Nietzsche's writings were concerned with stressing the role of becoming over the role of being is common knowledge. Claims to this effect abound: 'Heraclitus will remain eternally right with his assertion that being is an empty fiction';[59] '... everything has evolved; there are no eternal facts nor are there any absolute truths';[60] 'It is of time and becoming that the best parables should speak: let them be a praise and a justification of all impermanence';[61] 'The character of the world in a state of becoming as incapable of formulation, as "false," as "self-contradictory."'[62] But what is perhaps unique to Deleuze's discussion of this theme is the stress he places on the 'self-contradictory' nature of becoming, or the double structure of becoming. In *Logic of Sense*, for example, Deleuze claims that there is

> a simultaneity of becoming whose characteristic is to elude the present ... becoming does not tolerate the separation or the distinction of before and after, or of past and future. It pertains to the essence of becoming to move and pull in both directions at once: Alice does not grow without shrinking, and vice versa.[63]

The reference to Alice is to Alice in *Through the Looking Glass*, for when 'Alice becomes larger,' she becomes larger than she was and is yet smaller than she becomes. Or, as Deleuze puts it, 'she is not bigger and smaller at the same time. She is larger now; she was smaller before.'[64] The claim is thus not that Alice *is*, at some 'present' moment, bigger and smaller at the same time, but rather that in becoming larger she is simultaneously becoming smaller than she becomes. Becoming entails this double structure, this being pulled in both directions at once, and this 'at once' is not an identifiable, present moment, but is a 'self-contradictory' moment that will forever 'elude the present.'

As that which forever eludes the present, is non-identifiable and 'self-contradictory,' becoming must in turn elude being 'known,' at least if knowledge is assumed to be a manner of grasping and identifying something. And this is precisely what Nietzsche, after stating that becoming is 'self-contradictory,' claims: 'Knowledge and becoming exclude one another.'[65] But if we are to get on with our lives, we must also, as we have discussed earlier, have 'knowledge,' or the strange and unfamiliar (i.e., becoming as 'self-contradictory') must be reduced to the habitual and the familiar (i.e., being as non-contradictory). 'Consequently,' as Nietzsche continues, 'there must first of all be a will to make knowable, a kind of becoming must itself create the deception of beings.'[66] This will is the 'will to power': 'To impose upon becoming the character of being: that is the supreme will to power.'[67] Yet, as 'a kind of becoming,' will to power must itself be 'self-contradictory,' or have the double structure of being simultaneously pulled in two directions at once; and, indeed, this is what we, following Deleuze, have argued is the case with respect to Nietzsche's notion of the will to power. The will to power, as we will now clarify, is simultaneously pulled in the directions of becoming *both* affirmative *and* negative, becoming and being, chance and necessity. It is, in other words, 'the world defined and determined according to its "intelligible character."'

As that which interprets, or as the non-identifiable will which *evaluates* while itself remaining 'unapproachable' and incapable of being evaluated, will to power is to be interpreted, and this is Nietzsche's strategy, with respect to that which is *evaluated*, or that which is valued. The will which wills and affirms 'being,' for example, the 'will to make knowable,' is for Nietzsche a *negative* will. The reason for this is that this will affirms being, it says yes to being, yet it simultaneously negates becoming, and negates it in order to have knowledge; but since the will to power, even the 'will to make knowable,' is a 'kind of becoming,' this will consequently negates itself. It is a will directed against itself, or, as Nietzsche refers to this, 'the condemnation of life is only a value judgment of life ...'[68] And this leads Nietzsche to the conclusion that this condemnation is symptommatic of a 'declining, weakened, weary, condemned life.' This is a will and life that does not have the 'strength of spirit'[69] to endure the 'truth' of itself – that is, the 'truth' of becoming. Consequently, this is a will that simply reacts to and affirms things as the result of a fundamental negation, and thus this affirmation is not, as Deleuze points out, an affirmation of strength, or even an affirmation that affirms what *is* (i.e., being). This is the affirmation of the ass in *Zarathustra* (IV, 'The Awakening'): 'He carries our burden, he took upon himself the form of a servant, he is the patient of heart and never says No.'[70] In other words, as a result of negating its own becoming, the will to power is left merely repeating this fundamental negation, and thus the ass's 'Yea-Yuh' is an affirmation that does not know how to say 'no' to this fundamental negation (i.e., nihilism). The ass's 'Yea-Yuh' reacts to, or is a servant of, the consequence of this negation (i.e., the affirmation of 'being,' 'reality'), or, as Deleuze puts it, 'he always answers yes, but answers yes each time nihilism opens the conversation.'[71] The ass bears the load of 'reality' and 'being.'

But the will to power is not simply pulled in the direction of becoming a negating will, it is also simultaneously pulled towards becoming an affirming will; and that which is affirmed is will to power itself, or, since will to power is a kind of becoming, it is the affirmation of becoming. Furthermore, since the world, nature, and life are understood by Nietzsche to be '"will to power" and nothing else,' the affirmation of will to power is therefore simultaneously the affirmation of all that there *is* – namely, being as a whole. However, because the will to power is the non-identifiable medium which evaluates, affirms, and wills, it can only be affirmed, Deleuze argues, if another will affirms it. Deleuze thus claims that Nietzsche has a conception of being, but that this being entails a 'double affirmation': 'It is primary affirmation (becoming) which is being, but only as the object of the second affirmation. The two affirmations constitute the power of affirming as a whole.'[72] Dionysian affirmation, in order to be raised to the level of being, must itself be affirmed, and it is for this reason that Deleuze feels Nietzsche had to discuss not only Dionysus's affirmation, but also Ariadne's affirmation of Dionysus. Ariadne's affirmation is a repetition or recurrence of Dionysus's affirmation. This is not, however, a repetition of an identifiable, static 'being,' and thus this is not a repetition understood in the manner of a 'habit' or 'memory' – that is, repetition of the same. Ariadne's repetition is also not a repetition that repeats at some 'present' moment something that has already happened in the past (as do habits and memories). The will to power as affirmation, as becoming, forever eludes the present, and it also, as we saw Deleuze claim, 'does not tolerate the separation or the distinction of before and after, or of past and future.' Ariadne's repetition is hence a repetition of that which is timeless, or that which forever eludes the understanding and identification of time as the passing of 'present' moments into the past; consequently, Ariadne's repetition is a recurrence of the timeless and eternal – it is 'eternal recurrence.' And this is precisely Deleuze's interpretation of Nietzsche's notion of eternal recurrence: 'Dionysian becoming is being, eternity, but only insofar as the corresponding affirmation is itself affirmed';[73] and this, in turn, is the reason for Nietzsche's claim that the eternal return 'is the closest approximation of a world of becoming to a world of being.'[74]

The double structure of will to power entails both affirmation and negation; however, between affirmation and negation there is not, as Deleuze points out, a 'univocal relation.'[75] The ass's affirmation, for example, begins with the negation of becoming, and it is with this that 'being' and 'reality' arises and is affirmed; thus what is positive and affirmed is the consequence of negation, or it is the 'positivity of the negative.' Dionysian affirmation, on the other hand, is a yes that says 'no' to nihilism, and to nihilism's negation of becoming: it is a negation of negation. But the positivity of this affirmation, the negation of negation, is not, and this is where Deleuze sees Nietzsche being radically anti-Hegelian, a consequence of negation; rather, the negative is itself a consequence of affirmation, of becoming, and of the self-differing double structure of becoming. It is 'the negativity of the positive.' In addition, this negativity is not opposed to affirmation, but is the expression of this affirmation, the expression of difference. Therefore, instead of saying yes to that which is the result of negation, or the result of a dialectical process, affirmation entails saying no (the Lion's 'no') as a consequence of the affirmation of difference. It is for this reason that Deleuze believes negation and affirmation are not univocally related: 'Negation is opposed to affirmation but affirmation differs from negation.' If we begin with negation, with *what is not* (e.g., becoming as negated for the sake of knowledge), then what comes to be affirmed as what is (being) is affirmed as that which is opposed to (or is *not*) *what is not*. 'Opposition,' Deleuze adds, 'is the essence of the negative as such';[76] and therefore we can see why he characterizes Hegel as the 'philosopher of the negative.' But if we begin with affirmation, with the double structured self-difference of becoming, then what is not, or negation, comes simply to be seen as what is different.[77] Deleuze thus contrasts Hegel's negation of negation which *results* in something positive, with Nietzsche's affirmation of affirmation – that is, eternal recurrence – which *is* positive, which is the being of becoming. As Deleuze summarizes this position, he notes:

> Being ought to belong to becoming, unity to multiplicity, necessity to chance, but only insofar as becoming, multiplicity and chance are reflected in the second affirmation which takes them as its object. It is thus in the nature of affirmation to return or of difference to reproduce itself. Return is the being of becoming, the unity of multiplicity, the necessity of chance: the being of difference as such or the eternal return.[78]

In looking at the world 'from inside,' what Nietzsche claims we find is will to power, but will to power, as Deleuze interprets it, is 'the differential element that produces and develops difference in affirmation, that reflects difference in the affirmation of affirmation and makes it return in the affirmation which is itself affirmed.' And the whole which harbours this 'difference in affirmation' (i.e., will to power) is a whole which forever eludes achieving equilibrium – that is, stable self-identity – and in the affirmation of this whole, will to power is precisely this difference and non-equilibrium that is affirmed: both necessity and chance, both being and becoming, both identity and difference.[79] And it is this affirmation of affirmation, or eternal recurrence, which is 'the closest approximation of a world of becoming to a world of being.'

But is not Plato's project, at least in *The Republic*, also that of finding 'the closest approximation of a world of becoming to a world of being'? For example, when Glaucon asks Socrates whether the 'city in speech' they are constructing, or 'fictioning,' to use an earlier term, could ever 'come into being' (471c), Socrates responds by accepting the difficulty of creating an actual city, a 'city in deed,' that would correspond exactly to the 'city in speech'; however, Socrates adds that 'if we are able to find that a city could be governed in a way most closely approximating what has been said [i.e., fictioned] ... (and) that we've found the possibility of these things coming into being ... won't you be content if it turns out this way? I, for my part, would be content' (473a–b). Analogously, if the philosopher-king (who, after Socrates confesses he is content with only an approximation, immediately becomes the topic of discussion) has as his goal the knowledge of the '*ideas*' (*eidos*), ideas that have in turn been fictioned by the gods in the place above heaven (*hyperouranios topos*), then perhaps he too will be content if it is possible for an approximation of these ideas to come into being. In the philosopher-king's attempt to rule the city in the best possible manner, is he not attempting to bring about in the world of becoming (i.e., in deed) the closest approximation of that which *is* in the world of being (i.e., the 'ideas' fictioned by the gods)? Whether or not the philosopher-king is able to leave the cave of becoming and look 'at that which *is* and the brightest part of that which *is*' (518c), it is nonetheless clear that Socrates feels the 'ideal' city could only be, as actualized in the world of becoming, an approximation of this 'ideal.'

Despite the apparent similarity between Plato's and Nietzsche's fundamental efforts to think an 'approximation of a world of becoming to a world of being,' there is, however, a crucial difference. For Plato this 'approximation' is understood to be the resemblance in the world of becoming to an already fictioned and created 'idea,' and the philosopher attempts to bring about this resemblance, or recognize it. For Nietzsche this 'approximation' of becoming to being is not an approximation of an already fictioned being; rather, it is an approximation of being insofar as becoming is essentially what is, and 'the brightest part of that which is,' but is being only as the object of a second affirmation, of an affirmation that returns to becoming as the being of becoming (i.e., eternal return). The eternal return is thus the return and affirmation of that which is non-identifiable, self-differing (i.e., double structure of becoming). The eternal return, in short, entails the non-identifiable, self-differing 'will to power' as the differential element which allows for the possibility of differentiating, deciding, evaluating, etc., and, as self-differing, allows for a different will which affirms itself, affirms its irreducible difference. The eternal return is therefore not the return of something that has already been created and fictioned, something which remains the same and can be identified (recollected); it is the return of difference itself, a difference that creates, fictions, becomes, and eludes all identification. Thus, for Nietzsche, the approximation of becoming to being entails creation, whereas for Plato it entails re-creation.

We are now in an even better position to understand Nietzsche's inversion and reversal of Plato. We have seen that for Plato the solution to the problem of the *Meno* entailed arguing for a knowledge that already exists in the soul, or that has already been stamped upon the soul. Consequently, when we come to know the ideas, we simply recollect something that was already there.[80] Nietzsche, on the other hand, since his concern is for the repetition and return of difference, and not for the repetition or recollection of the same, will be critical of the Platonic theory of recollection. Nietzsche will subsequently emphasize and praise forgetfulness in one of the preludes to *The Gay Science*. This particular prelude is titled, perhaps in reference to Plato, 'Dialogue':

A. Was I ill? Have I got well?
   Who was my doctor? Can you tell?
   Oh, my memory is rotten!
B. Only now you're truly well.
   Those are well who have forgotten.[81]

Only if we have forgotten something can we see it again for the first time, see it as something unique and different. Similarly, only if we forget who we are, or who we are supposed to be, can we then create ourselves – 'We, however, want to become those we are – human beings who are new, unique, incomparable, who give themselves laws, who create themselves.'[82] To do this, however, entails a continual overcoming of the tendency to settle into habits, yet this does not mean, as it did for Plato, that 'bad' habits are to be replaced by 'good' habits (*Republic* 401b); instead, it entails the affirmation of oneself as the fundamentally different, 'unique, incomparable' medium whereby these habits are created. In other words, what is affirmed is will to power as the differential element of forces; and habits, as understood here, are forces that come to be predominant, familiar, and predictable. Thus, to create and affirm ourselves as new, unique, and incomparable – that is, to restore 'the innocence of becoming' – the 'free spirit' thus 'hates all habits and rules, everything enduring and definitive; that is why, again and again, he painfully tears apart the net around him.'[83] Nietzsche's reversal of Plato, therefore, is not concerned with bringing about or restoring what is fundamentally and forever the same, but it is rather the attempt to restore what is fundamentally and eternally new, different, incomparable – 'the innocence of becoming.'[84]

Again, things are not so simple. In the relationship between 'Plato' and the poets, the rationale for the Platonic disenfranchisement of poetry and the imitative arts is that they tend to promote dispersal, or to instil a desire for multiplicity and otherness, a desire that results from the poets' ability 'to imitate all things' (398a). Poetry softens the plasticity of the soul and prohibits the stamp of good habits from solidifying. Without such habits, and with the tendency for dispersal and otherness, the principle of 'to each his own' becomes impossible to maintain, and hence so too does justice in the city and the soul. Despite their disenfranchisement, however, the poets, as Plato seems to be aware, are not dismissed so easily. Why this is so becomes clear when we look at the *Ion*. In this dialogue the poets are said to lack art (i.e., *techne*), and 'good epic poets' (533e) are simply the medium through which it is 'the god himself who speaks' (534d). It is thus 'not by art [that] they utter these [poems], but by power divine, since if it were by art that they knew how to treat one subject finely, they would know how to deal with all the others too' (535c). Since the poets do not know what they are doing, or because they do not have an art that can produce things *other* than poems, their efforts are not to be lauded but criticized. Yet it is precisely because the poets do not know but are inspired, or because it is 'the god himself who speaks,' that difficulties arise with respect to criticizing and dismissing the poets. In particular, if the 'ideas' are created and fictioned by the gods, and if it is the 'god himself who speaks' through the poets, then it would seem that the poets would be an exceptional resource for anyone who wishes 'to know' these 'ideas.' But this is not the case. The effort in *The Republic* to dismiss the poets from the city appears to show that they are not seen as such an exceptional resource. The reason for this is that the poets lack the art (*techne*) of applying the 'ideas' the gods fiction to the many. It is therefore precisely because of a concern for the realm of becoming, for the realm of the many, that the poets are of no use to the city. But why must we also get rid of the poets' poetry? If we are interested in knowing the 'ideas' that have been fictioned by the gods, can these same ideas not be gleaned from the poetry these gods have fictioned? More troubling, perhaps, is the difficulty of reconciling the claim that the gods speak through the 'good' epic poets, with the position in *The Republic* that we must censor all poetry which falsely portrays the gods as being liars, deceiving, changing forms, etc. Do the gods falsely portray themselves? Socrates would clearly reject this possibility, for the gods, he claims, have no reason to lie (*Republic*, 382e). Are these poets, therefore, such as Homer, whom Socrates cites as an example of one who portrays the gods falsely (379d–380a), to be deemed 'bad'? This, in turn, does not appear to be a response Socrates would accept, for he repeatedly applauds Homer, and in the *Ion* he declares Homer to be 'the best and most divine of all [the poets]' (530b). How, then, are we to account for these contrasting claims concerning the poets, and in particular the apparent difficulty in accounting for the relationship between the poets and the 'fictioning essence' of the 'ideas' – namely, the gods?

One possible way of clarifying the 'Platonic' attitude to poetry is to understand it as the result of a confrontation with the double structure of becoming. Plato both affirms and negates the poets, not because he is inconsistent or lacks rigour in his thinking, but precisely for the reason that Plato confronts and attempts to think the 'fictioning essence' of the ideas, or Plato is attempting to think difference. And since we have been arguing that this 'fictioning essence,' following Nietzsche, is the non-identifiable double structure of becoming which forever eludes the stability of the present, it should not be surprising that Plato's discussion of the poets, who are intimately related to this 'fictioning essence,' should repeat this double structure. In addition, as Plato attempts to explicate and think the fictioning process itself, or the process whereby the gods fiction both the ideas and poetry (via the 'good' epic poets), it is also not surprising that we find both being and becoming. On the one hand, the gods do not depart from their own idea, or they forever are what they are (*Republic* 380d–381c); and, on the other, the poets, with their ability 'to imitate all things,' consistently *become* other than what they are. The fictioning process, as with Nietzsche's notion of will to power, is the non-identifiable differential element whereby the differences between various fictions (forces, for Nietzsche) can be decided and evaluated, but it is not to be identified with these fictions. Similarly, for Plato the gods are the condition for differentiating between the ideas of justice, beauty, couch, etc., but they are not to be identified with these ideas. Nietzsche and Plato therefore confront this fundamental differential element, this fictioning process, and in doing this they both affirm the Being of becoming. However, whereas for Nietzsche the Being of becoming is the self-differing, self-affirmation (i.e., eternal return) of becoming, for Plato the Being of becoming is the self-identical, self-affirmation (i.e., repetition of the same) of Being (e.g., the gods as forever the same). But this decision of Plato's is itself made possible by the non-identifiable differential element which is both being and becoming; consequently, Nietzsche's reversal of Plato is not an opposition or negation, but rather a continuing attempt to think the fundamental difference Plato also sought to explicate (i.e., the fictioning process). Nietzsche's philosophy, as Deleuze would also argue, entails a positive affirmation of difference, not the affirmation of negation, and hence Nietzsche's reversal does not negate or oppose itself to Platonism. Nietzsche affirms, rather, a reversal of reversal, or what he referred to as the 'transvaluation of all values' (including the value of opposite values), and this entails affirming the non-identifiable differential medium which is the condition for such values, but is 'itself' absolutely different, unique, and incomparable. In short, Nietzsche's reversal of reversal implies restoring 'the innocence of becoming,' or the fundamental double structure (both/and) that is the condition for reversal, and for the logic of either/or (e.g., either Plato or Nietzsche). Nietzsche's philosophy does *differ* from Plato's; however, it is not the opposite of Plato's, its *negative* image, so to speak.

How are we to interpret the manner in which Nietzsche and Plato differ? In other words, what is left for interpretation to do in the wake of this confrontation with the non-identifiable differential element? To identify a 'proper' standard or task for interpretation would be to run counter to the very claim that what is crucial for any interpretive, evaluative task is precisely that which is non-identifiable and 'improper' – namely, the differential element. Are we left with relativism? On the one hand, no, we are not left with relativism, for the weight of the criticism which accuses a position of relativism resides in a faith in objective standards, or a faith in an either/or (either objective or relative); but the position we have been discussing is critical of this very either/or, and thus we would accuse the objectivist critic of 'Enlightenment blackmail.'[85] On the other hand, this response seems to leave the question of interpretation, or the question of how a philosophical discourse is to proceed, unanswered. But we have stated that there is an answer to these questions, and the answer, put briefly, was said to be will to power. To clarify this, therefore, we need to return to the notion of will to power; more precisely, we will return to the theme of the 'double structure' of will to power, or, as we have referred to it earlier in this chapter, the 'double bind.' To clarify the consequences the 'double bind' has for understanding the role of interpretation, or for how a philosophical discourse is to proceed, it will be helpful to refer to Gregory Bateson's theory of the double bind. Bateson, as we will argue, can be seen to be an important influence on Deleuze's work, and for this reason the consequences upon behaviour which Bateson claims result from a double bind will clarify what Deleuze feels is philosophy's 'proper' task.

Bateson argues that a double bind consists of two injunctions. The first or primary injunction says that one must or must not do so and so; the second injunction is more general, or more 'abstract,' and it conflicts with the first. For example, a mother might tell her son not to do so and so, but then might, by her more general behaviour – for example, by her gestures, intonation, or other non-verbal means of communicating – tell him not to submit to her prohibitions. Regardless what the son does, therefore, he will be in the wrong.[86] Subsequently, Bateson argues that in such a situation, a person is likely to choose one of several alternatives in response to his or her inability to judge what the other person 'really' means. To judge what a person 'really' means, Bateson refers to as being able to discern the 'metacommunicative level' of another's discourse, the level where we are 'able to comment directly or indirectly on an expression.' Most of the responses to this failure Bateson claims are pathological: for example, paranoia, when the person assumes that what is 'really' meant is ultimately harmful; hebephrenia, when the person gives up on attempting to distinguish between levels of meaning and hence either takes everything literally or takes nothing seriously; catatonia, when the person detaches from external communication and withdraws into internal processes; and even schizophrenia, in which hallucinations and delusions are *created* to resolve the double bind.[87]

Not all consequences of a double bind, however, are pathological. Bateson notes that just as the schizophrenic responds to the double bind by creating hallucinations, delusions, etc., so too, he claims, can this creativity be used as a means of resisting pathological consequences. Bateson thus observes 'that if this pathology can be warded off or resisted, the total experience [of the double bind] may promote creativity.'[88] Rather than submit or succumb to the 'pain and maladjustment' of the 'no-win' double bind, the resistance to this pain and maladjustment can be creative, a creativity which actualizes this pain while being counter to it; or, to put it another way, it 'counteractualizes' this pain.[89] Thus, although the double bind can result in the failure of communicative interaction, wherein either it collapses into being nothing other than a self-referring threat (paranoia), or it disrupts conventional forms of communication to the point where it no longer refers (schizophrenia); it can also result in the creation of new forms of communication, new conventions, that can reopen the lines of communication.

This creative response to the double bind is not simply a phenomenon of individuals but is one of cultures as well. In Bateson's analysis of Balinese culture, for example,[90] he claims that their cultural interactions differ greatly from those of traditional cultures of the West. In the West, for example, Bateson claims that cultural/individual forces and tensions are built up to a point where there is a release of tension, or a return to calm, order, and stability. This usually entails either some climactic release of tension, after which the intensity is greatly reduced (Bateson cites orgasm as an example), or some power or force that intervenes from outside to restrain the build-up of intensity. This build-up is thus seen to be incompatible with order and stability, and therefore for the sake of stability either there is to be a release from this build-up (orgasm) or it must be restrained from the outside (e.g., government intervention). The Balinese, by contrast, are confronted with a double bind: they demand order and stability on the one hand, and, on the other, that the instability, intensity, and dynamics of forces be maintained from *within*. In other words, their cultural interactions reflect an effort to maintain stability while allowing for neither a climactic resolution nor a restraining *outside* force.[91] The Balinese response to this challenge, or to this double bind, is the creation of what Bateson refers to as a 'plateau of intensity' (p. 113). For example, rather than building up sexual intensity to a climax and release of tension, the Balinese substitute a plateau of intensity that is maintained and stabilized without release (i.e., without orgasm); and with quarrels, to take another example, rather than resolving the quarrel, the two men 'will register their quarrel [formally], agreeing that whichever speaks to the other shall pay a fine or make an offering to the gods' (p. 113). This is not, Bateson observes, a means of resolving the hostility between the two, but rather a means of stabilizing it, or a recognition and maintaining of this hostility. The Balinese thus do not attempt to resolve the build-up of tension by transcending it and bringing it to a close, whether from within or from without, but they maintain a 'plateau of intensity' from within, a plateau without resolution.

We can now begin to see, especially with the notion of a 'plateau of intensity,' the influence of Bateson on Deleuze (and Guattari). In fact, the very title of Deleuze and Guattari's companion volume to *Anti-Oedipus*, *Thousand Plateaus* (*Mille plateaux*), is indebted to Bateson's discussion. They acknowledge this debt in the introduction to this work:

> A plateau is always in the middle, not at the beginning or the end. A rhizome is made of plateaus. Gregory Bateson uses the word 'plateau' to designate something special: a continuous, self-vibrating region of intensities whose development avoids any orientation toward a culmination point or external end ... It is a regrettable characteristic of the Western mind to relate expressions and actions to exterior or transcendent ends, instead of evaluating them on a plane of consistency on the basis of their intrinsic value ... We are writing this book as a rhizome. It is composed of plateaus.[92]

In contrast to what Deleuze and Guattari will refer to as the 'regrettable characteristic of the Western mind,' with its emphasis upon 'arboreal' roots and transcendent ends,[93] they propose to write plateaus, rhizomes, and planes of consistency. In their work, they are interested neither in arboreal roots (i.e., a single origin, beginning, or primary cause) nor in transcendent ends (i.e., a purpose, goal, or *telos*); rather, they map the plateaus within which such goals come to the fore – that is, come to be the predominant forces, intensities, etc. With this move, we find the continued link to Nietzsche, for this concern for plateaus and planes of consistency (i.e., consistency of intensities and forces) which one cannot get beyond, or which one is always already 'in the middle of,' and similarly with Bateson's discussion of the consequences of the double bind: these themes were already at work in Deleuze's book on Nietzsche.

In particular, these issues were at work in Deleuze's discussion of the will to power. As the non-identifiable differential element, it is impossible to decide, evaluate, or interpret the will to power, for such an evaluation would entail stepping outside or beyond it. Nevertheless, since all there is for Nietzsche is will to power and 'nothing else,' and since will to power is precisely what evaluates, differentiates, or is, in short, 'the difference which makes a difference,' it is also impossible not to evaluate and interpret. Furthermore, since the world and Nature, understood from within (since we can't get beyond it, or outside it), is also will to power and 'nothing else,' and because Nietzsche claims that the fundamental character of the world is 'chaos,'[94] we are subsequently led to a double bind with respect to the theme with which we began this chapter: the chaos in oneself. It is thus impossible to know and evaluate the chaos in oneself, and yet it is necessary to know it, to impose an order and 'knowledge' upon it. And it is precisely Nietzsche's response to this double bind, or what he thinks *ought* to be our response to it, which answers the question of interpretation, or the question of how a philosophical discourse ought to proceed.

Nietzsche's response, *à la* Bateson, is *to create*. Thus, rather than submit or succumb to the pain and suffering of our existence, or our double bind, one can *actively resist* this pain through creativity. We turn our pain and suffering into an active, creative suffering, or what Nietzsche calls the 'great suffering.' It is this 'great suffering' which Nietzsche believes 'has created all enhancements of man so far,' and it has done this as a result of 'its inventiveness and courage in enduring, persevering, interpreting, and exploiting suffering.'[95] As an active, creative suffering, this 'great suffering' is to be contrasted with the suffering of a passive 'creature' who simply accepts and succumbs to its suffering:

> In man creature and creator are united: in man there is material, fragment, excess, clay, dirt, nonsense, chaos; but in man there is also creator, form-giver, hammer hardness, spectator divinity, and seventh day: do you understand this contrast?[96]

It is with respect to the latter that Nietzsche has sympathy, or it is the 'great suffering' for which he has pity, and this pity is contrasted to the pity for the *passive* suffering of the creature within us. Nietzsche calls this pity a 'converse pity,' and 'thus,' he concludes, 'it is pity versus pity.' The 'great suffering' does call for pity, as did the 'pain and maladjustment' of Bateson's double bind, but this is not a pity for the creature who has succumbed to suffering, but rather a pity for that which creates in response to its suffering; it is a pity that is counter to this pity – that is, it 'counteractualizes' this pity.

A question arises here, however, for if we are both creature and creator, and if chaos is an aspect of the former, then what is the relationship between chaos and will to power? Had we not earlier roughly equated will to power with the chaos in oneself? Is chaos being contrasted with the will that creates, with the great suffering? This apparent difficulty arises only if we do *identify* will to power with chaos, but since both will to power and chaos are non-identifiable, non-interpretable, this problem is avoided. But how then, one might now ask, can we identify the contrast between them? Is not the claim that the will to power creates, or hammers out a form upon this chaos, an identification or interpretation? Indeed it is. Furthermore, Nietzsche, as is well known and readily apparent for anyone who reads him, is never lacking in evaluative comments, interpretations, criticisms, historical analyses, etc. However, what is to be stressed in Nietzsche's interpretation concerning the relationship between the will that creates and the chaos that is given a form, is that there is not *either* chaos in oneself *or* will to power; there is both: 'creature and creator are united.' Will to power is 'itself' also double, is the differential element, and is the non-identifiable difference which is the condition for *identifying* the difference between suffering and 'great suffering,' pity and converse pity. But to identify this difference, to state what the fundamental difference *is*, is precisely the thought of the eternal return; consequently, although Nietzsche does interpret, state, and identify fundamental differences – for example, Dionysian/Apollinian, noble/slave, high/low, affirmation/*ressentiment* – and even though he clearly favours and contrasts the former to the latter in each case, this is always a favouring (a converse pity) which affirms difference; it is not an affirmation of oppositions. In addition, as the differential, non-identifiable element, will to power both allows for the evaluation and interpretation of differences, and as 'self-differing,' or as that which is forever in a state of non-coincidence with 'itself,' will to power entails the possibility of *another* will, a will that affirms the non-identifiable difference of the first (i.e., it affirms the being of becoming). It is in this sense, then, that one must create and interpret oneself, or that one 'becomes what one is': that is, to create and identify oneself, to interpret ourselves, entails affirming our fundamental difference, that which is unique, new, and incomparable within us (i.e., the thought of the eternal return). And Nietzsche's converse pity for the 'great suffering' is likewise an affirmation of difference: 'Profound suffering makes noble; it separates.'[97] This 'profound suffering' is itself, as we have seen, the creative response to the dual impossibilities of identifying the fundamental difference and chaos in oneself, and of identifying, for the sake of survival, the chaos in oneself. To create oneself, to 'become what one is,' is therefore what Nietzsche believes ought to be our creative response to the double bind.

Yet not all responses to the double bind, as we saw with Bateson, are creative, and Nietzsche was well aware of this. Nietzsche recognizes, for example, the possibility of what he calls 'the greatest danger that always hovered over humanity,' this danger being 'the eruption of madness – which means the eruption of arbitrariness in feeling, seeing, and hearing ...'[98] In short, the danger is that the will will succumb and submit to chaos, to 'arbitrariness.' Nevertheless, this danger should not be eliminated, or we should not deny any rights to the chaos in oneself, for Nietzsche also stresses the need for madness, for the madness and chaos that is necessary to create: 'almost everywhere it was madness which prepared the way for the new idea, which broke the spell of a venerated usage and superstition.'[99] And thus madness is necessary to avoid what Nietzsche takes to be our other danger: the collapse of the will into the 'venerated' repetition of the *same* 'enduring habits,'[100] customs, and traditions. One must be a little crazy, or one must have a little chaos in oneself, in order to create, to 'throw off the yoke' of traditions.

There is thus a twofold danger associated with the delicate balance of creativity, or a danger inherent in the non-identifiable both/and structure of will to power. In short, the both/and of will to power runs the risk and danger of collapsing into a destructive either/or: either the eruption of madness, or the repetition of the same. In both cases, what is destroyed is the ability to create and impose order, or what Nietzsche will also speak of as the ability 'to promise.'[101] The ability to promise is, as Nietzsche points out, liberated from the 'morality of custom,' but it is also, and he recognizes the 'paradoxical' nature of this claim, not without a calculable, predictable order. Those who are subservient to custom and tradition would be unable to promise, for they would lack the ability to create, to be inventive and experimental, an ability which is often necessary to fulfil our promises (especially when contingencies arise); but one who is mad would also be unable to promise for he/she would lack the necessary order and regularity. Promising is thus a delicate, difficult, and dangerous undertaking – it forever risks collapsing into a destructive either/or.[102]

Nietzsche's critiques and interpretations are likewise threatened by such a collapse. Nonetheless, he attempts to affirm and evaluate the paradoxical instance – that is, the both/and of creativity – which gives birth to new ideas, to ideas that are likely to become 'venerated' and blindly repeated. In doing this, Nietzsche assumes that 'all our actions are altogether incomparably personal, unique, and infinitely individual [i.e., will to power as paradoxical and non-identifiable both/and]; there is no doubt of that.'[103] Nietzsche's critiques and interpretations will subsequently consist of pointing out the habits, necessities, and imposed order which form the basis for the reasons, purposes, and goals we attribute to these actions: 'morality and religion: the reasons and purposes for habits are always lies that are added only after some people begin to attack these habits and to *ask* for reasons and purposes.'[104] Furthermore, as Nietzsche looks at these habits, he is concerned with whether they are 'the product of innumerable little cowardices and lazinesses or of your courage and *inventive* reason.'[105] In other words, are these habits the result of a creative, unique, and singular act, or are they the consequence of submitting to custom and tradition? Are we creating ourselves, or are we allowing ourselves to be created?

Even if we do create ourselves, however, this creation entails continuously dancing the fine and dangerous line between tradition and madness, or between chaos and the repetition of the same: it is the dance of continual self-overcoming.[106] Nietzsche's interpretive strategy and criterion, consequently, is to affirm and reveal the unique, singular, and perspectival conditions for the possibility of identifiable habits, forces, values, for the repetitions of the same (this, as we saw, is his interpretation/criticism of Plato); and yet this interpretation itself forever risks the possibility of either simply repeating venerated customs and philosophical traditions, or collapsing into the arbitrariness of relativism.[107] One must, Nietzsche believes, *both* create new ideas *and* affirm the tradition. This is the dangerous both/and Nietzsche recognizes: 'He who strays from tradition becomes a sacrifice to the extraordinary; he who remains in tradition is its slave. Destruction follows in any case.'[108] To avoid this destruction requires the paradox of creativity wherein we have both chaos in ourselves, a chaos which we creatively affirm without forsaking order, 'knowledge,' and form; and we have the creator in ourselves which creates this order without disenfranchising chaos, and thus without succumbing to the repetition of the same.[109] To extend Nietzsche's metaphor, therefore, 'one must have chaos in oneself to be able to give birth to a dancing star,' yet this creative birth can result, not in a 'dancing star,' but in a collapse into a 'black hole' of forever repeating the same, or an explosion into a fiery 'supernova' of madness.

Much of Deleuze's work can be seen to be a similar extension of Nietzsche's metaphor. For example, in reference to the notion of an 'event' in *Logic of Sense*, Deleuze claims: 'This event is, of course, quickly covered over by everyday banality or, on the contrary, by the sufferings of madness.'[110] The double, paradoxical structure of the event, the event as both embodied in the state of affairs of some 'present,' and forever eluding this present, being simultaneously past and future; this unique and singular event thus risks collapsing either into the repetition of the same, or of dispersing into the chaos of madness. The fusion or 'black hole' of the same, or the fission of the supernova: these are the two poles that forever threaten the event, the destructive either/or which haunts it.[111]

This either/or, following Bateson once again, is the potential consequence of failing to respond creatively to the double bind, to the dual impossibility and necessity of both being unable to identify and interpret the chaos in oneself, and being unable not to identify and interpret this chaos. This creative response, furthermore, entails the affirmation of the differential both/and structure of will to power. In Deleuze's theory, this affirmation entails creating a plateau and plane of consistency that is both fusion and fission, or, to use Deleuze and Guattari's terminology, both territorialized and deterritorialized. If a plateau, assemblage, plane of consistency, or event were to be completely territorialized, this would result in the blind repetition of the same and would render it incapable of responding to the unpredictable, and hence it would ultimately be destroyed; and yet if it were to be completely deterritorialized, this would render the event incapable of acquiring the necessary order and stability to function, and it would likewise be destroyed. To avoid this consequence, there must be the continual, eternal return of the event, the return of that which is both past (i.e., tradition, territorializing, being) and future (i.e., progress, deterritorializing, becoming). The both/and of the event must eternally return in order to prevent or correct the destructive tendency this both/and has to settle into an either/or: either 'everyday banality' or 'the sufferings of madness.' The event is therefore the 'negentropic activity' (another term Deleuze uses) which actively resists the sedimentation of the both/and into the either/or.[112]

This theme becomes even more important in Deleuze and Guattari's last co-written work, *Qu'est-ce que la philosophie*? In this book they recognize the impossibility of identifying and ordering chaos, but they also, in turn, recognize the necessity of this identification and ordering.

This is the double bind they explore, and what interests them are the creative responses scientists, artists, and philosophers take with respect to this double bind. The artist, for example, creates what Deleuze and Guattari refer to as a 'chaosmos,' or an ordered chaos: 'art isn't chaos, but a composition of chaos which gives rise to sight or sensation, with the result that it constitutes a chaosmos, as Joyce said, a composed chaos – neither predicted or anticipated.'[113] Art is thus both chaotic and unpredictable, and it is ordered and composed. In confronting chaos, therefore, the artist creates a composed chaos,[114] but this creative act also risks the possibility of being either a mere cliché or a chaotic piece which lacks the order necessary for 'sight or sensation,' for something new and determinate to be seen rather than something that is mere indeterminate, non-differentiated porridge. The artist is thus both for and against chaos: he/she is against chaos insofar as it needs to be ordered, given a form, etc., and she/he is for chaos as that which allows the artist to create something that is not a repetition of the same, a cliché. This both/and is not only true of the artist (the scientist, the philosopher) but is true of all creative responses to the double bind which resist its 'pain and maladjustment,' and thus resist the tendency to submit to the pain and destruction of an either/or. Our 'proper' activity, therefore, or the 'proper' task of philosophy, science, art, etc., is to create a plateau, plane of consistency, assemblage, work, or self that is both for and against the 'chaos in oneself.'

Critique without Redemption

What is new, however, is always evil, being that which wants to conquer and overthrow the old boundary markers and the old pieties; and only what is old is good. The good men are in all ages those who dig the old thoughts, digging deep and getting them to bear fruit – the farmers of the spirit. But eventually all land is exploited, and the ploughshare of evil must come again and again.

– Nietzsche, *The Gay Science* (§4)

Entropy will take its toll, and a once fertile soil, a soil that could give rise to healthy fruits, to new ideas, will soon lie dead. When this happens, the ploughshare of evil must necessarily come again and again; it must rip open the land, separating and overturning long-standing soil. Nietzsche's thought of the eternal return is his vision of this necessary return, the return of a creative act, a 'negentropic act' – the eternal return of the ploughshare.

Plato also called for the return of the ploughshare, or for the necessity of an activity which would overturn opinion and separate it from knowledge, from the truth of what is (i.e., *eidos*). Socrates the physician must return, again and again, to administer his medicine (*pharmakon*) and return the knowledge of ideas that have been long since forgotten. If this fails, as it often does, Socrates rests content with at least having the remedy for dogmatism: namely, dialectics. With the dialectical method, people become cured of their enduring opinions, of their long-standing yet mistaken belief that they know. Theaetetus, for example, after agreeing with Socrates that they have 'brought to birth all we have to say about knowledge,' and that he himself had 'given utterance to more than I had in me,' is urged by Socrates to 'henceforth try to conceive afresh, Theaetetus, [and] if you succeed, your embryo thoughts will be the better as a consequence of today's scrutiny, and if you remain barren, you will be gentler and more agreeable to your companions, having the sense not to fancy you know what you do not know' (*Theaetetus*, 210b–c). Socrates' remedy is therefore both an effort to overturn dogmatism and an attempt to give birth to ideas that are already there. Socrates' task is thus one of restoration and redemption, the recovery of forgotten ideas. Nietzsche's task is also one of restoration and redemption, but, and this is where he *differs* from Plato, this is not an effort to recover forgotten ideas, but rather an effort to give birth to new ideas. Nietzsche's ploughshare, as with Plato, is necessary both to overturn dogmatism and to give birth to ideas, but this birth is not the return of an idea that has remained the same; it is the return of that which forever differs, the difference that cannot be identified – in short, Nietzsche's ploughshare of evil is necessary 'to restore the innocence of becoming.'

Although they do indeed differ, Plato and Nietzsche both seem to be motivated by an effort to restore something that has been lost, and their critiques are consequently to be seen as critiques with some redemptive aim. For Plato the aim is to restore and recover being, whereas for Nietzsche it is becoming that is to be restored. Thus, if the tradition of metaphysics is understood to be primarily concerned with restoring and recovering some fundamental truth or reality that has been forgotten, or is at least constrained and held captive, then are not Nietzsche and Plato both a part of this tradition? In particular, is not Nietzsche's effort to liberate and restore the innocence of becoming simply a version of the modern 'enlightenment' project of restoring the captive liberty and freedom (i.e., becoming) of human beings? If this is so, then is the contemporary 'critique of metaphysics,' a critique that we have seen to be largely motivated by Nietzsche, also part and parcel of the tradition of metaphysics? Is it doing anything different, or has it, as Heidegger would argue, kept the redemptive motivation of metaphysics while only changing that which is to be recovered: namely, a non-identifiable becoming rather than an identifiable being? A brief summary of the path we have travelled might clarify the sense in which we take Nietzsche *not* to be concerned with recovering something that has been lost. This will further demonstrate that Nietzsche's critique, his ploughshare of evil, is a critique without redemption.

In Derrida's well-known critique of metaphysics, a critique he acknowledges continues the work of Nietzsche and Heidegger, metaphysics is indeed characterized as being concerned with redemption: in short, metaphysics is the attempt to restore to 'presence' some simple, ideal, normal, self-identical origin. Derrida's subsequent 'deconstruction,' his critique of metaphysics, consists in demonstrating the inevitable play of an 'undecidable' which prevents such a simple return, recovery, and liberation of some lost 'presence.' These undecidables, as we saw, entail a fundamental both/and which cannot be decided or identified by the logic of either/or, for it is precisely this both/and which allows for the possibility of deciding with respect to an either/or. The both/and is thus what a text must acknowledge and suppress in order to function, that is, decide and identify. In Plato, for example, the *pharmakon* is the undecidable that is both acknowledged and suppressed. Throughout Derrida's writings, these undecidables (e.g., supplement, hymen, gram, spacing, incision, iteration, etc.)[115] will play the crucial role in his critique of metaphysics, or in his effort to explicate that which makes metaphysical decisions possible while forever eluding such decisions, or forever eluding restoration and redemption.

A fundamental consequence of this critique is that Derrida will not see the task of interpretation as being one of recovering and revealing some fundamental meaning (e.g., a transcendental signified). Derrida criticizes hermeneutics for attempting just such a task, but neither does he feel that there are no standards or criteria for interpretation, or that one interpretation is as good as the next. An interpreter cannot, Derrida argues, 'add any old thing' to the text that has not been 'rigorously prescribed' by the text, 'by the logic of *play*'[116] of this text. Furthermore, to follow this logic in a text is for Derrida to remain 'true' to the text, whereas if this logic is not followed a reading will likewise be, as Derrida claims is often the case in interpretations of his writings, 'false.' 'The value of truth,' Derrida points out, 'is never contested or destroyed in my writings.'[117] But this logic which one is to follow to remain 'true' to the text, even though Derrida admits that it entails 'protocols of reading' which will act as guard rails to prevent any reading whatsoever from being advanced, is itself left undecided. Thus, when pressed to state what such protocols might be, or the logic one is to remain 'true' to, he confesses that 'I have not yet found any that satisfy me.'[118] Consequently, despite Derrida's claim that 'undecidability is always a *determinate* oscillation between possibilities ... [and that] they are *pragmatically* determined,'[119] if the protocol and standard whereby such determinations can be judged is not clarified, one is again left wondering whether any '*determinate* oscillation' will do. How are we to know when the deconstructionist has gone too far?

Deleuze is less hesitant to state and attempt to clarify what this protocol might be, and, as with Derrida, he feels that it is *pragmatically* determined; however, there are some crucial differences between them. First, although Derrida claims the 'oscillation between possibilities' is 'pragmatically determined,' he then admits that the nature of this pragmatic determination itself needs further elaboration, elaboration he has not yet given.[120] Deleuze and Gauttari, on the other hand, go to great lengths in their two-volume work, *Capitalism and Schizophrenia*, to set forth their version of 'pragmatics' (also referred to as 'schizoanalysis,' 'rhizomatics,' and 'nomadology') and with it to clarify the process of pragmatic determination. Secondly, whereas Derrida focuses almost exclusively upon the 'determinate oscillations' of some written text, Deleuze and Guattari are interested in the oscillations (i.e., between fusion and fission, paranoia and schizophrenia, black hole and supernova, etc.) of activity in general, both natural and human activity.

Part of the reason for Deleuze's more developed clarification and concern for the nature of the 'pragmatic determination' of activity can be traced to Nietzsche; in particular, to Nietzsche's claim, quoted above, that we need 'to impose upon chaos as much regularity and form as our practical needs require.' Consequently, the protocol which is to serve a critique for Deleuze is, following Nietzsche, determined by the practical needs of the functioning assemblage, whether this assemblage be human, social, natural, etc.; and thus the protocol reflects the creative response to the double bind, a response which resists the tendency to collapse into a destructive either/or. Deleuze's more explicit dependency on or repetition of Nietzsche is therefore to be seen as an advantage rather than a detriment,[121] for it is because of this that Deleuze is better equipped to grapple with, unlike Derrida, the problem of clarifying the pragmatic determination of the protocols of activity, including interpretive, natural, and revolutionary activities.

To briefly summarize how this pragmatic determination is clarified, it must first be stressed that the protocol which results is *both* an attempt to impose a form, order, and regularity upon chaos, *and* an attempt 'to institute,' as Deleuze puts it, 'the chaos which creates.'[122] Without a protocol which demands order, form, and regularity, the corresponding activity would collapse into non-sense; but without instituting the chaos which creates and gives rise to that which is unpredictable, then again nothing is said or done: '... what we call the meaning of a statement is its point. That's the only definition of meaning, and it amounts to the same as the novelty of statement ... the problem isn't that what someone says is wrong, but that it's stupid or irrelevant – that it's already been said a thousand times.'[123] With this claim, we can see an interesting parallel with contemporary chaos theory, in particular, information theory. Claude Shannon, for example, has argued that the more chaotic a message is, the more random and unpredictable, the more information it has. Shannon does make a distinction between meaning and information, and thus would not follow Deleuze in claiming that chaos gives rise to meaning. Robert Shaw, however, a more recent proponent of chaos theory, does go so far as to say that chaos is the source of everything that is new, and thus he would agree with Deleuze.[124] Chaos theorists also argue, as does Deleuze, that there is a necessary form and order to chaos, but that this order cannot be used to predict what a given dynamical system will do next (the 'strange attractor' is their famous example). Similarly, Deleuzean pragmatics will argue for a necessary order, form, protocol, etc., but will likewise claim that such a protocol cannot, nor should it, be used to determine what the order will be like in the future. There is thus a purposiveness to Deleuzean pragmatics, for there is the creation of a necessary order and protocol in response to the double bind, but there is no purpose or goal which transcends this purposiveness.

As a purposiveness without purpose, Deleuzean pragmatics proceeds to attempt to clarify the plateaus, planes of consistency, and assemblages that are themselves constitutive and constituted exemplifications of this purposiveness without purpose. In other words, pragmatics has no prior agenda (i.e., purpose), nor is it without purpose; what it is to do, they argue, is to make a plateau, a rhizome:

Schizoanalysis, or pragmatics, has no other meaning: Make a rhizome. But you don't know what you can make a rhizome with, you don't know which subterranean stem is going to make a rhizome, or enter a becoming, people your desert. So experiment.[125]

Experiment. A Nietzschean theme for sure, but we are still left with the question of how we are to go about experimenting? Deleuze and Guattari are aware of this question and admit that their 'experimentation imperative' is 'easy to say' but might be hard to follow, especially since there are no 'preformed logical orders to becomings,' to rhizomes and plateaus, an order that can be used to guide such experimenting. Nevertheless, they do claim that 'there are *criteria*' that are to be adhered to in experimenting, or in making a rhizome – that is, for pragmatics. For example, pragmatics is not to be used after the fact, but is to be applied 'in the course of events ... [and it should] be sufficient to guide us through dangers,'[126] such as the danger of collapsing into one of the two poles of the either/or. Secondly, pragmatics will 'reject the idea of an invariant immune from transformation.'[127] There is nothing, in short, following Nietzsche, that is not part of becoming, and hence susceptible to becoming other than what it is. It is for this reason that Deleuze and Guattari will stress the importance of becoming-x (e.g., becoming-animal, imperceptible, woman, etc.). Third, pragmatics will explicate the internal reasons which will not allow something (e.g., language) 'to close itself off,'[128] or to be immune to transformation. And finally, though not exhaustively, pragmatics will trace and map processes of transformation whereby non-formed flows and processes of becoming are selected, territorialized, and stratified, and will then show how these territorializations are in turn susceptible to deterritorializing flows, to 'lines of flight' that will transform them again.[129] Every assemblage, every plateau, has both its elements of territorialization and its deterritorializing flows. For example, in discussing genetics, Deleuze and Guattari note that for any genetic or structural identity that is passed through hereditary succession, there coexists a simultaneous de-coding, an ever-present becoming-other (i.e., transformation). There is 'no genetics,' they conclude, 'without "genetic drift."'[130] And it is precisely the task of pragmatics, its protocol, to note both the territorializing and deterritorializing poles within which all assemblages, according to Deleuze and Guattari, oscillate. These poles are not to be understood as binary opposites, but rather as the both/and which is constitutive of these assemblages (there is 'no genetics [territorialization] without "genetic drift" [deterritorialization]). Pragmatics, furthermore, notes these constitutive both/ands for the express purpose, or purposiveness, of resisting the dangerous tendency the both/and has to settle into one of the poles of an either/or, a pole which would bring about the destruction of the assemblage (e.g., *either* the genetic succession repeats the same to the point where the organism cannot adapt and thus becomes extinct, *or* it transforms and mutates into an organism that cannot adapt and dies).

Deleuze and Guattari discuss these constitutive both/ands, or what they refer to in *Anti-Oedipus* as 'inclusive disjunctions,' throughout *A Thousand Plateaus*; or, as the title suggests, they make a thousand plateaus. They also set forth a criterion or protocol for this enterprise – that is, for pragmatics – both a protocol for resisting the tendency to collapse into an either/or, and one which helps to clarify the manner in which differentiations are pragmatically determined. It is this latter clarification which is lacking in Derrida. Derrida does indeed demonstrate the limits of oppositional differentiation, or the logic of either/or, but he leaves unanswered the question of how a positive, non-binary mode of differentiation *ought* to proceed, or what protocol it is to follow. With Deleuze and Guattari's pragmatics, however, we have both a critique of binary oppositions, the logic of either/or, and we have a protocol which clarifies how one can positively differentiate, evaluate, judge, etc. Pragmatics is thus a critique with no goal or purpose of restoring and liberating something that has been held captive. It is a critique as resistance, for it resists the double bind that conditions it (i.e., purposiveness without purpose); but it is neither a critique which transcends and resolves this double bind, nor a critique with a 'pre-existing' logic and order for resisting the double bind; it is, in other words, a critique without redemption. Consequently, rather than having an order, form, or idea (*eidos*) in ourselves, an order that *ought*, à la Plato, to remain the same, this critique, following Nietzsche, claims that we ought to have chaos in ourselves, a chaos that gives birth to a dancing star; and this dancing star is not a repetition of the same, but is a repetition of the difference that is constitutive of it, a difference whose destructive consequences *ought* to be resisted. For if we are not careful and diligent, if we slack in our rigour and resistance, then the chaos in ourselves might not give birth to a dancing star, but, as a result of either collapsing into a black hole or exploding into a fiery supernova, this chaos might die.

Deleuze and Guattari's critique without redemption is indeed a part of traditional metaphysics insofar as it launches (e.g., through pragmatics, schizoanalysis, etc.) a critique and interpretive project with a determinate protocol, or insofar as it is a critique which accepts the wisdom (or lack thereof) of a given position. Their position is also a further elaboration of a Kantian-styled critique in that, as with Kant, it attempts to reveal the conditions for the possibility of knowledge (i.e., identifications, territorializations). However, whereas Kant reveals identifiable categories and forms of experience which are the conditions for the possibility of knowledge, Deleuze and Guattari encounter the non-identifiable both/and condition (e.g., will to power). It is on this point that they break with the tradition which traces its lineage to Plato. This break is not, moreover, one of opposing the tradition, but rather it reveals the double bind whereby the tradition itself is made possible, yet through which its success (i.e., its attempt to successfully redeem or restore a lost identity) is rendered impossible. The condition for the possibility of the tradition of metaphysics is also its condition of impossibility. A critique without redemption, therefore, and this should not be surprising at this point, is *both* for *and* against traditional metaphysics. In fact, as we will explore more fully in chapters 5 and 6, Deleuze unabashedly pursues and carries out metaphysics, what we will call a metaphysics of dynamic systems. Before we turn to discuss Deleuze's metaphysics of dynamic systems, however, we will first examine Heidegger's critique of metaphysics, or more precisely his critique of Aristotle and the metaphysical tradition Aristotle largely initiates. This discussion will further extend our examination of the philosophical effort to think difference, and it will set the stage for illustrating why a metaphysics of dynamic systems is able to overcome some of the shortcomings which continued to haunt Heidegger (and Derrida, as we will see in chapter 5).

4 Thinking Difference: Heidegger and Deleuze on Aristotle

Difference has been an important theme in contemporary philosophy, especially contemporary Continental philosophy, where many of the key players put an enormous amount of emphasis upon an understanding of difference. There is Derrida's well-known discussion of *differance*, for example, but there is also Jean-François Lyotard's concept of the 'differend'; Luce Irigaray explores the theme of sexual difference in her book *An Ethics of Sexual Difference*; and Gilles Deleuze attempts to set forth a philosophy of difference in his book *Difference and Repetition*. An important theme which circulates throughout these works, and which seems to characterize much of contemporary Continental thought, is that an adequate understanding of difference would be one which does not reduce difference to the conditions or logic of identity. More to the point, they argue that although thought and understanding itself is indeed of identities, the condition for the possibility of thinking and understanding identities is not itself identifiable, or it is a fundamental difference which cannot be thought in terms of identity. This claim immediately gives rise to some important questions: How can difference be thought if it is not to be thought in terms of identity? Or, if it cannot be thought, how can we know that it is the condition for the possibility of thought unless we grasp it as such – that is, think difference as this condition? In short, what is the relationship between difference and thinking?

To avoid repeating what many others have said concerning these themes and questions, this chapter shall take as its point of departure a comparison and contrast of how two of the more important figures in Continental philosophy understand difference – Heidegger and Deleuze. In particular, we will examine how Heidegger and Deleuze each sets his own understanding of difference apart from that of Aristotle. This analysis should clarify the differences between Heidegger's understanding of the ontological difference and Deleuze's attempt to set forth a philosophy of difference. The differences between Heidegger and Deleuze regarding their understanding of difference have received little attention, but considering the importance of difference to contemporary Continental thought, it seems this discussion can facilitate a greater understanding of what is at stake in contemporary Continental philosophy. Furthermore, by placing this discussion in the context of Aristotle's understanding of difference, we can see how Heidegger's and Deleuze's approaches do or do not differ from that of traditional metaphysics.

I

In his *Metaphysics*, Aristotle understands difference in two ways. First, he defines difference as that which is said of something that is 'the same in some respect, only not in number but in kind or in genus or by analogy' (1018a14–15).[1] Things are different in this first sense, therefore, only if they are the same in some other respect. What I am as a human being is different from what my cat is, though we are also the same insofar as we are both mammals. To understand the difference between human being and cat we must, according to Aristotle, have a common ground to work from – namely, a common genus such as mammal, animal, etc. The second definition of difference is that things can also be different in the sense of being 'contraries,' whereby contraries are those things which either 'differ according to genus and cannot at the same time be present in the same thing,' or those things which 'differ most in the same genus' (ibid.). For example, I am different from my car, not because we differ with respect to something which is the same (i.e., a genus), but because we differ in kind; or, though I and my wife are of the same genus, as man and woman we can be said to be different insofar as we 'differ most in the same genus.' The key to this second understanding of difference is that one cannot be both a man and a car, or a man and a woman. These differences are differences of kind and are irreconcilable, whereas with the first understanding of difference, the differences are reconciled by, or understood and made possible by, a common genus which is the same despite these differences.

One could argue, however, that differences according to genus, as well as the greatest differences within a genus, are reconcilable: they are reconcilable insofar as they all have 'being' in common. Whatever the differences between humans, cats, cars, men and women, we can say of all of them that they *are*. To put this in Aristotle's well-known terminology, one might say that just as the difference in species between cats and humans is a difference with respect to a common genus (mammal), so too one could argue that differences in genus are differences with respect to a common being. Being, in other words, would be the genus of all genera. Yet this argument is one that Aristotle rejects:

> It is not possible for either 'unity' or 'being' to be a genus of things; for each differentia of any genus must be and also be one, but it is impossible either for the species of a genus or for that genus alone to be a predicate of the proper differentiae of the species. Thus, if unity or being is indeed a genus, no differentia will be either a being or one. (998b22–28)

To clarify by way of example, Aristotle repeatedly refers to the human being as a rational animal. The differentia of the species 'human' is the predicate 'rational,' or when rationality is predicated of the genus 'animal' we have a human being. Genus is thus determined by the differentia of the species, but in itself the genus is simply the unity of the many differentia – that is, there is no animal in itself, only many species of animal. Put in other terms, the 'genus' animal does not make a human being what it *is* as a human being, or a cat as a cat, for it does not include the content that makes these things what they are. If 'animal' were to include the differentia 'rational,' it would be redundant to define a human being (species) as a rational animal. The differentia is thus not included within the genus but rather adds something or is a differentiation with respect to a common genus (i.e., it *is* a differentia), and it is this differentia that makes some-*thing* the thing it *is*. Similarly, if being were to be a genus, then it too would not include the content that makes something what it is, but this is contradictory for, as Aristotle argues, the 'differentia of any genus must be'; consequently, being is not a genus.

Aristotle's effort to understand and think difference thus brings him to the central problem of his *Metaphysics*: what is being? Or, to put the problem differently, how can we consistently maintain the view that things can be irreconcilably different and yet both be? Aristotle's initial answer: being is one, though it is said and meant in many *different* ways, for example, as quantity, quality, relation, etc. Despite these many senses, however, Aristotle argues 'that of these the primary sense is whatness, and used in this sense it signifies a substance' (1028a14). To clarify how being is both one and said in many ways, we must clarify the primary sense of being, substance. The question 'what is being?' becomes, for Aristotle, 'what is a substance?' (1028b4).

In his discussions of substance, one of the more important characteristics of substance that Aristotle repeatedly emphasizes is that substance individuates matter as such-and-such a thing, or it individuates matter as a this of a certain type. In the *Categories*, for instance, Aristotle claims, 'Every substance is thought to indicate a *this*' (3b10); and with this claim Aristotle contrasts his notion of substance with the Platonic conception of Ideas as universals, for, Aristotle argues, 'if they [principles or Platonic Ideas] are universal, they will not be substances; for none of what is common signifies a *this* but only a *such*, and a substance is a *this*' (*Metaphysics*, 1003a7–10). In other words, if the Ideas were to be a universal and a this, that is, an individual, then the problem this gives rise to is how the two different individuals are related to one another – for example, how is the Platonic Idea of beauty as an individual and a *this*, related to the existent individual or to the *this* that is beautiful? There must be a third thing (i.e., the third man), Aristotle argues, whereby these two are related to one another; but this in turn gives rise to the problem of the relationship between this third thing as an existent *this* and the essence or Idea of this third thing. In short, to avoid the famous third-man argument, a universal is not to be confused with a substance, a *this*.

What is a substance, then, if it is not a universal? Simply put, as that which individuates, substance determines an individual, a this, as such and such an individual. By individual Aristotle means 'that which is numerically one' (1000a1), and by numerically one Aristotle means that whose 'matter is one' (1026b32). Therefore, insofar as the matter that constitutes me as an individual is not the same as the matter which constitutes someone else, I and the other are then numerically distinct individuals, or we are two individuals, not one. However, if this other person is a human being, we may then be numerically distinct individuals, but in species we are one, wherein something is 'one in species if the formula is one' (ibid.). The formula is that which forms the matter as such-and-such a thing, or makes it to be a certain type of thing, namely, a human being. This, however, leads to an apparent ambiguity in Aristotle's thinking, for the substance of a thing appears both to be the *matter* which constitutes the numerical individuality and thisness of a thing, and it appears to be the *form* which constitutes the individual as a certain type of thing. In the first sense, substance is the underlying subject of predication, or the *this* which receives attributes and qualifications (e.g., this is red, loud, smart, etc.). In the second sense, substance is the form that allows us even to identify an individual as an individual, an identification which presupposes grasping the form or type of individual being presented. Aristotle recognizes these two meanings of substance: 'The term "a substance," then, has two senses: it means the ultimate subject which is not predicated of something else, and also that which is a *this* and is separable, such being the *shape* or *form* of each thing' (1017b23–26).

We can resolve the apparent ambiguity when we consider the role of matter in Aristotle's metaphysics. If matter is the underlying subject which receives the form or shape of a given species, then we would once again confront the third-man problem, for how would we account for the relationship between species and matter unless by some third thing, a third thing which in turn involves a subject which bears a certain form. To avoid the third-man problem and the infinite regress it generates, Aristotle argues that there is a point where the essence or form of the thing is the same as the thing itself, a point where the subject and its form are one and the same. This point Aristotle refers to as primary substance, and it is this thesis which Aristotle attempts to establish in the crucial yet difficult Book Z of the *Metaphysics*. In brief, to avoid the third-man problem, Aristotle must show that primary substance is indeed some-*thing* that is the same as its essence (i.e., form).

To establish this claim, one of the first orders of business is to reject the claim that substance is matter. In recognition of the ambiguity we noted above, Aristotle first admits that 'from what has been said, it follows that matter is a substance [or it is the primary subject],' but he immediately goes on to reject that this is so: 'But this is impossible; for to be separable and a this is thought to belong most of all to a substance' (1029a27–30). It is not the matter which allows us to pick out something as a this separable from another this; rather, it is the form, or what Michael Loux has referred to as the 'forming function' of substance,[2] which allows us to pick out some matter as a *this*. Aristotle will emphasize this point again later in Book Z, though this time he explicitly rejects the possibility that matter is primary (or first) substance:

> In some cases the essence of a thing and the thing are the same, as in first substances. For example, curvature and its essence are the same if curvature is a first substance ... But things which exist as matter, or which include matter, are not the same as their essence. (1037b1–8)

Why does Aristotle reject matter as substance? There are two important and related reasons. The first is Aristotle's adherence to the law of non-contradiction. Everything that exists in truth and actuality is what it is and is not simultaneously its opposite. I cannot in actuality be in my office and home on my sofa at one and the same time. Matter, however, is for Aristotle pure potentiality, as opposed to substance, which is actuality, and in this way 'the same thing [as matter] can be potentially both contraries at the same time, but it cannot be so in actuality' (1050b28). I cannot actually be at work and home at the same time, but I simultaneously possess the potential for both; similarly, matter has the potential both to be or not to be actualized according to a particular form. Substance, therefore, if it is the primary sense of being or of what is, must be what it is without contradiction, and hence it cannot be matter. Matter we can refer to as the genetic element, or that which is only potentially an actualized, non-contradictory, *this*. Aristotle is clear on this point:

> What is called 'a form' or 'a substance' is not generated, but what is generated is the composite which is named according to that form, and that there is matter in everything that is generated and in the latter one part is this and another that. (1033b16–20)

Later in Book Z Aristotle reiterates much this same point, though he emphasizes here the actuality/potentiality distinction:

> Now a substance is an underlying subject; and in one sense, this is matter (by 'matter' I mean that which is not a *this* in *actuality* but is *potentially* a *this*); in another sense it is the formula or the form, which is a this and separable in formula. (1042a27–30)

The ambiguity is by this point resolved. Substance is the underlying subject or matter only as potentiality, as genetic element, whereas true and primary substance is an actual this. Nevertheless, the question remains: how does substance as actual relate to the production of composite substances? What is the relationship between actual and potential? Unless these questions are adequately addressed, one can accuse Aristotle of simply repeating the errors he found in Plato. In other words, to account for how the actuality of substance can transform the potentiality of matter into the actuality of composite substances, must Aristotle presuppose a mediating third party which facilitates the pro-

duction of composite things? Clearly Aristotle would deny the need
for such a mediating third party, though what he says to clarify the
relationship between the actual and the potential does not do much to
address our questions. What Aristotle offers is an analogy which he
believes makes the relationship between the actual and potential intuitively obvious. Exploring the implications of this analogy should help
us to further trace the trajectory of Aristotle's thought with respect to
substance, and more precisely to show the consequences of this view
with respect to Aristotle's understanding of difference. Here is what
Aristotle offers us:

> What we mean [by distinguishing between actual and potential] is clear by
> induction from individual cases, and we should not seek a definition of
> everything but should also perceive an object by means of an analogy;
> thus, as that which builds is to that which is capable of building, so is that
> which is awake to that which is asleep, or that which is seeing to that which
> has its eyes shut but has the power to see, or that which is separated from
> matter to matter itself, or the finished product to the raw material. Let the
> term 'actuality' signify the first part of each of these differences and 'the
> potential' signify the second part. (1048a36–b7)

Does this analogy help? It is clear at least what Aristotle is saying. Just
as the finished product is related to the raw material which went into
the product, so too 'that which is separated from matter' (i.e., substance
as form) is related 'to matter itself.' With respect to the relationship
between finished products and raw material, however, there is an
important mediating factor: namely, the artisan. This mediating factor
is one of Aristotle's four causes – efficient cause. The relationship
between finished product (final cause) and raw material (material
cause) is indeed one which is mediated by a third party, the artisan.
What fills this role with respect to the relationship between that which
is separate from matter and matter itself? Aristotle's analogy does not
answer our earlier questions, but rather places its significance in clearer
focus. Moreover, in Book Z Aristotle uses yet another, similar analogy
when arguing for the claim that substance is the cause of a thing:

> 'Why is the matter some one thing?'; for example, 'Why are these materi-
> als a house?' Because to them belongs this, which is the essence of a
> house; and because a man is this, or, this body has this. Thus, we are seek-
> ing the cause (and this is the form) through which the matter is a thing;
> and this cause is the substance of the thing. (1041b5–10)

A thing, therefore, as with a house, entails a productive process whereby some material is put together in such and such a way, that is, in accordance with a form, so that it is this individual and not another. As Aristotle puts it, 'a thing is a threshold,' where threshold entails the composition of matter in 'such-and-such a position,' as a house is a thing defined as 'bricks and timber in such-and-such a position' (1042b27–1043a10). When Aristotle uses the analogy of building, for example, building a house, he is thus not simply thinking of human production; rather, he is arguing that all things, as composites of matter and form, are generated and produced. The key, then, is to understand how this generative process is carried forward without in turn falling into the problems Aristotle recognized in Plato.

Aristotle's effort to do this centres around, as we have seen, substance, whereby substance is the cause of the thing, or it is the cause which oversees the productive process through which matter is arranged and composed in 'such-and-such a position.' Substance, however, or at least primary substance, is free from matter, and is to matter much as the finished house is to the raw material of bricks and timber. Primary substance, therefore, must be a non-composite substance, for only non-composite substances, Aristotle argues, are 'neither generated nor destroyed' (1051b29). If they were generated, they would have to have not been at one time, and this would violate the law of non-contradiction. Only non-composite substances exist as pure actuality, whereas composite substance has the potential to exist or not to exist. It is non-composite, primary substance which is both essence and subject, both *what* this is and *that* this is, and it is this primary substance which in some way causes the composite things. How does it do this?

According to Loux, the primary substance is to be understood as 'substance-species,' and it is the substance-species which allows for the existence of a subject as a subject of a particular kind. Thus, as Loux contrasts the substance-species with a universal, he claims 'the universals in virtue of which something is musical, walking, or white require subjects in which they might be present; and the existence of these subjects turns on their membership in their respective substance-species.'[3] These substance-species themselves, moreover, 'can be viewed,' Loux argues, 'as forming functions,' or 'functions that take as their arguments appropriate parcels of matter' and then generate the subjects which can then be the bearers of universal predicates. It is these substance-species which are the actualities which precede the things which are the result of their forming function. These substance-species are therefore presupposed by every generative process, or, as Aristotle puts

.it, 'actuality is prior to potency and to every principle of change' (1051a4).

We can now begin to see how Aristotle addresses the question of 'What is being?' and, in turn, how he thinks difference. First, being, we saw, could not be a genus for a genus is simply a common term or universal applicable to many different things. In itself the genus does not contain what it is to be a human being, for example, but is simply a predicate that can be accurately applied to humans, cats, dogs, etc. Similarly, if being were a genus, then it too would not contain what it is that makes humans, cats, and dogs be; but since being is taken precisely to be that which humans, cats, and dogs presuppose such that they *are*, then being must not be a genus. If being is not a genus, then it is something else, and this something else is substance. As substance, the forming function of substance-species does indeed contain what makes a human being what he/she is, and as substance-species the term is not a genus which applies to many things, but just to that one substance-species. One could argue that this is not so. After all, the students in my classes are human beings, and thus do I not apply the species-term to many different things? Aristotle's point, however, as we have tried to show, is that although the species-term can be applied to many composite substances generated in accordance with the form of the substance-species, the substance-species itself is a non-composite free from matter. The many different students in my class are therefore different materially, but not in species; in species they are numerically one.

We can now return to our earlier discussion of Aristotle's attempt to think difference. Aristotle repeatedly claims that difference must forever be understood with respect to something that is the same. To quote from Book I of the *Metaphysics*, Aristotle argues, 'But that which differs is different from something else in some respect, so that there must be something which is the same with respect to which there is a difference. And that which is the same is the genus or the species' (1054b26–28). The students in my class are indeed different, but this difference is thought on the basis of that which remains the same, namely, their substance-species. As for things that are different in genus, Aristotle argues that these things 'have no way of proceeding to each other but are far removed and noncomparable' (1055a8), and he adds later that 'there is no difference in relation to things outside of a genus' (1055a27). In other words, because there is no basis for comparison between genera, or nothing which remains the same with respect to both, we cannot think or discuss this difference, and thus for all intents and purposes there is no difference here.

Aristotle, however, is not content simply to let this irreconcilable difference between genera stand. Aristotle recognizes that being is an inadequate concept with which to compare the different genera. The primary sense of being, we saw, is substance, or more precisely substance-species, and this substance is the actuality which precedes potentiality and change, and it is the actuality which causes actual, composite things. There are many different substance-species, however, and in many different genera. There is the substance-species 'human being' as well as the substance-species 'gaseous planet,' and the two are, from Aristotle's point of view, non-comparable because they are each in a different genus. Nevertheless, as substance-species, they are pure actualities which are prior to the composites which they make possible. Primary substance, recall, can neither be generated nor destroyed, for this would violate the law of non-contradiction. But it is at this point where we encounter a problem. If the substance-species is that which is the actuality that is free from the potentiality of matter, then is Aristotle committed to the viewpoint that the human substance-species is eternal and hence existed long before humans ever evolved? To make such a claim would risk reinstating the Platonic doctrine of the Forms, something Aristotle was loath to do; yet to claim that such substance-species had not always existed, or had come into being at some point, would seem to violate the law of non-contradiction.[4] With regard to this last point, Aristotle would claim that this is not necessarily the case. If the substance-species 'human being,' for example, were at some point merely a potential substance-species, then it would violate the law of non-contradiction, for the same thing would both be something and potentially not be something. Likewise, if the substance-species as actuality were to come into being from non-actuality, or from non-being, then this too would violate the law of non-contradiction, for the same thing would come into being from non-being. If, however, there is a pure actuality which generates other actualites such as the human species-substance, then although this substance-species is generated, it is not merely a potentiality waiting to be generated, nor is it generated from nothing. It is simply one actuality that is the effect of another.

This leads us to Aristotle's famous argument for the unmoved mover. The substance-species of a human being is, Aristotle argued, a mover in that it is the cause which allows for the generation of composite human beings. This mover or actuality is, in turn, made possible by another mover or actuality. However, if there is to be any motion at all, there must be a first mover which is itself unmoved; otherwise, the series of causes would stretch back to infinity and nothing, Aristotle argues, could then ever be caused or moved (see 994b1-10). To avoid violating the law of non-contradiction with respect to the many different species, including the many different genera to which they belong, Aristotle argues that there must be a single, unmoved mover, or there must be a single heaven (see 1074a33-38). Aristotle's science of being, his theory of substance, thus leads him to the science of the single, overarching cause, the cause which remains one and the same despite the many different species, genera, etc. Aristotle's metaphysics, or his science of being (since he does not use the word 'metaphysics'), leads to theology, and he himself recognizes this:

> The first science, however, is concerned with things which are both separate and immovable ... if there were no substances other than those formed by nature [i.e., movable substances], physics would be the first science; but if there is an immovable substance, this would be prior, and the science of it would be first philosophy and would be universal in this manner, in view of the fact that it is first. And it would be the concern of this science, too, to investigate being qua being, both what being is and what belongs to it qua being. (1026a15–32)

The differences in genera, therefore, are not maintained as irreconcilable differences, for all species and genera which can be thought and discussed must, Aristotle argues, presuppose some one thing. If these are differences between things, then this referential same is either the species or genus; and if the differences are between genera, then either they cannot be thought or they are to be thought in terms of the identity of the unmoved mover. Without this identity, of either heaven (unmoved mover) or substance, no thing could be thought or communicated. Aristotle is clear on this point. To think and communicate, one must be thinking and communicating some one, identical, self-same thing:

> For not to signify one thing is to signify nothing, and if names have no meanings, then discussion with one another, and indeed even with oneself, is eliminated; for it is not possible for anyone to conceive of anything if he does not conceive of one thing, and if it is possible, he could then posit one name for this one thing. (1006b8–12)

And again, later in the *Metaphysics*, Aristotle reiterates the same point:

> Now those who are to have a discussion with each other must also *understand* each other; for if this does not happen, how can they communicate

with each other? Accordingly, each name used must be known and signify something, but only one thing and not many. (1062a12–15)

Consequently, it is by now clear that if we are to conceive of difference, we must conceive it with respect to some one thing, and this is either a genus or a species; and with respect to the differences between genera, since there is no one thing to compare them to, these differences cannot be thought and conceived, unless they are thought in the theological sense with respect to the one unmoved mover. Aristotle is quite straightforward, then, in holding to the position that difference can only be thought in terms of identity.

II

Moving now to Heidegger's reading of Aristotle, Heidegger will stress the significance for Aristotle of the distinction between potentiality and actuality. In his study of Aristotle's *Metaphysics* Θ, 1–3, Heidegger recognizes the importance of substance-species as the overseer of the process from potentiality (δύναυις) to actuality (ἐνέργεια). The substance-species, *eidos* (εἶδος), is for Heidegger that which gathers together the elements necessary for a thing to become such-and-such a thing. As discussed above, the *eidos* is thus the forming-function that defines a thing according to its threshold, such as a house, to quote Aristotle, is the threshold wherein 'bricks and timber [are] in such-and-such a position' (1043a10). As Heidegger reads Aristotle:

> In producing something, the thing to be produced must necessarily be previewed even though it is not yet finished or perhaps not even begun. It is simply represented, in the genuine sense of the word, but not yet brought about and produced as something at hand. This representing and previewing of the ἔργου in its eidos is the real beginning of producing ... Eidos is a kind of being gathered together and selected, a legomenon; it is logos. Eidos is also telos, the ending end.[5]

This eidos, or representation, which gathers and selects what is necessary in order for the end (telos) of the productive process to be actualized, is not simply a representation which guides human productivity. Aristotle's point, as Heidegger correctly points out, is that this eidos (substance-species) is 'the real beginning' of all productive processes, both natural and human. It is true that flowers and trees are not produced in the same way that houses and violins are, and Heidegger notes that Aristotle distinguishes between *phusis onta* and *techne onta*, whereby the former 'produces itself by arising out of itself; *techne onta* is produced by human planning and production.'[6] As a natural being (*phusis onta*), flowers and trees are not in need of another in order to be produced, or they contain within themselves the principle which governs their emergence as flowers and trees; houses and violins, on the other hand, do not contain their own principle of emergence, or they only emerge because of humans' ability (i.e., *techne*) to execute their ideas. The substance-species, therefore, and to re-emphasize an earlier point, is inseparable from the natural objects which emerge by means of it. Nevertheless, these natural objects which are not in need of an external principle to govern their production are, as Heidegger argues, still understood by Aristotle in the sense of 'having been produced':

> For even that which is not in need of production, and precisely this, is also understood with respect to its being in terms of the essence of having been produced. This is the sense of the basic fact that such concepts as eidos, telos, and peras (i.e., threshold), as fundamental moments of beings, are not restricted to the things which have been produced, but rather concern the full array of beings.[7]

At this point we could introduce the standard Heideggerian critique of eidos: namely, that by thinking beings in terms of eidos, Aristotle thinks them in terms of their presence, their substance-species, rather than as the presencing of presence, or as Being. Aristotle, in other words, fails to think Being as the presencing of presence. This will be Heidegger's ultimate critique of Aristotle, but Heidegger recognizes that Aristotle's position is not as straightforwardly susceptible to the critique as might first appear. This becomes clear as Heidegger examines Aristotle's critique of the Megarian thesis.

The Megarian thesis, put briefly, denies potentiality and states that potentiality can only be judged or known when actualized. If I have the potential to be an excellent musician, the Megarians would argue, then this potential can only be known, or can only be, once it is actualized; otherwise, this potential as potential simply does not exist. The non-actualized, therefore, is, according to the Megarians, *nothing*. This position, however, as Heidegger reads Aristotle's critique of it, fails to recognize that the actual (i.e., substance-species as the actuality which guides the productive process) is not a simple presence, but is rather an active presencing and gathering: 'The Megarians comprehend the "non" [non-actualized] as pure negation – rather than as a distinctive privation. That which is negated, enactment itself, they comprehend only as the presence of something – rather than as transition, that is, as kinesis.'[8] The eidos as substance-species is thus not understood by Aristotle as a simple presence, but it is that which allows for the proceeding forth and gathering in, and this proceeding forth and gathering in is also a point Heidegger will emphasize when setting forth his own understanding of Being. The actuality of substance-species, the actuality which is the cause or principle of the production of things themselves, is not then 'a thing or property from which something proceeds (as the Megarians understand it),' but is to be understood as 'an origin for something other [that] is in itself a proceeding to the other.'[9]

Despite Aristotle's critique of the Megarian thesis, however, Heidegger maintains that he did not go far enough. Aristotle continued to think of the 'proceeding forth and gathering in' of eidos as a process which can be named and thought in terms of the logic of identity: that is, the process is identifiable as one thing, as a process of such-and-such a type; and as one thing this process can have a corresponding word to name it. Aristotle, in other words, ultimately subordinated the presencing of eidos to the identity of logos, or to logic.[10] Consequently, although Aristotle made great strides by understanding the presence of beings in terms of eidos as 'proceeding forth and gathering in,' when eidos itself was subordinated to logos, the moves here were lost. As Heidegger put it in his *Introduction to Metaphysics*, 'being as unconcealment [is] the very thing that has been lost by logic,' and this 'logic arose in the curriculum of the Platonic-Aristotelian schools.'[11] Thus, by subordinating eidos to logos, Aristotle presupposes the presence of that which 'lingers awhile in unconcealment,'[12] or that which lingers long enough so that it can be identified as one thing of such-and-such a kind, a thing that can be named. Aristotle thinks Being, not as the presencing of Being, but as the presence of being, or, to use one of Heidegger's oft-quoted terms, Aristotle thinks 'beings as such ontotheologically.'[13]

Returning to our theme of thinking difference, it now becomes even clearer that Aristotle thinks difference in terms of identity. If eidos or substance-species is fundamentally something that can be said, then what can be said, as we saw above, must be one and non-contradictory. Substance-species therefore equals the identity of actuality rather than the contrariety of potentiality; and yet this is precisely the point Aristotle argued for repeatedly. But by arguing this point, Aristotle reveals his bias for thinking difference in terms of identity, a bias which, from Heidegger's point of view, leaves him unable to think Being.

As we turn now to Heidegger, we find Heidegger much more willing to embrace a fundamental contradiction with respect to Being; or, Heidegger does not, as Aristotle does, shy away from accepting a fundamental both/and. In fact, Heidegger explicitly argues that when it comes to Being, there is an admitted and accepted contradiction:

> The word 'being' is indefinite in meaning and yet we understand it definitely. 'Being' proves to be totally indeterminate and at the same time highly determinate ... we have here an obvious contradiction ... we find ourselves standing in the middle of this contradiction, and this 'stand' of ours is more real than just about anything else that we call real; it is more real than dogs and cats, automobiles and newspapers.[14]

With this recognition of a fundamental contradiction, Heidegger launches an effort to think difference as difference, and not as subordinate to identity; and in doing this, Heidegger makes moves towards overcoming the tradition of metaphysics as 'ontotheological.'

III

Heidegger is quite forthright in claiming that he wants to think difference as difference, and not difference as identity. In his book *Identity and Difference*, Heidegger claims that 'the matter of thinking is the difference as difference.'[15] Earlier in this same book, however, Heidegger seems to repeat Aristotle's claim that difference is to be understood in terms of identity: 'The Reader is to discover for himself in what way difference stems from the essence of identity.'[16] Heidegger will qualify this statement, though, by referring to the essence of identity as being 'the Same,' whereas the Same is understood by Heidegger to be the difference between Being as presencing and beings as presence – that is, the Ontological Difference. Thus, prior to stating that the matter of thinking is 'difference as difference,' Heidegger claims, 'For us, the matter of thinking is the Same, and this is Being – but Being with respect to its difference from beings.'[17] Heidegger, in fact, will later contrast identity, or the identical, with the same:

> The equal or identical always moves toward the absence of difference, so that everything may be reduced to a common denominator. The same, by contrast, is the belonging together of what differs, through a gathering by way of the difference.[18]

Consequently, when Heidegger states that 'difference stems from the essence of identity,' he means that the difference between identifiable beings stems from the essence of Being as the gathering by way of difference; or the proceeding forth and gathering in of Being allows for the presence of beings, and hence the difference between beings. This is quite different from what Aristotle argued. Aristotle recognized the importance of the 'proceeding forth and gathering in' of eidos, as we saw, but this proceeding and gathering occurs, not 'by way of the difference,' but rather by way of logos, or by way of what can be said. Heidegger's understanding of the gathering in of Being does not presuppose the lingering presence of the identifiable, the identifiable that can be named, but is the very condition for the possibility of lingering presence. Heidegger thus continues Aristotle's project of attempting to think being qua being, but for Heidegger this involves thinking difference as difference, or it involves thinking the ontological difference between Being and beings, presencing and presence.

In thinking the difference between Being and beings, Heidgegger is clear that such a thinking does not entail answering the question 'what is Being?' by pointing to some identifiable thing as Being. Rather, Being is the very condition for the unconcealedness and identity of beings. 'The disclosedness of Being,' Heidegger maintains, 'alone makes possible the manifestness of being.'[19] Consequently, to think the difference between Being and being is not to think the difference between an identifiable Being and an identifiable being. This latter thinking of difference already presupposes the ontological difference, which allows for the emergence of identifiable entities, entities which form the basis of identifiable differences. This was Aristotle's understanding of difference, and Heidegger is clear that such an understanding is made possible by the ontological difference, a difference Aristotle failed to think: 'A is differentiated from B – with the "is" we already maintain the older difference.'[20]

What, then, does thinking difference as difference entail if it is not thinking the difference between identifiable things? How do we think the disclosedness of beings? Are we to turn our backs on beings and enter a meditative state of openness, a state free of thoughts regarding beings? Although Heidegger would not be opposed to a meditative openness, he would not urge the abandonment of beings. The reason for this is that Being and beings essentially presuppose one another. It is true that identifiable beings presuppose the disclosedness of Being, or Being is in this way the ground of beings, but Heidegger adds that 'not only does Being ground beings as their ground, but beings in their turn ground, cause Being in their way. Beings can do so only insofar as they "are" the fullness of Being: they are what *is* most of all.'[21] Being and beings are thus involved in what Heidegger calls 'reciprocal reflection,' or 'the circling of Being and beings around each other.' Moreover, this circling implies for Heidegger a free space, an empty region, which allows for the lingering presence and presencing – that is, circling of presence and presencing – of beings. This circling is simply the ontological difference, and it is precisely this, Heidegger claims, that is to be thought: 'Being essentially occurs in that it – the freedom of the free region itself – liberates all beings to themselves. It remains what is to be thought by thinking.'[22]

To think Being, therefore, and to think the ontological difference between Being and beings, does not require for Heidegger the abandonment of beings; instead, we are to think beings with respect to the nothingness which they presuppose, or we are to think beings with respect to what they are 'not.' This 'not' is not a simple negation of beings, a negation which leaves us with an empty void. The thinking of this negation is a thinking that confronts the *non*-identifiable condition for the possibility of identifying beings, a condition which, precisely because it cannot be identified, provokes anxiety. Thus, in his *Introduction to Metaphysics*, Heidegger argues that 'anxiety is being "at one with" beings that are slipping away as a whole,' and adds that 'in anxiety nothing is encountered at one with beings as a whole.'[23] To think Being as the negation or nothingness essentially related to beings is not to abandon beings, for this nothingness is at 'one with beings as a whole'; instead, this thinking confronts the non-identifiable condition for the possibility of identifying beings, and in doing so this thinking involves anxiety.

Is this discussion of anxiety in the face of thinking nothingness to be seen as a product of Heidegger's early, subject or Dasein-oriented work, a discussion which becomes irrelevant in his later works? Such a dismissal would be unwarranted, we argue, for what Heidegger refers to in 1943 as the 'narcotization of anxiety in the face of thinking' will continue implicitly as the basis for his critique of technology, a critique Heidegger continued to set forth up to the end of his career. This will become especially clear as we compare and contrast Deleuze and Heidegger, especially their views regarding technology and capitalism. It is therefore to this discussion that we now turn.

IV

One issue which Deleuze and Heidegger initially appear to be in agreement on, or even an issue some could argue Deleuze simply appropriated from Heidegger, is the notion of the 'event.' It is well known among Deleuze scholars that the concept 'event' is one of the more important within the Deleuze (and Deleuze-Guattari) corpus. As Deleuze understands 'event,' such as sense, which is for him an event, it is neither to be identified with states of affairs in the world or with the propositions which refer to these states of affairs; rather, an event is the non-identifiable, unique singularity which allows for the possibility of identifying and relating states of affairs to propositions. An event thus functions as what Deleuze refers to as a 'differenciator of difference;' that is, as differenciator, an event allows for the recognition and identification of difference, for example, the difference between states of affairs and propositions.

But was this not already Heidegger's position? The ontological difference, as we saw, is not a difference between identifiable entities – Being and beings – but is rather the condition of possibility for identifying and differentiating between beings. The ontological difference is itself, to use Deleuze's terminology, a differenciator of difference. Furthermore, Heidegger will also refer to the ontological difference in its capacity as differenciator of difference by the term 'event' (*Ereignis*). Thus, in *Time and Being*, Heidegger claims, 'What determines both, time and Being, in their own, that is, in their belonging together, we shall call: *Ereignis*, the event of Appropriation.'[24] This event, moreover, is not simply one state of affairs among others, or one identifiable occurrence among others, but as the differenciator of difference the event is the condition of possibility for identifiable occurrences: an '"event" is not simply an occurrence, but that which makes any occurrence possible.'[25] Heidegger also refers to these events, as does Deleuze, as singularities, or as a condition which is non-identifiable, unique, and incomparable: 'The term event of appropriation here no longer means what we would otherwise call a happening, an occurrence. It now is used as a *singulare tantum*. What it indicates happens only in the singular, no, not in any number, but uniquely.'[26]

These obvious parallels between Heidegger and Deleuze did not go unnoticed by Deleuze. In *Difference and Repetition*, for example, Deleuze argues that with Heidegger's notion of the ontological difference he appears to set forth an understanding of the differenciator of difference, though Deleuze believes that ultimately Heidegger did not follow through on this attempt to set forth a philosophy of difference which thinks difference as difference. To see why Deleuze makes this claim, it will be helpful if we first turn to Deleuze's critique of Aristotle. This will prove useful, for although both Deleuze and Heidegger believe Aristotle never adequately thought difference as difference, an examination of Deleuze's critique of Aristotle will ultimately reveal why Deleuze feels this same criticism applies to Heidegger as well.

Deleuze's criticism of Aristotle occupies only a few pages of his work *Difference and Repetition*; and yet the significance of these pages, especially as they relate to Deleuze's criticism of Heidegger, should not be underestimated. Deleuze's criticism of Aristotle, in short, is that while Aristotle recognizes the importance and productive nature of difference, this difference nonetheless is subordinate to identity, and in two fundamental ways. The first way in which the productive nature of difference, that is, the differenciator of difference, is grounded in identity is with the identity of substance-species, or what Deleuze refers to as infima species:

> The determination of species links difference with difference [i.e., difference which determines species – e.g., rationality – with difference which constitutes genus – e.g., animal vs. non-animal, etc.] across successive levels of division, like a transport of difference, a diaphora of diaphora, until a final difference, that of the infima species, condenses in the chosen direction the entirety of the essence and its continued quality, gathers them under an intuitive concept and grounds them along with the term to be defined, thereby becoming itself something unique and indivisible [atomon, adiaphoron, eidos].[27]

As a species, difference determines human beings by differentiating them from other animals – humans have rationality. As an animal, however, humans are different from non-animals such as geometric figures, rocks, etc. In the Aristotelian scheme, therefore, difference is productive of the categories within which things are identified, yet this productive power of difference is limited by the ultimate determination of an identifiable substance-species, the *infima species*. Difference is thus subservient to the end of determining an ultimate identity, a non-difference [adiaphora].

The second way in which difference is subservient to identity is more complex, although initially it is straightforward enough. Put simply, the determination of species and the productive power of difference is limited by the genus within which these differences occur. Aristotle, we will recall, argued that difference within genus is the greatest difference, and beyond that there was no difference because differences between genera had no basis for comparison and hence could not be discussed or thought (except theologically). Differences within a genus – that is, species – do have such a basis for comparison and are therefore the only differences that can be thought. Deleuze recognizes that for Aristotle 'specific difference is maximal and perfect, but only on condition of the identity of an undetermined concept [i.e., genus].'[28] However, this leaves the question of the difference between genera unanswered. Perhaps it could not be answered since such an answer would entail the identity of a concept, and since the difference between genera are not subsumed by such a concept an answer is not possible. Deleuze recognizes this possible approach to understanding difference: 'genera as ultimate determinable concepts (categories) ... are not subject to the condition that they share an identical concept or a common genus.'[29] The reason for this, of course, is that being is not a genus. There opens up, then, as Deleuze reads Aristotle, a fracture within Aristotle's thought between a difference that is subservient to the identity of a concept (species difference) and a difference that is not subservient to such an identity:

> It is as though there were two 'Logoi,' differing in nature but intermingled with one another: the logos of Species, the logos of what we think and say, which rests upon the condition of the identity or univocity of concepts in general taken as genera; and the logos of Genera, the logos of what is thought and said through us, which is free of that condition and operates both in the equivocity of Being and in the diversity of the most general concepts. When we speak the univocal, is it not still the equivocal which speaks within us?

With this fracture in Aristotle's thinking of difference, Deleuze feels that an opportunity for a philosophy of difference emerges – namely, a philosophy which does not think difference in terms of identity, but thinks difference as difference. Despite this opportunity, however, Deleuze goes on to say, 'Nothing of this kind occurs with Aristotle';[30] the opportunity for a philosophy of difference is missed.

What Aristotle does to turn away from this opportunity, as discussed above, is to understand generic difference with respect to the analogy of the productive relationship itself, a relationship that is established and assured by the identity of the unmoved mover, the one heaven; and furthermore, the essence of each and every productive relationship, regardless of the genus, is such that it can be named. In other words, despite the differences in genera, there persists the identity of productivity itself, and for this reason Deleuze concludes that Aristotle does not follow through on the opportunity to develop a philosophy of difference: 'The fact is that generic or categorial difference remains a difference in the Aristotelian sense and does not collapse into simple diversity or otherness. An identical or common concept thus still subsists, albeit in a very particular manner.'[31] This particular manner is precisely the analogical identity of the productive relationship, or it is the identity which allows itself to be named or expressed in the form of judgments. There is not a difference, in other words, that cannot be thought, named, and judged. Thus, Deleuze concludes:

> Whereas specific difference is content to inscribe difference in the identity of the indeterminate concept in general, generic (distributive and hierarchical) difference is content in turn to inscribe difference in the quasi-identity of the most general determinable concept; that is, in the analogy within judgment itself.[32]

Aristotle does not think difference as difference, and in fact, for Deleuze, Aristotle initiates a tradition in philosophy which is based upon a confusion that prevents thinking difference as difference. Deleuze claims that this occurs when

> assigning a distinctive concept of difference is confused with the inscription of difference within concepts in general – the determination of the concept of difference is confused with the inscription of difference in the identity of an undetermined concept.[33]

Rather than developing a concept of difference which gives credit to its productive nature, that is, differenciator of difference, and hence rather than thinking difference as difference, this task of thinking becomes confused with developing a concept of difference in terms of its inscription within the identity of an undetermined concept, such as genus or the analogy within judgment in the case of Aristotle. In Aristotle, therefore, 'we never discover,' according to Deleuze, a philosophical appreciation and thinking of the 'differenciator of difference.'[34]

We can now relate Deleuze's critique of Aristotle to his critique of Heidegger. At first such an attempt seems unwarranted, for, as Deleuze himself admits, Heidegger does appear to develop a notion of Being which appreciates difference as the differenciator of difference. 'Being,' Deleuze claims, 'is truly the differenciator of difference – whence the expression "ontological difference."'[35] Later in the same work, Deleuze reiterates this same point:

> In accordance with Heidegger's ontological intuition, difference must be articulation and connection in itself; it must relate different to different without any mediation whatsoever by the identical, the similar, the analogous or the opposed. There must be a differenciation of difference, an in-itelf which is like a differenciator, a Sich-unterscheidende, by virtue of which the different is gathered all at once rather than represented on condition of a prior resemblance, identity, analogy or opposition.[36]

Deleuze's critique of Aristotle's failure to think difference as difference appears then merely to echo Heidegger's own critique of Aristotle. Their respective critiques of Aristotle are largely in agreement, but as Heidegger develops his understanding of Being as differenciator of difference, Deleuze finds two key problems which ultimately undermine Heidegger's efforts. His first objection is that Heidegger understands difference as a means for gathering into the same, or difference appears to be mediated by the primal and inviolable unity of a self-contained, pure and simple Being. His second objection is that Heidegger's tendency to contrast Being with the fullness of beings, or to strike through Being as the nothingness opposed to beings, has the consequence of denying reality and fullness to Being, or to the differenciator of difference, which is something Deleuze refuses to do.

As for the first objection, it is certainly clear that Heidegger emphasizes the role of the same, whereby the same is that which 'gathers what is distinct into an original being-at-one.'[37] However, Heidegger also stressed, as we saw, that this gathering into an original 'being-at-one' is not, à la Aristotle, subordinate to the identity of substance-species, to a one that can be named, but rather it allows for the lingering presence whereby one can identify a being. Similarly for the second objection, it is true that Heidegger contrasts Being as nothingness with the identity and fullness of beings. For example, Heidegger argues that scientists are concerned solely with 'beings, and beyond that – nothing,' and adds that 'when science tries to express its proper essence it calls upon the nothing for help. It has recourse to what it rejects.'[38] This nothing, moreover, is not to be confused with the beings science interrogates, and hence the nothing is not to be interrogated in the manner of science: 'Interrogating the nothing – asking what and how it, the nothing, is – turns what is interrogated into its opposite.'[39] Nevertheless, Heidegger stresses that the nothing is not an empty void, nor should it be understood to be in opposition to beings, for the nothing, as we saw, is reciprocally and essentially related to the beings it grounds; or the nothing is inseparable from beings, even though it is not to be confused or identified with them, or as one of them (and this is precisely how Deleuze characterizes the event).

It seems, then, that Deleuze's criticisms of Heidegger might not stand up to a more thorough examination of Heidegger's texts. We argue that this is not the case. A more thorough examination of Heidegger's texts, and in particular a close analysis of his criticisms of the West's technological, capitalist-dominated society, will show that Deleuze's criticisms are indeed valid. To gain a better understanding of these criticisms, therefore, and to clarify further the sense in which Deleuze sets forth a philosophy of difference, we turn now to their critiques of capitalist society.

V

We begin this section with an appeal Heidegger makes to refrain from turning away from the nothing, or from Being: 'The more we turn toward beings in our preoccupations the less we let beings as a whole slip away as such and the more we turn away from the nothing. Just as surely do we hasten into the public superficies of existence.'[40] The more we get caught up in beings, in the everyday superficies of life, the less we attend to what is essential, to Being (the nothing). More to the point, the dominance of capitalism and technological expansion and control in Western cultures represents for Heidegger a frenzied attempt to make up for the lack of what is essential by excessively controlling and arranging the everyday world of beings:

> The consumption of all materials, including the raw material 'man,' for the unconditioned possibility of the production of everything is determined in a concealed way by the complete emptiness in which beings, the materials of what is real, are suspended. This emptiness has to be filled up. But since the emptiness of Being can never be filled up by the fullness of beings, especially when this emptiness can never be experienced as such, the only way to escape it is incessantly to arrange beings in the constant possibility of being ordered as the form of guaranteeing aimless activity.[41]

To return to our earlier theme of the 'narcotization' in the face of the anxiety provoked by nothingness, we can see here a similar theme and concern being expressed: in the face of the emptiness of Being, the resulting anxiety inspires a mad, futile effort to fill this emptiness with an ever-increasing ordering of beings. This futile effort finds its greatest expression in technology and capitalism; however, the technological/capitalist exploitation and ordering of beings does not attend to Being; but, rather, it is precisely the turning away from Being which accounts for the rampant success of technological expansion. And it is this failure to attend to Being, to the nothingness, which concerns Heidegger. The reason for this is that Heidegger believes that a proper attunement to Being would lead to a respect for the intrinsic limitations and possibilities of Being. Because the technological/capitalist world view is one that turns away from Being, the result is a transgression of these intrinsic limitations and possibilities. The consequence for Heidegger is that 'technology drives the earth beyond the developed sphere of its possibility into such things which are no longer a possibility and are thus the impossible.' And, a few lines later, Heidegger adds:

> It is one thing just to use the earth, another to receive the blessing of the earth and to become at home in the law of this reception in order to shepherd the mystery of Being and watch over the inviolability of the possible.[42]

It is at this point where Deleuze's criticism of Heidegger becomes more clear, though on first reading one might not think so since Deleuze, too, will criticize the excesses of capitalism, or the excesses of capitalist/technological processes of appropriation.[43] The basis for Deleuze's criticisms, however, is quite different from Heidegger's. Whereas Heidegger accuses technological/capitalist expansion of violating the simplicity and limitations of Being, Deleuze argues that capitalism improperly staves off its condition of possibility – chaos.

The key here is clearly the term 'chaos' (as was also true in the previous chapter). Deleuze and Guattari discuss chaos at greatest length in their last collaborative work, *What Is Philosophy?* In this work, they define chaos and explicitly contrast it with nothingness:

> Chaos is defined not so much by its disorder as by the infinite speed which every form taking shape in it vanishes. It is a void that is not a nothingness but a virtual, containing all possible particles and drawing out all possible forms, which spring up only to disappear immediately, without consistency or reference, without consequence.[44]

It is true that Heidegger also thought of Being as a nothingness which is not simply the lack of being; however, Deleuze's point is that Heidegger's tendency to use the word 'Being,' and to strike through Being, leads one to the conclusion that whereas beings are the fullness of Being, Being itself is empty. Deleuze claims quite the opposite: it is not beings that are full, but Being as chaos which is the fullness that gives rise to beings when the infinite speeds and inconsistencies are limited and slowed to a level where consistency, and hence beings, can emerge. Heidegger was right to claim that Being should not be thought in terms of beings, but not because it is the nothingness which allows for the presencing of full presence; rather, it is because Being is the chaotic fullness which exceeds the intrinsic limitations of finite beings.

In the context of their discussion of capitalism, many of these same points are made. For example, Deleuze and Guattari argue, along with Heidegger, that capitalism is excessive, and to the extent that it is excessive, it merely recapitulates its condition of possibility – chaos. In other words, capitalism institutes chaos as part of its process of creating an increasing number of new markets, products, etc., and this is a process which necessarily involves the undermining of (Deleuze and Guattari use the word 'deterritorializes') old markets, or at least the transformation of these markets. Yet it is precisely chaos which for Deleuze and Guattari is the condition of possibility for such creative changes and transformations. At the same time, however, if capitalism is to function, it must forever avert completely realizing its condition of possibility, for if it were to do so the markets would lack the consistency and predictability necessary to make profits. This point is made quite explicitly in *Anti-Oedipus*, though here they use the word 'schizophrenia' in much the same way they will later use the word 'chaos':

> One can say that schizophrenia is the exterior limit of capitalism itself or the conclusion of its deepest tendency, but that capitalism only functions on condition that it inhibit this tendency, or that it push back or displace this limit, by substituting for it its own immanent relative limits, which it continually reproduces on a widened scale.[45]

Deleuze's critique of the excessive controls of capitalism, therefore, will not be based, as with Heidegger, on the theory that it transgresses the inviolability of Being, or the mystery of the Same; to the contrary, Deleuze's criticisms are based on the assumption that capitalism improperly staves off chaos, or that it improperly limits a chaos that always already transgresses whatever limitations might be set forth.

What would properly staving of the chaos entail? Simply put, chaos is understood as the differenciator of difference, or that which produces and creates difference without being mediated in any way by identity. Chaos is what is to be instituted for the possibility of change, or for the possibility of thinking and feeling differently. Such change is clearly necessary, as is stability, for in a world of change and becoming we must forever dip into the chaos to be able to initiate and carry forward change. Without sufficient stability, we lack the consistency necessary to survive; without sufficient chaos, we lack the ability to change and adapt (see the previous chapter). A proper use of chaos, therefore, would function as a dynamical system and hence stave off chaos for the sake of being able to function, while remaining attuned to Being, to chaos, as the ever-present possibility of difference, of thinking, feeling, acting differently, etc. An improper use of chaos, from Deleuze's point of view, would therefore be one that holds the differentiating power of chaos subservient to identity. And this is precisely what occurs in capitalism, and even according to the self-acknowledged admission of capitalists themselves, such as Peter Lynch, the legendary one-time Magellan fund manager at Fidelity. Lynch clearly recognizes that the processes of capitalism are subservient to the production of homogeneity and sameness rather than difference: 'The very homogeneity of taste in food and fashion that makes for a dull culture also makes fortunes for owners of retail companies and of restaurant companies as well. What sells in one town is almost guaranteed to sell in another ...'[46]

We can now make better sense of Deleuze's criticism of Heidegger. First, just as Deleuze criticizes the capitalist appropriation of difference for the sake of producing the same – that is, the same consumers coming back again and again; so too does Deleuze criticize Heidegger's claim that difference is the means whereby an 'original being-at-one' is gathered. By arguing for this 'gathering by way of the difference,' Heidegger is continuing in the tradition which fails to think difference as difference, that is, as the differenciator of difference. This is further exacerbated by Heidegger's tendency to refer to Being as a simple unity with intrinsic limitations of possibility. This was exemplified most in Heidegger's critique of the technological exploitation of the earth. The problem with this, for Deleuze, is that Heidegger again seems to call for a difference that is subordinate to a more fundamental unity and identity; and it is hard not to come to this conclusion when Heidegger himself uses the word 'the Same' to characterize Being. Deleuze will thus conclude that by contrasting the same with the identical, rather than contrasting the same and identical with the different, Heidegger betrays his continued adherence to a philosophical tradition which has failed to think difference as difference.[47] Deleuze's criticism of Aristotle, namely, that difference is thought only as inscribed within the identity of a general concept, can in turn be directed towards Heidegger's understanding of difference as that which is self-inscribed within the inviolable unity and purity of Being.[48]

Despite these differences, it is important to note, as we close this chapter, that in many ways Deleuze is continuing the Heideggerean tradition, in particular Heidegger's understanding of authenticity. Heidegger and Deleuze will each lambast against the preponderance of homogeneity and samenenss in daily life. In a passage from *Being and Time*, for example, Heidegger argues that this homogeneity is a result of the 'dictatorship of the they':

> We take pleasure and enjoy ourselves as *they* take pleasure; we read, see, and judge about literature and art as *they* see and judge; likewise we shrink back from the 'great mass' as *they* shrink back; we find 'shocking' what *they* find shocking. The 'they,' which is nothing definite, and which all are, though not as the sum, prescribes the kind of Being of everydayness.[49]

Deleuze, as we have been arguing, disagrees sharply with the ultimate justification Heidegger gives for his critique of the homogeneity of the everyday. By basing this critique on the Sameness of Being rather than the differenciating difference of Chaos, Deleuze feels that Heidegger ultimately remains within the tradition of philosophy which fails to think difference. When one takes this criticism into account, and if one accepts Deleuze's claim that Being is ultimately a Chaos of infinite, inconsistent speeds which is not the emptiness and nothingness that conditions the fullness of beings, but rather the excessive fullness that only allows for the emergence of beings when slowed and limited; if this is all taken into account, then Deleuze and Heidegger sound remarkably similar. Deleuze thus echoes Heidegger:

> For there is no other aesthetic problem than that of the insertion of art into everyday life. The more our daily life appears standardized, stereotyped and subject to an accelerated reproduction of objects of consumption, the more art must be injected into it in order to extract from it that little difference which plays simultaneously between other levels of repetition, and even in order to make the two extremes resonate – namely, the habitual series of consumption and the instinctual series of destruction and death.[50]

At this point we could return to the themes of the previous chapter – that is, realizing the chaos within, or injecting art into everyday life, while avoiding the dual dangers of cliché and madness. We could then focus upon the notion of chaos in Deleuze's work and see in what way it moves beyond Heidegger, or how it is to be understood in the context of thinking difference. Before turning to these themes, however, in the next chapter we will first examine the work of a near contemporary of Deleuze – Derrida. Derrida will also emphasize the importance of a fundamental difference that cannot, nor should not, be subsumed by the logic of identity. Furthermore, Derrida is clearly following in the footsteps of Heidegger, more so than Deleuze at least; and in many ways Derrida's critique of metaphysics extends Heidegger's own critique. And finally, Derrida also stresses a theme that is dear both to Heidegger and Deleuze, and a theme that has been central to this work – that is, the role of doing philosophy as thinking the uncommon within the common. A discussion of Derrida will therefore bring together many of the themes and issues that have been the concern of this work, and it will further highlight the differences between what we argue is Deleuze's dynamical systems approach to doing philosophy and the approaches of philosophers such as Heidegger and Derrida. The next chapter will also begin addressing the problems that remain, problems that will be taken up most fully in chapter 6 when we rethink system.

5 Thinking and the Loss of System: Derrida and Deleuze on Artaud

I

In our critique of Heidegger in the previous chapter, we did not adequately address some important themes which, in light of Derrida's work, may very well take the wind out of the sails of our critique. In particular, by arguing as we did that chaos is the fullness of being, the excessive fullness that allows for the *identification* of beings when this excessiveness is slowed and limited, we appear to endorse a position that Derrida subjects to critique and deconstruction – namely, the fullness or *presence* of being. Derrida's critique of presence, in short, is implicitly a critique of our (and Deleuze's) position. To take the fullness of chaos as the condition for the possibility of identifying beings, Deleuze, Derrida would argue, would continue in the metaphysical tradition which understands identity and truth in terms of an always presupposed, unquestioned, metaphysical presence.[1] By basing an understanding of the emergence of stable forms and identities on the grounds of the fullness and excessiveness of chaos, we seem then to be open to Derrida's objection that identity is being understood in terms of an unquestioned, presupposed identity (chaos as fullness and presence). We have failed to think difference. Moreover, in Derrida's extension of Heidegger's critique of presence, Derrida explicitly utilizes this critique in an effort to think difference, or to think/write the uncommon within the common and self-evident. Derrida states this openly in his work *Of Grammatology*: 'To make enigmatic what one thinks one understands by the words "proximity," "immediacy," "presence," ... is my final intention in this book.'[2] Consequently, in order to show that our critique of Heidegger is not susceptible to Derrida's (and Heidegger's) own critique of the metaphysics of presence, we must further elaborate upon Derrida's critique of presence and then compare this with Deleuze's critique of the metaphysical tradition.

Derrida's critique of metaphysics surfaces primarily, as we stated above, as a critique of presence, or, to be more precise, it is a critique of the simultaneity and self-presence the metaphysical tradition presupposes. Related to this critique is the critique of the fundamental either/ ors and dualities which are the stock and trade of metaphysics. If the purity and inviolability of truth is taken, as Derrida believes it is, within the metaphysical tradition to be equivalent to the presence and fullness of that which is 'self-evident,' then that which lacks this self-evidence and purity is impure, vulgar, or false. The pure/impure, true/false, original/copy, transcendent/worldly distinctions are the either/ors and dualities which are the unquestioned givens that for Derrida both founds the tradition of metaphysics and continues to circulate throughout it. On this point Derrida follows Heidegger; in particular, Derrida recognizes that the reason Heidegger referred to Nietzsche as the 'last metaphysician' was precisely because Nietzsche continued to adhere to an unquestioned duality. To recall our earlier quote, Heidegger notes that in his reversal of Plato's understanding of the relationship between the sensuous and the supersensuous (i.e., the Forms), Nietzsche continues to adhere to the sense of an 'above and a below'; he only reverses the priority of the two, and thus 'as long as the "above and below" define the formal structure of Platonism, Platonism in its essence perdures. The inversion does not achieve what it must ... namely, an overcoming of Platonism in its very foundations.'3

Derrida accepts Heidegger's critique of metaphysics, but he does not read Nietzsche as one who necessarily falls into this Platonic tradition. In Derrida's attempt 'to save Nietzsche from a reading of the Heideggerian type,' he claims that in reading Nietzsche one must

accentuate the 'naieveté' of a breakthrough which cannot criticize metaphysics radically without still utilizing in a certain way, in a certain type or a certain style of text, propositions that, read within the philosophic corpus, that is to say according to Nietzsche ill-read or unread, have always been and will always be 'naievetés' incoherent signs of an absolute appurtenance. Therefore, rather than protect Nietzsche from the Heideggerian reading, we should perhaps offer him up to it completely [and then discover that] [h]e [Nietzsche] has written that writing – and first of all his own – is not originally subordinate to the logos and to truth.4

In reading Nietzsche, or in extending Heidegger's reading of Nietzsche, Derrida argues that one recovers the 'absolute strangeness' of what he has written. This writing is not a reversal of metaphysics in the sense that it offers something other to replace this tradition; instead, one encounters what Derrida will refer to as a 'trace,' an undecidable, an excess of metaphysics [i.e., a trace] which is not strictly to be identified within the parameters of metaphysics [i.e., and thus be susceptible to a Heideggerian reading], nor is it something identifiably other than metaphysics. It is a both/and, or it is a writing that is 'not originally subordinate to the logos and to truth,' and hence to the either/or this implies.

In his essay on Bataille, Derrida finds in Bataille's notion of the 'sovereign' an operation or writing which is in excess of a writing based in a metaphysics of identity (what Bataille calls the Lord function), yet 'this transgression of discourse [and metaphysics] must,' Derrida continues, in some fasion 'conserve or confirm that which it exceeds.'[5] In contrast to the Hegelian *Aufhebung*, which also surpasses and conserves, the Hegelian transgression and excess is always subordinate to the identity of the system which is coming into self-realization (i.e., the Lord function). For Bataille, to the contrary, and similarly for Derrida's reading of Nietzsche, the transgression and excess which preserves is an 'empty form of the Aufhebung,' or it is used 'in an analogical fashion, in order to designate, as was never done before, the transgressive relationship which links the world of meaning to the world of non-meaning.'[6] In other words, Bataille and Nietzsche, in their writing, do not write an excess which would point to another writing, an alternative to metaphysics. Their writing is an excess of metaphysics which confirms and preserves it by unsettling it, or by the 'absolute strangeness' of the trace whereby this metaphysics is inextricably tied to non-metaphysics, presence is tied to absence, purity to impurity, truth to falsity, etc. As Derrida reads Nietzsche, therefore, he does not follow the Heideggerean reading which assumes a continued adherence to an either/or; rather, Derrida finds in Nietzsche a writing which is critical or beyond such either/ors.

Moreover, in Derrida's most extended treatment of Heidegger, Derrida argues that in his reading of Aristotle, Heidegger himself presupposes the dualities of metaphysics he finds in Aristotle (and in Nietzsche as we saw). Despite this eventual criticism, Derrida largely accepts and endorses what he sees, in his essay 'Ousia and Gramme,' as Heidegger's attempt to think 'Being and time otherwise than on the basis of the present.' More to the point, Derrida adds that for Heidegger 'it is not a question of proposing that we think otherwise, if this means to think some other thing. Rather, it is thinking that which could not have been, nor thought, otherwise. There is produced in the thought of the impossibility of the otherwise ... a certain difference, a certain trembling, a certain decentering that is not the position of an other center.'[7] It is in this manner, then, that Derrida reads Heidegger's long footnote towards the end of *Being and Time*. In the note, Heidegger briefly sketches the manner in which Hegel's philosophy of Nature extends and is indebted to Aristotle. In particular, Hegel's understanding of time in terms of the 'now' follows Aristotle's placing of the essence of time in the *nun* (present). In doing this, Heidegger claims that by showing the 'connection between Hegel's conception of time and Aristotle's analysis, we are not accusing Hegel of any "dependence" on Aristotle, but calling attention to the ontological import which this filiation has in principle for the Hegelian logic.'[8]

It is this latter point which is key, both for Derrida and Heidegger, and the 'ontological import' of the filiation between Aristotle and Hegel reveals its significance, for Derrida, with Aristotle's aporia regarding time. In the *Physics*, Aristotle asks whether time belongs to beings or non-beings. When time is understood on the basis of the now, the present (*nun*), time is not. The reason for this is that each instant, each now, is *simultaneously*[9] both what is becoming past, or is no longer, and coming into being, or not yet is. If one thinks of time from the perspective of passing presents, or what Derrida calls the vulgar, everyday conception of time, then time is not. Nevertheless, by virtue of the fact that we attribute temporal characteristics to things and events, we presuppose that in some sense time is. Derrida will later point out that Aristotle, in the context of discussing Zeno's paradox, will repeat this aporia, but he does so 'without deconstructing it.'[10] As Derrida puts Aristotle's point: 'Time is not (among beings). It is nothingness because it is time, that is a past or future now.'[11] In other words, if time is thought in terms of the now, presence, then time is not, and yet this very argument presupposes what time is (i.e., 'a past or future now [present, presence]'). It is for this reason that Derrida will claim that for Aristotle 'Being is non-time, time is nonbeing insofar as being already, secretly has been determined as present, and beingness (ousia) as presence.'[12] It is this latter secret determination, the presupposition of presence, which Aristotle fails to deconstruct. And to deconstruct this presupposition involves, for Derrida, revealing the necessary connection between presence and absence, being and non-being, time and non-time. In short, Derrida will read in Aristotle, as he did with Nietzsche, the 'absolute strangeness' or excess which is not subordinate to logos, truth, and presence. Derrida will carry forward the deconstruction Aristotle failed to.

In subjecting Aristotle's understanding of time to a deconstructive reading, Derrida will, as discussed above, render the self-evident enigmatic, or reveal the 'absolute strangeness' within what is taken to be obvious. In the text of Aristotle, this reading focuses upon a single word:

> Aristotle's text comes down upon a word so small as to be hardly visible, and hardly visible because it appears self-evident, as discreet as that which goes without saying, a word that is self effacing, operating all the more effectively in that it evades thematic attention. That which goes without saying, making discourse play itself out in its articulation, that which henceforth will constitute the pivot of metaphysics, the small key that both opens and closes the history of metaphysics in terms of what it puts at stake, the clavicle on which the conceptual decision of Aristotle bears down and is articulated, is the small word hama.[13]

Hama is the Greek word for 'together,' 'all at once,' 'at the same time.' This word appears five times in the crucial passage from the *Physics* where Aristotle puts forward the aporia regarding time (218a). It is this word, and the presupposed, unquestioned, and unthought duplicity associated with 'at the same time,' 'simultaneous,' etc., which is what allows for the possibility of the aporia as aporia. Consequently, if time does not participate in being, this is because time is thought in terms of nows; thus, one now cannot follow another by immediately destroying it, for then there would be no time (recall, time is past and future nows); nows cannot follow one another with overlapping simultaneity, for here too there would be no time, or no temporal distinction between past and present; and finally, past and future nows cannot coexist 'at the same time' in a single now, for then events distant in time would be simultaneous. As Derrida concludes, the absurdity of the latter point is made possible by virtue of 'the self-evidence of the "at the same time," that constitutes the aporia as aporia.'[14]

This presupposed, unquestioned self-evidence of the 'at the same time' results, as Derrida continues his reading of Aristotle, in some strange conclusions. If time is not to be understood in terms of being, then what truly is is not in time. This is precisely what Aristotle says regarding the pure actualities, the Being in act, which is the presupposed actuality which allows for the possibility of potential Beings, or for the possibility that something has the potential to come into Being and be actualized (recall our earlier discussion of this in the previous chapter when we examined the distinction between *dynamis* and *energeia* in greater detail). Since these eternal beings are what truly is, they cannot be in time since time does not participate in Being: 'Thus it is evident that eternal Beings (*ta aei onta*), as eternal, are not in time' (*Physics* 221b).[15] But Aristotle's very aporia is based on an assumption of what time is – namely, it is a past or future now: 'One part of it has been and is no longer; another part will be and is not yet. Such are the components of time – of infinite time and of time considered in its incessant return. Now it seems impossible that that which allows non-beings in its composition participates in beingness' (217b–a). This impossibility, as we have seen Derrida point out, is an impossibility because of the presupposed self-evidence of the 'at the same time.' But because the nature of what time is, is itself taken as a given, 'time,' Derrida continues, 'is not non-Being, and non-Beings are not in time.'[16] In other words, for something to be in time it must have come into being, or it must have begun a process whereby it becomes what it was not, or was only *in potentia*. These beings that are in time, that are in various processes of becoming, do not lack being according to Aristotle. These beings are not pure Beings, for if they were they would not be 'in time' – they would be eternal beings. Therefore, something which is not yet, or only potentially is, is thus a non-Being which is not in time *yet*. Aristotle's conclusion, then, as Derrida notes, is that 'it is evident that non-Being will not always be in time' (221b). In short, and this is where Derrida's deconstructive reading leads him, an understanding of time based on presence (Being) necessarily involves and presupposes its other, absence (non-Being).

This is why the term *hama* ('at the same time') is so important in Derrida's reading of Aristotle, 'the pivot of metaphysics.' Aristotle's aporia was constituted by, or based upon, the self-evidence that two different things cannot *be* at the same time – for example, past/future now and present now could not coexist at the same time. But the very term *hama* presupposes the coexistence, the duplicity, of different things at the same time. What Aristotle failed to recognize, according to Derrida, is that while this unquestioned self-evidence of the term *hama* allowed for the possibility of the conclusion that eternal Beings are not in time, it simultaneously led Aristotle to the conclusion that non-Beings 'will not always be in time,' or that an understanding of time based on presence simultaneously entails an understanding of time in terms of its other. Derrida refers to the simultaneity of these two conclusions as 'a formal rule for anyone wishing to read the texts of the history of metaphysics.'[17] In the context of Aristotle, this rule involves reading the term *hama*, for example, as something that is simultaneously submitted as the unquestioned premise upon which Aristotle bases his understanding of time as well as his metaphysics. This self-evident given lays the foundation, then, for the distinction between a pure Eternal Being that is not in time and a fallen, temporally bound being, or a being that has fallen from its pure state and is, but only 'barely and obscurely' is (*Physics* 218a). The term *hama* is submitted as the unquestioned ground for the dualities of metaphysics (e.g., eternal being vs. finite, temporal being), or it is, as Derrida says, the pivot of metaphysics. By contrast, and by necessity, the presupposed duality and duplicity of the term *hama* must be subtracted from what is acceptable or passes as truth in metaphysics – for example, past and future cannot be at the same time, something cannot both be and not be. In reading Aristotle, therefore, Derrida shows that *hama* is both submitted as the basis for thinking time and it is subtracted from this thinking as the manner in which time is not to be thought, or the manner in which it is impossible to think time. Derrida's deconstructive reading does not offer an other reading, a pure as opposed to an impure reading, but it reads a text in order to reveal the impossible presupposed by the possible, or the enigmatic within the self-evident. By following the formal rule Derrida proposes in reading the texts of metaphysics, one does not leave metaphysics behind for something else, a better alternative; one instead finds within metaphysics itself that which exceeds it, or that which transgresses it while preserving it.

Derrida will also apply this same formal rule to his reading of Heidegger. For Derrida, despite the 'extraordinary trembling to which classical ontology is subjected in *Sein und Zeit* [this book] still remains within the grammar and lexicon of metaphysics.'[18] The reason for this is that Heidegger, too, appears to presuppose the incompatibility of two different times being at the same time, or of a pure and a fallen time. It is true that Heidegger recognizes the metaphysical tendency to think the Being of beings as presence rather than presencing, and for this Derrida greatly admires Heidegger, but then Heidegger refers to the time that is thought in terms of beings (presence) as a falling from, or a forgetfulness of, Being as presencing.[19] This falling from an authentic to an inauthentic temporality is built in, so to speak, to the nature of temporality itself. In other words, for Heidegger temporality includes both its authentic and inauthentic modes. Heidegger has thus moved beyond Aristotle (and Hegel) by explicitly recognizing what was implicitly at work in Aristotle (i.e., the presupposed duality of time, or *hama*). Where Derrida claims Heidegger continues within the lexicon of metaphysics is with his use of the term 'fallen' (*Verfallen*). Derrida asks of Heidegger: 'is not the opposition of primordial to derivative still metaphysical? ... Why determine as fall the passage from one temporality to another? And why qualify temporality as authentic – or proper (*eigentlich*) – and as inauthentic – or improper – when every ethical preoccupation has been suspended?'[20] For Derrida, Heidegger continues to utilize the traditional metaphysical parameters and dualities, and rather than read the excess or nonsense which both submits and is to be subtracted from the meaning of these traditional terms, Heidegger instead inquires into the meaning of being. This, in Derrida's view, accounts for the significance of Heidegger's closing question in *Being and Time*, a question concerning 'whether this primordial temporality constitutes the horizon of Being, [or] if it leads to the meaning of Being.'[21] Such a question betrays, for Derrida, a continued adherence to the metaphysical notions of purity, systematic totality, and completeness or closure; consequently, it is an assumed primordial temporality that leads Heidegger to ask whether it constitutes the 'horizon of Being,' or whether it is the standard whereby the meaning of being is fulfilled. To push Heidegger beyond metaphysics, therefore, will not involve offering an alternative to Heidegger, but rather it will read in Heidegger the excess or nonsense which is necessarily presupposed by, and accompanies, the notions of completeness, purity, etc. And this excess does not destroy Heidegger's metaphysics – to the contrary, it is the excess that is submitted and subtracted by the metaphysics it makes possible.

On reading Heidegger in accordance with his formal rule, Derrida argues that the plentitude and fullness of authentic, primordial temporality is made possible by the 'absolute strangeness' of an enigmatic, undecidable trace; and it is this trace which must be subtracted, excluded, and suppressed if the metaphysical text is to achieve completeness. Heidegger's thought of a primordial temporality and the horizon of Being is therefore a thought based on the fullness and plentitude of presence. Consequently, Derrida's critique of presence will apply to Heidegger as well, for Heidegger continues to take, much as Aristotle did, as unquestioned the self-evidence of plentitude, presence, purity, and completeness. Derrida's critical response to this metaphysical approach, therefore, or his effort to think difference, involves revealing the 'absolute strangeness,' the enigmatic, which the self-evidence of metaphysics presupposes. The plentitude, as Derrida will argue, is conditioned by the undecidable trace, or what he also calls *differance*. As Derrida puts it: 'The (pure) trace is differance. It does not depend on any sensible plentitude, audible or visible, phonic or graphic. It is, on the contrary, the condition of such plentitude.'[22] As its condition of possibility, however, differance is also the presupposed difference which defers and subverts efforts to overcome difference by virtue of the purity and plentitude of something that is self-identical. Differance is thus the condition of impossibility for any complete, total, self-contained system. In short, what Heidegger failed to recognize, as Derrida reads (or deconstructs) him, is the *impossibility* of thinking 'the meaning of Being.'

We can now further extend our earlier critique of Heidegger. Earlier it was argued that Heidegger's definition of the Same as that which 'gathers what is distinct into an original being-at-one' betrayed an adherence to an ideal of simplicity, purity, and self-containment. Difference, we argued, was reduced to the primordiality and simple identity of this self-contained 'being-at-one.' Heidegger failed to think difference. Similarly, Derrida also sees in Heidegger the ideal of a primordial plentitude from which other states fall or are derived (e.g., forgetfulness of being), but then Heidegger does not recognize the fundamental difference (or differance, trace, etc.) which is the presupposed condition for the possibility of this plentitude. Because he fails to recognize this presupposed condition, he also fails to realize the *impossibility* of thinking a complete, pure, self-contained meaning of Being whereby everything is gathered into an 'original [primordial] being-at-one.' Because of this, Heidegger continues to hold to the *possibility* of thinking the meaning of Being, a meaning which expresses the essence of Being as the systematic gathering of elements (i.e., differences) into an original being-at-one. From Derrida's perspective as well, then, Heidegger fails to think difference. Difference, and this was true of Hegel as well, is ultimately gathered by and subordinate to a fundamental identity – for Heidegger this was the primordiality and inviolability of the Same (Being), and for Hegel this was Spirit.

Derrida would clearly reject Hegel's view of system as well. Because Hegel explicitly affirms an understanding of system whereby all differences between elements are related to one another by virtue of their being subordinate to the self-identity of Spirit, then Derrida's deconstructive reading would uncover the enigmatic presupposed by Hegel's system. While Heidegger explicitly rejects understanding the differences between beings (i.e., beings as presence) in terms of another being (e.g., the self-presence or being of Spirit), his understanding of the presencing of Being as the Same which gathers differences into an original being-at-one ultimately repeats, if only implicitly, Hegel's position regarding system. Derrida will subsequently argue that systems, as with any complete, full presence and plentitude, presuppose the trace (or differance) as their condition. Moreover, if we take into consideration Derrida's claim that differance is 'an economic concept designating the production of differing/deferring,'[23] then we can extend this concept so as to understand more clearly Derrida's position regarding systems. For instance, in *Of Grammatology*, while discussing the linguistic system presupposed by linguists such as Hjelmslev and Saussure, Derrida claims:

> It is because arche-writing, movement of differance [i.e., differance as 'production of differing/deferring'], irreducible arche-synthesis, opening in one and the same possibility, temporalization as well as relationship with the other and language, cannot, as the condition of all linguistic systems, form a part of the linguistic system itself and be situated as an object in its field. (Which does not mean it has a real field elsewhere, another assignable site.)[24]

It is the movement of differance, the production of differing/deferring, which allows for the possibility that the terms of a language can be related to the *other* terms of the language.[25] This is not to deny Saussure's claim, and later Hjelmslev's, that there are systematic relationships among the terms of a language. In his essay where he discusses Saussure at length, Derrida recognizes the significance and validity of Saussure's claim that the meaning of a word in a language is not a self-identical entity, an entity independent of other words and meanings, but rather it involves a necessary relationship to the other words of the language (*la langue* as system). Much of Derrida's efforts at deconstructing texts, or following his 'formal rule,' involves showing that any claim to have achieved a pure self-identity and presence necessarily presupposes (i.e., submits) and yet denies (i.e., subtracts) a fundamental difference, an *other* or absence which is inseparable from the proposed self-identity and presence. What Derrida rejects in Saussure and Hjelmslev is that they transfer the meaning of a word from the self-identity and completeness of a meaning-in-itself to the self-identity and completeness of the linguistic system. In either case, they fail to recognize the movement of differance which allows for the possibility of thinking a system as a complete, self-identical totality, but a movement that renders it impossible to think system as a complete, self-identical totality.

With this critique of Hjelmslev's and Saussure's understanding of system, we seem to find common cause between Derrida and Deleuze. In an earlier chapter, we showed how important the notion of a double bind can be in understanding what is at work in Nietzsche, and then with Deleuze as he extends Nietzsche's work. Likewise, with the Derridean claim that differance allows for the possibility and impossibility of thinking a system as a complete, self-identical totality, we once again encounter an apparent double bind. Without repeating our earlier discussions in showing how Derrida and Deleuze agree in so many ways (which we could do), it will be more helpful at this point to focus upon some issues where they appear to differ. In particular, Deleuze will often speak of the 'plane of consistency [*plan de consistence*]' in terms that seem to echo Heidegger's references to the horizon of Being; more importantly, Deleuze also accepts a view of completeness which Derrida would reject. For example, in discussing the schizo-revolutionary in *Anti-Oedipus*, Deleuze and Guattari argue that the processes associated with genius may appear incomplete to others, though this is only because, 'from the moment there is genius, there is something that belongs to no school, no period, something that achieves a breakthrough – art as a process without goal, *but that attains completion as such.*'[26] Moreover, in reference to the artistic and schizo-revolutionary art experiments of Artaud, and to the completion inherent in the process of such experiments, Deleuze and Guattari return to the use of the metaphysical duality Derrida criticized in Heidegger – that is, the pure/impure duality:

> It is here [with Artaud for instance] that art accedes to its *authentic modernity*, which simply consists in liberating what was present in art from its beginnings, but was hidden underneath aims and objects, even if aesthetic, and underneath recodings or axiomatics: *the pure process that fulfills itself, and that never ceases to reach fulfillment as it proceeds* – art as 'experimentation.'[27]

By focusing on these apparent differences, therefore, we can confront directly the possibility that Deleuze's understanding of chaos may simply be a repetition of Heidegger's understanding of Being, and hence be susceptible to a Derridean critique. To examine this possibility, we will examine more closely Deleuze's and Derrida's interpretations of Artaud. Both Derrida and Deleuze devoted much time to writing on Artaud, and although Deleuze and Guattari may be better known for adopting Artaud's phrase 'Body without Organs,' Derrida himself has consistently, and throughout his career, returned to the writings of Artaud.[28] A brief discussion of Deleuze's and Derrida's interpretations of Artaud, and in particular Artaud's use of the phrase 'Body without Organs,' will, it is hoped, allow us to address the potential problems with our earlier (Deleuzean) critique of Heidegger.

II

There has been a continuing fascination with the writings of Artaud. This is no doubt in large part due to the rare combination of having tremendous writing and poetic skills coupled with a constant and almost obsessive process of self-examination regarding the mental illness one is suffering. The result, in the case of Artaud, is a fascinating and disturbing look into the mind of a schizophrenic. This same rare combination was present in Daniel Schreber, and hence the continued interest in his *Memoirs of My Nervous Illness*. This fascination with Artaud was present from the beginning. In his famous correspondence with Artaud, for example, Jacques Rivière noted the striking contrast between 'the extraordinary precision of your [Artaud's] self-diagnosis and the vagueness, or at least the formlessness, of your creative efforts.'[29] How could Artaud be so precise, so exacting in his self-examination, and yet submit poetry for publication which, in the words of Rivière, fails to 'succeed in creating a sufficient unity of impression.'[30] It was precisely this striking contrast, or the window which Artaud's writings opened onto the mind of a schizophrenic, which ultimately led Rivière to ask Artaud to publish their correspondence. This interest in Artaud has continued unabated.

From our perspective, Artaud's writings are no less interesting. As both Deleuze and Derrida note, the problem for Artaud was one of thinking, of being able to think something. Thus, when responding to Rivière's criticism that his poems lack a 'unity of impression,' Artaud says that it 'must be attributed not to a lack of practice, a lack of control over the instrument I was handling ... but to a central collapse of the soul, to a kind of erosion, both essential and fleeting, of the thought ... to an abnormal separation of the elements of thought.'[31] What is needed, Artaud says later, is to in some way 'restore to my mind the concentration of its forces, the cohesion that it lacks, the constancy of its tension, the consistency of its own substance.'[32] In other words, the elements of thought need to be systematically gathered together to form the cohesion and consistency which would then crystallize into the creation of something that is thought, or a poem with 'unity of impression.' Artaud states this need explicitly: 'A man possesses himself in flashes, and even when he possesses himself, he does not reach himself completely. He does not realize *that constant cohesion of his forces without which all true creation is impossible.*'[33] And again in another letter, Artaud complains that at

> the moment the soul is preparing to organize its wealth, its discoveries, this revelation, at that unconscious moment when the thing is on the point of coming forth, a superior and evil will attacks the soul like a poison, attacks the mass consisting of word and image, attacks the mass of feeling, and leaves me panting as if at the very door of life.[34]

It is for these reasons that Artaud opened his first letter to Rivière with the confession that

> I suffer from a horrible sickness of the mind. My thought abandons me at every level. From the simple fact of thought to the external fact of its materialization in words. Words, shapes of sentences, internal directions of thought, simple reactions of the mind – I am in constant pursuit of my intellectual being.[35]

Artaud's observations of his mental state, and his interpretations of what is going on, are echoed by many psychologists who have studied schizophrenia. Andras Angyal, for example, in an essay written on schizophrenia in 1939, argues that 'the thinking of the schizophrenic patient is not impaired so far as apprehending of relationships is concerned; the schizophrenic – when he fails in the solution of an intellectual task – fails in the apprehension of system-connections.'[36] More recently, Anton Ehrenzweig has reaffirmed this view of what is going on in schizophrenic thought processes. What is interesting in Ehrenzweig's work, however, is that he explores the workings of the schizophrenic mind by examining artworks, and in doing this he will come close to the position Deleuze and Guattari put forward. As he puts it,

> Psychosis and creativity may be two sides of the same coin. Both are in a sense self-destructive. But while the creative man can absorb the ego's

temporary decomposition into the rhythm of creativity and achieve self-regeneration, the psychotic is left only with the first schizoid phase of creativity. He has not learned to dedifferentiate the scattered fragments of his surface ego.[37]

In order to think, or in order to create (which are for Deleuze one and the same thing),[38] the elements of thought must be gathered into a coherent system of interconnections, or they must be 'dedifferentiated.' Artaud recognized this need, as well as his inability to attain it; or, in the words of Angyal and Ehrenzweig, Artaud recognized his inabiltity to apprehend 'system-connections,' 'to dedifferentiate the scattered fragments of his surface ego.' Where Derrida's and Deleuze's interest with these issues is most relevant, is not with the causes or reasons why the schizophrenic has lost his/her hold on system, but rather with the philosophical implications the schizophrenic brings to bear on understanding the relationship between thought and system. In particular, what they focus on are Artaud's statements concerning what he believes needs to go right for him to be 'normal,' for him to find and establish his 'intellectual being.' What, in other words, is the condition which allows for the possibility of systematic unity, coherence, and consistency, and thus for the possibility of thought and creativity? These are obviously important philosophical questions, and it is therefore no surprise that Derrida and Deleuze (who are simply two among many) will attempt to mine philosophical insights out of the writings of Artaud.

When Artaud expresses himself regarding what is needed to generate the systematic coherence he so desperately wants yet lacks, he will often speak of a 'powerlessness' or impower (*impouvoir*) of thought which is closely tied in some way to a process whereby the elements of thought are 'crystallized.'[39] Expressed in other terms, Artaud says, 'Everything depends on a certain flocculation of things, on the clustering of all these mental gems around a point which has yet to be found.'[40] What is this point, or what is the seed or imperfection that 'crystallizes' the elements of thought into a systematic, coherent, and complete whole? Artaud struggled with this issue throughout his life. He clearly saw the nature of his own incapacities (as Rivière and others saw), and he continually attempted to express the hope and desire for the missing point, the missing crystallizing seed, that would enable him to overcome these incapacities. In his late writings, this hope was expressed as the desire to become a body without organs, as in the following lines from the radio broadcast 'To Have Done with the Judgment of God':

Man is sick because he is badly constructed.
We must make up our minds to strip him bare in order to scrape
off that animalcule that itches him mortally,

god,
and with god
his organs.

For you can tie me up if you wish,
but there is nothing more useless than an organ.

When you will have made him a body without organs,
then you will have delivered him from his automatic reactions
and restored him to his true freedom.

Then you will teach him again to dance wrong side out
as in the frenzy of dance halls
and this wrong side out will be his real place.[41]

Deleuze and Guattari will read much into Artaud's call to become a
body without organs. An entire chapter from *A Thousand Plateaus* is
titled 'How Do You Make Yourself a Body without Organs?' and the
date preceding this title is 28 November 1947, which was the date originally planned for the radio broadcast of 'To Have Done with the Judgment of God.' But before clarifying the manner in which Deleuze and
Guattari read Artaud, it is nonetheless clear that one can easily be led to
conclude that they, too, as with Artaud, long for a lost homeland, a
deeply buried purity and freedom which has since been covered over by
layers of impurities (in this case, organs) which only serve to hinder the
freedom necessary for thought and creativity. If this is how Artaud is to
be read, it is evident, then, that his longing is a metaphysical longing, a
striving to regain a lost presence. This is precisely the reading Derrida
has of Artaud (at least in his early writings on Artaud).[42] Before turning
to Deleuze and Guattari's reading of Artaud, or, better put, to their use
of Artaud, we will first address Derrida's reading of Artaud. In this way,
we can better focus upon whether Derrida's critique of Artaud applies
to Deleuze and Guattari as well, and in turn to their critique of Derrida
(or, at least, our interpretation of what their critique would be).

On an initial reading of Artaud, Derrida sees in Artaud a profound
critique of the metaphysical tradition. In his critique of traditional the-

atre (discussed at greatest length in *Theater and Its Double*), Artaud sets forth the notion of a theatre of cruelty. This theatre, Derrida argues, reacts against 'the differences upon which the metaphysics of Occidental theater lives (author-text/director-actors), its differentiation and its divisions, transform the "slaves" into commentators, that is, into organs.'[43] The resulting theatre would have no text which actors would rehearse and repeat, over and over again; the emphasis, instead, will be on the living gestures of the person on stage. With this move, Derrida believes that although Artaud seeks to undermine the traditional duality between author-text/director-actors, what he calls to replace it is simply the pure presence of an actor to himself, a presence without interior differences.

To support this reading, Derrida turns to Artaud's comments concerning the body without organs. Derrida notes that for Artaud 'the division of the body into organs, the difference interior to the flesh, opens the lack through which the body becomes absent from itself ...'[44] He cites Artaud: 'The body is the body, / it is alone / and has no need of organs, / the body is never an organism, / organisms are the enemies of bodies, / *everything one does transpires by itself without the aid of any organ*, / every organ is a parasite, / it overlaps with a parasitic function / destined to bring into existence a being which should not be there.'[45] The 'organ,' Derrida adds, 'thus welcomes the difference of the stranger into my body: it is always the organ of my ruin ...' Moreover, since 'everything one does transpires by itself without the aid of any organ,' it is therefore the body without organs which possesses the autonomous means of doing something – that is, thinking and creating. The desire for a pure theatre of cruelty, a theatre without the metaphysical dualities of the past, is of a piece, according to Derrida, with Artaud's desire to become a body without organs, or the free, autonomous body which does not suffer from internal divisions and the attendant possibility that something strange or other might insinuate itself by virtue of these differences. Derrida thus concludes by arguing that for Artaud, 'the reconstitution of the body must be autarchic; it cannot be given any assistance and the body must be remade of a single piece.' He then quotes Artaud: 'It is / I / who / will be / remade / by me / myself / entirely / ... by myself / who am body / and have no regions within me.'[46] The theatre of cruelty is Artaud's answer, as Derrida reads him, to this call to the 'reconstitution of the body.' It is with this theatre, finally, that all difference will be purged: 'Restored to its absolute and terrifying proximity, the stage of cruelty will thus return me to the autarchic immediacy of my birth, my body and my speech. Where has Artaud better defined the stage of cruelty than in Here Lies, outside any apparent reference to theater: "I, Antonin Artaud, am my son, / my father, my mother / and myself."'[47]

Derrida will return to this last quote in another essay devoted to Artaud written at around the same time, 'The Theater of Cruelty.' Here, too, Derrida argues that the quote is exemplary of Artaud's effort to restore a lost presence and purity. In this essay, Derrida reiterates the point that Artaud 'wanted to save the purity of a presence without interior difference and without repetition ... Is it not Artaud who wants to reduce the archi-state [i.e., reduce it to "the purity of a presence without interior difference"] when he writes in Here Lies: "I Antonin Artaud, am my son, / my father, my mother, / and myself."'[48] Therefore, despite his critique of the traditional metaphysical dualities of the theatre, Artaud's theater of cruelty is in the end, according to Derrida, a theatre which in turn repeats the metaphysical tradition which thinks in terms of a pure, self-identical presence. Much as Aristotle's metaphysical understanding of time presupposes another, non-metaphysical understanding, so too, in Derrida's summation of Artaud, does Artaud's nonmetaphysical theatre of cruelty rely on metaphysics: 'One entire side of his [Artaud's] discourse destroys a tradition which lives within difference, alienation, and negativity without seeing their origin and necessity. To reawaken this tradition, Artaud, in sum, recalls it to its own motifs: self-presence, unity, self-identity, the proper, etc. In this sense, Artaud's "metaphysics," at its most critical moments, fulfills the most profound and permanent ambition of Western metaphysics.'[49]

In light of Derrida's critique of Artaud, the question we turn to now is whether Deleuze and Guattari's call to become a body without organs is susceptible to a similar critique. In Difference and Repetition, Deleuze repeatedly argues for a philosophy of difference, for a philosophy which does not, as he argues traditional metaphysics has done, reduce an understanding of difference to a fundamental identity. He calls for a philosophy which thinks 'difference in itself.' If Derrida's critique of Artaud applies to Deleuze and Guattari, then it would seem that they ultimately do think difference in terms of identity, or they fail to see the persistence of metaphysics within Artaud (and hence in their own theory of chaos as the excessive fullness which is the condition for the possibility of identity). Yet Deleuze and Guattari do recognize that Artaud's statements are open to a Derridean-style critique. In the chapter previously mentioned, 'How to Become a Body without Organs,' Deleuze and Guattari, in speaking of Artaud's play *Heliogabalus*, claim that 'heliogabalus and experimentation have the same formula: anarchy and unity are one and the same thing, not the unity of the One [i.e., body without organs as One], but a much stranger unity that applies only to the multiple.' In a footnote connected with this passage, Deleuze and Guattari recognize that 'it is true that Artaud still presents the identity of the One and the Multiple as a dialectical unity, one that reduces the multiple by gathering it into the One ... but this is a manner of speaking, for from the beginning multiplicity surpasses all opposition and does away with dialectical movement.'[50] As Deleuze and Guattari understand Artaud's call to become a body without organs, then, it is not a call to become that which would unify and encompass the organs (which Derrida recognized as well), nor is the body without organs *other* than the organs (as Derrida does imply).[51] Derrida acknowledges Artaud's aversion to the organization and differentiation inherent to the body with organs,[52] but for Derrida the way Artaud avoids this organization is to call for a body without organs that is completely undifferentiated, that is a pure presence to itself. This, we saw, was the significance for Derrida of Artaud's enigmatic utterance 'I Antonin Artaud, am my son, my father, my mother, and myself.' Deleuze and Guattari, on the other hand, agree that the body without organs is offered as an alternative in opposition to the organization of the body with organs, but it is not put forward as something that is in itself undifferentiated: 'The BwO is opposed not to the organs but to that organization of the organs called the organism ... the BwO and its 'true organs,' which must be composed and positioned, are opposed to the organism.'[53] The BwO is not undifferentiated, but has its own inner differentiation, its composed and positioned "true organs," and it is in this manner, then, that Deleuze and Guattari can read Artaud's call for a BwO as not being a call for a One in opposition to the multiple.

But what is this BwO, if it is neither the pure, self-identical One in opposition to the multiple, nor the organization that is the organism? In *Anti-Oedipus*, the BwO is defined as matter and substance: 'The body without organs is the matter that always fills space to given degrees of intensity, and the partial objects [e.g., organs] are these degrees, these intensive parts that produce the real in space starting from matter as intensity = 0. The body without organs is the immanent substance, in the most Spinozist sense of the word ...'[54] This view is reiterated again in *A Thousand Plateaus*: 'The BwO is that glacial reality where the alluvions, sedimentations, coagulations, foldings, and recoilings that compose an organism ... occur.'[55] The organs are conditioned by this immanent substance, this glacial reality, or the organs are, to use Artaud's wording, 'parasitic' upon this BwO.[56] The BwO, as we will see, is understood by Deleuze and Guattari to be the 'strange unity' which neither is opposed to the organs, nor is the unity of the One; and it is this 'strange unity' which is key to how the BwO as immanent substance is used to clarify the relationship between the organs and their condition of possibility.

In *Anti-Oedipus*, where Deleuze and Guattari first develop the notion of a body without organs, they stress the role of the BwO in the processes of production, in particular, the productions of desire. Within these processes, the BwO is not a pre-existent ether or substance which makes production possible, and likewise the identity of that which is produced; rather, the BwO is itself produced within the production process itself: 'The body without organs is nonproductive; nonetheless it is produced, at a certain place and a certain time in the connective synthesis, as the identity of producing and the product ... It is perpetually reinserted into the process of production.'[57] It is the nature of the BwO as the identity of 'producing and the product' which is important in this context. As Deleuze and Guattari elaborate, 'Producing, a product: a producing/product identity. It is this identity that constitutes a third term in the linear series: an enormous undifferentiated object. Everything stops dead for a moment, everything freezes in place – and the whole process will begin over again.'[58] In the series between producers and products, a product can only in turn become a producer, or continue the series, if it is both product and producer. The body without organs is the condition which allows for the connective links and series to continue, or as they put it, 'The body without organs, the unproductive, unconsumable, serves as a surface for the recording of the entire process of production of desire.'[59] In other words, identifiable processes of production presuppose a condition that allows for the relationship between producer and produced to be identified, and yet this condition is not to be identified with the producer (it is non-productive), nor with the produced, if by this it is meant that it is produced by something other. Deleuze and Guattari's notion of the body without organs is an effort to account for the connections between producer and produced without presupposing a transcendent, organizing Law which predetermines the connections that will occur (e.g., the Judgment of God).[60]

To clarify by means of an example, Deleuze and Guattari claim early on that capital is a body without organs: 'Capital is indeed the body without organs of the capitalist, or rather of the capitalist being.'[61] In a traditional market economy, buyers and sellers enter into mutual agreements that are assumed to benefit both parties. Market forces of supply and demand determine the price a seller can ask and expect to receive, as well as the price a buyer can expect to pay. In a barter-based market economy, transactions are determined by what specific needs the potential parties can satisfy (i.e., do they have what I need, such as wheat, wool, fish, etc.?). With the advent of money, the condition for successful transaction has been abstracted from specific needs, and thus money becomes a condition for unrestricted transactions between buyers and sellers (or they are only restricted by the amount of money one has). As money becomes capital, money becomes abstracted from a market-based economy where price is largely determined by the relationship between supply and demand. Capital becomes a means of determining and fixing the prices which buyers and sellers ultimately agree to. By amassing a large storehouse of a given commodity, the capitalist can cause a shortage and then sell his stockpile for a profit, and with this profit he can turn around and amass another quantity of goods and repeat the same process over again. It does not matter what the commodity is. As capital it is merely a means of determining and fixing prices in order to create more capital. This is where we can see why Deleuze and Guattari refer to capital as the 'body without organs of the capitalist.' Capital is neither to be identified with the capitalist who buys the goods and commodities, nor is capital a commodity.[62] Capital is what allows for the possibility of the relationship between the capitalist and these goods and commodities. Capital is the presupposed condition for the relationships that emerge between capitalists and commodities, or capital is the recording surface for the various connections these relationships will establish. Similarly, capital is related to other bodies without organs, which in turn creates the possibility for yet other relationships and connections to be established. For example, capitalists may set up relationships with people's desires, or they may establish relationships with weather-related phenomena (such as an agricultural commodites speculator might do), or even with genetic material (as in capitalist investment in genetic research). The point for Deleuze and Guattari is that capital, as body without organs, is the unstructured, unformed medium, or it is the fundamental both/and (producer and produced) which is presupposed by the structured, formed, and identifiable relationships between capitalist and commodity, or the relationships which emerge when capital connects with other unstructured flows (BwOs), such as with the dynamic relationship between the hydrosphere and atmosphere which is the BwO presupposed by the hurricanes, pressure systems, wind currents, and temperature gradients (e.g., El Niño) which emerge upon (i.e., are recorded on) this BwO. A capitalist connects with this BwO, for instance, when speculating on coffee futures (e.g., a capitalist might risk losing a fortune if there is a bad freeze in Brazil).[63]

We are now in a better position to understand why Deleuze and Guattari consistently referred to the BwO in terms of 'matter' or 'immanent substance.' The BwO is not a conceptual matter, or a heuristic device (or what Kant might call a regulative principle) which enables one to understand the processes one observes and identifies; rather, the BwO is through and through a material condition for the possibility of identifying a producer and a product, capitalist and commodity, or even for identifying hurricanes, as discussed above. This material condition, however, although inseparable from those things which come to be identified, is not to be confused with them. Thus, while capital is inseparable from capitalist and commodity, it is not strictly to be identified with either; similarly, while the dynamic relationship between hydrosphere and atmosphere is inseparable from hurricanes and pressure systems, it is also not to be confused with them. The BwO, instead, is to be understood as the 'strange unity' these identifiable entities and relationships presuppose. The BwO is indeed a unity, but not a unity in the traditional, metaphysical sense – namely, a unity whereby diverse elements are gathered by a transcendent and/or privileged element (e.g., the Judgment of God). Thus, the BwO is not an other which restores a lost unity or presence; it is the 'strange unity' whereby 'anarchy and union are one,' or it is the consistency necessary for the emergence of identifiable, non-strange unities. To clarify this latter point, we need to turn to the *self-engendering* aspect of the BwO, or to what Derrida saw as yet another metaphysical attempt on the part of Artaud to purge all difference and otherness.

In Deleuze and Guattari's reading of Artaud's statement that he is his son, father, mother, and himself, they do not follow Derrida and claim that this is evidence that the BwO lacks differentiation. To the contrary, they see the BwO as self-engendered, or as autarchic, and thus while it is not to be seen as a product of a distinct producer, it is, as the self-engendered condition for identifying producers and products, the strange unity which is inseparable from all potentially identifiable producers and products. Deleuze and Guattari are clear on this point:

The full body without organs is produced as antiproduction, that is to say it intervenes within the process as such for the sole purpose of rejecting any attempt to impose on it any sort of triangulation implying that it was produced by parents. How could this body have been produced by parents, when by its nature it is such eloquent witness of its own self-production, of its own engendering of itself ... Yes, I have been my father and I have been my son. 'I, Antonin Artaud, am my son, my father, my mother, and myself.'[64]

As the strange unity presupposed by all identifiable processes of production, including identifiable producers and products, the BwO is affirmed within each and every different process. Far from being a rejection of difference, a purging of otherness, the BwO is the very affirmation of difference, or it is what is affirmed anytime something identifiable is produced (or identified as producing). What the BwO does reject, as Deleuze and Guattari made clear, is the view which claims that the processes of production presuppose a transcendent other, an other that is identifiably distinct. Deleuze and Guattari thus reject a transcendent other and difference, or they follow Artaud in being done with the judgment of God, and argue instead, in Spinozist fashion, for an immanent other and difference, a non-identifiable difference which is immanent to the processes of production. This is why the BwO is referred to as an 'immanent substance.' Moreover, as a self-produced, self-engendered substance which is immanent to, and affirmed within every identifiable process, the BwO will by its nature be complete. As the immanent difference and substance presupposed and affirmed within processes of production, the BwO is not complete by virtue of a reference to an objective marker or goal. Deleuze and Guattari reject, as we have seen, an understanding of the BwO in terms of such transcendent objects; nor is the BwO complete by virtue of some other that has come to complete it, for this too would presuppose a transcendent other. The BwO is complete precisely because it is the self-produced substance which is the condition for the possibility of conceiving transcendent objects and goals.[65] The BwO is complete in itself, and not because of some other. Again, Deleuze and Guattari are clear on this point as well:

For the new earth is not to be found in the neurotic or perverse reterritorializations that arrest the process or assign it goals; it is no more behind than ahead, it coincides with the completion of the process of desiring-production, this process that is always and already complete as it proceeds, and as long as it proceeds.[66]

Much of Deleuze and Guattari's later work, in particular, in *A Thousand Plateaus* and *What Is Philosophy?*, can be understood as a continuing elaboration upon this theme of the BwO as the self-produced, complete-in-itself condition for processes whereby goals and products are produced and identified. An important addition to these later works is the notion of a 'plane of consistency.' We have mentioned earlier that the strange unity of the BwO was to be understood as the consistency which allowed for the emergence of identifiable unities and objects (e.g., producers and products). With the notion of a plane of consistency, this theme becomes explicit. Thus, in *A Thousand Plateaus*, Deleuze and Guattari argue that 'a plateau is a piece of immanence. Every BwO is itself a plateau in communication with other plateaus on the plane of consistency. The BwO is a component of passage.'[67] If we will recall our earlier reference to the BwO as being composed of 'true organs,' organs which are themselves positioned, the plane of consistency is the standard or criterion they offer for a BwO which can successfully maintain and increase its connections with other BwOs, or with other unformed flows. And in the processes which presuppose a BwO, the plane of consistency is only one manner in which the BwO can be expressed and composed, and more precisely it is how Deleuze and Guattari believe it ought to be expressed: 'all becomings are written like sorcerer's drawings on this plane of consistency, which is the ultimate Door providing a way out for them. This is the only criterion to prevent them from bogging down, or veering into the void.'[68] In other words, the self-production of the BwO does not necessarily result in a consistency which allows for the emergence of identifiable processes. The self-production can, to reintroduce a theme from chapter 3, either get bogged down or veer into the void. The plane of consistency is what is drawn when the BwO avoids either of these two alternatives. As Deleuze and Guattari put it,

... the totality of all BwOs can be obtained on the plane of consistency only by means of an abstract machine capable of covering and even creating it [i.e., the plane of consistency], by assemblages capable of plugging into desire, effectively taking charge of desires, of assuring their continuous connections and transversal tie-ins. Otherwise, the BwO's of the plane will remain separated by genus, marginalized, reduced to means of bordering, while on the 'other plane' the emptied or cancerous doubles will triumph.[69]

Or again,

> The material problem confronting schizoanalysis is knowing whether we have it within our means to make the selection, to distinguish the BwO from its doubles: empty, vitreous bodies, cancerous bodies, totalitarian and fascist ... distinguishing within desire between that which pertains to stratic proliferation, or else too-violent destratification, and that which pertains to the construction of the plane of consistency.[70]

The concept of a BwO being drawn into a plane of consistency in contrast to the cancerous and fascist bodies is where we see Deleuze and Guattari developing the notion of a dynamic system. A dynamic system that is in process is complete in itself as process, and not because of some objective, transcendent goal or other. A dynamic system, however, is a system in accordance with the 'criterion' of the plane of consistency. Deleuze and Guattari's concern, or 'the material problem confronting schizoanalysis,' is to discern and hopefully avoid the stratified, closed systems, the systems whereby the multiple is gathered under the unity and dictatorship of the One. A dynamic system is thus not a system as Hegel understood it, nor even as Heidegger implicitly understood it. On the other hand, a dynamic system is a unity, a 'strange unity,' such that the elements are in a relationship of consistency with one another, and it is this consistency that allows the dynamic system to continue functioning, or to continue its processes of becoming. A dynamic system that veers towards the void becomes a cancerous system, a system whereby the unity explodes into an uncontrolled process that results in death. With the notion of a plane of consistency, therefore, Deleuze and Guattari have further clarified the manner in which a BwO is to be understood as the 'strange unity' which is neither the unity of the one, nor is it a chaos which lacks unity altogether. The BwO is a dynamic system, or we might say it is chaosmos, a system at the edge of chaos.[71]

With this understanding of a BwO as a dynamic system, we can further address the criticism Manfred Frank made of Derrida's work (discussed in chapter 1). Frank, it will be recalled, argued that in his rejection of Saussure's notion of system, Derrida left himself without any sense of completion or self-identity, and without this Derrida was unable to account for the emergence of meaning altogether. Derrida agreed with Saussure's move which rejected the intrinsic meaning of a word while arguing instead for the dependency of this meaning on a word's relationship to all the other words in the language. Where Derrida broke with Saussure, as we saw, was with Saussure's replacement of the self-identity and completeness of a word's meaning with the self-identity and completeness of the system of language. What Derrida argues for, instead, is a notion of *differance* which is an 'economic concept designating the production of differing/deferring.'[72] But this production of differing/deferring is a production without end, a necessarily incomplete production, as Derrida would admit; yet it is precisely this production of differing/deferring without completion that leaves Derrida, according to Frank, unable to account for any identifiable meaning. With Deleuze and Guattari's notion of the BwO as a dynamic system, we can see that this problem is avoided. Quite simply, the BwO is complete in itself, or it is a 'process that is always and already complete as it proceeds, and as long as it proceeds.' Identifiable meanings can be accounted for, then, if one sees them as conditioned by language as a dynamic system. At the same time, language is not a closed system, or a system that is objectively complete and immune to change and variability. Far from it, language, as a dynamic system, is complete only insofar as it proceeds, or only to the extent that it is constantly becoming other. A language that is objectively complete, such as Latin, is dead. Deleuze and Guattari thus appear to avoid some of the criticisms that have been directed at Derrida.

But have we successfully salvaged Deleuze and Guattari from a Derridean-style critique? We have illustrated, by means of comparing their readings of Artaud, the clear differences between Deleuze and Derrida, but has this resolved the critical question concerning whether Deleuze's project presupposes notions Derrida himself criticized as demonstrating an unquestioned adherence to a metaphysics of presence? Before we turn to a further discussion of dynamic systems in Deleuze's work, we should first consider, then, some recent criticisms of Deleuze. These criticisms can be seen as an extension of Derrida's critique of the metaphysics of presence, but in this case they are directed at the heart of what is taken to be the unquestioned premise of Deleuze's approach to systems (or what we call his implicit theory of dynamic systems). Since Deleuze's theory is part of an effort to think difference without reducing it to identity, and if this theory presupposes an unquestioned identity, as the criticism we will discuss suggests, then Deleuze's theory of dynamic systems would indeed fall prey to the type of criticism we have seen Derrida put forward. It is to this criticism, and to the possible response to it, that we now turn.

III

The first major criticism of Deleuze is one that Derrida and others have directed at Bergson. Deleuze, as Constantin Boundas correctly points out, consistently incorporated Bergson's ideas throughout his writings; consequently, a critique of Bergson might quite logically be extended to Deleuze. In particular, the criticism is that Bergson's theory of time follows the Aristotelian model by thinking of time in terms of presence;[73] or, in applying this to Deleuze, Deleuze's conception of chaos as the excessive plentitude which is slowed in order for identifiable entities to emerge, this too can be taken to be an understanding in terms of presence. The argument against Begson, as found in Derrida, is that while Bergson criticized the notion of the 'possible as possible,' a notion which subordinates the possible to the actual and thus understands time in terms of the realization (actualization) of the possible, Bergson nevertheless maintained a duality between the virtual and the actual which largely repeats Aristotle. The primary difference between Bergson and Aristotle is that whereas Aristotle claims the possible lacks reality until actualized, Bergson argues that both the virtual and actual are real. The resulting question, then, is to account for the difference between the virtual and the actual, or how can this difference be understood in a non-Aristotelian manner? Boundas noted this problem when he stated that 'Deleuze-Bergson will have to account for the formation of closed, "extended" or "cool" systems inside the open-ended, intensive chaosmic virtual.'[74] To put this in terms we will discuss below, how do equilibrium systems arise from dynamic, far-from-equilibrium systems?

The answer Deleuze develops in his book *Difference and Repetition* to explain the actualization of the virtual centres around the dual terms differentiation/differenciation. Deleuze defines these terms as follows: 'Whereas differentiation determines the virtual content of the Idea as problem, differenciation expresses the actualization of this virtual and the constitution of solutions (by local integrations).'[75] To better clarify Deleuze's understanding of this process, we can turn now to Deleuze and Guattari's discussion of chaos, which they will also describe as the virtual which is real though not actual, that is, identifiable; or, in the words of Boundas, it is the 'chaosmic virtual.' Deleuze and

Guattari explicitly define chaos in their last collaborative work, *What Is Philosophy?*:

> Chaos is defined not so much by its disorder as by the infinite speed with which every form taking shape in it vanishes. It is a void that is not a nothingness but a virtual, containing all possible particles and drawing out all possible forms, which spring up only to disappear immediately, without consistency or reference, without consequence.[76]

Chaos is thus not to be understood in terms of an order or identity which it negates – that is, dis-order. Chaos will lack consistency, not because it is the negation of consistency and order, but rather because it contains elements of infinite speed that exceed consistency. Chaos is therefore not a lack or negation of consistency and order; it is an excess that has not been caught within the paramaters of consistency. More importantly, chaos is the condition for the possibility of the consistent systems which emerge by virtue of what Deleuze and Guattari will call abstract machines, the machines which allow for the slowing down of infinite speeds, and hence for the possibility of consistency.

To explain how there can be such infinite speeds in the first place, and then how they can be transformed into finite, consistent speeds, Deleuze will frequently refer to differential calculus. In discussing the French mathematician Albert Lautman, for example, Deleuze notes that Lautman makes a fundamental distinction between the 'distribution of individual points in a field of vectors,' and 'the integral curves in their neighborhood.'[77] The manner in which these points are distributed in the field is the central issue. Chaos, on Deleuze's reading, consists of infinitesimal vectors which cannot be reduced to a level of consistency, or in the language of differential equations, these points cannot be integrated. The distribution of individual points must therefore be transformed into an integrable distribution of points, or points consistent enough for the integral curves to be drawn in their neighbourhood. The abstract machine, as we will further clarify below, performs the function of filtering the field of vectors (chaos), and transforms it into an integrable distribution. This integrable distribution is what Deleuze refers to as *differentiation*, or the virtual content of the Idea as problem. The integration of these distributed points, or the integral curve in their neighbourhood, is, as Deleuze makes clear, 'the thing that brings about or *actualizes* relations between forces.'[78] Or, it is the *differenciation* of the integrable distribution, an integration which constitutes solutions to the problem.

Speaking in much these same terms in his work on Leibniz, Deleuze refers to a sense of 'anxiousness' arising from a confrontation with the non-integrable forces or vectors of chaos. What is needed, therefore, is a taming or subduing of this chaos, or what Deleuze will call an 'accord':

> I produce an accord each time I can establish in a sum of infinitely tiny things differential relations that will make possible an integration of the sum – in other words a clear and distinguished perception. It is a filter, a selection.[79]

These differential relations or series from which an integral curve is possible are not, however, differential series or relations that could, if taken *in toto*, converge upon a complete and total picture of the universe. To assume this would be to attribute a comprehensive unity or identity to the universe, an identity the differential series would approximate. It is clear this is the assumption Leibniz makes, for in discussing the monads in his *Monadology*, Leibniz uses the analogy of the perspectives upon a city to show that although there are an infinite number of monads that are different from one another (or, to use our terms, an infinite number of differential series), each monad nevertheless is a different expression of one and the same universe. Thus, 'as the same city regarded from different sides appears entirely different ... [similarly] there are an infinite number of universes [i.e., monads or differential series] which are, nevertheless, only the aspects of a single one.'[80] Deleuze, however, breaks with this faith in a pre-existent totality or identity, and it is with his notion of chaos that he will argue instead for a non-identifiable inconsistency which exceeds identity and is only identified once the chaos is filtered, or once an accord is produced. Consequently, for Deleuze, the relationship between differential series is not one of accord, as it was for Leibniz, but one of divergence wherein the excess of chaos entails the possibility of undermining the consistency and unity. Deleuze is explicit on this point:

> Each series tells a story: not different points of view on the same story, like the different points of view on the town we find in Leibniz, but completely distinct stories which unfold simultaneously. The basic series are divergent: not relatively, in the sense that one could retrace one's path and find a point of convergence, but absolutely divergent in the sense that the point or horizon of convergence lies in a chaos or is constantly displaced within that chaos.[81]

These divergent series are nonetheless put into relation with one another, or, despite their divergence lines of communication are opened. In his early work *Difference and Repetition*, for example, Deleuze speaks of the 'dark precursor' as that which, 'by virtue of its own power ... puts them [the heterogenous differential series] into immediate relation to one another ...'[82] Deleuze then immediately addresses the logical criticism of this position: if there is a 'dark precursor' which enables the heterogenous series to communicate, must there not then be an identity to this precursor, or to the abstract machine Deleuze and Guattari refer to later, and a resemblance between the two series which enables them to communicate with one another? Deleuze's response is that indeed 'there is an identity belonging to the precursor, and a resemblance between the series it causes to communicate. This "there is," however, remains perfectly indeterminate.' Deleuze will then ask, 'Are identity and resemblance here the preconditions of the functioning of the dark precursor, or are they, on the contrary, its effects?' Deleuze's answer will be that identity and resemblance are the effects of the dark precursor, and not vice versa; in other words, the precursor is the indeterminate, the absolutely indeterminate substance as discussed in chapter 2, that is real though neither individuated nor determined, and it is 'this' which makes individuation and determination possible.[83] The dark precursor thus functions much as Deleuze and Guattari will come to understand the BwO drawn into a plane of consistency: it is the virtual real which functions as a 'component of passage,' or it establishes connections between heterogenous series.

An example which Deleuze spends some time on to clarify these issues concerns the psychoanalytic theories surrounding the effect of repressed memories on present behaviour. The past, according to Deleuze, does not have the same status or identity as the present (i.e., just a past present). The past is therefore not related to the present in the sense that it is part of the same extended series of identities (i.e., presents). Nor does the past act on the present through resemblance – for example, the resemblance between a person in the past (one's mother for example) and a person in the present as an explanation for the repetition of certain (childlike) behaviours. Deleuze argues that this repetition of behaviour 'is constituted not from one present [past present] to another [present present], but between the two coexistent series [series of past and present] that these presents form in function of the virtual object [the dark precursor, or BwO].'[84] It is not the resemblance between the mother and a present person which accounts for the repetition of childhood patterns; rather, the virtual object is the indeterminate object which is to be identified with neither the mother nor the present person, and yet it is the condition which allows for the possibility of seeing the resemblance, and hence for the repetition of the behaviour.

The virtual is therefore not to be confused with an Aristotelian understanding of the possible. First, the virtual is real, whereas the possible is not; and secondly, the virtual does not resemble the actual, while the possible (in the manner of a blueprint) does resemble its actualization. The virtual is the indeterminate reality, or what Deleuze will often refer to as the paradoxical instance, which is presupposed by any integrable series, a series that can in turn be actualized (through differenciation). The reason the virtual is then able to draw a plane of consistency is precisely because it differs from itself, or it is the heterogeneity in itself (difference in itself) which allows for the possibility of drawing heterogenous points into a plane of consistency (or a BwO as discussed above). One should not conclude from this that there is a pre-existent chaos upon which these paradoxical, self-differing instances draw planes of consistency; rather, Deleuze's point is that when a BwO is composed, it will in turn compose a plane of consistency; however, an immanent possibility in this process is the drawing of a line that leads to chaos (cancerous bodies) or the line that bogs down in a proliferation of strata (fascist, empty bodies). When a BwO is composed, and not a fascist or cancerous body, then this composition necessarily presupposes, as a condition of possibility, the paradoxical, self-differing instance which is inseparable from the virtual, integrable BwO. Boundas makes much this same point concerning the virtual when he comments on what is necessary if the virtual is to be differenciated (i.e., integrable): 'What is differenciated must, first of all, differ from itself, and only the virtual is what differs from itself.'[85]

This last point brings us to one final criticism. Lutz Ellrich, in a recent article on Deleuze, has recognized the significance Deleuze places on the self-differing nature of the virtual. But this is just what causes problems for Deleuze, according to Ellrich. In Ellrich's reading of *Difference and Repetition*, the dark precursor (difference in itself) is able to relate difference to difference (i.e., relate heterogenous series) by virtue of difference itself.[86] For Ellrich, however, if this is the basis for a philosophy of difference, a philosophy which does not think difference in terms of identity, then Deleuze failed miserably. The reason for this is the presupposed identity of difference to itself, or difference must have identified itself as that which it is relating to in the process which draws heterogenous series into a plane of consistency. As Ellrich puts it, 'Difference can exclude identity from its referential figures only if it identifies the different, to which it connectively refers, as precisely what it itself is.'[87] Ellrich concludes by saying that 'in the final analysis, the inevitable band that joins what differs to what differs has no other alternative but to rely on precisely those mediating instances that anti-representational thought condemns.'[88] In other words, in the very process of setting forth a philosophy of difference which condemns and attempts to avoid relying upon the identity of representations, Deleuze ultimately had to rely upon this very identity – namely, the representational identity of difference to itself. Deleuze has not avoided what he thought could be avoided, and to this extent Ellrich believes Derrida at least recognized the necessity of falling prey to the illusions of identity, or, as we have discussed it above, the impossibility of setting forth an alternative philosophy, one which avoids repeating the metaphysics of presence.[89]

We can best respond to this criticism if we return to our understanding of the virtual as a dynamic system. In particular, we turn to an important passage from Deleuze where Deleuze discusses positivity (i.e., reality of the virtual). The key part of the passage reads as follows: 'But the fact, that real space has only three dimensions, that time is not a dimension of space, really means this: there is an efficacity, *a positivity of time that is identical to a "hesitation" of things and, in this way, creation in the world*.'[90] The important phrase in this quote is the positivity that is identical to 'a "hesitation" of things.' In terms of dynamic systems, this hesitation of things is equivalent to the edge of chaos, or it is that critical point (threshold point) in a dynamic system that is far from equilibrium where the possibility for bifurcating into a stable state is greatest. At a critical temperature, for example, and under the right conditions, heated oil will spontaneously generate a series of vortices. Prior to reaching this new, stable state, the heated oil will be in a period of transition far from the previous equilibrium state (when the oil was at room temperature), and yet not be at the new stable state either. This transition state, or what is called a phase transition state in dynamic systems theory, is best characterized as being at the edge of chaos. Such a state is not chaos, for it possesses enough consistency and order that it can settle into a stable state through bifurcation. An edge-of-chaos state is what we have been discussing, in Deleuze's terms, as the virtual BwO, and with this notion we can also begin to sketch our understanding of dynamic systems and then turn to address some of Ellrich's (and by extension Derrida's) criticisms.

First, a dynamic system at the edge of chaos is not strictly identifiable. That is, it is not a stable, identifiable state, but a state of 'hesitation,' a state that is neither the previous stable state nor yet the stable bifurcated states it might become. At the same time, such a dynamic system is not pure, undifferentiated chaos. Pure undifferentiated chaos would, as we saw Deleuze define it, lack all consistency and hence be incapable of being actualized into a stable, identifiable state. A dynamic system is not chaos but is at the edge of chaos, or it is chaosmos. Second, such dynamic systems are clearly inseparable from the identifiable, stable states which presuppose them. The heated oil at the edge of chaos is clearly inseparable from the oil which has entered the stable state (e.g., the vortices). Third, the virtual, non-actualized dynamic system is only non-actualized insofar as it has not settled into a stable state, but it is not something other, a possibility which lacks the reality of the actual. By prioritizing dynamic systems, we are not setting forth on behalf of Deleuze an alternative to the representational philosophies of presence. We are doing much the same as Derrida; we are simply arguing the point that stable, identifiable states and systems presuppose, as a condition of possibility, dynamic, virtual systems. Where criticisms such as Ellrich's gain their force is by assuming that this self-differing condition of possibility (the virtual) is something other than, or distinct from, identifiable states and systems. To the contrary, the virtual, dynamic system is self-differing precisely because it inheres or subsists in concrete, identifiable systems and states. The virtual, dynamic system is the condition for the possibility of becoming and change in such an identifiable system.

In Deleuze's first major work, a book on Hume, he sets forth a notion of transcendental empiricism. By traditional methodolgy and philosophical thinking, a transcendental empiricism is an oxymoron. For Deleuze, however, the oxymoron arises because of a tendency to succumb to what one might call, following Kant, a 'transcendental illusion.'[91] The illusion results, in this instance, from the tendency to assume that what is actual must resemble, in some way, the condition which allowed for these particular forms to emerge. With this illusion began the metaphysical tradition of differentiating between the possible and the actual, whereby the possible is subordinate to the actual which it in some manner resembles. Plato's Ideas are the classic case of an actual, true reality which is related, by means of resemblance, to the possible manifestations of these ideas in the world. Insofar as Ellrich assumes that the differentiating condition, the virtual difference in itself, is distinct from, or other than, the states it conditions, Ellrich too understands the virtual in terms of identity (he succumbs to this version of the transcendental illusion). It is clear Ellrich makes this assumption for he assumes that Deleuze, in his effort to think difference without recourse to identity, must think difference in a manner *distinct* and *separate* from traditional metaphysics and philosophy.

Deleuze, on the contrary, understands identifiable states and systems in terms of the virtual (i.e., dynamic systems), and this virtual is not a separate, identifiable existent apart from these identifiable systems; the virtual is inseparable from identifiable things and states. Moreover, and to return to our earlier point, the virtual is the hesitation in things which is the self-differing differentiating condition which allows for the possibility of identifying new states and things. Because this condition is inseparable from empirical states of affairs, including empirical systems, Deleuze will refer to his study of these conditions as a 'transcendental empiricism.' To repeat the words of Deleuze, this condition is a transcendental condition for the possibility of identifiable states and systems, but it is not other than these states and things; it is a '"hesitation" in things' which allows for the possibility of 'creation in the world'; it allows, as was Artaud's quest, for the engendering and creation of thought and its 'unity of impression.'[92]

To explain this notion of a dynamic system further, and to understand the manner in which a rethinking of system as dynamic system can further elaborate our earlier criticisms of Heidegger and Derrida – that is, Heidegger's continued adherence to system as self-identical and complete, and Derrida's rejection of system and turn to a self-differing function without completion – we will need to clarify further how a dynamic system is both self-differing and complete. It is to this rethinking of system that we now turn.

PART TWO

Rethinking System

6 Rethinking System

As our discussion of Derrida has pointed out, there is an acknowledged need (acknowledged by Derrida himself as well as many others) for a criterion whereby meaning can gain a foothold. Derrida is understandably hesitant to offer up the 'guard rails' and 'logic' that would legitimate one reading as acceptable and true and another as unacceptable and false. Any such offering would itself fall prey to a deconstructive reading, a reading that undermines and subverts the legitimacy and self-identity of the proposed criterion. Consequently, Derrida will read texts closely, and dare I say accurately, and he will accuse others (e.g., Searle) of a false reading of his own writings; yet despite this, he offers no basis for rendering these judgments and admits to being 'unsatisfied' with any criteria offered so far, regardless of the need for them and Derrida's own *implicit* reliance on them.

It is precisely Derrida's resistance (some would say *failure*) to setting forth an *explicit* logic and criterion for reading a text and interpreting its meaning which has been the source of much criticism of deconstruction. The standard objection is that with deconstruction (and, by association, Derrida) truth has been thrown out the window, and hence any reading goes. Interpretation is merely playing with a text, and it is a play without rules of right and wrong, true or false. Frank's objections to Derrida, discussed earlier, thrust at the very core of what Frank believes is a central inconsistency or failing in Derrida's philosophy. This failing is a natural consequence of there being no criteria whereby it can be judged whether or not one has grasped the meaning of a text. The criticism, to recap briefly, is that by exploding the system of Saussure (i.e., Saussure's theory that the meaning of a given word in a language depends upon its relationship to, and difference from, all the other words in the language), Derrida denies his theory the conditions which make identifiable meanings possible. For Derrida language is not a completed system or totality, a system which conditions (*à la* Saussure) the meaning of a word; as a result, Frank argues, Derrida is unable to account for meaning at all.

We have seen how most of these objections to Derrida, including Frank's, do not pay proper attention to the sophisticated and subtle attempts by Derrida to give a non-metaphysical account of meaning. Most notably, the critics have not given due notice to Derrida's admitted adherence to system, a system of 'traces' which functions as the condition for identifiable meanings. Such a system is greatly different from Saussure's understanding of system, but by continuing to rely upon a notion of system, Derrida makes great strides in setting forth a criterion which avoids the dual pitfalls of absolute relativism and irrationalism, on one side, and dogmatism, on the other. What is needed, we argue, is to develop further this understanding of system. Derrida's own efforts concerning system are, as we have seen (and as Gasché argues so well), part of an attempt to rethink, or deconstruct, Hegel's system. However, in the process of overturning Hegel's view of a system as something that is subordinate to a *self-identical* Idea, Derrida does not give adequate emphasis to the importance of *identity* within systems (or system as identity); and it is this lack of emphasis which we believe has left the door open to Derrida's critics.

What we shall do in this chapter is to reconsider, rethink, system. We will argue for a view of system wherein a system is complete and self-identical (or self-similar, as we will prefer to call it), but not in the sense that its identity is subordinate to a single or sole Idea. A system, we will claim, is to be understood as a chaosmos; that is, it *both* involves the identity and completeness of cosmos, *and* it entails a chaos which subverts this identity and completeness, and thus renders the system open, or, as we will see, dynamic. As a dynamic system, chaosmos is necessarily self-identical (self-similar) and complete, for without the integrity of this self-identity, a system could not function and perdure; and yet chaosmos is forever open to an outside it presupposes, an immanent chaos which both threatens the system and allows it to create novel adaptations. Adaptations to what? one may ask: to the chaos within/without, or to the chaos chaosmos *is*, and hence a dynamic system is a system that creates itself – that is, it creates and constitutes the identity it *is* in response and adaptation to the chaos it *is*. To be, in other words, is to become.

To elaborate this last point and further detail our understanding of system, and to relate this to issues discussed earlier in the context of Aristotle, Heidegger, Nietzsche, and Derrida, we will focus on the theme of expression and self-cause. In relating chaosmos to the themes of expression and self-cause, we will clarify the manner in which chaosmos both involves the identity necessary to account for meaning and interpretation (and therefore to address the concerns of Derrida's critics), and involves the chaos of non-sense which subverts a final, ultimate meaning and truth. In developing this argument, we will first explore the significance of system and self-cause within Whitehead's philosophy, in particular, his work *Process and Reality*. This should set the stage for Deleuze's discussions of self-cause, system, and expression, and in doing this, it will become clear both why Deleuze considers himself a Spinozist and why he admired Whitehead as one of the most important philosophers of the twentieth century.[1] With these philosophical themes in place, we will turn next to a discussion of chaos theory and self-organization (i.e., self-cause). Recent research in science lends further support to the notion of chaosmos we are developing here – namely, that chaosmos is a dynamic, self-organized system that is simultaneously complete and open. At this point we will be able to address the concerns with which we were left upon completing our discussion of Derrida. Within a self-organized, dynamic system, a criterion necessarily emerges which enables this system to continue to be, and it is with this criterion that one can say, for a given system, that this does or does not work, this is true or false. And with this, finally, we will turn to discuss how philosophy itself can be a dynamic system. Such a philosophical system would not be a completed work which is offered to the reader as a *fait accompli*, but instead its intent would be to engender philosophizing (to 'engender "thinking" in thought' as Deleuze put it), or it will be a process which, if successful, will be further developed in creative, novel ways as it is appropriated by readers and deployed as one of their own tools in their own processes of growth as a dynamic system.

Whitehead

The notions of 'process,' 'system,' and 'self-cause' are integral to the philosophy of Alfred North Whitehead and most especially to his work in *Process and Reality*. Whitehead states quite bluntly in beginning *Process and Reality* that speculative philosophy, which is what he will be engaging in, should attempt 'to frame a coherent, logical, necessary system of general ideas in terms of which every element of our experience can be interpreted.'[2] And in founding such a system, a speculative philosophy then seeks for an ultimate entity with which to found, relate, and interpret 'every element of our experience.' For Whitehead, 'in *all* philosophic theory there is an ultimate which is actual in virtue of its accidents. It is only then capable of characterization through its accidental embodiments, and apart from these accidents is devoid of actuality' (10). In Locke, for example, what is ultimate is substance, but this underlying reality is only actual 'in virtue of' its secondary properties (e.g., colour, shape, etc.). In traditional philosophy, such as Locke's, though Whitehead also discusses Aristotle, Hume, and Spinoza, what is taken to be ultimate is a subject that *is* in virtue of its predicates. Whitehead, to the contrary, argues that in his 'philosophy of organism this ultimate is termed "creativity."' (ibid.). In other words, rather than a static subject which bears its predicates, Whitehead argues that it is creativity, and creative process, which is in virtue of the accidents which actualize this process – and for Whitehead the exemplar accident to actualize creativity is God: 'and God is its [creativity's] primordial, non-temporal accident' (ibid.). Whitehead thus knowingly places his philosophy of organism in opposition to traditional Western philosophy and aligns it with 'some strains of Indian, or Chinese, thought,' and with Spinoza as we read him – 'One side [i.e., Eastern tradition] makes process ultimate; the other side [i.e., Western tradition] makes fact ultimate' (ibid.).

At the heart of Whitehead's efforts to develop the system of a philosophy of organism is the notion of an 'actual entity.' The 'actual world,' Whitehead explains, 'is a process, and the process is the becoming of actual entities' (27). And this process of becoming an actual entity involves the actualization, or what Whitehead calls concrescence, of many potentials: 'in the becoming of an actual entity, the *potential* unity of many entities – actual and non-actual – acquires the *real* unity of the one actual entity; so that the actual entity is the real concrescence of many potentials' (ibid.). As Whitehead will elaborate, an actual entity is simply the process of becoming actual, and in this process there is involved three distinct things. First, there is the actual entity *that* appropriates or prehends (Whitehead's term) the potentialities which become actual within the actual entity. Second, there is that which is prehended, or *what* it is that is being appropriated. And finally there is the manner in which this datum is prehended, or *how* the actual entity prehends it (28). Yet, as the subject involved within this process, Whitehead is quick to point out that an actual entity is not a static, self-identical entity which remains the same throughout the process of becoming actual. To the contrary, the actual entity creates itself, or is both the subject actualizing by means of prehension and it is the subject that is actualized upon completing this process. In order to capture this distinction between actualizing and actualized subject, and to distance himself from traditional Western philosophy, Whitehead introduces the distinction subject-superject:

> It is fundamental to the metaphysical doctrine of the philosophy of organism, that the notion of an actual entity as the unchanging subject of change is completely abandoned. An actual entity is at once the subject experiencing and the superject of its experiences. It is subject-superject, and neither half of this description can for a moment be lost sight of ... 'subject' is always to be construed as an abbreviation of 'subject-superject.' (34)

Each actual entity, in other words, is self-caused: it is its own reason and means for existence. As Whitehead puts it: 'It is to be noted that every actual entity, including God, is something individual for its own sake; and thereby transcends the rest of actuality ... To be *causa sui* means that the process of concrescence is its own reason for the decision in respect to the qualitative clothing of feeling' (106). An actual entity is both the subject that chooses what is prehended and how, and it is the superject that becomes by means of this decision. At the same time, however, an actual entity never becomes what it is; rather, it is by virtue of its becoming. Put another way, an actual entity is by virtue of the process whereby entities are prehended within its own self-actualization (i.e., its own self-causation). To say of an actual entity that it is, that it is complete, is to say that it is no longer in process, and hence its life is complete. Whitehead will consequently say that 'an actual entity has perished when it is complete' (99). Although its temporal life as process is complete, however, the specific manner in which an actual entity prehends and integrates elements within its own self-formation can in turn be prehended by other actual entities within their own processes of self-formation. An actual entity can live on, then, within other actual entities as part of what they appropriate in creating themselves. Whitehead refers to this as the objective immortality of an actual entity.

This notion of an objective immortality further clarifies how Whitehead's philosophy is a departure from traditional Western philosophy. By becoming that which another actual entity prehends in its own process of becoming, an actual entity is thus that which allows for the possibility of creativity. In other words, as the ultimate category for Whitehead, creativity is, to recall our earlier discussion, by virtue of its accidents – in this case, these are the actual entities which instantiate creativity in themselves and contribute to the creativity of other actual entities (i.e., objective immortality). Creativity and process are not to be understood in terms of the entities they serve – the traditional Western view; rather, actual entities are to be understood in terms of the creativity and process they serve.

Another point on which Whitehead breaks with traditional Western philosophy concerns the relationship between the temporal and the eternal. To some extent, Whitehead would list himself as being simply one in a series of footnotes to Plato, and in this case because he, Whitehead, claims that 'the things which are temporal arise by their participation in things which are eternal' (53). Where Whitehead breaks with the tradition, including Plato, is in arguing that the temporal and the eternal coexist within actual entities. This is a clear departure from Plato, who placed the eternal ideas in a separate realm from that of the temporal; but Whitehead would add that because the entire tradition of Western philosophy has seen facts as ultimate, it is subsequently condemned to see the eternal in terms of eternal things, whether Plato's Ideas, Spinoza's substance,[3] or Descartes' *res cogitans*. Whitehead, on the other hand, by emphasizing the ultimate nature of creativity, will subsequently understand the eternal as that which is inseparable from temporal, creative processes, but which is nevertheless not to be identified with these creative processes. Whitehead will most often refer to this as the mental pole of an actual entity – that is, it is the potentiality prehended within the self-formation of an actual entity, and a potentiality which can only be said *to be* (in contrast to Plato) when it is involved in such a process. This mental pole of potentiality and conceptuality (Whitehead's term) is inseparable, within an actual entity – and recall that in Whitehead's system there is nothing but actual entities – from its physical, temporal pole: 'each actuality is essentially bipolar, physical and mental. The integration of the physical and the mental side into a unity of experience is a self-formation which is a process of concrescence, and which by the principle of objective immortality characterizes the creativity which transcends it' (128). And again: 'Every actual entity is "in time" so far as its physical pole is concerned, and is "out of time" so far as its mental pole is concerned' (290).

Each actual entity, in summary, then, is a self-caused both/and – that is, both physical and mental, 'in time' and 'out of time.' And it is on the basis of this understanding of actual entities that Whitehead then turns to examine the traditional philosophical notion of facts. In short, rather than argue, as we have seen, that facts are what is ultimate, Whitehead will claim that facts are derivative of actual entities, or they are complexes and societies of actual entities: 'The philosophy of organism is a cell-theory of actuality. Each unit of fact is a cell-complex ...' (256). To say of something, to use Whitehead's favourite example, that this is a grey stone is not to refer to an actual entity, but instead to an objective complex and society of such entities. A society, as Whitehead defines it, is 'a nexus of actual entities' which are ordered in one of various ways. Without going into details, the grey stone is a nexus of actual entities which exemplifies a highly homogenous order with little diversity, but which can, subsequently, endure as this society, despite the many changes that might occur around it to less stable, though more highly structured and diverse, societies (e.g., a flower). This aspect of Whitehead's thought has been widely discussed and examined.[4] For our purposes, however, the importance of the notion of societies is that with this concept Whitehead comes close to setting forth the notion of what we have called chaosmos:

> Spread through the environment there may be many entities which cannot be assigned to any society of entities. The societies in an environment will constitute its orderly element, and the non-social actual entities will constitute its element of chaos. There is no reason, so far as our knowledge is concerned, to conceive the actual world as purely orderly, or as purely chaotic. (131)

The world, in fact, is composed of nothing but actual entities, and to the extent that these entities are integrated within the nexus of a society we have order, and the degree to which we have free-floating, nomadic actual entities we have chaos. The world, however, involves both, or it is chaosmos. Moreover, on this point Whitehead again cites his closeness to Plato: 'There is another point in which the organic philosophy only repeats Plato. In the *Timaeus* the origin of the present cosmic epoch is traced back to an aboriginal disorder, chaotic according to our ideals. This is the evolutionary doctrine of the philosophy of organism' (114). In other words, the origin of our 'cosmic epoch' is simply the result of the integration of nomadic actual entities into societies, and societies with ever-increasing diversity, structure, and (for Whitehead) intensity.

It is with this 'evolutionary doctrine' where the significance of God for Whitehead appears with its full force. First, according to Whitehead, it is 'the immanence of God [that] gives reason for the belief that pure chaos is intrinsically impossible' (131). Secondly, for Whitehead, God is the very 'principle of concretion,' by which he means that God is 'that actual entity from which each temporal concrescence receives that initial aim from which its self-causation starts' (286). God thus guarantees that the creative process, the process whereby an actual entity creates itself, can initiate and be successful. God's role in Whitehead's system is therefore quite crucial. 'God,' Whitehead states, 'is the presupposed actuality of conceptual operation, in unison of becoming with every other creative act' (406). By conceptual operation, Whitehead means the infinite possibilities of conceptual qualities, qualities abstracted from their physical, actual instantiations. For example, as a conceptual, abstract quality, red is boundless, or harbours an infinite number of possible realizations. Such conceptual qualities, however, and this is central to Whitehead's criticism of Plato, among others, do not pre-exist independently of the concrete, actual entities in which they inhere. To the contrary, the conceptual operation is the process wherein the abstract qualities are actualized, but actualized always within the constraints laid down by pre-existing actual entities – that is, the objective immortality of such entities. There is not, in itself, an infinite, boundless realm of abstract possibilities. As Whitehead argues, 'The "boundless, abstract possibility" means the creativity considered solely in reference to the possibilities of the intervention of eternal objects, and in abstraction from the objective intervention of actual entities belonging to any definite actual world, including God among the actualities abstracted from' (258) But such abstractions are precisely that: an abstraction from the 'objective intervention of actual entities'; and, as such, they presuppose the actual entities from which the abstract qualites are derived. Ultimately, however, there is nothing but actual entities, and the conceptual operation is simply the manner in which conceptual possibilities become realized within actual entities. And what assures that there is no boundless abstract realm is God, or God is presupposed by every novel, creative advance. Whitehead is clear on this point:

The universe includes a threefold creative act composed of (i) the one infinite conceptual realization, (ii) the multiple solidarity of free physical realizations in the temporal world, (iii) the ultimate unity of the multiplicity of actual fact with the primordial conceptual fact. If we conceive the first term and the last term in their unity over against the intermediate multiple freedom of physical realizations in the temporal world, we conceive of the patience of God, tenderly saving the turmoil of the intermediate world by the completion of his own nature. (408)

It is therefore the unity of God, or God as an actual entity, and hence God both as the subjective potentiality seeking realization and the subject (superject) that is realized and completed; it is this unity which is the condition which assures the harmony and systematic unity of the world of physical multiplicity and diversity. God therefore assures that the diversity of the world will not slip into boundless chaos and 'turmoil,' or God assures that nomadic actual entities will never gain the upper hand and will remain forever subordinate to the processes that result in ordered, structured societies. It is for this reason, then, that Whitehead claims God 'does not create the world, he saves it' (ibid.). It is with this latter point that our notion of chaosmos diverges, as we shall see.

Chaosmos and Expression

Before elaborating on this divergence, we will first sketch some key similarities and differences between Whitehead's notion of an actual entity and our use of the term 'expression.' As for a key similarity, the term 'expression,' as with Whitehead's understanding of an actual entity, implies a fundamental both/and – in particular, a subjective and objective component. An expression entails both a subject expressing itself by means of an expression, and that which is the expressed within the expression, or that which one hopes to express in any complete and successful expression, something someone else can in turn express to another, perhaps even in a foreign tongue. A second key similarity concerns the notion of self-cause; therefore, just as an actual entity is self-caused, so too is chaosmos, or we might say it expresses itself. In claiming that chaosmos expresses itself, or actualizes itself within its expressions, we in turn reiterate Whitehead's threefold division of the creative act (in this case, the expressive act). There is (i) chaosmos as expresser, or the boundless potentiality which seeks to be constrained and limited to a degree which allows for the possibility of identification (i.e., for some*thing* to be expressed); there is (ii) the expression itself, or the physical realization of an act of expression, a realization that can assume an indefinite variety (e.g., different languages); and finally, there is (iii) chaosmos as expressed, the identifiable, objective sense which can be translated from one language to another (one form of expression to another). It is the middle term, expression, which is significant for us, for expression, we will argue below, is the both/and that allows for the identification of an expresser (subjective-pole) and an expressed (objective-pole). Where this differs from Whitehead's threefold division is that whereas Whitehead argues that God is the condition which guarantees that the multiplicity of actual entities will be integrated into orderly societies and structures, we shall argue that there is no such condition. Order does emerge out of free, nomadic actual entities (or what we earlier referred to as the non-integrated points or vectors), but it is not guaranteed by a single, privileged condition (i.e., God as actual entity); rather, the chaos of nomadic entities and singularities self-organizes into ordered structures, and does so without a guiding, ordering condition. We will elaborate on this point in greater detail below when we discuss work in chaos theory and dynamic systems, but for now our concern has been simply to sketch where our approach differs from that of Whitehead. Despite this important difference, however, we remain indebted to Whitehead's work, and largely follow him in applying the threefold division to chaosmos. Consequently, the notion of chaosmos as boundless, infinite potentiality, corresponds to chaos; chaosmos as the expressed, the identifiable and objective, corresponds to cosmos; and the both/and aspect of expression is what we have called chaosmos. In the discussion to follow, we will argue that it is the both/and of expression (chaosmos) which is the condition of possibility for identifying the subjective and objective poles. Chaosmos, in other words, is, as expression, the condition for the possibility of asking the questions: who/what expresses chaosmos? And what is expressed in these expressions?

Our approach is clearly at odds with the traditional understanding of expression. An expression, as usually understood, presupposes the subject (expresser) / object (expressed) dualism, rather than the reverse. An expression, this argument runs, presupposes a subject who has something to say, and who realizes this intention within an expression. The problem with this argument, however, surfaces when one attempts to account for the relationship between what a subject intends or means by an act of expression and the meaning itself that completes this act. This problem haunted Husserl's efforts to account adequately for the relationship between the intentionality of consciousness and the objects intended by this consciousness; most notably this gives rise to the problem of accounting for an-other consciousness that is not merely a correlate, or analogue, of one's own intending consciousness.[5] One way to resolve this problem, and this is the tactic Husserl and others have taken, is to posit a paradoxical entity which is simultaneously intending and intended, subject and object, expresser and expressed, and then to argue that it is this paradoxical element which is the condition for differentiating between an intending and intended consciousness, subject and object, expresser and expressed.[6] With respect to the latter distinction, which is our primary concern here, the famous linguist Louis Hjelmslev takes just this approach when he argues that the sign, or what he also calls sign-function, paradoxical as it may be, is the condition for distinguishing and relating both expresser and expressed:

> The sign is, then – paradoxical as it may seem – a sign for a content-substance and a sign for an expression-substance. It is in this sense that the sign can be said to be a sign for something. On the other hand, we see no justification for calling the sign a sign merely for the content-substance, or (what nobody has thought of, to be sure) merely for the expression-substance. The sign is a two-sided entity, with a Janus-like perspective in two directions, and with effect in two respects: 'outwards' toward the expression-substance and 'inwards' toward the content-substance.[7]

The sign, as with our notion 'expression,' is a two-sided entity, or a both/and entity; it is directed towards both expresser (expression-substance) and expressed (content-substance). This understanding of expression is a philosophically useful concept for several reasons. First, the concept 'expression' provides an intuitively straightforward way of approaching the problem of one and many – that is, the problem, as discussed earlier with respect to Aristotle, of several entities maintaining their individuality and differentiation from others, but at the same time continuing to be, and hence be One with everything else that is (*ousia*). In expression such a relationship between one and many occurs as a matter of course: many different expressions, in many different languages, can express one sense or meaning. A second use of the concept 'expression' echoes Hjelmslev's use of the notion 'sign.' In short, it answers the question of how to relate the expressions we utter to the intention of a speaker and the intended meaning being expressed. As a paradoxical both/and, an expression is turned both towards the subject who expresses him/herself and towards the objective content that is being expressed. When I express myself, I both take my expressions to be an adequate expression of my subjective state (if I have expressed myself well, that is) and I take them to bear an objective content that *others* can understand. This everyday use of expressions as a means of relating one's self to others emerges, then, as a solution to the problem left by Descartes. This well-known problem follows upon Descartes' claim that the mind (*res cogitans*) and fact of thinking cannot be doubted since it is known in and through itself; however, when it comes to knowledge of other things, or things that we know through their attributes, the difficulty is to show that the mind can come to know things *other* than itself. Descartes' solution to this problem entailed knowing the cause through the caused, and hence knowledge of an effect expresses knowledge of its cause; or, to narrow in on Descartes' argument, knowledge of an infinite perfection expresses a knowledge of the cause of this knowledge, namely, God. But to know God is to know something other, and with this move the door to knowledge of the world of extended things (*res extensa*) is opened.

This solution to the problem was inadequate from the perspective of both Leibniz and Spinoza. Their criticism, put briefly, is that to know God through our knowledge of the idea of infinite perfection is to know God through an attribute of God; but the problem was precisely to show how we can know something through its attributes. In other words, Descartes assumes precisely what he hopes to justify. To resolve this problem, then, both Spinoza and Leibniz, as Deleuze has shown, use the concept 'expression.' Leibniz, for example, in a letter to Arnaud, will claim that 'every individual substance [i.e., monad] *expresses* the whole universe in its own manner';[8] and Spinoza claims in his *Ethics*, 'By God I understand a being absolutely infinite, i.e., a substance consisting of an infinity of attributes, of which each one *expresses* an eternal and infinite essence.'[9] Their reason for this move to the use of the concept 'expression,' according to Deleuze, is that it adequately explains how two heterogenous series may nevertheless be related. Mind and body, therefore, may be two different monads, but they each express the one world, according to Leibniz; and Mind and Body may be two different attributes, as Spinoza understands them, but they in turn express the one substance. Therefore, just as the sign was able, as Hjelmslev understands the sign-function, to bring an expression-substance (i.e., physical utterances, signs, etc.) into relation with a content-substance (i.e., intended meaning, concept, etc.), so too does an expression bring a series of mental entities into relation with a series of physical entities. This relation, however, is, as Deleuze will clarify this point, a non-causal relationship. That is, although the expression-substance is related to the content-substance, neither one causes, or is dependent upon, the other.[10] They are each, Hjelmslev claims, functives of the paradoxical sign-function. Similarly, with the concept of expression one can explain how mind and body are related without arguing that one is dependent upon the other. As Deleuze puts it, 'the relation between the two series [i.e., mind/body, corporeal/spiritual], and their relation to what is invariant between them, depends on noncausal correspondence. If we then ask what concept can account for such a correspondence, that of expression appears to do so.'[11] It is on this conceptual basis, then, that Spinoza develops his famous theory of the parallelism of mind and body, and Leibniz develops his notion of the pre-established harmony. These theories of pre-established harmony and parallelism recognize the close ties between mind and body, and yet they attempt to explain the relationship between them without resorting to a causal explanation. The problem of knowing how mind and body are related is now simply a matter of recognizing mind and body as expressions of an invariant (i.e., the pre-established harmony of the world for Leibniz, and substance for Spinoza).

The concept 'expression' is also useful in accounting for a knowledge of that which is other, or for the problem Descartes left behind. The importance of the concept here is that when one gains a greater and more detailed knowledge of the attributes of God, for example, one is not coming to a knowledge of God through something other than God, such as the attribute of infinite perfection. As expressions, these attributes are not other than, or distinct from, God, but are God and substance as expressed (for Spinoza); or the monads are not other than the world, but each is a different way in which the world is expressed. It is precisely this aspect of expression that Deleuze finds to be most significant – that is, the expressed 'inheres or subsists' in the expression. As Deleuze argues this point in *Logic of Sense*, sense, following the Stoics,

> does not exist outside the proposition which expresses it; what is expressed does not exist outside its expression. This is why we cannot say that sense exists, but rather that it inheres or subsists. On the other hand, it does not merge at all with the proposition, for it has an objective (*objectité*) which is quite distinct.[12]

One does not come to a knowledge of God through something other, for example, the attributes of God, but instead one knows God in these attributes, as that which is not to be confused with these attributes in the sense of being wholly identified with them, but nonetheless as that which does not properly exist independently of these attributes. God 'inheres and subsists' in these attributes as what is expressed. To resolve the Cartesian problem, therefore, of accounting for a knowledge of something other that does not itself depend upon a knowledge of attributes that are other than God, Leibniz moves to a concept of expression whereby God (or God-created world for Leibniz) is not truly other than the monads (i.e., as separable existent), but rather 'inheres and subsists' in the monads as what is expressed therein. Deleuze will subsequently restate the claims of the previous quote, but will state it later in *Logic of Sense* in Leibnizean terms:

> It is indeed true that the expressed world does not exist outside of the monads which express it, and thus that it does exist within the monads as the series of predicates which inhere in them. It is no less true, however, that God created the world rather than monads, and that what is expressed is not confused with its expression, but rather inheres and subsists.[13]

At this point a comparison with Whitehead will be beneficial. As is well known, Whitehead's own 'cell-theory of actuality'[14] mirrors in many respects Leibniz's monadic theory of actuality. There is, however, an important difference between the two theories. As Whitehead expressed the difference, Whitehead's own theory of monads 'differs from Leibniz's in that his [Leibniz's] monads change. In the organic theory, they merely become.'[15] In other words, Whitehead's monads, as discussed earlier, are in his system referred to as 'actual entities'; however, one cannot say of these actual entities that they are, or that they are an identifiable fact, for once their process is complete and they are identified, they perish and then assume an objective immortality insofar as they are prehended by other actual entities in their own process of becoming. Leibniz's monads, on the other hand, *are* undestood in the manner of an ultimate fact, or something that is. Consequently, for Leibniz change is something that occurs to monads that are (and they change following their own internal principles), whereas Whitehead's actual entities only come to be seen as identifiable facts and entities that change (e.g., the grey stone) when they converge and are organized into a society of such entities. Thus, actual entities *become*, but to say that they change would imply that they change from *being* in one state to *being* in that of another, and this is something that can only be said of facts.

Despite this important difference between Leibniz and Whitehead, both are generally agreed that 'actuality' entails a convergence and system of monads whereby the world as a whole is expressed. To rephrase Whitehead's claim, the monads are the accidents (i.e., expressions) by virtue of which the world is actualized; similarly, for Whitehead, God is the accident by virtue of which the world, or facts, can be actualized.[16] And it is with respect to the presuppositions implied by this common ground between Whitehead and Leibniz that Deleuze breaks with Leibniz and that we, by extension, break with Whitehead. To understand this break, we must first set forth Deleuze's notion of 'the two stages of passive genesis,' for it is on the basis of this distinction that Deleuze will criticize and break with Leibniz.

By 'passive genesis,' Deleuze simply means the genesis of actualities, a genesis that is passive because there is no active, creative agent directing the process. In Leibniz, for example, the world and its pre-established harmony would be the result of an active genesis, but the monads which express the created world would be the result of passive genesis. This passive genesis, however, is, as we saw, the means whereby the created world is actualized when the monads converge into a system, a system which expresses the pre-established harmony and identity of the world (i.e., the fact that God created the best of all possible worlds). The monads, in other words, are subordinate to, and are organized with respect to, a world which determines what can and cannot be grouped together within the system of monads. This systematizing and passive genesis is what Deleuze refers to as the first stage of passive genesis. As Deleuze makes the distinction, 'First, beginning with singularities-events [i.e., monads] which constitute it [the world], sense engenders a first field wherein it is actualized: the *Umwelt* which organizes the singularities in circles of convergence; individuals which express these worlds; states of bodies; mixtures or aggregates of these individuals ...' 'Then,' Deleuze adds, 'a second, very different field appears, built upon the first; the *Welt* common to several or to all worlds; the persons who define this "something in common"; synthetic predicates which define these persons ... Just as the first stage of the genesis is the work of sense, the second is the work of nonsense, which is always co-present to sense (aleatory point or ambiguous sign).'[17] And with respect to Leibniz, Deleuze claims that 'no matter how far he may have progressed in a theory of singular points and the play, [Leibniz] did not truly pose the distributive rules of the ideal game and did at best conceive of the pre-individual very much on the basis of consti-

tuted individuals.'[18] In other words, along with the strictures and structures of an identity which organizes singularities, singularities which
express this world (i.e., the world is the sense expressed in these singularities), there is, for Deleuze, a simultaneous presence of nonsense, an
aleatory point which eludes and undermines the stable identities and
structures necessary for the first stage of passive genesis. Leibniz,
according to Deleuze, recognized only the first stage of passive genesis,
and not only did he not recognize the second stage, he outright
shunned it, and hence Deleuze's critical reference to 'Leibniz's shame-
ful declaration: he assigns to philosophy the creation of new concepts,
provided that they do not overthrow "established sentiments."'[19] We
can further clarify this critique, and the two stages of passive genesis,
by placing Whitehead's discussion of actual entities within the context
of Deleuze's critique of Leibniz. We will then be able to clarify the manner in which our understanding of chaosmos breaks with Whitehead's
understanding of God.

From Deleuze's perspective, although he never actually made this
argument, Whitehead is a clear advance over Leibniz. The reason for
this is that Whitehead recognized the necessity of what he called the
'non-social actual entities,' or chaos. These were the actual entities that
had not been integrated within the nexus of a society; they were free,
nomadic entities, or what Deleuze will call the nomadic singularities
and aleatory points. Leibniz, on the other hand, does not recognize the
possibility of free, nomadic monads: all monads express the pre-established harmony of the world (i.e., first stage of passive genesis). It was
because Leibniz rejected the possibility of such nomadic monads that
he believed in the possibility of a *mathesis universalis*. Leibniz, therefore, will argue for a system of monads, but a system that is pure order,
or a completely lawful cosmos. Whitehead argued, as we saw, that
there are always some free, non-social actual entities, that there is
never pure order, nor is there ever pure chaos; rather, there is both
order and chaos, or what we have termed chaosmos. It is this move to
chaosmos which is an advance over Leibniz's continued adherence to
cosmos.

Whitehead's view of chaosmos is not in complete agreement with our
understanding of it. To see where we break with Whitehead, we need to
recall his 'threefold' division of the creative act, and trace where
Deleuze does and does not follow Whitehead. There was first the 'one
infinite conceptual realization,' or a pure potentiality that is 'free, complete, primordial, eternal, actually deficient and unconscious' (407).

Then there is 'the multiple solidarity of free physical realizations in the temporal world,' or the actualization of this potentiality, an actualization that is now limited by the existence of what is already actual. And finally, there is 'the ultimate unity of the multiplicity of actual fact with the primordial conceptual fact' (408). The intermediate or second stage was, as we saw, saved by God, 'by the completion of his own nature' (Ibid.). Deleuze will follow much this same model, though rather than stressing the saving nature of God, Deleuze will emphasize the nature of the event. This concept of an 'event' is perhaps Deleuze's most important concept. For this reason, it is worth quoting in full one of Deleuze's most straightforward definitions of an 'event':

> With every event, there is indeed the present moment of its actualization, the moment in which the event is embodied in a state of affairs, an individual, or a person, the moment we designate by saying 'here, the moment has come.' The future and the past of the event are only evaluated with respect to this definitive present. On the other hand, there is the future and past of the event considered in itself, sidestepping each present, being free of the limitations of a state of affairs, impersonal, pre-individual, neutral.[20]

We can now restate Whitehead's threefold division of the creative act. There is first what Deleuze will most often call a transcendental field of pre-individual singularities. Within this transcendental, 'unconscious' field, Deleuze claims these pre-individual singularities 'are distributed in a "potential" which admits neither Self nor I, but which produces them by actualizing or realizing itself, although the figures of this actualization do not resemble the realized potential.'[21] In other words, in agreement with Whitehead, this first stage is a field of potentiality that is 'actually deficient and unconscious.' The second stage is the actualization of these pre-individual singularities, the actualization which produces Self and I, or it is the event as 'embodied in a state of affairs, an individual, or a person.' And finally, there is the objective form, structure, or assemblage within which an event occurs. For example, a battle is an event which, following Deleuze's example, both inheres and subsists in the individual bodies and states of affairs, and there is the persistent event as pre-individual and neutral which 'inheres or subsists' in the individual bodies and states of affairs while not being confused with them. This both/and structure of the event, however, also occurs within a larger structure and assemblage, such as being part of a larger war (or war-machine). An actualized event, in other words, is actualized within a certain assemblage or form, or within a certain structure. Even an event that may not be 'captured' by a larger assemblage or structure, an isolated, nomadic event so to speak, will necessarily arise with a certain form and consistency. An actualized event, in short, is both form and content, pre-individual and individual, 'here and now' while forever 'sidestepping each present' here and now. The question, then, is how the actual *becomes* actual, and with a certain form and structure?

For Whitehead the answer to this question is God. For Whitehead, God is the form of Self which guarantees successful actualization because the 'completion of his own nature [i.e., Self]' makes it possible for all other entities to achieve self-completion (actualization). Deleuze explicitly breaks with this understanding of actualization:

> A consciousness is nothing without a synthesis of unification, but there is no synthesis of unification of consciousness without the form of the I, or the point of view of the Self [e.g., God for Whitehead]. What is neither individual nor personal are, on the contrary, emissions of singularities insofar as they occur on an unconscious surface and possess a mobile, *immanent principle of auto-unification* through a nomadic distribution, radically distinct from fixed and sedentary distributions and conditions of the syntheses of consciousness.[22]

Deleuze thus posits an 'immanent principle of auto-unification' that is 'radically distinct' from Whitehead's understanding of a synthesis and unification that is under the direction of the form of an I or Self (God). What is this immanent principle? In *Logic of Sense* Deleuze refers to this principle of auto-unification as the 'paradoxical element' which traverses the singularities and draws them into relationships that allow for the possibility of being actualized. The actualization of the event, the immanent principle which allows for the possibility that an event will have the double structure form/content, pre-individual/individual, etc., is the paradoxical element which brings the two heterogenous sides into relationship with one another (and hence for the actualization which includes both sides). As Deleuze argues, 'It seemed to us that the event, that is, sense, referred to a paradoxical element, intervening as nonsense or as an aleatory point, and operating as a quasi-cause assuring the full autonomy of the effect [i.e., event as self-identical, or self-completed, individual, state of affairs, etc.].'[23]

To understand this concept of a 'paradoxical element,' and its role as 'quasi-cause' of actualized events, we need simply recall Hjelmslev's concept of the paradoxical sign-function. The sign-function, we saw, was what allowed for a non-causal correspondence between heterogenous series. That is, one series did not function as the cause of another that was its effect; rather, both series are non-causally related by virtue of the sign-function, and thus the sign can be called, as Deleuze does, a 'quasi-cause' of the resulting relationships. In the context of Hjelmslev, the sign-function is paradoxically both form and content, or it is more properly the condition for the possibility of distinguishing between a form and a content, or more precisely it allows for the possibility of distinguishing between an expression-substance and content-substance, as well as the corresponding expression-form and content-form. For example, the sign-function which engenders the sign 'I don't know' has both an expression-substance and expression-form. The expression-substance is the physical utterance, or the written sign. The expression-form would be, among other things, the accent with which the words are spoken, the tone, inflection, or even a written word that is *italicized* for emphasis. The content-substance is the meaning expressed by the expression, a meaning that can be expressed in a number of ways in a number of languages (e.g., *je ne sais pas* in French). The content-form is the grammatical, linguistic structure of a language, as well as the structure and traditions of a culture, which determine what can be meant.[24] The sign-function is precisely the function which allows for the relationship between form and content, expression and content (meaning), to occur, or to be actualized. Similarly, for Deleuze, the paradoxical element is the condition of possibility for similar relationships to occur within actualized events. Consequently, the content would be the pre-individual, non-personal singularities and nomadic points; the form would be the consistency, or set of integrable points, which allows for the possibility of drawing a line through these points, a plane of consistency or plateau. The singularities and nomadic points can be understood, then, to be as points scattered across a Cartesian graph. The use of differential equations allows one to plot the points on the graph, and the integration of these differential equations results in a solution or formula that enables one to draw an integral curve and determine where the next point, or any point, will be. In other words, what may initially appear as a random set of points on a graph acquires a consistency by means of the differential equations as such, and the integration of these equations gives us the identity of a rule or formula that removes the spectre of randomness.[25] The paradoxical element thus allows the points to be drawn into relationship with one another, or for what Deleuze also calls a 'plane of consistency' or 'circle of convergence.' And with this consistency, with this form, the actualization of an individual which embodies this form is made possible.

We can now more adequately clarify Deleuze's claims regarding the two stages of passive genesis. The first stage was the stage goverened by 'the work of sense.' Here Deleuze refers to the primordial form, or *Umwelt*, which 'organizes the singularities in circles of convergence; individuals which express these worlds; states of bodies; mixtures or aggregates of these individuals.' This stage of passive genesis is the work of sense, that is, sense as event, because sense/events entail both the pre-individual and an objective form. The intermediary stage of Whitehead's threefold division – 'the multiple solidarity of free physical realizations' – is possible because there is a form or consistency to the work of sense, and when this consistency is worked upon the pre-individual singularities, this allows for the possibility of actualization (integration). Leibniz, we saw, recognized only this type of actualization; however, we can see that Whitehead, to the extent that he privileges the guiding form and 'self-completion' of God, is also working with this understanding of actualization. Deleuze offers another understanding of actualization, one that occurs not by the work of sense, but rather by the work of nonsense, the paradoxical element and aleatory points. Such points are not separable from the first stage, from the work of sense; they are, as Deleuze said, 'always co-present to sense.'[26] To clarify the manner of this co-presence to sense, let us return to the theme of chaosmos as expression.

Our discussion to this point should make it much clearer what is meant by saying chaosmos is to be understood as expression. First, as expression, as an event, chaosmos entails a fundamental both/and structure. Chaosmos, as we have been repeating throughout this work, is both chaos, or a field of free, nomadic singularities (Whitehead's non-social actual entities), and chaosmos is cosmos, order, individuals, identity, structure, and the interrelationship of all these in accordance with law. To this point, then, we are simply setting forth an understanding of chaosmos that corresponds to the first stage of passive genesis, and we are not saying anything very different from what Whitehead has already argued. However, we shall follow Deleuze in his claim that there is a second stage, that of nonsense, aleatory points, or a paradoxical element that is in disequilibrium with itself, absent from its own place, and is yet the condition for the possibility of a non-causal correspondence between chaos and cosmos (i.e., paradoxical element as 'quasi-cause'). As Deleuze puts it, 'The metamorphoses or redistributions of singularities form a history; each combination and each distribution is an event [first stage of passive genesis]. But the paradoxical instance is the Event in which all events communicate and are distributed [second stage].'[27] The paradoxical instance allows for the communication and non-causal relationship between singularities, and hence for the circles of convergence and consistencies which allow for the integration and actualization of events. In this sense, the paradoxical instance, or what we have defined as paradoxa, is the condition of possibility for chaosmos, or for any functioning assemblage, and it is chaosmos which is the expressed within events, or within the first stage of passive genesis.[28]

This discussion of circles of convergence, consistency, and integrable forms reveals some important concepts in the work of Deleuze that he uses in attempting to offer a 'radically distinct' understanding of synthesis, auto-unification, and actualization. The notion of a circle as a condition for the possibility of actualization is not a new concept, and it has been of particular importance in accounting for systems. In Hegel's system, for example, all notions and determinations are one with the unfolding and return of Spirit to itself. This leads Hegel to say that 'the image of true infinity, bent back into itself, becomes the circle, the line which has reached itself, which is closed and wholly present, without beginning and end.'[29] And in the *Phenomenology of Spirit*, in the context of discussing system as the whole, and absolute knowledge as knowledge of system or whole, Hegel claims: 'The True is the whole. But the whole is nothing other than the essence consummating itself through its development.'[30] Actualization is part and parcel of a larger circle: the consummating return of Spirit to itself. For Whitehead, too, the notion of a circle (circling self-completion) is important. God is the actual entity whose form of self-completion guarantees the possibility of sucessful self-completion by other actual entities. Unlike Hegel, Whitehead argues that each actual entity, including God, is self-caused, though God is given, as we have shown, a privileged status over other actual entities.

For us, every circle of convergence, every event which expresses chaosmos, is interrelated in that each is made possible by the Event, or paradoxa. Chaosmos, therefore, is a system; however, this is an understanding of system quite distinct from that of Hegel or Whitehead. Although Hegel and Whitehead argue for system, their system is not,

Deleuze would say, truly univocal. By arguing that the formal properties and characteristics of a system (i.e., the nature and interrelationship
of the entities which constitute a system) are made possible by a condition which is similar to that which is conditioned – for example, the
self-completion of God is comparable to the self-completion of other
actual entities – one is left with the necessity of privileging a particular
form or identity as the condition of possibility for all other identities.
The conditioned identities thus do not express themselves in quite the
same way as the privileged or conditioning identity does. Despite the
fact that Whitehead claims God is one actual entity *just* as any other,
these other actual entities are 'saved by' God, and therefore God does
not express him/herself in the same way, or actual entities are
expressed equivocally, depending on whether the actual entity is God
or not. In following Deleuze, we claim chaosmos is systematic in the
sense that each event, each actual entity (including chaosmos itself), is
conditioned by that which in no way resembles it – namely, paradoxical
instance, or paradoxa. In saying this, we are not privileging one identifiable event as sufficiently self-expressed whereby all others are only
sufficiently self-expressed (or actualized) on the condition of this first;
rather, the paradoxical instance is what allows for the possibility of an
actualized event, an event with a dual form/content structure (i.e.,
event as expression of chaosmos, or first stage of passive genesis), but
the paradoxical instance does not itself have this structure, or it is non-
identifiable. The paradoxical instance is not a privileged form or identity, a privileged individuality, precisely because it is pre-individual,
a-formal, and non-identifiable. And since Whitehead does view God
both as a privileged actual entity, by which the multiplicity of other
actual entities is 'saved,' and as the self-identical and self-complete
actual entity which guarantees the emergence of new, identifiable entities, we can see, finally, where Deleuze, with his notion of the paradoxical instance, ultimately breaks with Whitehead. In our terms, then,
paradoxa is the condition of possibility all actual events presuppose, or
it is the condition that does not exist independently from, or in separation from, these events. Paradoxa is the immanent, non-identifiable
condition that inheres or subsists in all identifiable events, or it is
'always co-present to sense.' As Deleuze defines univocity,

> if Being is the unique event in which all events communicate with one
> another, univocity refers both to what occurs and to what is said. Univocity
> means that it is the same thing which occurs and is said: the attributable to
> all bodies or states of affairs and the expressible of every proposition.[31]

Paradoxa, or Event and paradoxical instance, is the immanence pre-supposed by all actual entities, whether states of affairs or propositions, but it is at the same time the immanent outside of every state of affairs and every proposition, because it is both not to be confused with the identities and actualities it makes possible (it is non-identifiable), *and* it is the condition of impossibility that must remain outside the syntheses which allow for the expression (actualization) of a given identity, for without doing so the system will collapse into nonsense and cease func-tioning altogether. All actualized entities, therefore, are systematically interrelated in that they immanently and univocally express paradoxa, both as its condition of possibility and its condition of impossibility. This does not mean that there is just a single system, or a whole which contains all things; to the contrary, there is a multiplicity of systems, and more precisely there is a multiplicity of *dynamic systems*. It is these dynamic systems which presuppose and express paradoxa as the con-dition of possibility for a system which is constantly changing and in flux, that is, which is dynamic. At the same time, such a dynamic system expresses paradoxa as the limit it must avoid (its condition of impossi-bility) if it is to remain a dynamic, functioning system. It is this view of system that we believe Deleuze to be setting forth.

To illustrate further our claim that Deleuze is developing a metaphys-ics of dynamic systems at the edge of chaos, we shall look at some of the principles of self-organization (auto-unification) as they have been put forth within contemporary dynamic systems theory; and we will look at complementary work in chaos theory, work which is often used to sup-port the dynamic systems approach. This discussion of dynamic sys-tems should clarify two important philosophical points. The first point arose in response to Frank's criticism of Derrida. By doing away with a closed, self-identical system (such as Saussure offered), Derrida was left with an open system that was unable, according to Frank, to account for any identifiable meaning. To respond to this criticism, we argued that what was needed was an understanding of system as simultaneously complete and open. Related to this view of a system as simultaneously complete and open is the notion of self-identity. In particular, the view of dynamic systems we will be sketching below will argue that these systems are both self-differing (i.e., constantly changing and becoming different) and self-identical, though in this context we will adopt the concept of self-similarity (following chaos theory and its understanding of the self-similarity of fractals). The second point that our discussion of dynamic systems should clarify is the role of the paradoxical instance, or paradoxa. As those working in chaos theory and dynamic systems theory have been arguing, there is no fixed, privileged form or identity which governs the processes of organization. Rather, dynamic systems are self-organized in such a way that they both exhibit the presupposition of a paradoxical, aleatory point which conditions them, and they exhibit this same condition as a limit to be avoided. What we have to this point referred to as chaosmos, we will now discuss as dynamic systems, and in this way better connect with other fields and with their efforts to account for self-organization and the emergence (actualization) of stable identities, forms, and patterns.

Dynamic Systems

A guiding question of recent work in dynamic systems is how order – that is, the sophisticated, stable patterns which are readily apparent – are able to emerge despite the second law of thermodynamics, which states that order tends to move to chaos, or that systems in disequilibrium tend to move to equilibrium. Returning to our earlier analogy of the random points on a graph, we see that this question relates directly to our effort to explain how consistency and hence identifiable order is able to emerge and be actualized from within a random set of points. What researchers in dynamic systems theory and chaos theory will most often point to is the fact that such order does emerge (obviously), but only under certain circumstances, in particular circumstances that are far from equilibrium. To take a frequently cited example, oil, when heated, will suddenly exhibit convection rolls and vortices as it is heated and before it boils. Before the oil is heated, the oil is in an equilibrium state in which entropy is at a maximum; in other words, the oil molecules are randomly scattered throughout the container such that no order or consistency is present. One section of the container would be indistinguishable from another. We thus have chaos, or a random set of points with no identifiable order, what is called 'equilibrium thermal chaos.' When heated, however, the oil moves away from equilibrium, and it is under these conditions that the convection rolls and vortices appear. Once the oil is in a full boil, chaos reappears, or 'non-equilibrium thermal chaos,' and subsequently one section of the boiling water is indistinguishable from any other. Dynamic systems and chaos theorists will pay particular attention to far-from-equilibrium conditions, and more precisely to the order which emerges at the critical threshold between equilibrium and non-equilibrium chaos.

The far-from-equilibrium conditions which give rise to spontaneous order most often occur during what is called a phase transition. A phase transition is a transition between two steady and stable equilibrium states, such as liquid and gas, or liquid and solid. As these systems approach a phase transition, they enter a far-from-equilibrium state wherein self-organized patterns tend to emerge, and at a critical point (e.g., of temperature), there is a discontinuous jump to the new phase. Related to these phase transitions, and also occuring in far-from-equilibrium conditions, is the phenomenon of bifurcations. As Ilya Prigogine and Isabelle Stengers discuss bifurcations in their well-known book *Order out of Chaos*, a bifurcation point arises at a critical point where a system is poised to transition and when not just one stable state but, rather, 'two new stable solutions emerge.'[32] For example, at the critical point where the stable solution of a convection roll appears in the heated oil, the rolling motion may assume either a clockwise or counterclockwise direction – both solutions are possible. Which solution, or which branch of the bifurcation the system will 'choose,' is impossible to predict: 'How will the system choose between left and right? There is an irreducible random element; the macroscopic equation cannot predict the path the system will take ... We are faced with chance events very similar to the fall of dice.'[33] As the oil is heated, further bifurcations appear, rolls within rolls, in what is called a process of 'cascading bifurcations,' which then leads to turbulent chaos. A bifurcation diagram of such a process between 'equilibrium thermal chaos' and 'non-equilibrium thermal chaos' is surprisingly ordered, or 'order or coherence is sandwiched between thermal chaos and non-equilibrium turbulent chaos.'[34] If one enlarges a portion of a bifurcation diagram, for example, one will find that it resembles the whole, and an enlarged portion of this would in turn resemble the whole. A bifurcation diagram, and the more commonly referred to Mandelbrot sets or fractals, exhibit the important feature of self-similarity, or a consistency and order which appears between 'equilibrium thermal chaos' and 'non-equilibrium thermal chaos.' In Stuart Kauffman's recent book, *At Home in the Universe*, as well as in the work of J.A. Scott Kelso, attention has shifted to this emergence of order within a dynamic system that is on the 'edge of chaos,' or a system that is poised between equilibrium and non-equilibrium chaos.

These findings in chaos theory have raised enticing possibilities regarding the study of the origins of life, human behaviour, and consciousness. It seems a natural extension of work in chaos theory and its study of the emergence of order amidst the turbulence in fluids, to turn next to living organisms, for they seem to be just the sort of dynamic system which inhabits the 'edge of chaos,' the ordered middle ground between thermal equilibrium (which would be death) and non-equilibrium chaos (which would also mean death).[35] Kauffman, in fact, will argue that life emerges and best maintains itself at the 'edge of chaos,' and it is with this notion, therefore, that Kauffman proposes we approach the difficulties in accounting for the origins of life which have plagued traditional approaches. For example, considering the number of random chemical reactions which must occur and be synchronized with one another to form a living being, and if you factor in the amount of time within which such random reactions may occur, the result is that the possibility such a chain of events will actually lead to life becomes astronomically remote. Since such a chain of events obviously did occur, the conclusion traditionally reached is that we human beings are extremely lucky – 'We, the improbable,' to quote Kauffman. What Kauffman argues, to the contrary, is that life did not emerge piecemeal, or through a process of gradual accumulation. Life arose at once. Kauffman's argument, in short, is that as the chemical reactions in a given pre-biotic soup increase, the number of catalysts which can enter into new reactions also increases, which in turn creates even newer catalysts. At a critical point, according to Kauffman's hypothesis, a phase transition occurred, a discontinuous emergence of life:

> Life, in this view, is an emergent phenomenon arising as the molecular diversity of a prebiotic chemical system increases beyond a threshold of complexity. If true, then life is not located in the property of any single molecule – in the details – but is a collective property of systems of interacting molecules. Life, in this view, is not to be located in the parts, but in the collective emergent properties of the whole they create.[36]

Kauffman gives a helpful example to illustrate the sense in which life is an emergent property. Imagine a number of buttons scattered randomly across the floor. If one begins randomly connecting two buttons at a time by means of a thread, one will at first have a random collection of connected buttons. Occasionally a button will be connected to more than one other button, and many others will remain isolated altogether. At a critical point (when the number of threads is roughly half the number of buttons), a rapid phase transition occurs after which almost all the buttons are interconnected to one another. Moreover, as the number of buttons which one begins with increases, Kauffman notes that the phase transition becomes even more discontinuous, such that 'were there an infinite number of buttons, then as the ratio of threads to buttons passed 0.5 the size of the largest component would jump discontinuously from tiny to enormous.'[37] The idea here is that at the critical phase transition, there suddenly emerges a global interrelation between all the buttons. In applying this idea to the growing number of catalytic reactions, Kauffman argues that when a critical phase transition is reached, the system suddenly becomes autocatalytic. Within the system, catalytic reactions occur as before, but after the phase transition these reactions occur within a dynamic system that is self-sustaining, or the catalytic reactions maintain the system and the system maintains these reactions, that is, the system appropriates the chemicals (food) necessary to feed the reactions. Life thus does not emerge slowly, or after a long process of tinkering and additions; life emerges discontinuously, as with the interconnected buttons, and as a whole or emergent property of its chemical constituents. Once it arises, Kauffman argues, this living, dynamic system will only continue to exist and maintain its stability and order (as with the bifuraction diagram) if it strikes a balance between order and chaos. This is perhaps Kauffman's most central thesis in his book:

> For what can the teeming molecules that hustled themselves into self-reproducing metabolisms, the cells coordinating their behaviors to form multicelled organisms, the ecosystems, and even economic and political systems have in common? The wonderful possibility, to be held as a working hypothesis, bold but fragile, is that on many fronts, life evolves toward a regime that is poised between order and chaos. The evocative phrase that points to this working hypothesis is this: life exists at the edge of chaos. Borrowing a metaphor from physics, life may exist near a kind of phase transition.[38]

We are now in a better position to clarify what is meant by our use of the notion 'paradoxa.' Key to the emergence of order, as we have seen, are the phase transitions that are far from equilibrium. Within such a state, and at a critical threshold, a bifurcation occurs such that the system suddenly, and discontinuously, moves into a stable attractor (i.e., state), or it unleashes a self-similar cascade of bifurcations poised between order and chaos. Both possibilities are, as we will see, integral to dynamic systems. In the first, a dynamic system settles into a stable state while being immune to slight perturbations. For example, a swinging pendulum, if perturbed slightly, will soon return to its attractor state (swinging back and forth); thus, a dynamic system will not be sent into chaos at the slightest provocation. In the second case, a dynamic system must be sensitive to changes which might call for an adaptive response, and it is here where the cascading bifurcations (the self-similar bifurcation diagram) comes into play. This is so because the cascading bifurcations have not 'chosen' either of two bifurcated alternatives, but rather continually generate further bifurcations and alternatives while avoiding a collapse into chaotic disorder. By doing this, a dynamic system is able to maintain the flexibility of choosing and selecting among the possible bifurcated states, and consequently is better able to adapt. In both cases, the primary operative mechanism is the discontinuous bifurcation and/or phase transition; for example, catalytic → autocatalytic, stable state → 2 bifurcated stable states. Paradoxa is precisely the critical threshold, the 'bifurcation point,'[39] which is a point of instability (or what Deleuze would call an aleatory point) that allows for the possibilty of a bifurcation to two steady states, a bifurcation wherein one cannot predict which of the two states will result. In terms of our earlier discussion of the Event, paradoxa is the point that is instantiated, the critical threshold that a scientist can measure and determine. At the same time, paradoxa is neither to be identified with the initial stable state – it is a point of instability between stable states – nor is it to be identified with either of the two bifurcated states it makes possible. Paradoxa is the condition of possibility for the bifurcation which allows for two different identifiable states, but in itself it is non-identifiable. Paradoxa is inseparable from the identifiable states which emerge and change, hence the possibility of measuring and determining the 'bifurcation point,' and paradoxa is not to be confused with the stable states which come to be identified.

Paradoxa is also the condition or limit a dynamic system must forever avoid, or it is this system's condition of impossibility. As the point of change, the aleatory point, which harbours an intrinsic instability that allows for the emergence of stable, identifiable order, paradoxa must neither be completely actualized as stable, ordered systems, nor must it be completely actualized as chaos and disorder. Paradoxa is the condition for the possibility of actualization which must remain unactualized. Put another way, by not being confused with the actuality of chaos (e.g., random distribution of points), or with the emergent properties of order which emerge as a result of interrelationships between these points (e.g., autocatalysis), paradoxa is the unactualized, heterogenous and/or discontinuous condition which allows for the relationships of consistency to emerge. Kauffman cites an intriguing experiment which elucidates this point. In a computer simulation, 100,000 lightbulbs are interconnected to one another, and they turn on or off by a simple rule – namely, the bulb switches on or off depending on whether the bulbs it is connected to are on or off. What Kauffman found was that if the bulbs were connected to only one other bulb, the network of bulbs quickly 'freezes up, saying the same thing over and over for all time.'[40] At the other extreme, if the bulbs are connected to every other bulb, the network is so susceptible to any slight change that the system never settles down, but continuously jumps from attractor to attractor, and because the number of potential attractors is so large the resulting changes are in effect random, and thus we have chaos. If the bulbs are connected to two others, then rather than a random, chaotic range of potential attractors, 100,000 bulbs will settle into one of 317 attractor states. Kauffman will note that the 100,000 proteins that make up DNA produce the 256 cell types that make up the human body. The point, in short, is that the virtually infinite number of connections and patterns which could have emerged from the interrelationships between 100,000 bulbs or proteins, settles instead into a much stabler, though still flexible, system with 317 patterns (or 256 for the human body). Kauffman is clear that this is an important factor for the stability of dynamic systems: 'For a dynamical system, such as an autocatalytic net, to be orderly it must exhibit homeostasis; that is, it must be resistant to small perturbation. Attractors are the ultimate source of homeostasis as well, ensuring that a system is stable.'[41] Paradoxa is the condition which allows for the possibility of patterned interrelationships among random points (i.e., attractors), but paradoxa is neither the attractor – or set and system of attractors, as is found within the human body – nor is paradoxa the random points brought into relationships of consistency and order with one another; moreover, paradoxa is the non-identifiable condition which should not be actualized, for to do so would be to actualize it as either the randomness of chaos, or the stifling order and stability of an unchanging attractor.

The importance of dynamic systems, or systems that are at the 'edge of chaos,' has emerged as an important new direction in science, some would call it a paradigm shift. In fields as diverse as quantum physics, political theory, child development, and biology, researchers are finding important conceptual tools within the theory of dynamic systems. In his own book, for example, Kelso argues that the notion 'edge of chaos,' what he also calls 'intermittency,' clarifies many of the observed phenomena concerning behaviour. With respect to perception, though later Kelso will extend this hypothesis to include consciousness and the processes of the brain as well, Kelso argues:

> Intermittency means that the perceptual system (and the brain itself?) is intrinsically metastable, living at the edge of instability where it can switch spontaneously among collective states. Rather than requiring active processes to destabilize and switch from one stable state to another (e.g., through changes in parameter(s), increases in fluctuations), here intermittency appears to be an inherent built-in feature of the neural machinery that supports perception.[42]

Esther Thelen, a leading reseacher in early cognitive and behavioural development, has also utilized the concepts of dynamic systems theory. In her book with Linda Smith, *A Dynamic Systems Approach to the Development of Cognition and Action*, Thelen and Smith reiterate Kelso's point that for a dynamic system to maintain its flexibility and order, it must be at the edge of chaos, or at the point of instability between stable states, which in turn conditions the actualization of a stable state. In borrowing an example from P.J. Beek, Thelen and Smith note that 'skilled jugglers, while having to execute highly phase-entrained movements of both hands, stop short of complete phase-locking. Rather, they operate just on the borders of phase-locking, so to speak. This gives them the flexibility to adapt to even small fluctuations that are inevitable in each catch and throw.'[43] Similarly, in the cognitive and behavioural development of children, Thelen and Smith will argue that their actions are quite often at the 'borders of phase-locking,' and this becomes apparent as one studies a child's growth and development.[44] The concepts of dynamic systems have also come to be used in work in cognitive science. In *Being There*, Andy Clark, in his efforts to overcome what he sees as a dualism in traditional cognitive science – that is, the tendency to see the brain as an input-output device with the resulting problem of relating this device to the actions of a body in the world – argues that the concepts of 'feedback loops and closely coupled physical systems ... [as found in] the province of standard Dynamical Systems theory'[45] are helpful. For example, in manoeuvring one's way through a cluttered room, one does not, so this theory goes, take the visual input, process it, and then create a map with which to direct one's manoeuvring through the room; rather, Clark argues that the perceiving agent and world are a 'coupled complex system ... whose joint activity solves the problem.'[46] Organized, controlled behaviour does emerge, and emerge as if an organizer controlled the process, but with the concepts of dynamic systems theory in hand, Clark prefers to see the organized behaviour as an 'emergent property' which is the result of the coupled, complex system of interactions between perceiver and perceived. In other words, and to repeat Kauffman's earlier point, the organized behaviour is an emergent property which arises after the number of perceiver-perceived reactions reaches a critical threshold or phase transition, and then suddenly the behaviour emerges. It was for this reason that Thelen argued that a child's developmental process is dependent upon being at the 'borders of phase-locking.' A child is a complex, dynamical system, and being at the edge of chaos allows the child to proceed through the phases of development.

Clark will extend his notion of a feedback loop to include not only the complex, developing interaction of perceiver and perceived, but also the interaction between speaking agent and language. In fact, Clark puts forth the notion 'scaffolding,' following suggestions of Vygotsky, and argues that the functioning of the brain and language, language as an external artifact or 'scaffolding,' is itself part of a complex dynamical process. As Clark puts it, 'The complementarity between the biological brain and its artifactual props and supports is thus enforced by coevolutionary forces uniting user and artifact in a virtuous circle of mutual modulation.'[47] One could see the development of the relationship between human beings and tools (including language as 'artifactual prop') in terms of an emergent property, where at some critical point of instability in the number of interactions between human beings and their tools, language suddenly and discontinuously appeared as an emergent property of these interactions.[48] Philosophy itself, as Merlin Donald argues and as Clark cites in his book, can be seen as a further development, or a new phase transition, in the development of the relationship between human beings and their tools. As an 'artifactual prop' which can be used to record memories and store knowledge, writing has led to a 'feedback loop' process whereby the knowledge base has exploded. Socrates likely expresses common knowledge when he recognizes the usefulness of writing as an 'artifactual prop,' though perhaps his suspicion of language for this very reason was not so common.[49] This use of writing had been around for centuries prior to the Greeks, with the Egyptians, Sumerians, etc. The novelty of the

Greeks' use of language, according to Donald, was that they 'were employing external memory devices to their fullest effect, in a way that was totally new. Although phonetic writing had been invented by the Egyptians and later refined in many cultures, it had never been used to record the thought process itself.'[50] The Greeks invented what Donald calls a new 'ESS [external symbolic storage] loop'; that is, rather than simply using language as an 'artifactual prop' for recording and storing data, it now becomes a medium for recording the processes of thought itself. This new loop initiates, for Donald, the birth of philosophy.

At this point we can return to the theme with which we began this book – the end of philosophy. Heidegger's discussion of this theme, developing upon some of Nietzsche's insights, maintained that to understand the end of philosophy one needed to rethink the moment of its birth. Without repeating this earlier discussion, we can now see that our argument brings us to the same conclusion, if from a different direction. We have argued that philosophy necessarily thinks the unique, uncommon, non-identifiable condition for the possibility of identifiable, common knowledge. Philosophy is inherently uncommon. This condition we have called paradoxa. More importantly, paradoxa is also the condition of possibility/impossibility for dynamic systems, and it is this latter notion which we argued overcomes some of the difficulties we found plaguing the contemporary critique of metaphysics (e.g., Derrida). Now as we come to Donald's work, and to his claim that philosophy is an emergent property expressive of the dynamic interaction between human beings and language as 'artifactual prop,' or what he calls external symbolic storage device, we can see that the significance of philosophy's beginning, its condition of possibility, is important for understanding whether philosophy has ended, or ought to. Moreover, we can see that as we think through philosophy, through its legitimate and/or illegitimate possibilities, we inevitably confront the condition for these possibilities – namely, paradoxa as the condition of possibility for a dynamic system. What is left, then, for philosophy to do, or how has this discussion resolved questions of what philosophy can or ought to do? We will answer these questions in detail in the next and final chapter, but for now we can say that what philosophy ought to do is to engender the conditions that allow for something to be thought. Deleuze will note Artaud's recognition of the difficulty of doing this: 'the problem [for Artaud] ... was to manage to think something,' and in his efforts to do this he was 'forced to think [thought's] own natural powerlessness which is indistinguishable from the greatest power.'

And to this Deleuze adds, 'To think is to create – there is no other creation – but to create is first of all to engender "thinking" in thought.'[51]

As we have been arguing throughout this work, what is necessary to 'engender "thinking" in thought' is that this thinking maintain itself as a dynamic system at the edge of chaos. Now as we draw this work to a close, we will, in the next and final chapter, first elaborate upon the sense in which we take philosophy to be a dynamic system, and how this might be translated into philosophical practice. For Deleuze, this practice was the transcendental project in which he engaged in his own works and in his work with Guattari, and key to the success of this project, as Deleuze and Guattari themselves admitted, was that they formulate concepts that were not too abstract and yet were abstract enough. It was a philosophy at the edge of chaos that accomplished this task. Secondly, we hope to show that an understanding of philosophy as a dynamic system, along with the concepts we have discussed which have been generated by the work being done within dynamic systems theory, are helpful tools in avoiding some of the pitfalls that we feel have often accompanied traditional philosophical approaches, pitfalls we have detailed throughout this work. And finally, we will discuss a possible example of a philosophy and philosophical approach that explicitly takes itself to be a dynamic system – an approach based on 'definitions.' Rather than an approach which inherently is a dynamic system, or might even speak of the importance of process and philosophy as process – (that is, that it represents philosophy as a dynamic process, or paints a stable picture of what philosophy is), this approach, to the contrary, would attempt to engender 'thinking,' or it will set forth points of instability (i.e., definitions) which may lead to further work and 'thinking' in other areas (possible bifurcations). This is doing philosophy.

Conclusion: Philosophy at the Edge of Chaos

In our discussions to this point, we have repeatedly emphasized the similarity between Derrida, Deleuze, and others, on the theme of a fundamental difference, or a non-identifiable, undecidable both/and. In the context of Derrida, this undecidable both/and was critical to the method of deconstruction; consequently, for Derrida every identity or presence, every attempt to establish the self-identical, self-present grounding and meaning from which all other meanings can then arise, presupposes its other, a difference and/or absence which perpetually defers the closure necessary to attain true self-presence. Deleuze and Guattari, as they too develop the philosophy of difference Deleuze began in *Difference and Repetition*, will set forth a similar position. As we have seen, Deleuze and Guattari argue for a fundamental differentiating condition (recall Deleuze's both/and reading of Nietzsche's notion of the 'will to power' discussed in chapter 3) which allows for the possibility of identity, an identity which presupposes that which cannot be identified. Thus, to put it in their terms, each stable, identifiable stratum presupposes its unstructured flows (i.e., a body without organs – BwO). As this both/and comes to be developed in *A Thousand Plateaus*, it is the concept of the 'abstract machine' which carries much of the weight of explicating a philosophy at the 'edge of chaos.' The abstract machine is the fundamental both/and condition for the possibility of dynamic systems (a condition we have to this point referred to as paradoxa, and what Deleuze referred to as the paradoxical instance, event, etc.). It is with this concept that we saw most clearly the key differences between Deleuze and Derrida, especially with Deleuze and Guattari's argument that abstract machines, as conditions for dynamic systems, require the completion necessary for the stability and functioning of such systems.

As we argued in the Introduction to this work, Deleuze and Guattari's concept of the abstract machine should be interpreted along the lines of Kant's transcendental categories. *A Thousand Plateaus*, we argued, is in many ways a Kantian critique which attempts to delineate the appropriate limits within which the abstract machine is the condition for a functioning, dynamic system, and is one of many concepts that accompanies the various experimental forays of Deleuze and Guattari that we can see now as attempts to determine the limits beyond which the abstract machine collapses into either the cancerous body or the fascist body. We are now in a much better position to understand how Deleuze and Guattari's project differs from Kant's as well as those of Heidegger and Derrida. As our previous chapters have shown, the philosophical trajectories of Heidegger and Derrida both fail, as did Kant, to think difference, or to engender 'thinking' in thought. What has been crucial to Deleuze's success, both in his own works and in his works with Guattari, we believe, is the ability to avoid being either *too abstract* or *not abstract enough*. Now that we have detailed the manner in which Deleuze's philosophy at the edge of chaos is able to think difference, we can turn to the theme with which we began this book – viz. thinking difference without being *too abstract* or *not abstract enough*.

To show how the concept of the abstract machine is abstract enough to apply to various phenomena without being too abstract, we must first recall the significant role Louis Hjelmslev's work plays as Deleuze and Guattari develop this concept, a concept which largely extends Hjelmslev's work, in particular, his concept of the sign-function.[1] For instance, just as Hjelmslev argues that a meaningful expression is made possible by a sign-function, so too are dynamic systems[2] understood by Deleuze and Guattari to be expressions of a machinic-function (i.e., abstract machine). In addition, as Hjelmslev argues that the sign-function is paradoxically *both* expression *and* content, so too is the abstract machine *both* differentiation *and* differenciation,[3] or what is referred to in *A Thousand Plateaus* as *both* a first *and* second articulation (double articulation). And finally, Deleuze and Guattari follow Hjelmslev's claim that expression and content each has a corresponding subtance and form; thus, the first articulation (differentiation) involves both substance and form, and the second articulation (differenciation) likewise has a corresponding substance and form. It is this understanding of abstract machines as expression, or as double articulation (both/and), which is abstract enough to apply to a multiplicity of circumstances. At this point examples will clarify how Deleuze and Guattari believe this is so.

I

The first example is Deleuze and Guattari's, and it comes from the important third chapter of *A Thousand Plateaus*, wherein they detail what is meant by a double articulation model (i.e., abstract machine).[4] To clarify this model, they give the example of sedimentation, or the processes that lead to the formation of the strata which are sedimentary rocks. In the first articulation (differentiation), a heterogeneous collection of sedimentary material (i.e., particles of varying size) is collected into a layer of largely homogeneous material. The process which filters the heterogeneous material into a series of largely homogeneous layers is the flow of water which, depending upon the intensity of the flow, carries particles at different rates downstream. Particles that are roughly the same size will be carried at the same rate downstream, and hence they will tend to form generally homogeneous layers as they reach their ultimate destination.[5] This first articulation has, as Deleuze and Guattari argue, a substance (the sedimentary particles) and a form (the homogeneity of the layers which results as the particles are sorted by the flow of the fluid which transports them to the sedimentary bed). In the second articulation, this homogeneous layer of sedimentary particles is transformed, through what geologists call cementation, into a new substance. The pores between particles which were previously filled by fluid, become replaced, as additional layers increase the gravitational pressure upon lower layers, by agents (e.g., silica and hematite in the case of sandstone) which act as a cement that binds the particles and creates a new entity – sedimentary rock (substance). Restating this example in the terminology Deleuze used in his early work, *Difference and Repetition*, the process which results in an identifiable entity (sedimentary rock) involves both differentiation – that is, the sedimentary particles are filtered into roughly homogeneous and consistent layers[6] – and differenciation – that is, the consistent, homogeneous layers are transformed (or actualized, as Deleuze often says) into a new, *identifiable* entity.

In Deleuze and Guattari's final work, *What Is Philosophy?*, published twenty-three years after *Difference and Repetition*, much this same approach is taken. The process of double articulation, or differentiation/differenciation, is discussed more straightforwardly in this work as the process of becoming. In the 'becoming' of sedimentary rock, for example, the process involves the transformation of one substance (sediment) into another (sedimentary rock). What interests Deleuze and

Guattari, of course, is the process itself, and on this point their late work largely reaffirms Deleuze's initial understanding of the process in *Difference and Repetition*. This later formulation is quite to the point: in the becoming of 'b' (e.g., sedimentary rock) from 'a' (e.g., sediment), Deleuze and Guattari argue that 'there is an area *ab* that belongs to both *a* and *b*, where *a* and *b* "become" indiscernible. These zones, thresholds, or becomings, this inseparability, define the internal consistency of the concept.'[7] It is precisely this 'internal consistency,' or what we discussed in chapter 5 as the 'plane of consistency' drawn on the BwO, which is key. The BwO is thus a body without organs because it is not to be strictly identified with the entities that become. It is this BwO as drawn into a plane of consistency which allows for the becoming of *b*, or it is the consistency resulting from the first articulation (differentiation) which then becomes actualized in the second articulation (differenciation).

In the case of sedimentary rock, the sedimentary particles play the role of BwO, or, relative to the structured entity – that is, sedimentary rock – the sedimentary particles comprise the unstructured flow which facilitates the possibility of sedimentary rock. However, for sedimentary rock to be actualized, to become, this flow must first be drawn into a plane of consistency (the homogeneous layer), and it is this consistency, namely, the indiscernibility of *ab*, which is in turn actualized by the second articulation. In itself, however, sediment is a highly structured chemical compound composed of various elements, including, for example, silica, carbon, magnesium, phosphate, etc. These elements, moreover, can in turn be understood in terms of dynamic processes – that is, as expressions of an abstract machine. To state this in another way, in the process of *a* becoming *b*, *a* (e.g., sediment) is not, for Deleuze and Guattari, a simple given, but is itself the result of a process of becoming, or it too presupposes its own BwO and 'internal consistency' as its own condition of possibility.

The dynamic process which gives rise to carbon is an important case in point. The current account which is given is that it is only within the furnaces of stars where there is sufficient energy to fuse the atoms which make up carbon, and hence become the flows (BwO) that become carbon-based life-forms. Carbon therefore first depends upon the origin of stars, and here again we find the applicability of the double articulation model (i.e., abstract machine). In the first articulation, the hydrogen and helium which are nearly all that exists in the universe soon after the Big Bang begin to coagulate and form points of condensation. Minor differences in the spread of these atoms lead, through gravitational attraction, to an aggregation of atoms sufficiently dense to become transformed (i.e., actualized) into a star. If this critical density and mass is not reached, a giant gaseous planet might be formed (e.g., Jupiter) rather than a star. Therefore, in the first articulation (differentiation), hydrogen (substance) is sorted and condensed by means of gravitational attraction to a critical point of density and mass (form); and this critical point of density and mass (form) is then transformed in the second articulation (differenciation) into a star (substance). The BwO in this instance is hydrogen, for it is, relative to the star, the unstructured flow which, when drawn into a plane of consistency (i.e., brought to a point of critical density by means of gravitational attraction), is the condition for the possibility of a star, a condition which is actualized through double articulation (abstract machine). It is only within stars, and in particular dying red giant stars, where one finds, according to current cosmological theory, the conditions necessary for the origin of carbon, and thus carbon and the other heavy elements that constitute the sedimentary flows (BwO) necessary for the origin of sedimentary rock are themselves actualized by a process of double articulation.[8]

Moving on to carbon-based life, most biochemists argue that carbon is a necessary precondition for life. The reason for this is that carbon, due to its atomic structure – it has a valence of 4 – can combine with four univalent atoms or groups of atoms (elements with a free electron), or it can combine with itself. There are other 4-valence elements (e.g., silicon, germanium, and tin), but the attraction these elements have for their valence electrons is increasingly weaker than that of carbon.[9] The result is that carbon has a high degree of flexibility and is able to combine with, and react with, many other elements and compounds. The significance of this flexibility becomes especially clear and important in recent theories concerning the origin of life. In Stuart Kauffman's theory, discussed in the previous chapter, he claims that the emergence of life, or what he calls an autocatalytic set, becomes inevitable once a critical threshold of molecular interactions occurs. In a normal molecular interaction, two molecules will interact if there is a sufficient amount of free energy to initiate the process. Within catalytic reactions, however, the catalyst lowers the amount of free energy necessary for the chemical reaction to occur.[10] The result is that the frequency and ease with which reactions can successfully occur is higher in catalytic reactions. Couple this catalytic process with the intrinsic flexibility of the carbon atom, and one has a situation where these catalytic reactions can reach unprecedented frequency and complexity. This is precisely what Kauffman argues. He states that given a sufficient degree and frequency of interdependent catalytic reactions, a critical threshold is reached and an autocatalytic set emerges; in other words, this autocatalytic set emerges as a self-sustaining, self-duplicating set which will maintain its functional identity as long as there is an adequate supply of chemicals (i.e., food) to maintain the catalytic reactions within the set.[11] Again, the double articulation model fits with this understanding of the origins of life. In the first articulation, the chemicals (substance) which react and catalyze with one another achieve a degree of interdependency and frequency (form) such that these interdependent reactions (form) emerge as a new entity – an autocatalytic set, or a living being (substance). The BwO in this double articulation is the molecular reactions themselves. The molecules and chemicals are in themselves obviously highly structured, as our previous discussion has made clear, but with respect to the autocatalytic set which emerges, these reactions constitute the unstructured flow (BwO) that becomes, through double articulation (abstract machine), the structured entity that is a living organism.

Deleuze offers an example, discussed earlier in the Introduction, of the double articulation / abstract machine model that applies to living organisms themselves, and in particular to the learning process of a monkey. At the time of *Difference and Repetition*, this example was discussed in terms of the process of differentiation/differenciation, which, as we have seen, is carried forward largely unchanged in *A Thousand Plateaus* (and *What Is Philosophy?*) under the terminology of the abstract machine of double articulation. Deleuze describes the example as follows:

> ... a monkey is supposed to find food in boxes of one particular color amidst others of various colors: [during the test] there comes a paradoxical period during which the number of 'errors' diminishes even though the monkey does not yet possess the 'knowledge' or 'truth' of a solution in each case.[12]

This critical, paradoxical period soon gives way to the 'knowledge' which enables the monkey to eliminate the errors altogether. What occurs in this learning process, according to Deleuze, is that for a solution (i.e., knowledge) to arise, what must first be established is a critical phase in which the exploratory behaviour acquires a *consistency* or coherence which is then capable of an integration (i.e., differenciation) that enables a solution. In his summary of this learning process, Deleuze describes it in terms that are now quite familiar: 'Learning is the appropriate name for the subjective acts carried out when one is confronted with the objectivity of a problem (Idea [or what Deleuze also calls differentiation]), whereas knowledge designates only the generality of concepts or the calm possession of a rule enabling solutions [i.e., differenciation].'[13] In short, in the first articulation the choices of the monkey (substance) achieve a critical, paradoxical period when the number of errors is reduced (form – i.e., relationshp between right and wrong choices); and in the second articulation these reduced errors (form) find the solution which actualizes the rule that accounts for the reduced errors, and with this the monkey acquires knowledge of the correct choice (substance). The desire for food, and the flow of behaviours directed towards the acquisition of the energy necessary to maintain the living organism (i.e., as autocatalytic set), functions as the BwO in this instance. These food-oriented behaviours are filtered by means of a sorting mechanism (i.e., visual perception, including the ability to differentiate colours), which then allows for the double articulation to unfold (much as the flow of a river allows for the double articulation which creates sedimentary rocks).

This same double articulation model, to use one last example, can be seen at yet another level, or at another of a thousand plateaus as Deleuze and Guattari might put it. An important argument in American colonial history states that the colonies initially allowed for a high degree of social mobility. In the early days of settlement, when what was most important was carving out a living from the untamed wilderness, people with talent, energy, and resolve could easily find themselves rising to positions of importance, while those with less talent, energy, etc., did not. This flexibility was not present in Europe, where most privileges had long been established according to traditional hereditary and class distinctions. Early on, then, the colonies attracted those who sought to attain the privileges (i.e., power and wealth) that were closed to them in Europe. This freedom of social mobility did not last. By 1700 it was becoming increasingly difficult to move into the upper echelons of the social hierarchy. In a famous theory proposed by Charles Beard, Beard goes so far as to propose that the framers of the Constitution themselves sought, with this document, to formalize and institutionalize the disparity in privileges which had evolved. These framers, who were men from the upper echelons of American society, had supported the revolutionary war as a means of increasing their ability to maintain and enhance their economic advantage. They therefore invested in public securities in support of the war, and once the war was won they made sure, according to Beard, that the Constitution would protect their economic interests.[14] Gordon Wood has more recently qualified Beard's argument. Although Wood believes the economic motive was certainly at work, he claims it was not the sole factor at play as the framers ironed out the Constitution. Wood will stress the equal importance of ideological and pragmatic concerns, in particular, the concerns with how to establish a government which best serves the majority, even if this means that the majority does not get a say in the running of this government. Nevertheless, Wood supports Beard's basic premise that the Constitution formalized and institutionalized certain disparities in privilege (including economic and political privilege) that had gradually taken shape out of the earlier colonial context and its greater social mobility.[15]

The double articulation model is again applicable to this case. In the first articulation, the relationships between human beings (substance) are sorted by means of their talents and abilities to carve a successful living out of the frontier, and the result is that certain disparities (form) arise with respect to economic, political, and social privileges; and in the second articulation, these disparities (form) become actualized within a constitution, and with the institutions based upon this constitution (substance). The BwO in this case are the human beings themselves, or more precisely the economic, political, and social positions of human beings. These are the positions that are sorted within a double articulation which constitutes them as part of a new social structure (i.e., a class structure, or even a caste system).

II

At this point it will be helpful if we compare our reading of abstract machines (i.e., the double articulation model) with DeLanda's reading of Deleuze. In many ways, as we will see, we follow DeLanda's reading, and in fact much of this discussion has been in part indebted to DeLanda's understanding of abstract machines as he lays it out in *A Thousand Years of Nonlinear History* (1977) and, more recently, in *Intensive Science and Virtual Philosophy* (2002). There are, however, some important differences that we should examine, for in doing so we will gain a better understanding of what Deleuze and Guattari are doing, and ultimately clarify what we believe it means for them to be doing philosophy.

Our most significant agreement with DeLanda is with his reading of what Deleuze and Guattari mean when they claim that previous attempts to understand systems in terms of an abstract, transcendental, generative function have been both too abstract and not abstract enough. DeLanda argues that Deleuze and Guattari intend that the notion of an abstract machine (i.e., their transcendental, generative condition) should be both concrete enough to account for the variety of material factors which give rise to any given system (this, recall, was why Russell's logic and Chomsky's grammar were too abstract, for they were left unable to account for these factors); and the notion of an abstract machine should be abstract enough to be plugged into a variety of different circumstances, and yet continue to be equally relevant in each of these circumstances. DeLanda has applied this notion of an abstract machine (or what is discussed in his most recent book as the 'quasi-causal operator') to, in *A Thousand Years of Nonlinear History*, an understanding of the generative processes involved in economic, urban, biological, and linguistic history, and, in *Virtual Philosophy*, to mathematics and science. Our efforts here to apply this same approach to an understanding of the origins of sedimentary rocks, stars, autocatalytic sets, and the U.S. Constitution are thus largely in agreement with DeLanda. DeLanda, however, although he believes that the double articulation abstract machine (the model we have been using) was thoroughly developed in *A Thousand Plateaus*, argues for a second abstract machine – the self-consistent aggregate model. This abstract machine is, according to DeLanda, 'much less well developed than their double articulation model.'[16]

DeLanda accepts the first abstract machine, the double articulation model, and will on more than one occasion cite Deleuze and Guattari's example of the origin of sedimentary rocks as a case in point of such a model. The second abstract machine DeLanda calls for, the self-consistent aggregate model, is fundamentally different. Rather than the two-step model of double articulation, DeLanda argues that the self-consistent aggregate model involves three distinct elements. In the first, heterogeneous elements are brought together through 'an articulation of superpositions'[17] which establishes an interconnection of diverse but overlapping elements. For example, in the autocatalytic set a diversity of molecules (i.e., heterogeneous elements) is brought together by means of their ability to react with one another, or their ability to facilitate reactions by acting as a catalyst. In an ecosystem, you have a similar interconnection of heterogeneous elements. The plants and various species of animals are brought together through their role in the predator/prey food chain. And finally, DeLanda cites pre-capitalist markets as yet another example of a self-consistent aggregate. In this case, a heterogeneous collection of buyers and sellers, with a diversity of needs and products to sell, are brought together within the market by means of the role these products play in satisfying the demands of both buyers and sellers.[18] The second element of the self-consistent aggregate is the intercalary element, or the facilitator which allows for the interrelationship between the heterogeneous elements to be established more easily. In the autocatalytic set, this intercalary element is the catalyst (as we discussed above); in the ecosystem, DeLanda cites the bacteria which assist in the process of digestion; and in the pre-capitalist market, money functions as the facilitator of exchange. The third element of the self-consistent aggregate is the behavioural patterns and stability which constitute an 'emergent property' of the heterogeneous elements. The self-replicating behaviour of an autocatalytic set, for example, and the behaviours associated with this behaviour which maintain the autocatalytic set as a relatively stable state, is an 'emergent property' in that this stable state is not to be identified with the heterogeneous elements of which it is composed. Similarly, the stable state of a particular ecosystem is an emergent property which is greater than, or distinct from, the heterogeneous elements which make up an ecosystem; and again Braudel and others have noted that economic markets themselves exhibit stable states and patterns of behaviour which can in turn be understood as an emergent property of a heterogeneous set of individual decisions and exchanges.[19]

This self-consistent aggregate model is, according to DeLanda, quite different from the double articulation model. In the double articulation model, heterogeneous elements are not brought together, but rather they are sorted into homogeneous, consistent strata (e.g., sedimentary rocks). Rather than being the cementation of a homogeneous layer, the self-consistent aggregate represents the synthesis of heterogeneous elements, and it is the model that accounts for this synthesis that DeLanda believes Deleuze and Guattari only implicitly developed. To justify this position, DeLanda quotes Deleuze and Guattari's recognition that there is indeed a synthesis of heterogeneities, and draws our attention to their further claim that 'the term machinic is precisely this synthesis of heterogeneities as such.'[20] But Deleuze and Guattari immediately add to this claim that since 'these heterogeneities are matters of *expression*, we say that their synthesis itself, their consistency or capture, forms a properly machinic "statement" or "enunciation."'[21] As an expression, a machinic 'enunciation' or 'statement,' this synthesis (e.g., autocatalytic set, eco-system, pre-capitalist market) thus entails the paradoxical both/and structure of the abstract machine, or these expressions (following Hjelmslev) will exhibit, as we have discussed above, the abstract machine of double articulation. The double articulation model does seem, then, especially with the notion of a 'plane of consistency' drawn by the 'machinic-function' (abstract machine), capable of addressing DeLanda's concept of a 'self-consistent aggregate.'

Yet there is another, likely more important, reason why DeLanda calls for abstract machines and models other than the double articulation model. Of particular significance for DeLanda in this regard is the emergence of a living being that can search for its own food. DeLanda argues that a third abstract machine is necessary (in addition to the double articulation model and the self-consistent aggregate model) to account for this phenomenon. This machine he refers to as a 'probe head,' which he describes as a 'sorting device' coupled with an 'ability to replicate with variation.'[22] This third abstract machine is thus a com-bination of the first (i.e., its ability to sort and filter) and the second (i.e., self-replication of self-consistent aggregates) abstract machines, and furthermore this machine can better model behaviours which are clearly not shared by rocks. Moreover, even with respect to the second abstract machine (the self-consistent aggregate model), the emergent property of self-replication is not to be identified with the chemical reactions which constitute a living being, nor, more importantly, do sedimentary rocks even appear to possess such an emergent property. A sedimentary rock is generally taken to be nothing more than the sed-iment which constitutes it. To account for these clear differences, there-fore, DeLanda proposes that we use three (and eventually more) abstract machines to model the various phenomena of the world.

The key point we have been stressing, however, is that we need to understand dynamic systems as expressions of a machinic function (abstract machine, paradoxa), which consequently illustrate the double articulation which is immanent to these systems. Therefore, a dynamic system involves stability, slowness, and stratified elements, while also requiring the flexibility to adapt, transform, and destabilize these very elements. The first and second abstract machines DeLanda calls for are precisely the two heterogeneous elements that are brought together, paradoxically, as expressions of the abstract machine – Mechanosphere – or, all is an expression of an abstract machine and everything is con-sequently a dynamic system, a self-consistent aggregate, and a stratum. This is clearly the case in living organisms, such as human beings. As a living organism, a human being is a dynamic system, but he/she also has stable, slow to change strata – that is, the genetic code. This is not to say that the genes are not themselves dynamic. From the perspective of a human being, or even the human species, the genetic code is a stratum, but from the perspective of evolutionary time the genes are the vehicles of the dynamic process of evolution itself.[23] And even the elements which constitute DNA are constituted (e.g., carbon), as we have seen, within a dynamic process which encompasses an even larger scale of time and speed.

In *A Thousand Plateaus*, Deleuze and Guattari recognize the cosmic scope of the abstract machine, a scope in which differentiations occur based upon the speed and slowness of the flows which facilitate the emergence of various forms – for example, the flow of proteins which facilitates genetic mutation versus the flow of food which facilitates the growth, change, and development of a single organism. The plane of consistency, as we have seen, is the term Deleuze and Guattari give to that condition which allows for the emergence of new forms.[24] This consistency corresponds to the consistency of the first articulation, or the consistency (form) of differentiation which allows for the possibility that something can be actualized (i.e., the substance that emerges as a result of differenciation). In expanding the scope of this process, Deleuze and Guattari argue that

> the plane of consistency of Nature is like an immense Abstract machine ... there is therefore a unity to the plane of nature, which applies equally to the inanimate and the animate, the artificial and the natural [and this unity] is a plane upon which everything is laid out, and which is like the intersection of all forms, the machine of all functions ... It is a fixed plane, upon which things are distinguished from one another only by speed and slowness.[25]

This plane of consistency, as we saw in the previous chapter, is precisely the condition a BwO presupposes if an identifiable form is to emerge. Thus, the sediment was sorted into the homogeneous layers, which were then cemented and stratified into a new entity – sedimentary rock; a set of chemical reactions, with the aid of catalysts, achieves a state of high interdependence and overlap, and this in turn allows for the phase transition which results in the emergence of a new entity – a living organism; and a monkey searching for food under coloured boxes attains a state in which it consistently chooses the right box more than the wrong, and it is this consistency which then gives rise to a new stable state – knowledge. Relative to that new entity which ultimately emerges, the BwO is an unstructured flow, but for this flow to be able to allow for new substances to develop, this flow must achieve a state of consistency, or, as discussed above, the BwO must be drawn by the abstract machine of double articulation into a plane of consistency. And on this point, success is not guaranteed. Deleuze and Guattari recognize the possibility that either no consistency is drawn, with the result that the functioning system which requires that a plane of consistency be drawn by the BwO explodes into what Deleuze and Guattari call a cancerous body; or, on the other extreme, the BwO may fail to allow for consistency to be drawn from the unstructured flow by simply obstructing all flows whatsoever, resulting in what Deleuze and Guattari call a fascist body. In both cases, the unstructured flows of the BwO collapse in such a way that it is no longer possible for anything new to emerge, or for the double articulation to proceed. To restate this in terms used in our chapter on Spinoza, the absolutely indeterminate substance which exceeds and transgresses each and every determinate identity must be drawn into a plane of consistency (the attributes), or substance must be ironed out and avoid excessive differences, and then and only then can it be actualized into determinate, identifiable states (modes), states that are the determinate essence of substance itself. Or to rephrase Nietzsche's claim that one must have chaos in one's self to give birth to a dancing star, Deleuze and Guattari add Artaud's call that one needs to become a BwO, and a body that can be drawn into a plane of consistency so that something new can emerge, something new can be thought.

We can now understand the sense intended by Deleuze and Guattari when they claim that things are to be distinguished from one another 'only by speed and slowness.' The unstructured flow of proteins (BwO) through the process of genetic evolution occurs at a rate, or speed, which is slow in comparison to the rate of the unstructured flow of food (BwO) through a living organism as it grows, develops, and ages. Similarly, the unstructured flow of hydrogen (BwO) which gives rise to stars and, ultimately, carbon is slow in comparison to the rate at which carbon itself (as a component of protein) flows through genetic evolution. Expanding the perspective to encompass the entire natural universe, we see that here too anything which develops and differentiates itself from something else requires that a BwO be drawn into a plane of consistency. One should therefore read Deleuze and Guattari literally when they speak of the 'plane of consistency of Nature.' The natural universe, as a whole, is the field which conditions the possibility that new forms and entities can emerge. Furthermore, when Deleuze and Guattari add that this plane of consistency of Nature is like an 'immense Abstract machine,' and do so with a capital 'A,' we come then to understand that Nature itself must be understood as a dynamic system that is both stable and changing, or that requires both slow, stable elements and speeds and flows (i.e., BwOs) which allow for change. Consequently, when expanded to encompass the plane of consistency of Nature, the BwO is simply the flow or intensity from which a plane of consistency can be drawn, and in turn from which an identifiable, stable state can emerge, a state which can then serve as the BwO from which another plane of consistency, another dynamic system, is drawn, and so on, *ad infinitum*. The BwO that *becomes* the plane of consistency of Nature is thus the minimal condition or speed for the possibility that *any identifiable* entity or state can *be* – Deleuze and Guattari will refer to this BwO as *The* BwO – and for this reason Deleuze and Guattari argue that this BwO has an intensity equal to zero. In other words, relative to the external, *identifiable* states which function as the standard for measuring intensity (e.g., the speed of *identifiable* molecules as the standard presupposed by any measurement of 'heat'), *The* BwO, as the condition for the possibility of any external standard, is thus, relative to these standards, non-identifiable, or it has an intensity equal to zero. The BwO is thus not to be confused with Whitehead's view of God, for in this case God is the self-*identical* condition that guarantees the emergence of other identities, or God is an identity which conditions other identities. *The* BwO, to the contrary, is in itself non-identifiable, or has an intensity equal to zero. Yet by having an intensity equal to zero, this does not imply, as Deleuze and Guattari make clear, that the BwO is something negative:

> The BwO causes intensities to pass; it produces and distributes them in a spatium that is itself intensive, lacking extension. It is not space, nor is it in space; it is matter that occupies space to a given degree [i.e., measurable intensity] – to the degree corresponding to the intensities produced. It is nonstratified, unformed, intense matter, the matter of intensity, intensity = 0; but there is nothing negative about that zero, there are no negative or opposite intensities.[26]

A few lines later they ask, rhetorically, 'is not Spinoza's *Ethics* the great book of the BwO?'[27] This reference to Spinoza is significant, for

DeLanda was indeed correct to note the differences he sees in the different abstract machines he calls for. After all, sedimentary rocks and monkeys who learn are clearly different. However, these abstract machines are, as we have shown, themselves expressions, or they are repetitions of the Abstract machine which *expresses*, paradoxically, both the heterogeneous and the homogeneous, the stratified and the dynamic, the territorialized and the deterritorialized, differentiation and differenciation. This is where Deleuze's understanding of what he takes to be Spinoza's theory of the univocity of expression is crucial. By univocal expressions of the Abstract machine, Deleuze (on our reading) is not assuming that all abstract machines are one and the same; rather, as identifiably distinct, they presuppose the immanence of the Abstract machine, and the immanence of The BwO.

As we argued in the Introduction, Deleuze's work needs to be understood in light of the concepts of Spinoza and Nietzsche, and we see again why this is so. One of many problems commentators have had with Spinoza from the beginning has been in understanding the relationship between finite, actual modes and infinite substance and attributes. Similarly, critics of Deleuze such as Alain Badiou have found a major 'stumbling block' in Deleuze's theory of the virtual to be an accounting of the relationship between the virtual as completely determined and the actual of which the virtual is a part.[28] The basis for these criticisms is the same in both cases – viz. what is presupposed is the *identity* of, or the *identifiable* difference between, the modes and the attributes of substance for Spinoza, and the virtual and the actual for Deleuze. What was argued for in our chapter on Spinoza, however, and what subsequent chapters have argued with respect to Deleuze, is that the attributes are dependent upon the modes in order for the attributes to be identified as the actual, constitutive essence of substance; and for Deleuze the problematic of the Idea, the reality of the virtual and *The BwO*, is identifiable as such only within the actualities that are the solutions to this problematic. There is thus, to repeat, an indiscernible, nonidentifiable difference in itself – that is, a difference without mediation, without basis for comparison – and the problematic Idea is indiscernible from the actual precisely because there are real problems (reality of the virtual) that are yet to be solved, but which are inseparable from the actualities that are themselves solutions. Deleuze remained to the end, then, as he himself admitted, a Spinozist.

We can gain even further understanding of the terminology of Deleuze and Guattari by recalling our previous discussion of expression. Part of Deleuze's interest in Spinoza and Leibniz, and the great advance these two philosophers made over Descartes in his opinion, was their use of the concept 'expression.' Understood in the context of what we have been saying here, Hjelmslev's concept of the sign-function, the function that is paradoxically both expression and content, can now be seen to be expressed as the Abstract machine that paradoxically both is chaos, BwO, becoming, *and* is order, actualization, being. The Abstract machine, to state it in yet another way, is a dynamic system at the edge of chaos. Furthermore, since the Abstract machine is the paradoxical 'machinic-function' that is both chaos and order (it is chaosmos), the *identifiable* abstract machines are simply repetitions or further expressions of the Abstract machine.

It is here, as we also argued in the Introduction, that Nietzsche's concept of eternal recurrence becomes important. To restate briefly what was argued earlier, the Abstract machine of double articulation is itself a double affirmation, an eternal recurrence, in the sense that the first affirmation (the affirmation of Dionysus) is only identifiable as being an affirmation when it comes to be repeated by a second affirmation or articulation (the affirmation of Ariadne). Since the first affirmation is non-identifiable and hence outside the measurable time of *chronos*, this second affirmation is therefore the recurrence of the eternal, the return of *aion*. In a similar fashion, each of the abstract machines repeats the eternal recurrence of the Abstract machine, or each of the abstract machines, as identifiable, is an expression of the non-identifiable Abstract machine, much as the attributes are expressions of God for Spinoza. Moreover, the *identifiable* abstract machines, as expressions of the Abstract machine, express in their *own* way (i.e., *identifiable* way) the paradoxical double bind of determining and identifying the non-identifiable nature of becoming – these abstract machines are dynamic systems.[29] With this convergence of Spinoza and Nietzsche in the work of Deleuze and Guattari, and with their further elaboration of a transcendental project infused with the conceptual implications of univocity and eternal recurrence, we have, as was true for Nietzsche, 'the closest approximation of a world of becoming to a world of being.'[30]

III: Philosophy at the Edge of Chaos

In drawing this work to a close, we turn now to discuss what doing philosophy might mean, or how it might proceed if it were to be a dynamic system at the edge of chaos. By way of introduction, we will discuss again Merlin Donald's theory concerning the emergence of philosophy. With this discussion in hand, we should then be able to see the reason why we believe doing philosophy through definitions could constitute a dynamic system, or how this could be doing a philosophy at the edge of chaos. What we will be arguing below has an important precedent in Deleuze himself, for not only did Deleuze and Guattari write plateaus (more on this below), but in an important yet small book, *Spinoza: Practical Philosophy*, Deleuze devotes the majority of this book to setting forth definitions of key concepts in Spinoza. In following up on Spinoza's own philosophical labours that hinged on definitions, Deleuze thus appears to have found this effort to begin with definitions to be an important aspect of doing philosophy.

In Donald's analysis of the emergence of theoretic philosophy in ancient Greece, he emphasizes the role written language plays in this process, and more precisely he stresses the significance of a phonetic written language.[31] The ancient Greeks, of course, were neither the first to use language as a form of external storage, nor did they invent the phonetic alphabet (the Phoenicians, for example, had a phonetic alphabet, and it was their encounter with the Phoenicians around 900 B.C. which led to the reappearance of writing). The Greeks were not even the first to record their thoughts and observations on events (Donald notes that this was present in China, Egypt, and Mesopotamia); however, what Donald claims is the 'critical innovation' of the Greeks was to have 'developed the habit of recording the verbalizations and speculations, the oral discourses revealing the *process* itself in action. The great discovery here was that, by entering ideas, even incomplete ideas, into the public record, they could later be improved and refined.'[32] The Greeks thus began, and on this Donald believes they were the first, 'to record the thought process itself.'[33]

We can restate Donald's theory in terms of the double articulation model, and in fact by doing so we begin to draw in other factors not mentioned by Donald. In the first articulation, we have the written, externally stored record of oral commentary, a record that could, because of the phonetic alphabet, more accurately reflect the oral process associated with this commentary. As the Greek culture began to engage in increased trade and acquire greater influence throughout the Mediterranean, it became increasingly important to acquire the ability to record transactions in writing so as to keep track of this trade, and with this development more and more individuals acquired the ability to write, including, most importantly, individuals who may not have been from one of the traditional classes that would have acquired this skill – namely, the political or religious courts. The written thoughts and observations thus begin to take on a more secular, worldly tone. In time, with this increased recording of thought in writing, and with the external record of the process of thought itself, there emerged a critical point, a critical mass, from which emerged an activity concerned with thinking about the processes of thought themselves, a type of autocatalysis of thought. Thus, in the first articulation the external recording of thought in phonetic writing (substance) attains, because of increased economic activity by more and more individuals, a critical mass (form); and with the second articulation this critical mass (form) becomes transformed into a new activity (substance) – that is, thought about the processes of thought, or philosophy. More precisely, what emerged, especially with Socrates, was the attempt to *define* clearly the words used within the processes of thought. More to the point, Socrates not only sought to define the words used within the processes of thought, but sought a rule that could be used to account for each and every possible use of a particular word. It is this 'rule' that is the object of the second articulation, much as it was for the monkey who learned the rule.

To set forth a series of definitions as a dynamic system, one would in many ways be continuing within the Socratic tradition. However, there is an important difference between a philosophy at the edge of chaos and what Socrates (and Plato and much of the philosophical tradition which follows) attempts to do. In his conversations, Socrates sought to determine the true definitions of the topics being discussed – for example, justice, beauty, love, knowledge, etc. – and a true definition that was non-contradictory. If an interlocutor says justice is doing harm to enemies and good to friends, but later admits this is not what justice is, Socrates concludes that this person does not 'know' the true definition of justice. Underlying this approach is, as has been a central theme in this book, the assumption that the various instances of justice could be reduced to an *identifiable*, non-contradictory definition. We have repeatedly seen that this attempt to ground knowledge on the basis of a fundamental identity (e.g., a true definition) necessarily presupposes the non-identifiable condition for this identity, what Derrida, for example, referred to as *différance*. We have shown that this non-identifiable condition is to be understood as a fundamental difference, a non-identifiable both/and, which allows for the possibility of non-contradictory identities. We have referred to this condition by various names – will to power, chaosmos, paradoxa, and, most recently, the abstract machine of double articulation. We have argued that doing philosophy involves encountering this both/and condition, paradoxa, or that it involves thinking the different, the uncommon, within the *identity* of that which is common. We have also argued that philosophy ought to be systematic, or that it ought to concern itself with a systematic approach to the phenomena which can be thought, even if, as we saw, this equally involves encountering the non-identifiable condition for these phenomena, a condition which cannot be thought, and a condition that may lead to the transformation of the system. What we have claimed is needed is a philosophy that is systematic, though not in the Hegelian sense – that is, where the elements of the system are interrelated by means of their relation to a controlling, systematizing *identity* (e.g., Spirit), an identity one can know and think (e.g., Hegel's Absolute Knowledge); rather, what is needed is a philosophy that explicitly seeks to be a dynamic system, or a philosophy at the edge of chaos. Deleuze and Guattari's philosophy, or their writing of plateaus, is an instance of such a philosophy. By setting forth terms and definitions, they too set the stage for the actualization of their philosophy, the second articulation of their plateaus, within an indeterminate number of determinate contexts.[34]

It is the use of definitions that is key. In a philosophy at the edge of chaos, the definitions do not comprise a dictionary. As Umberto Eco has discussed this point in setting forth his notion of the 'Open Work,' the words of a dictionary lack the order and systematic interdependence which would allow one to read it like a novel.[35] If done right, the definitions would have a type of order and systematic interdependence, and thus they would be related to each other, but not in the sense that they are under the hierarchical governance and control of a first or dominant definition. Rather, each definition is to be understood as a repetition of the first definition, though not as a repetition of the same, but rather as a repetition of the non-identifiable differentiating condition (e.g., abstract machine ... double articulation ... chaosmos ... paradoxa ...), a condition which allows for the very possibility of identifying and defining the terms at all. In short, the pursuit of definitions is already a repetition of the non-identifiable condition, a repetition of the double bind of the abstract machine, and thus presupposes still other abstract machines (e.g., it presupposes machinic functions associated with language, academics, publishing, etc.). Therefore, the abstract machine, or the both/and condition of double articulation, will be univocally expressed in each of the definitions one would set forth, and for this reason there would be a type of relationship between them. Moreover, the interaction and relationship between these definitions may generate a systematic, consistent philosophy, but only a system that is an emergent property of the interactions and relationships between these definitions. There is no guarantee, of course. The definitions may fail to draw a plane of consistency, and hence they may fail to generate a consistent, dynamic whole, the result being just an inconsistent, incoherent, meaningless jumble of words and ideas; or again they may slip into platitudes and again fail to say something new, fail to generate the conditions which allow for the creativity of thought to appear. Deleuze and Guattari worked to create these conditions for the creativity of thought, and with the series of terms and definitions they offer us, they have presented a systematic philosophy, a series of plateaus, that should not be seen as a completed work or system; to the contrary, to the extent that their philosophy is successful, is doing what it *ought* to be doing, it will engender further thought, it will engender a thinking that will become other and still other philosophies. This is the work of doing philosophy.

Notes

Introduction

1 Gilles Deleuze, *Difference and Repetition*, trans. Paul Patton (New York: Columbia University Press, 1994), 147.

2 Ibid., xix. In the Preface, Deleuze states, 'We propose to think difference in itself independently of the forms of representation which reduce it to the Same, and the relation of different to different independently of those forms which make them pass through the negative.' This passing through the negative implies, according to Deleuze, that the 'subordination to the identical is maintained.'

3 Miguel de Beistegui, in *Truth and Genesis: Philosophy as Differential Ontology* (Bloomington: Indiana University Press, 2004), has recently focused on this concern of twentieth-century Continental philosophy to 'think difference.' In impressive readings of the philosophical tradition, especially Aristotle and Heidegger, Beistegui shows that Deleuze's effort to 'think difference' entails an understanding of immanent genesis which avoids problems Beistegui finds in Aristotle and Heidegger. We agree with much of what Beistegui is doing. Where this work differs is in stressing the influence of Spinoza and Nietzsche on Deleuze's effort to think difference, an influence we argue is most visible when Deleuze is read in line with a theory of dynamic systems.

4 Jacques Derrida, *Of Grammatology*, trans. Gayatri Chakravorty Spivak (Baltimore: Johns Hopkins University Press, 1976), 23.

5 This theme will be discussed thoroughly in the third chapter as we address the influence of Nietzsche's thought on the work of Deleuze.

6 Christopher Langton, a pioneer in the field known as 'artificial life,' uses the term 'edge of chaos' to describe the conditions necessary for the emer-

gence of new life forms. Langton arrived at this conclusion after simulating on a computer the interaction of numerous species in an ecosystem, and programming these entities such that they possess the ability to self-replicate with the possibility for variation (i.e., mutation). Langton could run a computer simulation which could quickly see what happens over the space of hundreds and thousands of generations. What he found was that if the parameters which determine the amount of variation between generations were set too low, the life forms would soon collapse into one or a few non-changing varieties – and hence no new forms would evolve and the ecosystem would eventually collapse. If the parameters were set too high, changes would be so rapid that stable forms could neither emerge or be maintained, and here too life forms, and hence the ecosystem, would die off. It was only when the parameters were set at a critical period, the 'edge of chaos,' that new, stable forms could emerge. The 'edge of chaos,' then, is for Langton both ordered and chaotic, stable and unstable. See Langton's introduction to *Artificial Life: An Overview* (Cambridge, MA: MIT Press, 1995). See also, from this same book, Kunihko Kaneko's essay, 'Chaos as a Source of Complexity.'

7 For more on the differences between Deleuze and Derrida, see *Between Deleuze and Derrida*, ed. Paul Patton and John Protevi (New York: Continuum, 2003). For works that interpret Deleuze's philosophy in light of dynamic systems theory (or complexity theory, as it is also known), see Brian Massumi, *A User's Guide to Capitalism and Schizophrenia: Deviations from Deleuze and Guattari* (Cambridge, MA: MIT Press, 1992); Manuel DeLanda, *A Thousand Years of Nonlinear History* (New York: Zone Books, 1997) and *Intensive Science and Virtual Philosophy* (London: Continuum, 2002); and Mark Bonta and John Protevi, *Deleuze and Geophilosophy: A Guide and Glossary* (Edinburgh: Edinburgh University Press, 2004). Where this book contributes to the understanding of Deleuze and dynamic systems is in detailing how Deleuze's dynamic systems approach enables him to address issues that have been persistent throughout the philosophical tradition. In short, the extended comparative analyses offered here examine the relationship between Deleuze's project and those of Plato, Aristotle, Spinoza, Nietzsche, Heidegger, and Derrida, and in doing this show how Deleuze's dynamic systems approach is better able to 'think difference' (see note 3 above).

8 Bonta and Protevi, in *Deleuze and Geophilosophy*, make a similar point. They argue that 'just as Kant's Critiques were in a sense the epistemology, metaphysics, ethics, and aesthetics for a world of Euclidean space, Aristotelian time, and Newtonian physics, Deleuze provides the philosophical concepts

that make sense of our world of fragmented space ... twisted time ... and the non-linear effects of far-from-equilibrium thermodynamics' (vii–viii).

9 *A Thousand Plateaus*, trans. Brian Massumi (Minneapolis: University of Minnesota Press, 1987), 148.

10 This is why Deleuze and Guattari prefer the socio-linguist William Labov to Chomsky. See *Thousand Plateaus*, 93–4.

11 Perhaps a similar criticism could be made of Derrida. A common crticism of Derrida has been that he looks at nothing but texts, and even when he discusses concrete phenomena (e.g., politics, art, etc.) he almost exclusively focuses upon the written texts which refer to them. For Deleuze and Guattari, on the other hand, their notion of an abstract machine as a double articulation (or both/and) can be used as a tool in thinking through and understanding concrete processes rather than simply texts. Bonta and Protevi point out this difference as well, arguing that Deleuze and Guattari should not be placed in the 'post-structuralist neighborhood,' if by that is meant the study and critique of 'discourses' and 'regimes of signs.' See *Geophilosophy*, 39.

12 *Thousand Plateaus*, 514.

13 Ibid., 40.

14 References to Spinoza's *Ethics* are from *The Collected Works of Spinoza*, vol. 1, ed. Edwin Curley (Princeton: Princeton University Press, 1985). As is standard in referring to Spinoza's *Ethics*, the first number corresponds to the Part, the letters to definitions (D) and propositions (P) – hence 1D4 is from Part 1, the fourth definition.

15 See chapter 2 below for our discussion of the problems commentators have had with Spinoza and how the reading offered here not only resolves these problems but also clarifies both Spinoza's and Deleuze's projects. Furthermore, the same problems commentators have had with Spinoza can also be found in the commentary on Deleuze. The most notable instance of this is Alain Badiou's criticisms of Deleuze in *Deleuze: The Clamor of Being*, trans. Louise Burchill (Minneapolis: University of Minnesota Press, 2000). It is precisely the relationship between the virtual and the actual –or more precisely, Deleuze's claim that the virtual is completely determined and yet defined 'as strictly a part of the real object' (51) – that Badiou finds to be the 'stumbling block for the theory of the virtual' (ibid.). By showing how the virtual depends upon the actual, much as the attributes of substance depend upon the modes of the attributes for Spinoza, we can resolve Badiou's criticism as well.

16 *Difference and Repetition*, 164.

17 *A Thousand Plateaus*, 153.

18 *Twilight of the Idols*, in *The Portable Nietzsche*, ed. and trans. Walter Kaufmann (New York: Penguin Books, 1954), 481.
19 *The Will to Power*, ed. and trans. Walter Kaufmann (New York: Vintage Books, 1967), no. 517 (p. 280).
20 Gilles Deleuze, *Nietzsche and Philosophy*, trans. Hugh Tomlinson (New York: Columbia University Press, 1983), 187.
21 See, for instance, *The Logic of Sense*, trans. Mark Lester (New York: Columbia University Press, 1990), 162–8 ('Twenty-Third Series of the Aion').
22 *Will to Power*, 330.
23 *A Thousand Plateaus*, 53.

1. Systematic Thinking and the Philosophy of Difference

1 Plato, *The Republic*, trans. Allan Bloom (New York: Basic Books, 1968), 168 (488d–e). This is a persistent theme in Plato's writings. Socrates will, on a number of occasions, identify his method of inquiry and questioning – that is, his philosophizing – as 'out of the common.' See, for instance, Plato's *Apology*, 20c. See also chapter 3 below for a more extended discussion of Plato.
2 It should be noted that Deleuze had little interest in the critique of metaphysics or the end of philosophy debates. In *Negotiations* (New York: Columbia University Press, 1995), for example, Deleuze states, 'I've never been worried about going beyond metaphysics or any death of philosophy' (136).
3 G.W.F. Hegel, *Hegel's Science of Logic*, trans. A.V. Miller (Atlantic Highlands, NJ: Humanities Press International, 1995), 843.
4 Ibid., 844.
5 Ibid., 843.
6 Ibid.
7 Friedrich Nietzsche, *Beyond Good and Evil*, trans. Walter Kaufmann (New York: Vintage Books, 1966), sec. 43.
8 *The Gay Science*, trans. Walter Kaufmann (New York: Vintage Books, 1974), sec. 335, p. 266. See also sec. 354: 'Fundamentally, all our actions are altogether incomparably personal, unique, and infinitely individual; there is no doubt of that.'
9 Kaufmann cites this passage in a footnote (*Gay Science*, sec. 270n). The quote is from *Reason in History*, trans. Robert S. Hartman (Indianapolis: Bobbs-Merrill, 1953), 69.
10 *Gay Science*, sec. 355.
11 Ibid., sec. 110.
12 See, for example, *Beyond Good and Evil*, sec. 39: 'it might be a basic characteristic of existence that those who would know it completely would perish, in which case the strength of a spirit should be measured according to

how much of the "truth" one could still barely endure – or to put it more
clearly, to what degree one would require it to be thinned down, shrouded,
sweetened, blunted, falsified.' Or, to put it in other terms, to what degree
do they need to 'know' it?

13 *On the Genealogy of Morals*, trans. Walter Kaufmann (New York: Vintage
Books, 1969), third essay, sec. 12, p. 119.

14 *Gay Science*, sec. 344, p. 285.

15 Ibid., sec. 347, p. 287.

16 Ibid., p. 287.

17 *Philosophy in the Tragic Age of the Greeks*, trans. Marianne Cowan (Chicago:
Regnery Gateway, 1962), 23.

18 Ibid., 25.

19 Ibid., 23–4.

20 *Beyond Good and Evil*, sec. 6, p. 13.

21 Ibid., p. 3

22 Ibid., sec. 259, p. 203.

23 Martin Heidegger, *Parmenides*, trans. André Schuwer and Richard
Rojcewicz (Bloomington: Indiana University Press, 1992), 58.

24 Martin Heidegger, *Nietzsche*, trans. David F. Krell (San Francisco: Harper-
Collins, 1991), vol. 3, p. 41.

25 Ibid., p. 46.

26 I refer, of course, to Leibniz's example, in the *Monadology*, trans. George
Montgomery (La Salle, IL: Open Court, 1988), of the various perspectives of
the same city. See section 57, p. 263.

27 *Nietzsche*, vol. 1, p. 215.

28 Ibid.

29 Ibid., vol. 2, pp. 199–200.

30 'The End of Philosophy and the Task of Thinking,' in *Basic Writings*, ed.
David Farrell Krell (New York: Harper & Row, 1977), 375.

31 Ibid., 391.

32 *Nietzsche*, vol. 2, p. 200.

33 *The Will to Power*, ed. and trans. Walter Kaufmann (New York: Vintage
Books, 1967), no. 617, p. 330. Quoted by Heidegger, ibid., p. 202.

34 *Beyond Good and Evil*, sec. 36, p. 48.

35 In *Nietzsche*, vol. 2, p. 187, Heidegger argues that metaphysics is guided by
a single question, What is being, or the beingness of being? and in answering this question it has forgotten Being as presencing unconcealment, as
self-concealing aletheia, and answers instead in terms of being: 'Being as a
whole has now [i.e., with metaphysics] become visible for the first time as
being and as a whole.'

36 *Nietzsche*, vol. 3, p. 156.

37 Ibid., p. 212.

38 Ibid., vol. 2, p. 205.

39 Ibid.

40 Ibid., vol. 1, p. 201.

41 *Parmenides*, 50.

42 Ibid., 50. Heidegger describes this as the imperial aspect of the Roman view, a view he claims 'springs forth from the essence of truth as correctness in the sense of the directive self-adjusting guarantee of the security of domination. The "taking as true" of ratio, of reor, becomes a far-reaching and anticipatory security. Ratio becomes counting, calculating, calculus. Ratio is self-adjustment to what is correct.'

43 Ibid., 53.

44 Ibid., 58

45 Ibid.

46 *Nietzsche*, vol. 4, p. 147.

47 Thus Nietzsche's famous phrase regarding Being as 'the last wisp of evaporating reality' (quoted in *Nietzsche*, vol. 4, p. 182).

48 *Parmenides*, 101.

49 Ibid., 50.

50 Ibid. (emphasis added).

51 Ibid.

52 Jacques Derrida, *Speech and Phenomena*, trans. David B. Allison (Evanston, IL: Northwestern University Press, 1973), 79.

53 Ibid., 82.

54 Ibid., 85.

55 Jacques Derrida, *Of Grammatology*, trans. Gayatri C. Spivak (Baltimore: Johns Hopkins University Press, 1974), 23.

56 Ibid., 62.

57 Ibid., 60.

58 Jacques Derrida, 'From Restricted to General Economy: A Hegelianism without Reserve,' in *Writing and Difference*, trans. Alan Bass (Chicago: University of Chicago Press, 1978), 259.

59 Ibid.

60 Ibid., 268.

61 Ibid., 272.

62 Ibid., 272–3.

63 Ibid., 274.

64 Ibid., 275.

65 Derrida, for example, will cite Nietzsche as an example of a systematic thinker who does not subordinate his system to a standard or presence which would complete and close the system.

66 *Speech and Phenomena*, 133.

67 Ibid., 139.

68 Ibid., 140. Quote is from Ferdinand de Saussure, *Course in General Linguistics*, trans. Roy Harris (La Salle, IL: Open Court, 1983), 118.

69 *Speech and Phenomena*, 140.

70 Ibid., 141.

71 Ibid.

72 Manfred Frank, 'Is Self-Consciousness a Case of *présence à soi?* Towards a Meta-Critique of the Recent French Critique of Metaphysics,' in *Derrida: A Critical Reader*, ed. David Wood (Oxford: Blackwell, 1992), 231.

73 Ibid. Quoting *Limited, Inc.*, trans. Samuel Weber and Jeffrey Mehlman (Evanston, IL: Northwestern University Press, 1988), 24–5.

74 *Dissemination*, trans. Barbara Johnson (Chicago: University of Chicago Press, 1981), 64.

75 *Limited, Inc.*, 146.

76 *Positions*, trans. Alan Bass (Chicago: University of Chicago Press, 1981), 63.

77 Frank, 'Self-Consciousness,' 232.

78 We have appropriated the term from Félix Guattari, who uses it extensively in his book *Chaosmosis*, trans. Paul Bains and Julian Pefanis (Bloomington: Indiana University Press, 1995); and Guattari appropriates the term from James Joyce. For a study of the term in Joyce's writing, see Umberto Eco, *The Aesthetics of Chaosmos: The Middle Ages of James Joyce*, trans. Ellen Esrock (Cambridge, MA: Harvard University Press, 1982).

79 Recall our earlier citation from *Of Grammatology*: 'The (pure) trace is differance. It does not depend on any sensible plentitude, audible or visible, phonic or graphic. It is, on the contrary, the condition of such a plentitude' (62).

80 Recall another earlier citation, also from *Of Grammatology*: 'entity and being, ontic and ontological, "ontico-ontological," are, in an original style, derivative with regard to difference; and with respect to what I shall later call differance, an economic concept designating the production of differing/deferring' (23). Todd May has offered a criticism of Derrida that is similar to ours, when he contrasts Deleuze's understanding of difference with Derrida's conception of differance: 'Deleuze's notion of difference is distinct from Derrida's notion of differance. The latter involves an inevitable play of presence and absence, a specific economy of the two, which, although issuing in any number of philosophical possibilities, nevertheless governs them with a certain type of logic that is necessary to all discourse' ('Difference and Unity in Gilles Deleuze,' in *Gilles Deleuze and the Theater of Philosophy*, ed. Constantin Boundas and Dorothea Olkowski [New York: Routledge, 1994], 40). In short, Derrida reduces the uncommon, the plenti-

tude and diversity, the chaos of a text, to being an 'effect' of a simple necessary function that is common to all texts.

81   *Of Grammatology*, 158.
82   See *Positions*, 62.

2. Ironing Out the Differences: Nietzsche and Deleuze as Spinozists

1   Friedrich Nietzsche, *Beyond Good and Evil*, trans. Walter Kaufmann (New York: Vintage, 1966), 24.
2   Ibid., 20.
3   Friedrich Nietzsche, letter to Overbeck, 30 July 1881, in *The Portable Nietzsche*, ed. and trans. Walter Kaufmann (New York: Viking, 1969), 92. Richard Schacht begins his essay on Spinoza and Nietzsche with this quote. See 'The Spinoza-Nietzsche Problem,' in *Desire and Affect: Spinoza as Psychologist*, ed. Yirmiyahu Yovel (New York: Little Room Press, 1999). In this essay, Schacht argues, among many other things, that Nietzsche saw in Spinoza a precursor because of the latter's naturalistic understanding of religion, morals, and psychology. Nietzsche's main criticism, according to Schacht, is that Spinoza didn't go far enough and develop a naturalistic understanding of reason. Schacht is probably correct, though our concern here is different in that we shall attempt to explicate the philosophical tendencies the two philosophers share, and then show how this goes some way in confronting problems many commentators have had with Spinoza.
4   See Martial Gueroult, *Spinoza I: Dieu (Ethique, I)* (Hildesheim: Georg Olms Verlagbuchhandlung, 1968), 9–12.
5   Edwin Curley, in *Behind the Geometrical Method: A Reading of Spinoza's 'Ethics'* (Princeton: Princeton University Press, 1988), takes this approach and claims that his own 'method will be to start from the philosophy of Descartes and to see how far the central themes of the *Ethics* can be derived from critical reflection on the Cartesian system' (3).
6   *Beyond Good and Evil*, 13.
7   *The Gay Science*, trans. Walter Kaufmann (New York: Vintage, 1974), 292.
8   *Beyond Good and Evil*, 109.
9   A well-known and representative instance of this view can be found in the collection of essays published under the title *Pourquoi nous ne somme pas nietzschéens* (Paris: Bernard Grasset, 1991). Vincent Descombes' essay in this collection, 'Le moment français de nietzsche,' faults Deleuze for glorifying in excess the sovereignty of the individual, a glorification he argues promotes irresponsibility and immorality (see 121–3).
10   Gilles Deleuze, *Expressionism in Philosophy*, trans. Martin Joughin (New York: Zone Books, 1990), 11.

11 *A Study of Spinoza's 'Ethics'* (Indianapolis: Hackett Publishing Co., 1984), 375.

12 Ibid., 362–3. The reference here is to Spinoza's closing words of the *Ethics*, when he claims that salvation can be achieved only with 'great effort' (5P42S). Citations from the *Ethics* are from Edwin Curley's translation, *The Collected Works of Spinoza*, vol. 1 (Princeton: Princeton University Press, 1985); and we will be following Curley's notation style when referring to the *Ethics* (e.g., 1P7 refers to Part 1, proposition 7).

13 Edwin Curley, *Spinoza's Metaphysics: An Essay in Interpretation* (Cambridge: Harvard University Press, 1969), 143.

14 *A Study of Spinoza's 'Ethics'*, 372.

15 There are a large number of commentators who have made this claim. Pierre Bayle, H.H. Joachim, and Bertrand Russell are among those who interpret Spinoza in this way.

16 Edwin Curley, for example, takes this position. See his *Spinoza's Metaphysics: An Essay in Interpretation*, chapter 1.

17 Alan Donagan, *Spinoza* (Chicago: University of Chicago Press, 1988), 177: 'Spinoza's position is both that the divine attributes are really distinct, and that they each express the same divine essence. Classical metaphysics puts down such a conjunction as impossible, self-contradictory.' By emphasizing the concept of expression, Donagan, along with others such as Gilles Deleuze (*Expressionism in Philosophy: Spinoza*), H.F. Hallett (*Benedict de Spinoza: The Elements of His Philosophy* [London: Athlone Press, 1957]), and Fritz Kaufmann ('Spinoza's System as a Theory of Expression,' *Philosophy and Phenomenological Research* 1 [1940]: 83–97), have offered interpretations of Spinoza that, although they differ in many other respects, argue for a way of understanding attributes that attempts to overcome the apparent inconsistency. They do not accept, in short, the dualistic assumption of 'classical metaphysics,' and as a result with the concept of expression they argue for a non-dualistic theory of the attributes and substance. It is this theory that is, from the perspective of classical metaphysics, 'self-contradictory.'

18 See Christiane Hubert, *Les premières réfutations de Spinoza: Aubert de Versé, Wittich, Lamy* (Paris: Presses Universitaires de France, 1994). See also Pierre Bayle's critique in his *Historical and Critical Dictionary*, ed. and trans. Richard Popkin (Indianapolis: Hackett Publishing, 1965), 288–338.

19 See H.F. Hallett, 'Substance and Its Modes,' in *Spinoza: A Collection of Critical Essays*, ed. Marjorie Grene (Notre Dame: University of Notre Dame Press, 1973), 139. We differ with Hallett in that we emphasize an understanding of self-cause as self-ordering becoming wherein the determinate order is already immanent to becoming itself. Hallett does not stress the immanence of determinate order to becoming (or to 'potency-in-act' to use

Hallett's phrase) but instead tends, as Donagan has pointed out (see Donagan, 'Essence and the Distinction of Attributes in Spinoza's Metaphysics,' in Grene, ed., *Spinoza: A Collection of Critical Essays*), to speak of absolutely indeterminate God as cause and the plurality of attributes as effects of God's naturing activity, or of potency-in-act. This would then make of the attributes something that are ultimately not known through themselves, but through another, which clearly is counter to Spinoza's understanding of attributes. By stressing the immanence of order to self-*ordering* becoming, we feel we can safely avoid Donagan's objections. We also feel our interpretation, although remaining true to the spirit of Hallett's, clarifies his points. This clarification is perhaps necessary, for we agree with C.L. Hardin's assessment that Hallett 'is at the same time the most profound and the most gratuitously obscure of all the Spinoza commentators' (Hardin, 'Spinoza on Immortality and Time,' in *Spinoza: New Perspectives*, ed. Robert W. Shahan and J.I. Biro [Norman: University of Oklahoma Press, 1978], n. 4).

20 Spinoza, *Letters*, trans. Samuel Shirley (Indianapolis: Hackett Publishing Co., 1995), 260.

21 For instance, in his appendix to his work on Descartes' *Principles of Philosophy*, I and II, Metaphysical Thoughts, Spinoza does not address the problem of becoming, or even appear to see it as a problem. For example, in Part II, chapter 4 ('Of God's Immutability'), Spinoza argues that it is 'as impossible for us to conceive that God can change his decrees as it is for us to think that the three angles of a triangle are not equal to two right angles' (*Collected Works*, 323.) This is true, however, with respect to the determinate order immanent to self-ordering becoming, but not, as we will see, to absolutely indeterminate substance.

22 Among the commentators who have interpreted Spinoza in this way are Bayle, Kant, Joachim, Russell, and more recently Curley. As for Curley, it must be stressed that although he distances himself from what he calls the Bayle-Joachim position as well as the Wolfson position, he nonetheless, as we will see below (see note 34), takes what A. Wolf has called the 'logico-mathematical' view of substance and the attributes, especially as this relates to his argument that the attributes are, in essence, the laws of nature.

23 Among the commentators in this camp is Kuno Fischer, who is probably one of the first to interpret the attributes as active, dynamic forces and who also influenced Nietzsche's reading of Spinoza. A. Wolf, H.F. Hallett, E. Giancotti, G. Deleuze, and P. Macherey are among more recent commentators who read Spinoza this way.

24 See, in particular, Elhanan Yakira, 'Ideas of Nonexistent Modes: Ethics II

Proposition 8, Its Corollary and Scholium,' in *Spinoza on Knowledge and the Human Mind*, ed. Yirmiyahu Yovel (New York: E.J. Brill, 1994), 159–70. Yakira recognizes the significance of this proposition as one that plays an important role in later arguments, most notably, for our purposes, 5P21D and 5P23D, where Spinoza argues for the eternity of the mind. Yakira, however, stresses the emergent understanding of logical relations implicit to this proposition. Although I do not take issue with her arguments *per se*, I stress the manner in which this proposition clarifies explicit concerns and themes of Spinoza rather than implicit themes.

25 As for the infinite modes, both immediate and mediate, I generally agree with Emilia Giancotti's argument that the infinite mediate modes were not important to Spinoza and that the infinite immediate modes served as regulating principles for the process of pluralization that Giancotti sees as key to Spinoza's understanding of substance. See 'On the Problem of Infinite Modes,' in *God and Nature: Spinoza's Metaphysics*, ed. Yirmiyahu Yovel (New York: E.J. Brill, 1991). Later (note 35) we will argue in a similar fashion that the infinite intellect (God's 'infinite idea') serves as a conceptual tool or useful fiction for Spinoza to explain how self-ordering becoming comes to be an actually ordered set of beings, or how becoming becomes stamped with the character of being (what Nietzsche will call 'will to power').

26 See H.A. Wolfson, *The Philosophy of Spinoza: Unfolding the Latent Processes of His Reasoning*, 2 vols (Cambridge, MA: Harvard University Press, 1962 [1934]); H.H. Joachim, *A Study of the Ethics of Spinoza* (New York: Russell and Russell, 1962 [1901]); George L. Kline, 'On the Infinity of Spinoza's Attributes,' in *Speculum Spinozanum, 1677–1977*, ed Siegfried Hessing (London: Routledge and Kegan Paul, 1977).

27 As Curley reminds us, Gueroult claims 2P21S and 3P2S provide the explanation lacking here. The second proposition, in particular, explicitly refers to 2P7 as a basis for accounting for the relationship between the mind and the body.

28 Letter 12, in *Collected Works*, 202.

29 See 1P31: 'The actual intellect, whether finite or infinite, like will, desire, love, etc., must be referred to Natura naturata, not to natura naturans.'

30 2P8C & S: '... it follows that so long as singular things do not exist, except insofar as they are comprehended in God's attributes, their objective being, *or* ideas, do not exist except insofar as God's infinite idea exists. And when singular things are said to exist, not only insofar as they are comprehended in God's attributes, but insofar also as they are said to have duration, their ideas also involve the existence through which they are said to have duration. Schol: If anyone wishes me to explain this further by an example, I

will, of course, not be able to give one which adequately explains what I
speak of here, since it is unique. Still I shall try as far as possible to illustrate
the matter ...'

31 See, among many of Pierre Macherey's works, *Introduction à l'Éthique de
Spinoza* (Paris: Presses Universitaires de France, 1998), 23–6, and 'The Prob-
lem of the Attributes' in *The New Spinoza*, ed. Warren Montag and Ted
Stolze (Minneapolis: University of Minnesota Press, 1998). This essay is a
translated chapter from Macherey's influential work *Hegel ou Spinoza*
(Paris: François Maspero, 1979).

32 See *Spinoza I*, 141–2 and 230–2.

33 See Donagan, 'Spinoza's Dualism,' in *The Philosophy of Baruch Spinoza*, ed.
Richard Kennington (Washington, DC: The Catholic University of America
Press, 1980), and 'Substance, Essence and Attribute in Spinoza, Ethics I,' in
Yovel, ed., *God and Nature*.

34 This is how we read Curley's argument, in *Spinoza's Metaphysics*, when he
addresses 2P8S. For Curley the idea of God that comprehends substance,
much as the idea of the circle comprehends the rectangles, is to be understood as the laws of nature. As he puts it, 'Just as the circle defines a class of
possible rectangles, so the laws of nature define classes of possible entities'
(141). This reading, however, assumes that substance is predetermined, or
limited to the 'logico-mathematical' (see note 22) possibilities of the laws of
nature, but this is to understand substance as limited rather than as absolutely indeterminate substance – as self-ordering becoming. It is for this
reason, among others, that we place Curley among the commentators who
does not interpret substance as dynamic.

35 A thorough justification of our claim that the infinite intellect is a 'useful
fiction' would take us too far afield of our primary concerns in this chapter,
for we would need to lay out Spinoza's philosophy of language, the relationship between common notions, beings of reason, and adequate ideas,
and then address the diverse claims of the many commentators who have
tackled these issues. Nevertheless, we believe a case can be made that
Spinoza recognized the limitations of language, and for a fundamental reason – language is by nature something that is common to the community of
language speakers, and yet the truth Spinoza is attempting to convey
through language is singular and unique. We have already seen this once
when Spinoza recognized that an analogy from geometry was inadequate
in conveying the uniqueness of the relationship between substance and the
attributes – namely, the uniqueness of self-cause. This is even more the case
with language. (For more on this line of argument, see David Savan,
'Spinoza and Language,' in Grener, ed., *Spinoza: A Collection of Critical*

Essays. See also G.H.R. Parkinson's dissenting view in his article 'Language and Knowledge in Spinoza' from the same volume.) In fact, it is perhaps not inappropriate to argue that much as Wittgenstein, in concluding his *Tractatus Logico-Philosophicus* (trans. Pears and B.F. McGuinness [London: Routledge and Kegan Paul, 1974]), a work whose title reflects the influence of Spinoza on Wittgenstein, claims that 'he must transcend these propositions, and then he will see the world aright'; so, too, for Spinoza one must move beyond the 'useful fictions' and the language of the *Ethics* and get to the point where, with the third kind of knowledge, one simply 'sees the world aright.' This reading is given even greater credibility when one examines the historical circumstances of Spinoza's *Tractatus Theologico-Politicus*. As Jonathan Israel has argued in his recent book, *Radical Enlightenment* (New York: Oxford University Press, 2001), the radical critiques of the Koerbagh brothers were in part motivated by a desire to show how the language that is used is itself a political tool to perpetuate the power of those with the requisite ability to use the terms correctly (*Radical Enlightenment*, 192). For Spinoza, too, who knew the Koerbagh brothers well, his work was also condemned, and for similar reasons. Spinoza argued that the writings of the Bible were not expressions of truth but simply 'useful fictions' that engendered obedience and right conduct. One could extend this argument to the *Ethics* and argue that there too the 'useful fictions' are, much as for Wittgenstein, to be moved beyond so as to acquire a proper view of the world, a view that in turn motivates proper conduct. Expanding upon these themes would reveal some of the reasons why the *Ethics* is an ethics, but it is again beyond the scope of this chapter.

36 H.A. Wolfson is perhaps most outspoken in his claim that the first definition is of minimal importance. Gueroult argues that D1 is important, but D6 is for him the definition that does much of the philosophical work in the *Ethics*. Bennett and Donagan find D1 to be problematic because they both feel Spinoza did not state his position clearly enough. For Bennett, 'that whose nature cannot be conceived as *existing*' must 'surely mean "that whose essence cannot be conceived except as *instantiated*"' (*A Study*, 74). For Donagan, Spinoza's first definition would have been much clearer had he more immediately tied it to the distinction between immanent and transient causation (*Spinoza*, 60–4).

37 *The Will to Power*, ed. and trans. Walter Kaufmann (New York: Vintage, 1967), 330.

38 *Beyond Good and Evil*, 48. For more on this aspect of Nietzsche's thought and its relationship to Deleuze, see the next chapter.

39 See *Short Treatise*, Part 2, Preface (I/52–3).

40 See 2D7: 'By singular things I understand things that are finite and have a determinate existence. And if a number of Individuals so concur in one action that together they are all the cause of one effect, I consider them all, to that extent, as one singular thing.'

41 In the *Short Treatise*, for example, Spinoza claims '... if other bodies act on ours with such force that the proportion of motion and rest cannot remain 1 to 3 [for example], that is death, and a destruction of the soul ...' (I/53).

42 This is yet another place of convergence between Nietzsche and Spinoza. In *The Gay Science*, for example, Nietzsche argues that knowledge is nothing but the need to select against excessive differences by reducing them to something common and familiar: 'Look, isn't our need for knowledge precisely this need for the familiar, the will to uncover under everything strange, unusual, and questionable something that no longer disturbs us? Is it not the instinct of fear that bids us to know?' (300–1). This is a central theme of the next chapter.

43 Much of Deleuze's work on Spinoza has been to stress the role of 'common notions' in Spinoza's work as part of an effort to explain how certain ideas or useful fictions aid the 'body's power of acting.' Deleuze believes that Spinoza recognized this near the end of his *Treatise on the Emendation of the Intellect* when he claimed that 'there seems to be considerable difficulty in our being able to arrive at knowledge of these singular things. For to conceive them all at once is beyond the powers of the human intellect ... So other aids will have to be sought' (§102). These other aids, on Deleuze's interpretation, are what come to be called the common notions (see note 46 below for more on the significance of common notions for Deleuze).

44 This lends further support to arguments concerning 'useful fictions' as sketched above in our earlier note (note 35).

45 Bennett argues that Spinoza denies any validity to teleological claims such as 'if it would help x to do A, x does A,' wanting instead to reduce them to claims such as 'if x does A, it is helpful to x to do A.' Bennett argues that Spinoza begins with the second claim but ultimately switches to arguments that are dependent upon the first (see 'Spinoza and Teleology: A Reply to Curley,' in *Spinoza: Issues and Directions*, ed. Edwin Curley and Pierre-François Moreau (New York: E.J. Brill, 1990]). We agree, though possibly for different reasons, with Lee Rice's criticism of Bennett on these points (see 'Spinoza, Bennett, and Teleology,' *Southern Journal of Philosophy* 23.2 [1985]: (241–53).

46 Gilles Deleuze has offered probably the most thorough analysis of why the *Treatise* was left unfinished. For Deleuze the reason is simple: 'when he discovers and invents the common notions, Spinoza realizes that the positions

of the *Treatise on the Intellect* are inadequate in several respects, and that the whole work would have to be revised and rewritten' (*Spinoza: Practical Philosophy*, trans. Robert Hurley [San Francisco: City Light Books, 1981], 120–1). Common notions, according to Deleuze, allow Spinoza to account for the development of knowledge from vague, random experiences to the knowledge of essences (see note 43 above). In short, and this is where we further extend Deleuze's argument, with common notions Spinoza is better able to explain the relationship between finite and determinate beings and the eternal, infinite enjoyment of existing that is substance.

47 G.H.R. Parkinson has pointed out the significance for Spinoza of understanding true ideas, not as representations but as activities of the mind that are in some way complete. See '"Truth Is Its Own Standard": Aspects of Spinoza's Theory of Truth,' in Shanan and Biro, eds, *Spinoza: New Perspectives*.

48 Early in the *Treatise*, Spinoza offers this alternative way of knowing the essence of something: 'there is the Perception we have when a thing is perceived through its essence alone, or through knowledge of its proximate cause' (§19, II/10).

49 See Spinoza's *Descartes' 'Principles of Philosophy,'* Part 1, Prolegomenon (II147–148).

50 A reference to our earlier citation from Nietzsche's notebooks: 'To impose upon becoming the character of being: that is the supreme will to power.'

51 2P13: 'The object of the idea constituting the human Mind is the Body, or a certain mode of Extension which actually exists, and nothing else.'

52 For a recent interpretation of Spinoza that emphasizes the concept of power, see Lorenzo Vinciguerra, *Spinoza* (Paris: Hachette, 2001).

53 This theme has been discussed by many commentators, though not quite in the manner that we have set forth. Yirmiyahu Yovel, for example, has discussed the significance of the third kind of knowledge as a qualitative shift which does not change the content of what is known (i.e., the essence of God), but represents a shift in perspective to seeing the individual as the embodiment of the eternal laws of nature grasped by the second kind of knowledge (see 'Third Kind of Knowledge as Alternative Salvation,' in Curley and Moreau, eds, *Spinoza: Issues and Directions*.) See also Charles Ramond, *Qualité et quantité dans la philosophie de Spinoza* (Paris: Presses Universitaires de France, 1995) for an extensive reading of Spinoza that pays close attention to the conceptual work the quality/quantity distinction plays in Spinoza's philosophy. Similar to the qualitative shift Yovel and others recognize, our reading emphasizes the shift as an existential shift, a shift that brings into focus the activities, emotions, and joy of existing (for a

similar account, an account that also supports some of our claims made in note 35, see Yosef Ben-Shlomo, 'Substance and Attributes in the *Short Treatise* and in the *Ethics*: An Attempt at an "Existentialist" Interpretation,' in Yovel, ed., *God and Nature*). The difference between our position and Yovel's becomes more clear when one sees how Yovel compares and contrasts Nietzsche and Spinoza (see 'Spinoza and Nietzsche: *Amor dei* and *Amor fati*,' in *Spinoza and Other Heretics* [Princeton: Princeton University Press, 1989]). Because Yovel sees the third kind of knowledge as a manner of living and experiencing the eternal, unchanging laws of nature, in contrast to our claim that it is coming to live existentially the absolutely indeterminate substance as the power of self-ordering becoming, Yovel concludes that despite the fact that each rejects a transcendent God, Nietzsche is to be contrasted with Spinoza because 'Nietzsche's experience of immanence leaves no room for order, permanence, fixed laws, inherent rationality, or truth ...' (107). We, to the contrary, find that on this point Spinoza is a profound precursor to Nietzsche, not a contrast. Another view similar to the one set forth here is that of Herman De Dijn. In a number of places, especially in *Spinoza: The Way to Wisdom* (West Lafayette, IN: Purdue University Press, 1996) and 'Wisdom and Theoretical Knowledge in Spinoza,' in Curley and Moreau, eds, *Spinoza: Issues and Directions*, De Dijn has argued that the third kind of knowledge is not a 'theoretical' knowledge but rather a type of lived experience, and an experience that parallels the experiences of enlightenment commonly found among Buddhist monks and sages.

A more traditional interpretation is offered by Alan Donagan, who bases his argument, as we do, on a reading of 2P8. Donagan argues that to be comprehended under an infinite idea of God is to exist as an already determined identity (i.e., the idea of the formal essence of the body) that simply lacks bodily existence (see 'Spinoza's Proof of Immortality,' in Grene, ed., *Spinoza*, 251). This does make sense of 5P23, but it is problematic, and hence on this point we agree with C.L. Hardin's objections to Donagan's arguments (see his essay 'Spinoza on Immortality and Time,' in Shahan and Biro, eds, *Spinoza: New Perspectives*). Hardin, however, and Allison, who admits to being a 'Hardinist' on this position (see Allison, 'Spinoza's Doctrine of the Eternity of the Mind: Comments on Matson,' in Curley and Moreau, eds, *Spinoza: Issues and Directions*), interprets 2P8 much as Curley does, arguing that to be 'comprehended under' entails being subject to 'a set of conjoined law-like propositions' (Hardin, 136). To this claim we can simply repeat our earlier criticism of Curley's position (see note 34). We feel our 'existential' interpretation of living eternally, coupled with our reading of 2P8, is more successful at giving 5P23 the full weight and significance we believe Spinoza intended it to have while at the same time placing it into the broader context of Spinoza's arguments and concerns.

54 *Expressionism in Philosophy: Spinoza*, 11.
55 *Gay Science*, 274
56 *Will to Power*, 330.
57 *Thus Spoke Zarathustra*, in *The Portable Nietzsche* (New York: Penguin Books, 1954), 435.

3. Philosophizing the Double Bind: Deleuze Reads Nietzsche

1 Plato, *The Republic*, trans. Allan Bloom (New York: Basic Books, 1991), 54. All references hereafter will be to this translation. References to the *Statesman* are from Seth Benardete's translation (Chicago: University of Chicago Press, 1986). All other Plato references are from *The Collected Dialogues of Plato*, ed. Edith Hamilton and Huntington Cairns (Princeton: Princeton University Press, 1961).
2 Friedrich Nietzsche, *Beyond Good and Evil*, trans. Walter Kaufmann (New York: Vintage Books, 1966), 49.
3 Friedrich Nietzsche, *The Gay Science*, trans. Walter Kaufmann (New York: Vintage Books, 1974), 254.
4 Friedrich Nietzsche, *Human, All Too Human*, trans. Marion Faber and Stephen Lehmann (Lincoln: University of Nebraska Press, 1984), 238.
5 Heidegger, Kaufmann, Nehamas, and Schacht have all discussed important similarities they have seen between Nietzsche and Plato, as well as their important differences. I will discuss some of their observations below, but my reasons for bringing in the similarities I have sketched here are quite different in intent, as will also be seen below.
6 *Beyond Good and Evil*, Nietzsche' preface, 3.
7 See Martin Heidegger, *Nietzsche*, vol. 1, trans. David Farrell Krell (San Francisco: Harper Collins, 1991), 201.
8 In *The Philosophical Discourse of Modernity*, trans. Frederick Lawrence (Cambridge, MA: MIT Press, 1987), Habermas cites Derrida's reference to Heidegger's claim that the Nietzschean reversal 'and demolition remains dogmatic and, like all reversals, a captive of that metaphysical edifice which it professes to overthrow' (166). Habermas then claims that such a claim is equally valid of Heidegger and Derrida themselves. In particular, he feels that they are both within 'the constraints of the paradigm of the philosophy of the subject,' a paradigm they claim to be criticizing.

Searle's inclusion on this list should perhaps be elaborated. In his criticism of Derrida, Searle does not directly criticize Derrida's critique of metaphysics, nor does he explicitly claim that Derrida is committed to the very tradition he criticizes. However, in criticizing Derrida's reading of Austin, this is implicitly at work. First of all, Derrida is clear in saying that his critique of Austin is in line with his critique of metaphysics, which entails showing the untenability of 'returning, "strategically," ideally, to an origin or to a "priority" held to be simple, intact, normal, pure, standard, self-identical, in order then to think in terms of derivation, complication, deterioration, accident, etc.' (*Limited, Inc.* trans. Samuel Weber and Jeffrey Mehlman [Evanston, IL: Northwestern University Press, 1988], 93). Derrida will then criticize Austin's 'strategic' exclusion of 'non-serious,' 'non-ordinary,' 'fictional' discourse that was designed to aid in understanding 'serious,' 'ordinary' discourse. Searle's criticism is therefore implicitly directed towards Derrida's critique of metaphysics. Furthermore, for Searle's arguments to carry any weight one must remain committed to the very distinctions Derrida questions. Derrida thus asks rhetorically: 'how can one oppose to it [Derrida's article 'Signature, Event, Context'], qua dogma, what it seeks to call into question?' (*Limited, Inc.*, 72). Searle therefore presupposes that Derrida, if not at least actually committed to a tradition of metaphysics that he has simply misunderstood (e.g., Searle argues that Derrida has failed to understand that fiction is logically dependent upon ordinary, 'simple' discourse), then he ought to be so committed. In either case, Searle has both failed to understand Derrida's critique of metaphysics and has assumed that Derrida is or ought to be committed to the very tradition he is criticizing, and thus the inclusion of Searle on this list.

Fredric Jameson, in *Postmodernism, or, The Cultural Logic of Late Capitalism* (Durham: Duke University Press, 1991), claims that 'postmodernism [which includes for Jameson poststructuralism and the critique of metaphysics] is not the cultural dominant of *a wholly new social order* ... but only the reflex and the concomitant of yet another systemic modification of capitalism itself' (xii, emphasis added). The critique of metaphysics remains committed to, and is simply the latest form of, capitalism.

For more criticisms along these lines, see Luc Ferry and Alain Renaut, *French Philosophy of the Sixties* (Amherst: University of Massachusetts Press, 1990); and Ferry and Renaut, eds, *Pourquoi nous ne sommes pas nietzschéens* (Paris: Bernard Grasset, 1991), in particular, Vincent Descombes' article 'Le moment français de Nietzsche' (96–128).

9 Friedrich Nietzsche, *Twilight of the Idols* ('The Problem of Socrates,' 11), in *The Portable Nietzsche*, ed. and trans. Walter Kaufmann (New York: Penguin Books, 1954), 478.

10 Alan Schrift, *Nietzsche and the Question of Interpretation: Between Hermeneutics and Deconstruction* (New York: Routledge, 1990), 104.

11 Jacques Derrida, *Dissemination*, trans. Barbara Johnson (Chicago: University of Chicago Press, 1981), 125.

12 Ibid., 125–6.

13 Ibid., 98–9.

14 Ibid., 103. This quote is a concluding summary of the following long quote from the *Phaedrus*, which details King Thamus's rejection and suppression of Theuth's claim that writing is a *pharmakon*: 'But the king said, "Theuth, my master of arts, to one man it is given to create the elements of an art, to another to *judge the extent of harm and usefulness it will have* [i.e., good vs. evil] for those who are going to employ it. And now, since you are father of written letters, your paternal goodwill has led you to pronounce the very *opposite* of what is their real power [claimed it is helpful when it is harmful]. The fact is that this invention will produce forgetfulness in the souls of those who have learned it because they will not need to exercise their memories, being able to rely on what is written, using the stimulus of external marks that are alien to themselves rather than, from within [i.e., inside vs. outside] their own unaided powers to call things to mind. So it's not a remedy [*pharmakon*] for memory [as Theuth claimed], but for reminding, that you have discovered. And as for wisdom, you're equipping your pupils with only a semblance of it, not with truth [appearance vs. reality]. Thanks to you and your invention, your pupils will be widely read without benefit of teacher's instruction; in consequence, they'll entertain the delusion they have wide knowledge, while they are, in fact, for the most part incapable of real judgment [knowledge vs. ignorance]. They will also be difficult to get on with since they will be men filled with conceit of wisdom, not men of wisdom"' (274e–275b; quoted by Derrida in *Dissemination*, 102).

15 *Beyond Good and Evil*, 10.

16 Ibid. This was already Nietzsche's position at the time of *Human, All Too Human*, when Nietzsche distanced himself from the tradition which 'denied the origin of the one from the other (i.e., its opposite) ... [and Nietzsche offers instead a] historical philosophy [which pursues] a chemistry of moral, religious, aesthetic ideas and feelings [which might] end with the conclusion that, even here, the most glorious colors are extracted from base, even despised substances' (13–14).

17 *Twilight of the Idols* ('Morality as Anti-Nature,' 5), in *The Portable Nietzsche*, 490. In *Beyond Good and Evil*, Nietzsche identifies life with will to power: 'life simply is will to power' (203); and again, in *Twilight of the Idols*, he associates 'dionysian frenzy' with will to power: 'that wonderful phenomenon

which bears the name of Dionysus: it is explicable only in terms of an excess of force' (560), where excess of force is one of the ways in which Nietzsche defines 'will to power.' I will discuss will to power more fully in the third section ('Thumos') and bring in Deleuze's interpretation of it as the 'differential element' – that is, the element which is the condition, *à la* Derrida, for differentiating between good and evil, etc.

18 See *Beyond Good and Evil*, §259: '... life simply *is* will to power.'

19 I will discuss some of these criticisms below, but I am here referring to note 8 above, where I discuss Habermas, Searle, Jameson, and other's criticisms of the contemporary critique of metaphysics.

20 Michel Foucault, 'What Is Enlightenment?' in *The Foucault Reader* (New York: Penguin Books, 1984), 43.

21 Michel Foucault, 'Space, Knowledge, and Power,' an interview with Paul Rabinow in March 1982, in *The Foucault Reader* (New York: Pantheon Books, 1984), 248–9. The Habermas quote is on page 249.

22 For a good study of the close relationship between Nietzsche's and Foucault's critiques, see Michael Mahon, *Foucault's Nietzschean Genealogy* (Albany: State University of New York Press, 1992).

23 Our use of the term 'double bind' comes from Gregory Bateson. We will further clarify the connection between Bateson's understanding of double bind, and its implications for philosophy, below. See Gregory Bateson, *Steps to an Ecology of Mind* (New York: Ballantine Books, 1972). In particular, see the essay 'Double Bind,' 271–8.

24 Seth Benardete, for example, argues that Plato was indeed aware of this impossibility. See *Socrates' Second Sailing: On Plato's Republic* (Chicago: University of Chicago Press, 1989). Derrida also claims that Plato was aware of such impossible both/and's, but argues that he merely made note of them 'in passing, incidentally, discreetly' (*Dissemination*, 126). Our point, however, is that such an awareness was not 'incidental' to Plato's thought, but one of the central problems of his entire corpus.

25 Friedrich Nietzsche, *The Will to Power*, trans. Walter Kaufmann (New York: Vintage Books, 1967), 278. This fragment is dated March–June 1888.

26 *Gay Science*, 300–1: 'What is it that common people take for knowledge? What do they want when they want "knowledge"? Nothing more than this: Something strange is to be reduced to something familiar ... Look, isn't our need for knowledge precisely this need for the familiar, the will to uncover under everything strange, unusual, and questionable something that no longer disturbs us? Is it not the *instinct of fear* that bids us to know?'

27 *Will to Power*, 278.

28 Heidegger, *Nietzsche*, vol. 1, p. 584 (German edition); quoted by Phillippe

Lacoue-Labarthe in *Typography: Mimesis, Philosophy, Politics*, ed. Christopher Fynsk (Cambridge, MA: Harvard University Press, 1989), 70.

29 Ibid., 585; quoted by Lacoue-Labarthe in *Typography*, 71. See *The Republic*, 597c–d.

30 Heidegger, *Nietzsche*, vol. 1, trans. David Farrell Krell, 201.

31 Ibid., 202. Heidegger claims this questioning first occurred in a section in *Twilight of the Idols* entitled 'How the "True World" Finally Became a Fable: The History of an Error.' In this section, Nietzsche claims that not only is the 'true world' to be abolished, but 'along with the true world we have also abolished the apparent one!' With this move, Heidegger believes that Nietzsche conducts himself 'for the first time into the brilliance of full daylight ... Thus the onset of the final stage of his own philosophy' (208). It is for this reason that Heidegger devotes much of his long work on Nietzsche to an analysis of the late notes to *Will to Power*, the notes of his 'final creative year.'

32 *Human, All Too Human* (§1, 'Chemistry of concepts and feelings'), 13–14.

33 Jacques Derrida, *Of Grammatology*, trans. Gayatri Chakravorty Spivak (Baltimore: Johns Hopkins University Press, 1974), 19.

34 I am indebted to Lacoue-Labarthe's work for pointing this out, and for much else that has been influential in my thinking through the themes of this section.

35 Quoted by Lacoue-Labarthe in *Typography*, 48.

36 Ibid., 49; also in *Nietzsche: A Self-Portrait from His Letters*, ed. Peter Fuss and Henry Shapiro (Cambridge: Harvard University Press, 1971), 77.

37 *On the Genealogy of Morals; Ecce Homo*, trans. Walter Kaufmann (New York: Vintage Books, 1969), 258 (emphasis added).

38 Recall our earlier quote in which Nietzsche claimed that 'a basic characteristic of existence [might be] that those who would know it completely would perish, in which case the strength of a spirit should be measured according to how much of the "truth" one could still barely endure.' In other words, the more strength a spirit has, the fewer the fictions and lies it will need, and thus Nietzsche will evaluate our judgments (i.e., beliefs and values), not on the basis of their truth or falsity, but, as we will discuss in the next section, on the basis of whether they were created (fictioned) from a position of strength or weakness.

39 *Beyond Good and Evil*, 229 (emphasis added).

40 *Twilight of the Idols*, 497. See also: *Beyond Good and Evil*, 216; *Gay Science*, 205, 249.

41 *Beyond Good and Evil*, §259.

42 *Twilight of the Idols*, 500.

43 By infinite variability, I mean there is an infinite variation or number of perspectives that can be taken upon this whole. It is this understanding of infinite which Nietzsche refers to in *The Gay Science* (§374, 'Our new "infinite"'): 'the world [has] become "infinite" for us all over again, inasmuch as we cannot reject the possibility that *it may include infinite interpretations*. Once more we are seized by a great shudder; but who would feel inclined immediately to deify [i.e., form into a unity] again after the old manner this monster of an unknown world? And to worship this unknown henceforth as "the Unknown One"?'

44 *Twilight of the Idols*, 517.

45 *The Gay Science*, 168.

46 *Twilight of the Idols*, 518 (emphasis added).

47 See, for example, *Beyond Good and Evil*, §13: 'A living thing seeks above all to discharge its strength – life itself is *will to power* ...'

48 Gilles Deleuze, *Nietzsche and Philosophy*, trans. Hugh Tomlinson (New York: Columbia University Press, 1983), 50.

49 See Heidegger, *Nietzsche*, vol. 2, p. 86: 'What is the pervasive character of the world? The answer is: "force."'

50 Ibid., 87: 'What Nietzsche calls "force" becomes clear to him in later years as "will to power."'

51 Gilles Deleuze, *Logic of Sense*, trans. Mark Lester (New York: Columbia University Press, 1990) 228. Deleuze is speaking of 'sense' subsisting or inhering in propositions and states of affairs in this context, but for him sense is an event, and thus the same applies for events more generally.

52 Ibid., 151.

53 *Nietzsche and Philosophy*, 50.

54 Ibid., 51.

55 Ibid., 43–4. Deleuze refers to the following relevant passages from *Will to Power*: 'We cannot help feeling that mere quantitative differences are something fundamentally distinct from quantity, namely that they are *qualities* which can no longer be reduced to one another' (565); 'Mechanistic interpretation: desires nothing but quantities; but force is to be found in quality. Mechanistic theory can therefore describe processes, not explain them' (660); 'The reduction of all qualities to quantities is nonsense' (564).

56 Ibid., 53.

57 Ibid., 53–4.

58 Ibid., 54.

59 *Twilight of the Idols*, 481.

60 *Human, All Too Human*, 15.

61 *Thus Spoke Zarathustra* ('Of the Blessed Isles'), in *The Portable Nietzsche*, 198–9.

62 *Will to Power*, no. 517.

63 *Logic of Sense*, 1.

64 Ibid.

65 *Will to Power*, no. 517, p. 280.

66 Ibid.

67 Ibid., no. 617, p. 330.

68 *Twilight of the Idols*, 490. We referred to this section earlier in our discussion of Derrida.

69 This refers to our earlier quote from *Beyond Good and Evil* (p. 49) wherein the 'strength of a spirit should be measured according to how much of the "truth" one could still barely endure ...'

70 *Thus Spoke Zarathustra*, 424.

71 *Nietzsche and Philosophy*, 182.

72 Ibid., 186.

73 Ibid., 187. Deleuze also argues that this is why Nietzsche refers to the eternal return as a wedding ring – the marriage of Dionysus and Ariadne (see *Zarathustra*, III, 'The Seven Seals').

74 *Will to Power*, no. 617, p. 330; quoted by Deleuze (ibid.).

75 *Nietzsche and Philosophy*, 188.

76 Ibid.

77 We see in this the well-known contrast between master and slave morality. Whereas master morality affirms what Nietzsche refers to as a 'pathos of distance,' or it affirms one's own difference and distance from others as 'good,' and on this basis negates or denies that which is different, or that which is 'bad,' weak, sickly, declining, etc.; slave morality negates what is other – that is, master morality – and on this basis affirms itself as what is 'good,' and the negated other comes to be seen as the *opposite* of good, or 'evil.' Good and bad differ, but good and evil are opposed. See *Genealogy of Morals*.

78 *Nietzsche and Philosophy*, 189.

79 Since the will to power is the differential element which produces the differences between, and allows for the identification and evaluation of, forces, it is consequently this 'difference in affirmation' which also prevents these forces from coming into equilibrium, or into a static identity. Thus Nietzsche claims, 'That a state of equilibrium is never reached proves that it is not possible' (*Will to Power*, 547).

As an aside, which will be developed in later chapters, this position is very similar to that of chaos theory (see, in particular, Ilya Prigogine and Isabelle Stengers, *Order out of Chaos* [New York: Bantam Books, 1984]). In chaos theory, also known as complexity theory, non-linear theory, or dynamic systems theory, the focus is upon systems that are in a 'far-from-equilibrium' condition. It is only as a consequence of such a condition, Prigogine and Stengers argue, that the distinction between past and future comes about: Only when a system behaves in a sufficiently random way may the difference between past and future ... enter into its description' (16). In far-from equilibrium conditions, furthermore, complexity theorists argue that there is both being and becoming, necessity and chance, predictability and unpredictability, multiplicity and unity. In addition, a fundamental claim of complexity theory is that far-from-equilibrium conditions are not uncommon deviations from a universe that would otherwise be at or near equilibrium; rather, they argue the reverse: far-from-equilibrium conditions are the rule, and equilibrium states are the exceptions which arise from them.

80 See our earlier discussion. See also the *Theaetetus*, 191c-d.

81 *The Gay Science*, 41.

82 Ibid., 266.

83 *Human, All Too Human*, §427, p. 206. See also §228.

84 It is for this reason that Nietzsche rejected Rohde's remark, discussed earlier, that 'Plato created his Socrates and you your Zarathustra.' Socrates is the figure of recollection, the return of the same, but Zarathustra is the figure of forgetfulness, the return of difference; consequently, Nietzsche claimed that 'everything in it [*Zarathustra*] is mine alone, without model, comparison, or precursor ...'

85 This phrase is from Foucault (we mentioned it earlier), but it should be noted that Richard Bernstein makes use of this notion in his book *The New Constellation* (Cambridge: MIT Press, 1991). He also notes, and I will echo this, that despite the poststructuralists' emphasis upon a 'both/and' which eludes the constraints of the Enlightenment blackmail's 'either/or,' one 'cannot avoid asking...[regarding the poststructuralist critique] ... "critique in the name of what?"' (318). For example, Bernstein argues that Foucault's critique implicitly affirms, or is in the name of, an 'ascetic-aesthetic mode of ethical life,' but that he never says why such a life is 'desirable' (164), or why it should be affirmed. Bernstein calls for this type of affirmation, but he recognizes the necessity of a 'double attitude,' or what I would prefer to call a 'double bind,' which calls both for the necessity of affirmation and the recognition 'that any affirmation can be called into question' (318). I am very sympathetic to Bernstein's position – one could even say that he calls for a critique without redemption – but there are important differences which I will clarify in the concluding section of this chapter.

86 Bateson describes the following example: '.. if he responds to his mother's simulated affection, her anxiety will be aroused and she will punish him ...

if he does not make overtures of affection, she will feel that this means she is not a loving mother and her anxiety will be aroused. Therefore, she will either punish him for withdrawing or make overtures to the child to insist that he demonstrate that he loves her.' But if he does this, obviously, he will arouse her anxieties and be punished; hence, the 'no-win' situation of the double bind (*Steps to an Ecology of Mind*, 212–13).

87 See Gregory Bateson, 'Toward a Theory of Schizophrenia,' in *Steps to an Ecology of Mind*, 201–27. As an example of the latter, Bateson cites an experiment of Erik Erickson's. Erickson was 'able to produce a hallucination by first inducing catalepsy in the subject's hand [through hypnosis] and then saying, "There is no conceivable way in which your hand can move, yet when I give the signal, it must move" ... When Erickson gives the signal, the subject hallucinates the hand moved, or hallucinates himself in a different place and therefore the hand was moved' (223).

88 'Double Bind,' in *Steps to an Ecology of Mind*, 278.

89 Bateson cites 'play therapy' as one means of working through, or 'counter-actualizing,' the effects of the double bind (see 'A Theory of Play and Fantasy,' in *Steps to an Ecology of Mind*). Bateson also notes that the double bind can be used against itself. He cites a therapeutic situation in which Frieda Fromm-Reichmann placed her client into a double bind in order to engage her in the therapeutic process; and once engaged, the client was then able to confront the symptoms which resulted from her initial double-bind situation (i.e., she counteractualized them).

90 See 'Bali: The Value System of a Steady State,' in *Steps to an Ecology of Mind*, 107–27.

91 Ibid., 119–20. Bateson points out that the Balinese do not have an understanding of 'laws' which transcend individual interactions, or that are dictates from someone on high 'who made the rules' which require one to treat him- or herself, as well as others, in a particular way; rather, they view wrongs as being 'against the natural structure of the universe,' against its stability, order, etc., of which they are a part.

92 Gilles Deleuze and Félix Guattari, *A Thousand Plateaus*, trans. Brian Massumi (Minneapolis: University of Minnesota Press, 1987), 21–2.

93 For a discussion of the distinction between rhizomatic and arboreal perspectives, see 'Rhizome,' in *Thousand Plateaus*, 3–25.

94 *Gay Science*, §109: 'The total character of the world ... is in all eternity chaos ...'

95 *Beyond Good and Evil*, §225, p. 154.

96 Ibid.

97 Ibid., §270, p. 220.

98 *Gay Science*, §76, p. 130.
99 Friedrich Nietzsche, *Daybreak*, trans. R.J. Hollingdale (Cambridge: Cambridge University Press, 1982), §14, pp. 13–14.
100 See *The Gay Science*, §295, for Nietzsche's critique of 'enduring habits.'
101 See *Genealogy of Morals*, second essay, section 2; and also *The Gay Science*, 303.
102 Vincent Descombes, in his article 'Le moment français de Nietzsche,' in Ferry and Renaut, eds, *Pourqoui nous ne sommes pas nietzschéens*, argues that this discussion of promising shows that 'Nietzschean philosophy does not have principles other than those of the modern project; theirs is only another version of these principles' (126, translation mine). This applies, he adds, to contemporary interpretations and approaches to Nietzsche, in particular that of Deleuze. He claims that Deleuze's stress upon 'irresponsibility' in *Nietzsche and Philosophy*, and the resulting claim that Nietzsche eliminates 'all subjection of the superior individual,' whereby this individual is a 'sovereign and legislator' without being subject to this legislation – these claims show that the individual is 'irresponsible' with respect to such legislation (123–5). Descombes' criticisms would have some force if Nietzsche's notion of self-creation were simply a 'repetition' of the 'modern project'; however, since he is interested, as we have shown, in the non-identifiable both/and (e.g., both creator and creature) which allows for the distinction to be made between irresponsibility and responsibility, Descombes' criticisms prove to be misdirected. We are responsible, Nietzsche (and Deleuze) would claim, but we are responsible, not for repeating 'venerated' ideas and customs, but rather are responsible for actively creating in response to the chaos in oneself. This responsibility is thus not to be understood as the opposite of irresponsibility, if irresponsibility is understood to be the absence of obligation or duty (this is Descombes' interpretation); but neither is this a responsibility obligated to the 'morality of custom.' This is a responsibility whose obligation is to create in response to the chaos in oneself, and thus it is to be understood as a 'converse responsibility,' or a 'counteractualized' responsibility. This is the sense Nietzsche, and Deleuze, give to irresponsibility.
103 *The Gay Science*, 299.
104 Ibid., 102.
105 Ibid., 246 (emphasis added).
106 The themes of dancing and self-overcoming are to be found throughout Nietzsche's writings, though they are particularly evident in *Thus Spoke Zarathustra*.
107 Despite Nietzsche's avowed perspectivism, he argues that this is not to be

confused with relativism. For example, in *The Gay Science* (§345), concerning the opposition between those who argue that these 'principles must be unconditionally binding also for you and me' and those who hold 'that among different nations moral valuations are *necessarily* different and then infer from this that no morality is at all binding,' Nietzsche comments that 'both procedures are equally childish.'

108 *Human, All Too Human*, §552.

109 With this interpretation, we can respond to Luc Ferry and Alain Renaut's criticisms of Nietzsche in 'Ce qui a besoin d'être démontré ne vaut pas grand-chose,' in *Pourquoi nous ne sommes pas nietzschéens*. They argue that Nietzsche's attempt to merge what is independent of tradition with tradition is an impossible one. For example, in *Twilight of the Idols* Nietzsche claims that 'democracy has ever been a form of decline in organizing power ... [and the primary reason for this is that there is no longer] the will to tradition, to authority, to responsibility for centuries to come, the solidarity of chains of generations, forward and backward *ad infinitum*' ('What the Germans lack,' 39). What Nietzsche is critical of is the rejection of the past, of tradition, for the sake of some future state. For example, Nietzsche criticizes Socrates' rejection of the Hellenes in order to obtain some future recognition of the truth by means of the dialectic; or the Christians' denial of their finite mortal selves in order to obtain future salvation. This is the modern malaise as Nietzsche sees it, and it entails two presuppositions he seeks to overcome: (1) a faith in opposite values, for example, past/future, appearance/reality, good/evil; and (2) an affirmation of one as superior to the other, an other that needs to be overcome – for example, tradition, appearance, and evil. The result of this move is an either/or: either you seek to maintain tradition, or you progress towards the emancipation of humanity (i.e., the modern, democratic move), but not both. Ferry and Renaut interpret Nietzsche in terms of such an either/or and consequently see problems in his position. For example, they see Nietzsche's notion of the eternal return as nothing more than a Hegelian *Aufheben*, or a resolution of the opposition between tradition and creative change. Ferry and Renaut thus feel Nietzsche is committed to the idea of progress, or to some future synthesis and transcendent state, but they note the idea of the eternal return 'negates by definition such an idea' (148). Nietzsche is thus attempting an impossible, contradictory task. What we have tried to show, however, is that Nietzsche's position is not one of founding positivity (i.e., eternal return) on a negation or opposition. Rather, he affirms the non-identifiable both/and which makes the opposition between past and future, tradition and modernity, possible. Thus, the

will to power wills both 'forward and backward,' or it is the paradoxical condition which is always already past (i.e., tradition), and always willing and creating that which is yet to come. It is this both/and which is the condition for, and always runs the risk of, collapsing into a destructive either/or: either a slave to tradition, or a sacrifice to the extraordinary.

110 *Logic of Sense*, 249.

111 Constantin Boundas, in his introduction to *The Deleuze Reader* (New York: Columbia University Press, 1993), refers to this notion of the two poles as Deleuze's *idée mère*. He notes 'that fusion and fission are the external limits of all functioning assemblages, natural or man-made ... [and that] assemblages ... that are still in operational order avoid these external limits through the preventive mechanism of a controlled repetition: they repeat the very conditions the extremes of which would have brought about their entropic *stasis* and death' (11). In other words, they repeat the paradoxical both/and (i.e., both fusion and fission, tradition and novelty, or, to use some of Deleuze's common polarities, intensity and extension, paranoia and schizophrenia, sense and nonsense, sedentaries and nomads), which is the condition for the destructive either/or.

112 This is yet another instance where Deleuze's work parallels chaos theory. One of the central claims of chaos theory is that the universe is not going to suffer an 'entropic' death; that is, the universe will not achieve a state of equilibrium wherein no heat is generated, heat being dependent upon a non-equilibrium condition. Rather, chaos theorists argue that the universe is sufficiently chaotic such that 'negentropic' activity can arise (order out of chaos), and some claim that the universe is expanding in the manner of a fractal, or is expanding infinitely within a finite area, and thus won't reach the point of entropic death. There will consequently always be room for, and perhaps the necessity for, negentropic activity.

113 Gilles Deleuze and Félix Guattari, *Qu'est-ce que la philosophie?* (Paris: Les Éditions de Minuit, 1991), 192.

114 The philosopher, similarly, creates a 'concept,' a concept being itself a creative response to the double bind of having to order that which cannot be ordered, make sense of that which makes no sense, etc.; and the scientist creates 'representations' which map the world to some function, a function which is an attempt, and this is the scientist's double bind, to predict the unpredictable. It is for this reason that Deleuze and Guattari stress the importance of 'strange attractors' in contemporary science (p. 194). The 'strange attractor' was a discovery of what has come to be called chaos theory, and its unique characteristic – although chaos theorists would say it is not unique but rather the norm – is that it is both predictable and unpredictable.

115 See Jacques Derrida, *Positions*, trans. Alan Bass (Chicago: University of Chicago Press, 1981), 42–3, for a discussion of these undecidables.

116 *Dissemination*, 64. This is from the brief introduction to the long essay 'Plato's Pharmacy,' an essay which is itself written 'by force of play' (65).

117 *Limited, Inc.*, 146. Derrida claims in this work that Searle, for example, sets forth a false reading of his texts.

118 *Positions*, 63.

119 *Limited, Inc.*, 148.

120 Ibid., 148n16: 'Grammatology has always been a sort of pragmatics, but the discipline which bears this name today involves too many presuppositions requiring deconstruction ... A programmatology (to come) would articulate in a more fruitful and rigorous manner these two discourses.'

121 Ferry and Renaut, for example, in *French Philosophy of the Sixties* will fault Deleuze for 'merely repeating the Nietzschean approach' (19), whereas we claim it is precisely this repetition which helps him and us to address key problems in contemporary philosophy.

122 'Plato and the Simulacrum,' in *Logic of Sense*, 266.

123 'Mediators,' in *Incorporations*, ed. Jonathan Crary and Sanford Kwinter (New York: Zone Books, 1992), 289.

124 See Claude Shannon, 'A Mathematical Theory of Information,' *Bell System Technical Journal* 27 (1948): 379–423, 623–56; and 'Prediction and Entropy of Printed English,' *Bell System Technical Journal* 30 (1951): 50–64. See also Robert Shaw, 'Strange Attractors, Chaotic Behavior, and Information Flow,' *Zeitschrift für Naturforschung* 36A (January 1981): 79–112.

125 *Thousand Plateaus*, 246.

126 Ibid., 251. The previous two quotes are from this page as well.

127 Ibid., 139.

128 Ibid., 82.

129 We will expand on this theme below, both in chapter 5, 'Thinking and the Loss of System: Derrida and Deleuze on Artaud,' and again in chapter 6, 'Rethinking System.'

130 *Thousand Plateaus*, 53.

4. Thinking Difference: Heidegger and Deleuze on Aristotle

1 All references to Aristotle's works in this essay will be from Hippocrates Apostle's translations, published by the Peripatetic Press.

2 Michael Loux, *Primary Ousia: An Essay on Aristotle's Metaphysics Z and H* (Ithaca, NY: Cornell University Press, 1991), 237.

3 Ibid., 40.

4 It is this Aristotelian bias which is widely regarded to have been one of

the obstacles to the formulation and acceptance of evolutionary theory.

5 Martin Heidegger, *Aristotle's Metaphysics Book Theta 1–3: On the Essence and Actuality of Force*, trans. Walter Brogan and Peter Warnek (Bloomington: Indiana University Press, 1995), 121.
6 Martin Heidegger, *Early Greek Thinking*, trans. David Farrell Krell and Frank Capuzzi (San Francisco: Harper & Row, 1975), 15.
7 *Arisotle's Metaphysics*, 154.
8 Ibid., 180.
9 Ibid., 85.
10 In *The Glance of the Eye: Heidegger, Aristotle, and the Ends of Theory* (Albany: State University of New York Press, 1999), William McNeill compares and contrasts Heidegger and Aristotle by way of the former's appropriation of the concept 'seeing,' or in this case 'foreseeing,' as an essential component of knowledge. By doing this, McNeill is able to detail the extensive and complex influence of Aristotle on Heidegger's thinking but also show how they differ. This difference, as we are discussing it here, is that foreseeing as Aristotle understands it, is predetermined by the identity of what can be said – that is, by logos or logic.
11 Martin Heidegger, *Introduction to Metaphysics*, trans. Ralph Manheim (New Haven, CT: Yale University Press, 1959), 121.
12 *Early Greek Thinking*, 38.
13 Martin Heidegger, 'The End of Philosophy and the Task of Thinking,' in *Martin Heidegger: Basic Writings*, trans. Joan Stambaugh, ed. David Farrell Krell (San Francisco: Harper & Row, 1977), 388.
14 *Introduction to Metaphysics*, 78.
15 Martin Heidegger, *Identity and Difference*, trans. Joan Stambaugh (New York: Harper & Row, 1969), 47.
16 Ibid., 21.
17 Ibid., 47.
18 Martin Heidegger, *Poetry, Language, Thought*, trans. Albert Hofstadter (New York: Harper & Row, 1971), 218.
19 Martin Heidegger, *Essence of Reasons*, trans. Terrence Malick (Evanston, IL: Northwestern University Press, 1969), 23.
20 *Aristotle's Metaphysics*, 20.
21 *Identity and Difference*, 68–9.
22 Martin Heidegger, *Nietzsche*, vol. 4, trans. David Farrell Krell (San Francisco: HarperCollins, 1991), 250.
23 'What Is Metaphysics,' in *Basic Writings*, 104.
24 *On Time and Being*, trans. Joan Stambaugh (New York: Harper & Row, 1972), 19.

25 Ibid.

26 *Identity and Difference*, 36.

27 *Difference and Repetition*, trans. Paul Patton (New York: Columbia University Press, 1994), 31. The differenciator of difference will be discussed in later chapters as the second articulation of the double articulation model (i.e., abstract machine).

28 Ibid., 32.

29 Ibid.

30 Ibid., 33.

31 Ibid.

32 Ibid., 34.

33 Ibid., 32.

34 Ibid.

35 Ibid., 65.

36 Ibid., 117.

37 '... Poetically Man Dwells ...' in *Poetry, Language, Thought*, 219.

38 'What Is Metaphysics,' 97.

39 Ibid., 98.

40 Ibid., 106.

41 Martin Heidegger, 'Overcoming Metaphysics,' in *The End of Philosophy*, trans. Joan Stambaugh (New York: Harper & Row, 1973), 106–7.

42 Ibid., 101.

43 For an extended discussion of these themes in Deleuze's work, see 'Postscriptum sur les sociétés de contrôle,' in *Pourparlers* (Paris: Les Éditions de Minuit, 1990).

44 Gilles Deleuze and Félix Guattari, *What Is Philosophy?* (New York: Columbia University Press, 1994), 118.

45 *Anti-Oedipus: Capitalism and Schizophrenia*, trans. Robert Hurley, Mark Seem, and Helen R. Lane (Minneapolis: University of Minnesota Press, 1983), 246.

46 Peter Lynch, *Beating the Street* (New York: Simon & Schuster, 1993), 152.

47 Our Deleuzian critique of Heidegger is largely in agreement with Miguel de Beistegui's. In *Truth and Genesis* (Bloomington: Indiana University Press, 2004), Beistegui argues that despite the moves Heidegger makes in his later work to move beyond the phenomenological tendency to assert the 'ontical privileging of human eixistence' (116), his thought nonetheless remains largely anthropocentric and does not reach the pre-individual in the way that Deleuze does. Where we differ is in our emphasis upon an excessive or chaotic nature of the pre-individual reality, an excess that cannot be captured by any 'privileged' limitations, and it is this chaos that becomes,

through the double articulation (difference in itself) of dynamic systems at the edge of chaos, identifiable.

48 Although we are not focusing upon Deleuze's political theory in this book, there are a number of important books that develop, with the concept 'mul-titude,' arguments quite in line with what we have set forth here. These arguments, moreover, draw their inspiration in large part from Spinoza. See, for instance, Antonio Negri, *The Savage Anomaly*, trans. Michael Hardt (Minneapolis: University of Minnesota Press, 1991); Negri and Hardt's col-laborative works, including *Labor of Dionysus* (Minneapolis: University of Minnesota Press, 1995), *Empire* (Cambridge, MA: Harvard University Press, 2000), and *Multitude: War and Democracy in the Age of Empire* (New York: Penguin Putnam, 2004); and Étienne Balibar, *Spinoza and Politics*, trans. Peter Snowdon (London: Verso, 1998).

49 *Being and Time*, 164.

50 *Difference and Repetition*, 293.

5. Thinking and the Loss of System: Derrida and Deleuze on Artaud

1 Derrida's well-known example of such a presupposed, unquestioned pres-ence is the self-presence of our thought within the sounds which express these thoughts. It is the plentitude of this sound, the physicality and self-presence of hearing ourselves speak, which is the unquestioned self-pres-ence one presupposes in understanding truth as the self-identity and coin-cidence of the world and our thoughts regarding the world.

2 *Of Grammatology*, trans. Gayatri C. Spivak (Baltimore: Johnson Hopkins University Press, 1974), 70.

3 Martin Heidegger, *Nietzsche*, vol. 1, trans. David F. Krell (San Francisco: HarperCollins, 1991), 2001.

4 *Of Grammatology*, 19

5 Jacques Derrida, *Writing and Difference*, trans. Alan Bass (Chicago: Univer-sity of Chicago Press, 1978), 274. See our earlier discussion of this topic in the Introduction.

6 Ibid., 275.

7 Jacques Derrida, *Margins of Philosophy*, trans. Alan Bass (Chicago: Univer-sity of Chicago Press, 1982), 38.

8 Ibid, from *Being and Time* (New York: Harper & Row, 1962), 500, n. xxx. For a more extended study of the interplay among Aristotle, Heidegger, and Derrida and their respective understandings of time, see John Protevi, *Time and Exteriority: Aristotle, Heidegger, Derrida* (Lewisburg, PA: Bucknell Uni-versity Press, 1994).

9 The importance of the notion 'simultaneity' for Derrida's reading here will be discussed below.

10 *Margins,* 50.

11 Ibid.

12 Ibid., 51.

13 Ibid., 56

14 Ibid.

15 Quoted by Derrida in *Margins,* 62

16 Ibid.

17 Ibid.

18 Ibid., 63.

19 Derrida quotes the following passage from Heidegger in support of this reading: '"Spirit" does not fall into time; but factical existence "falls" as falling from priomordial, authentic temporality. But this "falling" has its own existential possibility in a mode of its temporalizing – a mode which belongs to temporality' (*Being and Time,* 486).

20 *Margins,* 63.

21 Ibid. See *Being and Time,* 488: 'Is there a way which leads from primordial time to the meaning of Being? Does time itself manifest itself as the horizon of Being?'

22 *Of Grammatology,* 62.

23 Ibid., 23.

24 Ibid., 60.

25 It is useful to recall here Saussure's argument that the meaning of a term in a language is dependent upon the system of the language as a whole (*la langue*). The meaning is not a self-contained identity, but rather is dependent upon the identity of the system, and the relationship between this word and all the other words of the language.

26 *Anti-Oedipus: Capitalism and Schizophrenia,* trans. Robert Hurley, Mark Seem, and Helen R. Lane (Minneapolis: University of Minnesota Press, 1983), 370 (my emphasis).

27 Ibid., 371 (my emphasis).

28 In *Margins,* for example, published in 1968, two essays are devoted to Artaud, and thirty years later he published *The Secret Art of Antonin Artaud* (Cambridge, MA: The MIT Press, 1998).

29 Antonin Artaud, *Selected Writings,* trans. Helen Weaver, ed. Susan Sontag (Berkeley: University of California Press, 1988), 38.

30 Ibid., 33.

31 Ibid., 35.

32 Ibid.

33 Ibid., 43.
34 Ibid., 45.
35 Ibid., 31.
36 Andras Angyal, 'Disturbances of Thinking in Schizophrenia,' in *Language and Thought in Schizophrenia*, ed. J.S. Kasanin (New York: W.W. Norton & Company, 1939), 117.
37 Anton Ehrenzweig, *The Hidden Order of Art* (Los Angeles: University of California Press, 1967), 124–5.
38 See *Difference and Repetition*, trans. Paul Patton (New York: Columbia University Press, 1994), 146–8; for example: 'To think is to create – there is no other creation – but to create is first of all to engender "thinking" in thought' (147).
39 *Selected Writings*, 82: 'A powerlessness to crystallize unconsciously the broken point of the mechanism to any degree at all.'
40 Ibid.
41 Ibid., 570–1. These are the closing lines from 'To Have Done with the Judgment of God.'
42 In his more recent work on Artaud, Derrida has emphasized the aspect of Artaud's work which undermines the metaphysical tradition. Derrida recognized the necessary presence of such an undermining *differance* in his early writings on Artaud – part of his deconstructive approach, as we have seen (e.g., in his reading of Aristotle), is to show the necessary other, the repressed other, a metaphysical text presupposes. However, in his later writings, Derrida emphasizes the undermining *differance* rather than the continued adherence to metaphysics.
43 'La Parole Soufflée,' in *Writing and Difference*, 186.
44 Ibid.
45 Ibid.
46 Ibid., 187. Derrida follows this quote with the following, to show that the purging of differences involved with becoming a body without organs is part of the same process involved with the theatre of cruelty: 'Reality has not yet been constructed because the true organs of the human body have not yet been assembled and put in place. / The theater of cruelty has been created to complete this putting into place and to undertake, through a new dance of the body of man ...'
47 Ibid., 190.
48 'The Theater of Cruelty,' in *Writing and Difference*, 249.
49 Ibid., 194.
50 Gilles Deleuze and Félix Guattari, *A Thousand Plateaus*, trans. Brian Massumi (Minneapolis: University of Minnesota Press, 1987), 158.
51 This is precisely the duality in Artaud which Derrida criticized, and which

was simply Artaud's 'metaphysics.' Thus, the 'autarchic' body is the body which lacks organization and articulation, while the body with organs is organized and articulated – that is, has internal divisions and regions.

52 See *Writing and Difference*, 186.

53 *Thousand Plateaus*, 190.

54 *Anti-Oedipus*, 326–7. We can now begin to see the continuing significance and importance of Spinoza in Deleuze's work, especially with our reading of Spinozist substance as absolutely indeterminate becoming. We will draw out this comparison further in the conclusion.

55 *Thousand Plateaus*, 159.

56 Recall our earlier quote of Artaud, cited by Derrida: 'The body is the body, / it is alone / and has no need of organs, / the body is never an organism ... every organ is a parasite ...' (*Writing and Difference*, 186).

57 *Anti-Oedipus*, 8.

58 Ibid., 7.

59 Ibid., 11.

60 At this point our reading converges with other recent discussions that compare and contrast Derrida and Deleuze. Daniel Smith, for instance, in 'Deleuze and Derrida, Immanence and Transcendence: Two Directions in Recent French Thought,' in *Between Deleuze and Derrida*, ed. Paul Patton and John Protevi (London: Continuum, 2003), claims that Derrida's thought emphasizes transcendence, whereas Deleuze stresses immanence. Deleuze's critique of the Judgment of God, therefore, is ultimately an affirmation of immanence, whereas Derrida's understanding of differance, according to Smith, is of a notion that 'exceeds or transcends metaphysics' (49). John Protevi, in *Political Physics*, offers a similar contrast, arguing that Derrida, with his compelling critique of onto-theo-logo-centric identities, is a philosopher whose approach is 'top-down' in its focus; and Deleuze, with his emphasis upon offering an account of the emergence of identities through immanent processes, processes that are in line with complexity theory, sets forth a 'bottom-up' philosophy.

61 *Anti-Oedipus*, 10.

62 This is why capital is not to be identified with money, for money can and has been treated like a commodity. During the currency crisis in Asia of 1998, for example, the Malaysian prime minister blamed the collapse of his currency on large speculators who sold his currency short, which led to a devaluation and collapse of the currency, and ultimately to the enrichment of the speculators. In other words, currency traders buy and sell money as a commodity, and large speculators can use this commodity as capital, or as a means of determining prices that will translate into more capital.

63 I am largely following Manuel DeLanda here, from his book *A Thousand*

Years of Nonlinear History (New York: Zone Books, 1997). In particular, see pages 260–3. Here he argues that 'since what truly defines the real world are neither uniform strata nor variable meshworks but the unformed and unstructured flows from which these two derive, it will also be useful to have a label to refer to this special state of matter-energy information, to this flowing reality animated from within by self-organizing processes constituting a veritable nonorganic life: the Body without Organs (BwO).' DeLanda then discusses how the flow of energy from the sun is the BwO from which many of the self-organization processes on our planet derive, including weather phenomena, which presuppose their own BwO, according to DeLanda – 'the coupled dynamics of hydrosphere and atmosphere and their wild variety of self-organized entities: hurricanes, tsunamis, pressure blocks, cyclones, and wind circuits.' (262). In the conclusion, we will revisit DeLanda's theory and contrast it with our own.

64 *Anti-Oedipus*, 15.
65 We will discuss this further in the next chapter, 'Rethinking System,' as well as in the conclusion.
66 *Anti-Oedipus*, 382.
67 *A Thousand Plateaus*, 158.
68 Ibid., 251.
69 Ibid., 166.
70 Ibid., 165.
71 This ties in with our earlier chapter, chapter 3, on Nietzsche and the importance of chaos.
72 *Of Grammatology*, 23.
73 See *Margins*, 63n36. See also the earlier section of this chapter where this issue is discussed at some length, as well as the previous chapter.
74 'Deleuze-Bergson: An Ontology of the Virtual,' in *Deleuze: A Critical Reader*, ed. Paul Patton (London: Blackwell, 1996), 85.
75 *Difference and Repetition*, 209. For an excellent secondary source on *Difference and Repetition*, see James Williams, *Gilles Deleuze's Difference and Repetition: A Critical Introduction* (Edinburgh: Edinburgh University Press, 2004).
76 Gilles Deleuze and Félix Guattari, *What Is Philosophy?* (New York: Columbia University Press, 1994), 118.
77 Gilles Deleuze, *Foucault*, trans. Sean Hand (Minneapolis: University of Minnesota Press, 1988), 78.
78 Ibid., 79 (emphasis mine).
79 Gilles Deleuze, *The Fold: Leibniz and the Baroque* (Minneapolis: University of Minnesota Press, 1993), 130–1.
80 G.W. Leibniz, *Discourse on Metaphysics; Correspondence with Arnauld; Monadology* (La Salle, IL: Open Court Publishing Company, 1988), 263.

81 *Difference and Repetition*, p. 123.
82 Ibid., 119. The term 'dark precursor' Deleuze gets from the example of thunderbolts: 'Thunderbolts explode between different intensities [i.e., between the heterogenous series of positively and negatively charged particles], but they are preceded by an invisible, imperceptible dark precursor ... Likewise, every system contains its dark precursor which ensures the communication of peripheral series.' The following two quotes are from this same page.
83 Recall our earlier discussion of Spinoza, where this is discussed in detail.
84 *Difference and Repetition*, 104–5.
85 'Deleuze-Bergson,' 91.
86 Lutz Ellrich, 'Negativity and Difference: On Gilles Deleuze's Criticism of Dialectics,' *Modern Language Notes* 111 (1996): 463–87. Ellrich has the following passage in mind from *Difference and Repetition*: 'Given two heterogenous series, two series of differences, the precursor plays the part of the differenciator of these differences. In this manner, by virtue of its own power, it puts them into immediate relation to one another: it is the in-itself of difference or the "differently different" – in other words, difference in the second degree, the self-different which relates different to different by itself' (119).
87 'Negativity and Difference,' 484.
88 Ibid., 487.
89 Ibid., 463: 'Thought that remains directed toward the priority of the identical is charged with having fallen prey to an illusion, be it necessary (Derrida) or an avoidable one (Deleuze).' In a footnote to this, Ellrich adds that because of 'this assumed necessity, the illusion cannot be destroyed through aesthetic masquerades as Derrida argues, but only de-constructed, i.e., enacted *as* illusion.'
90 Gilles Deleuze, *Bergsonism*, trans. Hugh Tomlinson and Barbara Habberjam (New York: Zone Books, 1988), 104; emphasis mine.
91 Kant used this term in *Critique of Pure Reason* to refer to the tendency to attribute to regulative principles, principles which allow us to make sense of our world, the status of being a knowledge-constitutive principle.
92 For an interesting reading of the difference between Derrida and Deleuze that complements the reading set forth here, see Leonard Lawlor's essay 'The Beginnings of Thought: The Fundamental Experience in Derrida and Deleuze,' in Patton Protevi, eds, *Between Deleuze and Derrida*. Lawlor states the difference between the two quite succinctly: 'the fundamental principle of Deleuze's entire thinking' is 'immediate duality,' and for Derrida it is 'mediate unity' (79). Stated in our terms, and with our emphasis upon dynamic systems as the self-differing condition for identities (difference in

itself), Deleuze understands identity in terms of a fundamental difference that is inseparable from the identities themselves, or there is an *immediate* indiscernibility between this difference and the 'unity of impression.' For Derrida, by contrast, the 'unity of impression' is, as we have argued, the effect of, or is *mediated* by, differance as an 'economic concept designating the production of differing/deferring' (*Of Grammatology*, 23; cited in the introduction to the present work).

6. Rethinking System

1 In *Difference and Repetition*, trans. Paul Patton (New York: Columbia University Press, 1994), Deleuze claims that *Process and Reality* is 'one of the greatest books of modern philosophy' (284–5).
2 Alfred North Whitehead, *Process and Reality* (Boston: Free Press, 1969), 5. Hereafter all citations from Whitehead will be from this book and will be cited in the text (in parentheses). For perhaps the closest and most important reading of Whitehead to emerge in recent years, and a reading that is sympathetic to Deleuze's project, see Isabelle Stengers's *Penser avec Whitehead* (Paris: Gallimard, 2002).
3 Our reading of Spinoza differs with Whitehead's. Whitehead is yet another commentator on Spinoza's work who understands substance as static, and as a subject that bears predicates (attributes). Earlier we listed Bertrand Russell among those who read Spinoza this way, and, considering the close working relationship between Whitehead and Russell, it should not be surprising that Whitehead reads Spinoza this way too. We sided, by contrast, with those who read substance as dynamical, or as process.
4 For some good discussion on this topic, the best place to start is Nicholas Rescher's *Process Philosophy: A Survey of Basic Issues* (Pittsburgh: University of Pittsburgh Press, 2000).
5 For a detailed discussion of these problems, see my book, *The Problem of Difference: Phenomenology and Poststructuralism* (Toronto: University of Toronto Press, 1998).
6 Ibid., 33–48.
7 Louis Hjelmslev, *Prolegomena to a Theory of Language*, trans. Francis J. Whitfield (Madison: University of Wisconsin Press, 1961), 58.
8 G.W. Leibniz, *Discourse on Metaphysics; Correspondence with Arnauld; Monadology* (LaSalle, IL: Open Court Publishing, 1988), 69.
9 *Ethics* (1D6), in *The Collected Works of Spinoza*, vol. 1, ed. and trans. Edwin Curley (Princeton: Princeton University Press, 1985). See our discussion of this theme in chapter 2 for a more thorough treatment of Spinoza's use of the concept 'expression.'

10 It is on this point that Hjelmslev breaks with Saussure. Saussure maintained a causal relationship between the content-substance and the expression-substance that signifies this content. The expression-substance depends, according to Saussure, upon the content that it comes along to represent and signify, whereas Hjelmslev claims both are made possible by the paradoxical sign-function.

11 Gilles Deleuze, *Expressionism in Philosophy: Spinoza*, trans. Martin Joughin (New York: Zone Books, 1990), 327. The remaining part of this chapter will show how Deleuze's philosophy carries to fruition his Spinozism, or why Deleuze says he is a Spinozist. With immanent, dynamic substance, or dynamic systems, and with the importance of the concept of expression in Deleuze's work, it is not surprising that Deleuze thought of himself as a Spinozist.

12 *Logic of Sense*, trans. Mark Lester (New York: Columbia University Press, 1990), 21.

13 Ibid., 110.

14 *Process and Reality*, 256.

15 Ibid., 97.

16 Ibid., 10.

17 *Logic of Sense*, 116.

18 Ibid.

19 Ibid.

20 Ibid., 151.

21 Ibid., 103.

22 Ibid., 102 (emphasis mine).

23 Ibid., 95.

24 In a famous example of this, Sapir and Whorf have argued that the linguistic form and structure of the Navajo language, a structure that lacks the present tense of verbs, limits what can be said and meant in that culture. More recent studies have supported the Sapir-Whorf hypothesis.

25 See *Logic of Sense*, 54: 'in the theory of differential equations, the existence and distribution of singularities are relative to a problematic field defined by the equation as such. As for the solution, it appears only with the integral curves and the form they take in the vicinity of singularities inside the field of vectors.' Deleuze will use the conceptual tool of differential equations again in *Difference and Repetition*, and again much later in his book *Foucault*.

26 *Logic of Sense*, 116.

27 Ibid., 56.

28 Both Whitehead and Umberto Eco note that chaosmos is a balance between two extremes, either of which, if actualized alone, would render the identity and existence of a work (functioning assemblage) impossible.

29 G.W.F. Hegel, *Science of Logic*, trans. A.V. Miller (Atlantic Highlands, NJ: Humanities Press International, 1995), 149.

30 G.W.F. Hegel, *Phenomenology of Spirit*, trans. A.V. Miller (Oxford: Oxford University Press, 1976), 11.

31 *Logic of Sense*, 180.

32 Ilya Prigogine and Isabelle Stengers, *Order out of Chaos* (New York: Bantam Books, 1984), 161.

33 Ibid., 162. Recall the significance of 'chance' for Nietzsche, as discussed in chapter 3.

34 Ibid., 167.

35 Recall Deleuze and Guattari's notion of the cancerous and fascist BwOs, discussed in the previous chapter, or Nietzsche's concern with being able to give birth to a dancing star as discussed in chapter 3.

36 Stuart Kauffman, *At Home in the Universe* (New York: Oxford University Press, 1995), 24.

37 Ibid., 57.

38 Ibid., 26.

39 Prigogine and Stengers, *Order out of Chaos*, 160.

40 Kauffman, *At Home in the Universe*, p. 81.

41 Ibid., 79.

42 J.A. Kelso, *Dynamic Patterns* (Cambridge, MA: MIT Press, 1995), 223.

43 *A Dynamic Systems Approach to the Development of Cognition and Action* (Cambridge, MA: MIT Press, 1996), 68.

44 For example, Thelen and Smith argue that in studying the processes associated with learning to walk, a dynamic systems approach overcomes past failures to account adequately for the complexity of the data.

45 Andy Clark, *Being There* (Cambridge, MA: MIT Press, 1997), 99.

46 Ibid., 98.

47 Ibid., 213.

48 It is perhaps worth noting that Wittgenstein, in beginning his *Philosophical Investigations* (trans. G.E.M. Anscombe [Oxford: Basil Blackwell, 1953]), Wittgenstein stresses that in looking at language, 'it disperses the fog to study the phenomena of language in primitive kinds of application in which one can command a clear view of the aim and functioning of these words. A child uses such primitive forms of language when it learns to talk. Here the teaching of language is not explanation, but training.' (§5). See also Terrence Deacon, *The Symbolic Species* (New York: W.W. Norton, 1997).

49 See *Phaedrus*. See also our earlier discussion of Derrida.

50 Merlin Donald, *The Origins of the Modern Mind: Three Stages in the Evolution of Culture and Cognition* (Cambridge, MA: Harvard University Press, 1991), 343.

51 *Difference and Repetition*, 147.

Conclusion: Philosophy at the Edge of Chaos

1 For a more thorough discussion of the influence of Hjelmslev on Deleuze and Guattari's work, see the previous chapter.

2 Deleuze and Guattari do not actually use the term 'dynamic systems,' but their use of the terms 'assemblages' and 'abstract machines' is generally synonymous with this term, and we believe, based on what we have shown, that they likely would have had no objections to our use of this term, especially given the fact that they began to refer to work in chaos theory in their last work together, *What Is Philosophy?*

3 This distinction is from Deleuze's, *Difference and Repetition*. We discussed this in the previous chapter, though we will discuss it again below.

4 See *A Thousand Plateaus*, trans. Brian Massumi (Minneapolis: University of Minnesota Press, 1987), 40–1.

5 See Harvey Blatt, Gerard Middleton, and Raymond Murray, *Origin of Sedimentary Rocks* (Englewood Cliffs, NJ: Prentice-Hall, 1980), chapter 5.

6 Deleuze, as discussed earlier, often borrows an analogy from differential calculus, and thus the stage of differentiation draws a line of consistency between points on a graph. The stage of differenciation integrates this line and offers a solution which captures all possible points and allows one to determine and identify where the next point on the line will be.

7 *What Is Philosophy?*, trans. Hugh Tomlinson and Graham Burchell (New York: Columbia University Press, 1994), 20.

8 See John Barrow, *The World within the World* (New York: Oxford University Press, 1988), 354. It is only within a dying red giant star that a sufficient amount of carbon is produced because a star, once it has run out of its hydrogen fuel (which it has fused into helium), begins to die, and in this process the helium fuses with itself and other elements to form the heavier elements. It is to this latter process that we can apply the double articulation model to the origin of carbon. The current consensus on the origin of carbon within dying red giant stars is that there are two possible routes. In the first, three helium atoms, if in appropriate proximity and relation to each other, can fuse to form a carbon nucleus. The first articulation is the conditions within a dying red giant that places helium (substance) in just the right relationship to two other helium atoms (form). The second articulation is the fusion of the helium atoms in this 'just right' relationship (form) into carbon (substance). The second, more widely accepted view is that two helium atoms fuse to form a beryllium isotope which is unstable enough to fuse easily with helium to form carbon, but not too unstable such

that it flies apart before being able to fuse with helium. The second view is more widely accepted because it is better able to account for the amount of carbon in the universe. As for the double articulation model, we could expand the helium to carbon synthesis by breaking it into two double articulations, the first being the fusion of helium to form beryllium, and the second the fusion of beryllium and helium to form carbon.

9 See Carl Noller, *Chemistry of Organic Compounds* (Philadelphia: W.B. Saunders Company, 1957). There is some debate about the possibility, given different initial conditions, of whether life could originate based on silicon. The reason for this is that silicon, although it does not attract its valence electrons as strongly as carbon, is stronger than germanium and tin. The resulting speculation, then, is that while it is statistically less likely that life could originate from silicon, it is not necessarily impossible.

10 For example, methyl iodide (CH_3I) can react with water (H_2O) to produce methyl alcohol (CH_3OH) plus hydrogen iodide (HI). A bromide ion (Br^-), however, can act as a catalyst and react with methyl iodide to form a molecule of methyl bromide, which then reacts with water to give back the initial bromide ion and methyl alcohol. The catalyzed reaction requires less free energy than the uncatalyzed, and hence the catalyst will increase the speed with which these reactions can unfold (what chemists refer to as the 'kinetics' of a chemical reaction). For more on catalytic reactions, see Myron L. Ender and Lewis J. Brubacher, *Catalysis and Enzyme Action* (New York: McGraw Hill, 1973), chapter 1.

11 See Stuart Kauffman, *At Home in the Universe* (New York: Oxford University Press, 1995), Chapter 3. The term 'emergent property' is discussed more fully in the previous chapter, and will be discussed again below.

12 Gilles Deleuze, *Difference and Repetition*, trans. Paul Patton (New York: Columbia University Press, 1994), 164.

13 Ibid.

14 See Charles A. Beard, *An Economic Interpretation of the Constitution of the United States* (New York: Macmillan, 1935).

15 See Gordon Wood, *The Creation of the American Republic* (Chapel Hill: University of North Carolina Press, 1969), 393–6.

16 Manuel DeLanda, 'Immanence and Transcendence in the Genesis of Form,' *South Atlantic Quarterly* 96.3 (Summer 1997): 507.

17 Ibid.

18 DeLanda refers frequently to Fernand Braudel's analysis of pre-capitalist markets in Braudel's *Wheels of Commerce*. In this book, as well as the other two from this series, Braudel analyses the role of the markets in Europe (e.g., the markets at Champagne) between 1400 and 1800, and he examines the emergence of capitalism as what he calls an 'anti-market' system. In

capitalism, merchants use various techniques (such as hoarding in a warehouse) to manipulate prices to their benefit. See *Civilization and Capitalism*, vol. 2, *Wheels of Commerce*, trans. Sian Reynolds (Berkeley: University of California Press, 1984), 226–30.

19 With respect to this last example, DeLanda cites recent studies which have found that economic cycles can be understood in terms of what is called the 'economic long wave or Kondratiev cycle.' According to this view, economic downturns emerge in a pattern of 50-year cycles, and this pattern is an emergent property which reflects the interdependence of a series of heterogeneous elements. See J.D. Sterman, 'Nonlinear Dynamics in the World Economy: The Economic Long Wave,' in *Structure, Coherence and Chaos in Dynamical Systems* (New York: Manchester University Press, 1989), 389–414. Braudel also notes that the economy of fifteenth- and sixteenth-century Europe entered into patterned cycles which would occur throughout Europe, regardless of what might be happening at vastly removed locations in Europe. In *Wheels of Commerce*, for example, Braudel argues: 'Historically, one can speak of a market economy, in my view, when prices in the markets of a given area fluctuate in unison, a phenomenon the more characteristic since it may occur over a number of different jurisdictions or sovereignties' (227).

20 *A Thousand Plateaus*, 330–1.

21 Ibid. (Deleuze and Guattari's emphasis).

22 'Immanence and Transcendence in the Genesis of Form,' 511. See also 'Virtual Environments and the Emergence of Synthetic Reason,' in *Flame Wars: The Discourse of Cyberculture*, ed. Mark Derby (Durham: Duke University Press, 1994), 263–86.

23 See Richard Dawkins, *The Selfish Gene* (New York: Oxford University Press, 1989).

24 See previous chapter for more on this term.

25 *A Thousand Plateaus*, 254.

26 Ibid., 153.

27 Ibid.

28 Alain Badiou, *Deleuze: The Clamor of Being*, trans. Louise Burchill (Minneapolis: University of Minnesota Press, 2000), 51. See Introduction, note 15, where this was first discussed.

29 We can now see most clearly how our position differs from that of DeLanda. Although DeLanda's *identification* of three abstract machines does indeed further the work of Deleuze and Guattari, an effort, as we shall see below, that they would endorse, Deleuze and Guattari nonetheless recognize that whatever abstract machines are identified come to be this way as a result of the double articulation that allows for the identification of the

non-identifiable (double bind). Thus, although Deleuze and Guattari may leave the self-consistent aggregate model undeveloped, as well as the probe-head model, this is not because of an oversight (or perhaps it is), but rather it is because these models, as identified abstract machines, are repetitions and expressions of the Abstract machine, the double articulation model, and this is a model which they do thoroughly discuss.

This same point can be made with respect to DeLanda's more recent book, *Intensive Science and Virtual Philosohpy* (London: Continuum, 2002). Although DeLanda does great service to Deleuze's work by reconstructing Deleuze's concepts in light of complexity theory, and, in particular, with his application of the notion of a cascading of symmetry-breaking phase transitions, he admittedly recognizes that he does not discuss the notion of the 'edge of chaos' and its relevance to the actualization of abstract machines (or what he calls the quasi-causal operator). As DeLanda puts it: 'Finally, there is a term which refers to the actualization (or effectuation) of the quasi-causal operator itself. I did not discuss this in detail, but I did give an example in Chapter 2 of the neighborhood of a phase transition (or "edge of chaos")' (168). What we have done in this work is to focus upon the actualization of the abstract machine, arguing that it is precisely at the 'edge of chaos' where this actualization is able to be effected. More importantly, we have shown how by understanding the conceptual development of Deleuze's thought as being in line with the concepts associated with dynamical systems theory, and especially with the notion of the 'edge of chaos,' we have been able to address and clarify a number of issues related to the philosophical tradition. DeLanda dismisses Plato all too quickly as merely a thinker of transcendent essences. What we have shown, however, is that Plato's philosophy as itself an expression of the abstract machine, or more accurately as an effort to 'engender "thinking" in thought,' ultimately attempts to philosophize the double bind. Consequently, Plato's thought, and the same was true of Aristotle, as we saw, cannot be so quickly dismissed and bears in many ways profound similarities to Nietzsche (and, by extension, Deleuze). Another crucial difference between our project and DeLanda's results from the emphasis we placed upon Deleuze's Spinozism, and related to this the claim that the double articulation model is a crucial part of the abstract machine, or it is how the abstract machine becomes effectuated in actual entities. Thus, the two aspects of the quasi-causal operator that DeLanda discusses – namely, its (1) meshing of 'multiplicities by their differences,' or the drawing of a plane of consistency; and (2) its ability 'to generate the multiplicities by extracting them from actual intensive processes' (103) – are, from our perspective, another way of discussing double articulation, which DeLanda seems to view as distinct. The first task, drawing a plane of consistency, is precisely what we have discussed as the first articulation; or, as Spinoza discusses this, it is the attributes as expressions of God's essence. The second aspect of the quasi-causal operator, 'to generate the multiplicities by extracting them from actual intensive processes,' does appear to differ. However, if it is recognized, as we argued in our chapter on Spinoza, that the identifiable essence of substance, of God, is only made possible by way of the modifications of an attribute, then the infinite substance, the univocity of being, is inseparable from the actual, identifiable entities. Consequently, singularities, or multiplicities, are inseparable from the actual, and problems are inseparable from their solutions (as DeLanda correctly emphasizes). The abstract machine is therefore the condition of possibility for the actual insofar as the BwO is drawn into a plane of consistency, a plane of consistency that is then actualized by way of the second articulation; and yet the abstract machine is also the condition of impossibility for the continued identity of this actualization, for inseparable from this actualization are multiplicities that will, when actualized through yet another double articulation (eternal recurrence), transform the identity of the given actuality. Deleuze and Guattari thus say, in good Spinozist fashion, that God is a 'Lobster, or a double pincer, a double bind' (*A Thousand Plateaus*, 40).

30 *The Will to Power*, ed. and trans. Walter Kaufmann (New York: Vintage Books, 1967), 330.
31 This discussion can be found in Merlin Donald, *The Origins of the Modern Mind* (Cambridge, MA: Harvard University Press, 1991), 340–4.
32 Ibid., 342.
33 Ibid., 343.
34 To list just a few examples of some excellent work on Deleuze that has done just this, one could begin with DeLanda's book, but their have been others as well, such as Mark Bonta and John Protevi, *Deleuze and Geophilosophy: A Guide and Glossary* (Edinburgh: Edinburgh University Press, 2004). Note this book includes a 'glossary,' and hence the important role of definitions in doing philosophy. Other books include Gregory Flaxman, *The Brain Is the Screen: Deleuze and the Philosophy of Cinema* (Minneapolis: University of Minnesota Press, 2000); and, though not exhaustively, Keith Ansell Pearson, *Germinal Life: The Difference and Repetition of Deleuze* (New York: Routledge, 1999).
35 Umberto Eco, 'Poetics of the Open Work,' in *The Open Work*, trans. Anna Cancogni (Cambridge, MA: Harvard University Press, 1989).

Bibliography

Althusser, Louis. 'The Only Materialist Tradition, Part I: Spinoza.' In *The New Spinoza*, ed. Warren Montag and Ted Stolze, 3–19. Minneapolis: University of Minnesota Press, 1998.

Angyal, Andras. 'Disturbances of Thinking in Schizophrenia.' In *Language and Thought in Schizophrenia*, ed. J.S. Kasanin. New York: W.W. Norton and Company, 1939.

Ariew, Roger. 'The Infinite in Spinoza's Philosophy.' In *Spinoza: Issues and Directions*, ed. Edwin Curley and Pierre-François Moreau. New York: E.J. Brill, 1990.

Aristotle. *Metaphysics*. Trans. Hippocrates Apostle. Grinnell, IA: The Peripatetic Press, 1979.

Artaud, Antonin. *Antonin Artaud: Selected Writings*. Trans. Helen Weaver. Ed. Susan Sontag. Berkeley: University of California Press, 1988.

Badiou, Alain. *Deleuze: The Clamor of Being*. Trans. Louise Burchill. Minneapolis: University of Minnesota Press, 2000.

– 'Gilles Deleuze, *The Fold: Leibniz and the Baroque*.' In *Gilles Deleuze and the Theater of Philosophy*, ed. Constantin V. Boundas and Dorothea Olkowski. New York: Routledge, 1994.

Balibar, Étienne. 'Heidegger et Spinoza.' In *Spinoza au XXe siècle*, ed. Olivier Bloch, 327–44. Paris: Presses Universitaires de France, 1993.

– '*Jus-Pactum-Lex:* On the Constitution of the Subject in the *Theologico-Political Treatise*.' In *The New Spinoza*, ed. Warren Montag and Ted Stolze. Minneapolis: University of Minnesota Press, 1998.

– 'A Note on "Consciousness/Conscience" in the *Ethics*.' *Studia Spinozana* 8 (1992): 37–53.

– *Spinoza et la Politique*. Paris: Presses Universitaires de France, 1985.

Barrow, John D. *The World within the World*. New York: Oxford University Press, 1988.

Bateson, Gregory. *Steps to an Ecology of Mind*. New York: Ballantine Books, 1972.

Bayle, Pierre. *The Dictionary Historical and Critical of Mr. Peter Bayle. The Second Edition*. London, 1702.

Beard, Charles A. *An Economic Interpretation of the Constitution of the United States*. New York: Macmillan, 1935.

Beistegui, Miguel de. *Truth and Genesis: Philosophy as Differential Ontology*. Bloomington: Indiana University Press, 2004.

Bell, Jeffrey A. *The Problem of Difference: Phenomenology and Poststructuralism*. Toronto: University of Toronto Press, 1998.

Ben-Shlomo, Yosef. 'Substance and Attributes in the *Short Treatise* and in the *Ethics*: An Attempt at an "Existentialist" Interpretation.' In *God and Nature: Spinoza's Metaphysics: Papers Presented at the First Jerusalem Conference (Ethica I)*, ed. Yirmiyahu Yovel, 219–30. New York: E.J. Brill, 1991.

Benardete, Seth. *Socrates' Second Sailing: On Plato's Republic*. Chicago: University of Chicago Press, 1989.

Bennett, Jonathan. 'Response to Garber and Rée.' In *Doing Philosophy Historically*, ed. Peter H. Hare. Buffalo: Prometheus Books, 1988.

– 'Spinoza and Teleology: A Reply to Curley.' In *Spinoza: Issues and Directions*, ed. Edwin Curley and Pierre-François Moreau. New York: E.J. Brill, 1990.

– 'Spinoza's Metaphysics.' In *The Cambridge Companion to Spinoza*, ed. Don Garrett. Cambridge: Cambridge University Press, 1996.

– *A Study of Spinoza's Ethics*. New York: Hackett, 1984.

Bernstein, Richard. *The New Constellation*. Cambridge, MA: MIT Press, 1991.

Blatt, Harvey, Gerard Middleton, and Raymond Murray. *Origin of Sedimentary Rocks*. Englewood Cliffs, NJ: Prentice-Hall, 1980.

Bonta, Mark, and John Protevi. *Deleuze and Geophilosophy: A Guide and Glossary*. Edinburgh: Edinburgh University Press, 2004.

Boundas, Constantin V., and Dorothea Olkowski, eds. *Deleuze and the Theater of Philosophy*. New York: Routledge, 1994.

Braudel, Fernand. *Capitalism and Material Life, 1400–1800*. Trans. Miriam Kochan. New York: Harper and Row, 1973.

– *Civilization and Capitalism, 15th–18th Century*. 3 vols. Trans. Sian Reynolds. Berkeley: University of California Press, 1984.

Clark, Andy. *Being There*. Cambridge, MA: MIT Press, 1997.

Curley, Edwin M. *Behind the Geometrical Method: A Reading of Spinoza's Ethics*. Princeton: Princeton University Press, 1988.

– 'On Bennett's Spinoza: The Issue of Teleology.' In *Spinoza: Issues and Directions*, ed. Edwin Curley and Pierre-François Moreau. New York: E.J. Brill, 1990.

- *Spinoza's Metaphysics: An Essay in Interpretation.* Cambridge: Harvard University Press, 1969.

Dawkins, Richard. *The Selfish Gene.* New York: Oxford University Press, 1989.

De Dijn, Herman. 'Spinoza: Reason and Intuitive Knowledge.' *Philosophy* 13 (1989): 1–22.

- *Spinoza: The Way to Wisdom.* West Lafayette, IN: Purdue University Press, 1996.

- 'Wisdom and Theoretical Knowledge in Spinoza.' In *Spinoza: Issues and Directions: The Proceedings of the Chicago Spinoza Conference,* ed. Edwin Curley and Pierre-François Moreau, 147–56. New York: E.J. Brill, 1990.

Deacon, Terrence. *The Symbolic Species.* New York: W.W. Norton, 1997.

DeLanda, Manuel. 'Immanence and Transcendence in the Genesis of Form.' *South Atlantic Quarterly* 96.3 (1997).

- *Intensive Science and Virtual Philosophy.* London: Continuum, 2002.

- *A Thousand Years of Nonlinear History.* New York: Zone Books, 1997.

- 'Virtual Environments and the Emergence of Synthetic Reason.' In *Flame Wars: The Discourse of Cyberculture,* ed. Mark Derby. Durham: Duke University Press, 1994.

Deleuze, Gilles. *Bergsonism.* Trans. Hugh Tomlinson and Barbara Habberjam. New York: Zone Books, 1988.

- *Cinema 1: The Movement-Image.* Trans. Hugh Tomlinson and Barbara Habberjam. Minneapolis: University of Minnesota Press, 1986.

- *Cinema 2: The Time-Image.* Trans. Hugh Tomlinson and Robert Galeta. Minneapolis: University of Minnesota Press, 1989.

- *Difference and Repetition.* Trans. Paul Patton. New York: Columbia University Press, 1994.

- *Différence et répétition.* Paris: Presses Universitaires de France, 1968.

- *Empiricism and Subjectivity.* Trans. Constantin Boundas. New York: Columbia University Press, 1991.

- *Expressionism in Philosophy: Spinoza.* Trans. Martin Joughin. New York: Zone Books, 1990.

- *The Fold: Leibniz and the Baroque.* Trans. Tom Conley. Minneapolis: University of Minnesota Press, 1993.

- *Foucault.* Trans. Sean Hand. Minneapolis: University of Minnesota Press, 1988.

- 'He Stuttered.' In *Gilles Deleuze and the Theater of Philosophy,* ed. Constantin V. Boundas and Dorothea Olkowski. New York: Routledge, 1994.

- *Kant's Critical Philosophy: The Doctrine of the Faculties.* Trans. Hugh Tomlinson and Barbara Habberjam. Minneapolis: University of Minnesota Press, 1984.

– *Logic of Sense.* Trans. Mark Lester. New York: Columbia University Press, 1990.
– *Masochism: Coldness and Cruelty / Venus in Furs.* New York: Zone Books, 1989.
– 'Mediators.' In *Incorporations*, ed. Jonathan Crary and Sanford Kwinter. New York: Zone Books, 1992.
– *Negotiations, 1972–1990.* Trans. Martin Joughin. New York: Columbia University Press, 1995.
– *Nietzsche and Philosophy.* Trans. Hugh Tomlinson. New York: Columbia University Press, 1983.
– 'Nomad Thought.' In *The New Nietzsche*, ed. and introd. David B. Allison. Cambridge, MA: MIT Press, 1985.
– *Périclès et Verdi.* Paris: Les Éditions de Minuit, 1988.
– *Pourparlers 1972–1990.* Paris: Les Éditions de Minuit, 1990.
– 'Spinoza and the Three "Ethics."' In *The New Spinoza*, ed. Warren Montag and Ted Stolze. Minneapolis: University of Minnesota Press, 1998.
– 'Spinoza et la méthode générale de M. Gueroult.' *Revue de métaphysique et de morale*, 4 (1969): 426–37.
– *Spinoza: Practical Philosophy.* Trans. Robert Hurley. San Francisco: City Lights Books, 1981.
Deleuze, Gilles, and Félix Guattari. *Anti-Oedipus: Capitalism and Schizophrenia.* Trans. Robert Hurley, Mark Seem, and Helen R. Lane. Minneapolis: University of Minnesota Press, 1983.
– *Kafka: Toward a Minor Literature.* Trans. Dana Polan. Minneapolis: University of Minnesota Press, 1986.
– *Qu'est-ce que la philosophie?* Paris: Les Éditions de Minuit, 1991.
– *A Thousand Plateaus: Capitalism and Schizophrenia.* Trans. Brian Massumi. Minneapolis: University of Minnesota Press, 1987.
– *What Is Philosophy?* Trans. Hugh Tomlinson and Graham Burchell. New York: Columbia University Press, 1994.
Deleuze, Gilles, and Claire Parnet. *Dialogues.* Trans. Hugh Tomlinson and Barbara Habberjam. New York: Columbia University Press, 1987.
Derrida, Jacques. *Dissemination.* Trans. Barbara Johnson. Chicago: University of Chicago Press, 1981.
– 'Economimesis.' *Diacritics* 11 (1981): 3–25.
– *Edmund Husserl's Origin of Geometry: An Introduction.* Trans. John P. Leavey. Lincoln: University of Nebraska Press, 1978.
– *Limited, Inc.* Trans. Samuel Weber and Jeffrey Mehlman. Evanston: Northwestern University Press, 1988.
– *Margins of Philosophy.* Trans. Alan Bass. Chicago: University of Chicago Press, 1982.

- *Of Grammatology*. Trans. Gayatri C. Spivak. Baltimore: Johns Hopkins University Press, 1974.
- *Positions*. Trans. Alan Bass. Chicago: University of Chicago Press, 1981.
- *The Secret Art of Antonin Artaud*. Cambridge, MA: MIT Press, 1998.
- *Speech and Phenomena and Other Essays on Husserl's Theory of Signs*. Trans. David B. Allison. Evanston, IL: Northwestern University Press, 1973.
- *Spurs: Nietzsche's Styles*. Trans. Barbara Harlow. Chicago: University of Chicago Press, 1979.
- *Writing and Difference*. Trans. Alan Bass. Chicago: University of Chicago Press, 1978.
Donagan, Alan. 'Essence and the Distinction of Attributes in Spinoza's Metaphysics.' In *Spinoza: A Collection of Critical Essays*, ed. Marjorie Grene. Notre Dame: University of Notre Dame Press, 1973.
- 'Homo Cogitat: Spinoza's Doctrine and Some Recent Commentators.' In *Spinoza: Issues and Directions: The Proceedings of the Chicago Spinoza Conference*, ed. Edwin Curley and Pierre-François Moreau, 102–12. New York: E.J. Brill, 1990.
- *Spinoza*. Chicago: University of Chicago Press, 1988.
- 'Spinoza's Dualism.' In *The Philosphy of Baruch Spinoza*, ed. Richard Kennington, 89–102. Washington, DC: Catholic University of America Press, 1980.
- 'Spinoza's Theology.' In *The Cambridge Companion to Spinoza*, ed. Don Garrett. Cambridge: Cambridge University Press, 1996.
Donald, Merlin. *The Origins of the Modern Mind: Three Stages in the Evolution of Culture and Cognition*. Cambridge, MA: Harvard University Press, 1991.
Eco, Umberto. *The Aesthetics of Chaosmos: The Middle Ages of James Joyce*. Trans. Ellen Esrock. Cambridge, MA: Harvard University Press, 1982.
- *The Open Work*. Trans. Anna Cancogni. Cambridge, MA: Harvard University Press, 1989.
Ehrenzweig, Anton. *The Hidden Order of Art: A Study in the Psychology of Artistic Imagination*. Los Angeles: University of California Press, 1967.
Eisenberg, Paul. 'On the Attributes and Their Alleged Independence of One Another: A Commentary on Spinoza's Ethics IP10.' In *Spinoza: Issues and Directions*, ed. Edwin Curley and Pierre-François Moreau. New York: E.J. Brill, 1990.
Ellrich, Lutz. 'Negativity and Difference: On Gilles Deleuze's Criticism of Dialectics.' *Modern Language Notes* 111 (1996): 463–87.
Ender, Myron L., and Lewis J. Brubacher. *Catalysis and Enzyme Action*. New York: McGraw Hill, 1973.
Ferry, Luc, and Alain Renaut. *French Philosophy of the Sixties*. Trans. Mary S. Cattani. Amherst: University of Massachusetts Press, 1990.

– eds. *Pourquoi nous ne sommes pas nietzschéens*. Paris: Bernard Grasset, 1991.

Flaxman, Gregory. *The Brain Is the Screen: Deleuze and the Philosophy of Cinema*. Minneapolis: University of Minnesota Press, 2000.

Foucault, Michel. *The Order of Things*. New York: Vintage Books, 1972.

Garrett, Don, ed. *The Cambridge Companion to Spinoza*. Cambridge: Cambridge University Press, 1996.

– 'ETHICS IP5: Shared Attributes and the Basis of Spinoza's Monism.' In *Central Themes in Early Modern Philosophy*, ed. J.A. Cover and Mark Kulstad. Indianapolis: Hackett Publishing Company, Inc., 1990.

Giancotti, Emilia. 'On the Problem of Infinite Modes.' In *God and Nature: Spinoza's Metaphysics: Papers Presented at the First Jerusalem Conference (Ethica I)*, ed. Yirmiyahu Yovel, 97–118. New York: E.J. Brill, 1991.

Guattari, Félix. *Chaosmosis*. Trans. Paul Bains and Julian Pefanis. Bloomington: Indiana University Press, 1995.

Gueroult, Martial. *Spinoza I: Dieu (Ethique, I)*. Hildesheim: Georg Olms Verlagbuchhandlung, 1968.

– *Spinoza II: L'Âme (Ethique, II)*. New York: Georg Olms Verlag, 1974.

– 'Spinoza's Letter on the Infinite.' In *Spinoza: A Collection of Critical Essays*, ed. Marjorie Grene, 182–212. Notre Dame: University of Notre Dame Press, 1973.

Habermas, Jürgen. *The Philosophical Discourse of Modernity*. Trans. Frederick Lawrence. Cambridge, MA: MIT Press, 1987.

Hallett, Harold F. *Aeternitas: A Spinozistic Study*. Oxford: The Clarendon Press, 1930.

– *Benedict de Spinoza*. London: Athlone Press, 1957.

– 'On a Reputed Equivoque in the Philosophy of Spinoza.' In *Studies in Spinoza: Critical and Interpretive Essays*, ed. S.P. Kashap. Berkeley: University of California Press, 1973.

– 'Spinoza's Conception of Eternity.' *Mind* 37 (1928): 283–303.

– 'Substance and Its Modes.' In *Spinoza: A Collection of Critical Essays*, ed. Marjorie Grene. Notre Dame: University of Notre Dame Press, 1973.

Hampshire, Stuart. 'Truth and Correspondence in Spinoza.' In *Spinoza on Knowledge and the Human Mind: Papers Presented at the Second Jerusalem Conference (Ethica II)*, ed. Yirmiyahu Yovel, 1–10. New York: E.J. Brill, 1994.

Hardin, C.L. 'Spinoza on Immortality and Time.' In *Spinoza: New Perspectives*, ed. Robert W. Shahan and J.I. Biro, 129–38. Norman: University of Oklahoma Press, 1978.

Hardt, Michael. 'Spinoza's Democracy: The Passions of Social Assemblages.' In *Marxism in the Postmodern Age*, ed. Antonio Callari. New York: Guilford, 1994.

Harris, Errol E. 'Finite and Infinite in Spinoza's System.' In *Speculum Spinoza-num 1677–1977*, ed. Siegfried Hessing, 197–211. London: Routledge and Kegan Paul, 1977.

Hegel, G.W.F. *Hegel's Science of Logic*. Trans. A.V. Miller. Atlantic Highlands, NJ: Humanities Press International, 1995.

– *Phenomenology of Spirit*. Trans. A.V. Miller. Oxford: Oxford University Press, 1976.

– *Reason in History*. Trans. Robert S. Hartman. Indianapolis: Bobbs-Merrill, 1953.

Heidegger, Martin. *Aristotle's Metaphysics Book Theta 1–3*. Trans. Walter Brogan and Peter Warnek. Bloomington: Indiana University Press, 1995.

– *Being and Time*. Trans. Macquarrie and Edward Robinson. New York: Harper & Row, 1962.

– *Early Greek Thinking*. Trans. David F. Krell and Frank A. Capuzzi. San Francisco: Harper & Row, 1975.

– *The End of Philosophy*. Trans. Joan Stambaugh. New York: Harper & Row, 1973.

– *Identity and Difference*. Trans. Joan Stambaugh. New York: Harper & Row, 1969.

– *An Introduction to Metaphysics*. Trans. Ralph Manheim. New Haven: Yale University Press, 1959.

– *Martin Heidegger: Basic Writings*. Trans. Joan Stambaugh. Ed. David F. Krell. New York: Harper & Row, 1977.

– *Nietzsche*. 4 vols. Trans. David F. Krell. San Francisco: Harper Collins Publishers, 1991.

– *On Time and Being*. Trans. Joan Stambaugh. New York: Harper & Row, 1972.

– *Parmenides*. Trans. André Schuwer and Richard Rojcewicz. Bloomington: Indiana University Press, 1992.

– *Poetry, Language, Thought*. Trans. Albert Hofstadter. New York: Harper & Row, 1971.

– 'Who Is Nietzsche's Zarathustra?' In *The New Nietzsche*, ed. and intro. David B. Allison. Cambridge, MA: MIT Press, 1985.

Hjelmslev, Louis. *Prolegomena to a Theory of Language*. Trans. Francis Whitfield. Madison: University of Wisconsin Press, 1961.

Hubbeling, Hubertus G. 'The Third Way of Knowlege (Intuition) in Spinoza.' *Studia Spinozana* 2 (1986): 219–31.

Hubert, Christian. *Les premières réfutations de Spinoza: Aubert de Versé, Wittich, Lamy*. Paris: Presses de la Sorbone Nouvelle, 1994.

Israel, Jonathan I. *Radical Enlightenment: Philosophy and the Making of Modernity, 1650–1750*. Oxford: Oxford University Press, 2001.

Jameson, Fredric. *Postmodernism, or, The Cultural Logic of Late Capitalism*. Durham: Duke University Press, 1991.

Joachim, Harold H. *A Study of the Ethics of Spinoza*. New York: Russell and Russell, 1964.

Kaneko, Kunihko. 'Chaos as a Source of Complexity.' In *Artificial Life: An Overview*, ed. Christopher Langton. Cambridge, MA: MIT Press, 1995.

Kauffman, Stuart. *At Home in the Universe*. New York: Oxford University Press, 1995.

Kaufmann, Fritz. 'Spinoza's System As a Theory of Expression.' *Philosophy and Phenomenological Research* 1 (1940): 83–97.

Kaufmann, Walter. *Nietzsche: Philosopher, Psychologist, Antichrist*. New York: Vintage Books, 1968.

Kelso, J.A. *Dynamic Patterns*. Cambridge, MA: MIT Press, 1995.

Klever, Wim N.A. 'Actual Infinity: A Note on the Crescas-Passus in Spinoza's Letter (12) to Lodewijk Meijer.' *Studia Spinozana* 10 (1994): 111–19.

Kline, George L. 'On the Infinity of Spinoza's Attributes.' In *Speculum Spinozanum, 1677–1977*, ed. Siegfried Hessing. Boston: Routledge & Kegan Paul, 1977.

Kneale, Martha. 'Eternity and Sempiternity.' In *Spinoza: A Collection of Critical Essays*, ed. Marjorie Grene, 227–40. Notre Dame: University of Notre Dame Press, 1973.

Lacoue-Labarthe, Phillippe. *Typography: Mimesis, Philosophy, Politics*. Intro. Jacques Derrida. Cambridge: Harvard University Press, 1989.

Langton, Christopher, ed. *Artificial Life: An Overview*. Cambridge, MA: MIT Press, 1995.

Lawlor, Leonard. 'The Beginnings of Thought: The Fundamental Experience in Derrida and Deleuze.' In *Between Deleuze and Derrida*, ed. Paul Patton and John Protevi. London: Continuum, 2003.

Leibniz, Gottfried W. *Discourse on Metaphysics; Correspondence with Arnauld; Monadology*. Trans. George Montgomery. La Salle, IL: Open Court, 1988.

Lloyd, Genevieve. 'Spinoza's Version of the Eternity of the Mind.' In *Spinoza and the Sciences*, ed. Marjorie Grene and Deborah Nails, 211–33. Boston: D. Reidel, 1986.

Loux, Michael. *Primary Ousia: An Essay on Aristotle's Metaphysics Z and H*. Ithaca, NY: Cornell University Press, 1991.

Lynch, Peter. *Beating the Street*. New York: Simon & Schuster, 1993.

Macherey, Pierre. *Hegel ou Spinoza*. Paris: François Maspero, 1979.

– *Introduction à l'Éthique de Spinoza: La nature de choses*. Paris: Presses Universitaires de France, 2001.

- 'The Problem of the Attributes.' In *The New Spinoza*, ed. Warren Montag and Ted Stolze. Minneapolis: University of Minnesota Press, 1998.

Massumi, Brian. *A User's Guide to Capitalism and Schizophrenia: Deviations from Deleuze and Guattari*. Cambridge, MA: MIT Press, 1992.

Matheron, Alexandre. *Individu et communauté chez Spinoza*. Paris: Minuit, 1988.

May, Todd G. 'Difference and Unity in Gilles Deleuze.' In *Gilles Deleuze and the Theater of Philosophy*, ed. Constantin V. Boundas and Dorothea Olkowski. New York: Routledge, 1994.

McNeill, William. *The Glance of the Eye: Heidegger, Aristotle, and the Ends of Theory*. Albany: State University of New York Press, 1999.

Moreau, Pierre F. 'The Metaphysics of Substance and the Metaphysics of Forms.' In *Spinoza on Knowledge and the Human Mind*, ed. Yirmiyahu Yovel, 27–35. New York: E.J. Brill, 1994.

Negri, Antonio. 'L'Antimodernité de Spinoza.' In *Spinoza au XXe siècle*, ed. Olivier Bloch, 203–24. Paris: Presses Universitaires de France, 1993.

- *The Savage Anomaly: The Power of Spinoza's Metaphysics and Politics*. Trans. Michael Hardt. Minneapolis: University of Minnesota Press, 1991.

Negri, Antonio, and Michael Hardt. *Empire*. Cambridge, MA: Harvard University Press, 2000.

- *Labor of Dionysus*. Minneapolis: University of Minnesota Press, 1995.

- *Multitude: War and Democracy in the Age of Empire*. New York: Penguin Putnam, 2004.

Nietzsche, Friedrich. *Beyond Good and Evil*. Trans. Walter Kaufmann. New York: Vintage Books, 1966.

- *The Birth of Tragedy and The Case of Wagner*. Trans. Walter Kaufmann. New York: Vintage Books, 1967.

- *Daybreak*. Trans. R.J. Hollingdale. Cambridge: Cambridge University Press, 1982.

- *The Gay Science*. Trans. Walter Kaufmann. New York: Vintage Books, 1974.

- *Human, All Too Human*. Trans. Marion Faber. Lincoln: University of Nebraska Press, 1984.

- *On the Genealogy of Morals; Ecce Homo*. Trans. Walter Kaufmann. New York: Vintage Books, 1969.

- *Philosophy and Truth: Selections from Nietzsche's Notebooks of the Early 1870s*. Ed. and trans. Daniel Breazeale. Atlantic Highlands, NJ: Humanities Press, Inc., 1979.

- *Philosophy in the Tragic Age of the Greeks*. Trans. Marianne Cowan. Chicago: Regnery Gateway, 1962.

– *The Portable Nietzsche*. Ed. and trans. Walter Kaufmann. New York: Penguin Books, 1954.
– *Untimely Meditations*. Trans. R.J. Hollingdale. Cambridge: Cambridge University Press, 1983.
– *The Will to Power*. Ed. and trans. Walter Kaufmann. New York: Vintage Books, 1967.
Noller, Carl. *Chemistry of Organic Compounds*. Philadelphia: W.B. Saunders Company, 1957.
Parkinson, G.H.R. 'Language and Knowledge in Spinoza.' In *Spinoza: A Collection of Critical Essays*, ed. Marjorie Grene. Notre Dame: University of Notre Dame Press, 1973.
– '"Truth Is Its Own Standard": Aspects of Spinoza's Theory of Truth.' In *Spinoza: New Perspectives*, ed. Robert W. Shahan and J. I. Biro, 35–55. Norman: University of Oklahoma Press, 1978.
Patton, Paul. 'Anti-Platonism and Art.' In *Gilles Deleuze and the Theater of Philosophy*, ed. Constantin V. Boundas and Dorothea Olkowski. New York: Routledge, 1994.
– 'Conceptual Politics and the War-Machine in Mille Plateaux.' *SubStance* 44/45: (1984): 61–80.
Patton, Paul, and John Protevi, eds. *Between Deleuze and Derrida*. London: Continuum, 2003.
Pearson, Keith A. *Germinal Life: The Difference and Repetition of Deleuze*. New York: Routledge, 1999.
Plato. *The Republic*. Trans. Allan Bloom. New York: Basic Books, 1968.
– *Statesman*. Trans. with a commentary by Seth Benardete. Chicago: University of Chicago Press, 1986.
Prigogine, Ilya, and Isabelle Stengers. *Order out of Chaos*. New York: Bantam Books, 1984.
Protevi, John. *Political Physics*. London: Athlone, 2001.
– *Time and Exteriority: Aristotle, Heidegger, Derrida*. Lewisburg, PA: Bucknell University Press, 1994.
Saussure, Ferdinand de. *Course in General Linguistics*. Trans. Roy Harris. La Salle, IL: Open Court, 1983.
Savan, David. 'Spinoza and Language.' In *Spinoza: A Collection of Critical Essays*, ed. Marjorie Grene. Notre Dame: University of Notre Dame Press, 1973.
Schacht, Richard. *Nietzsche*. London: Routledge and Kegan Paul, 1983.
– 'The Spinoza-Nietzsche Problem.' In *Desire and Affect: Spinoza as Psychologist: Papers Presented at the Third Jerusalem Conference (Ethica III)*, ed. Yirmiyahu Yovel, 211–34. New York: Little Room Press, 1999.

Schrift, Alan. *Nietzsche and the Question of Interpretation: Between Hermeneutics and Deconstruction*. New York: Routledge, 1990.

Smith, Daniel. 'Deleuze and Derrida, Immanence and Transcendence: Two Directions in Recent French Thought.' In *Between Deleuze and Derrida*, ed. Paul Patton and John Protevi. London: Continuum, 2003.

Spinoza, Benedict de. 'Ethics.' In *The Collected Works of Spinoza*, Vol. 1, ed. and trans. Edwin Curley. Princeton: Princeton University Press, 1985.

– *The Letters*. Trans. Samuel Shirley. Introd. and notes by Steven Barbone, Lee Rice, and Jacob Adler. Indianapolis: Hackett Publishing Company, 1995.

– 'Parts I and II of Descartes' *Principles of Philosophy*.' In *The Collected Works of Spinoza*, Vol. 1, ed. and trans. Edwin Curley. Princeton: Princeton University Press, 1985.

– 'Short Treatise on God, Man, and His Well-Being.' In *The Collected Works of Spinoza*, Vol. 2, ed. and trans. Edwin Curley. Princeton: Princeton University Press, 1985.

– 'Treatise on the Emendation of the Intellect.' In *The Collected Works of Spinoza*, Vol. 1, ed. and trans. Edwin Curley. Princeton: Princeton University Press, 1985.

Stengers, Isabelle. *Penser avec Whitehead*. Paris: Gallimard, 2002.

Sterman, J.D. 'Nonlinear Dynamics in the World Economy: The Economic Long Wave.' In *Structure, Coherence and Chaos in Dynamical Systems*. New York: Manchester University Press, 1989.

Thelen, Esther, and Linda Smith. *A Dynamic Systems Approach to the Development of Cognition and Action*. Cambridge, MA: MIT Press, 1996.

Whitehead, Alfred N. *Process and Reality*. Boston: Free Press, 1969.

Williams, James. *Gilles Deleuze's Difference and Repetition: A Critical Introduction*. Edinburgh: Edinburgh University Press, 2004.

Wittgenstein, Ludwig. *Philosophical Investigations*. Trans. G.E.M. Anscombe. Oxford: Basil Blackwell, 1953.

– *Tractatus Logico-Philosophicus*. Trans. D.F. Pears and Bernard McGuinness. London: Routledge and Kegan Paul, 1976.

Wolfson, Harry A. *The Philosophy of Spinoza: Unfolding the Latent Processes of His Reasoning*. 2 vols. Cambridge: Harvard University Press, 1962.

Wood, David, ed. *Derrida: A Critical Reader*. Cambridge: Blackwell Publishers, 1992.

Wood, Gordon. *The Creation of the American Republic*. Chapel Hill: University of North Carolina Press, 1969.

Yakira, Elhanan. 'Ideas of Nonexistent Modes: *Ethics* II Proposition 8, Its Corollary and Scholium.' In *Spinoza on Knowledge and the Human Mind: Papers Pre-*

sented at the *Second Jerusalem Conference (Ethica II)*, ed. Yirmiyahu Yovel, 159–70. New York: E.J. Brill, 1994.

Yovel, Yirmiyahu. 'Spinoza and Nietzsche: *Amor fati* and *Amor dei*.' In *Spinoza and Other Heretics*. Princeton: University Press, 1989.

– 'The Third Kind of Knowledge as Alternative Salvation.' In *Spinoza: Issues and Directions*, ed. Edwin Curley and Pierre-François Moreau. New York: E.J. Brill, 1990.

Zourabichvili, François. 'Deleuze et Spinoza.' In *Spinoza au XXe siècle*, ed. Olivier Bloch, 237–46. Paris: Presses Universitaires de France, 1993.

Index